75¢

FEAR AND LOATHING:
ON THE
CAMPAIGN TRAIL'72

FEAR AND LOATHING:
ON THE
CAMPAIGN TRAIL '72

Dr. Hunter S. Thompson

Straight Arrow Books

The author gratefully
acknowledges permission to
reprint the following: Lines from
"Taxi" by Harry F. Chapin,
© 1972 **Story Songs Ltd;** used
by permission, all rights reserved.
"Eagleton Reveals Illness,"
"Vacation Ordeal" and "The
McGovern Course," by William
Greider, copyright © 1972
Washington **Post** Company,
by permission of the Washington
Post. "Be Angry at the Sun,"
copyright 1941, renewed 1969 by
Donnan Jeffers and Garth Jeffers;
reprinted by permission of
Random House, Inc. "The
McGovern Image," by James
Naughton © 1972 by The
New York **Times** Company;
reprinted by permission.

Library of Congress Catalog
Card Number: 72-88840

ISBN 0/87932/053/2

Third Printing

Straight Arrow Books
625 Third Street
San Francisco, CA 94107

Distributed by Quick Fox Inc.
33 West 60 Street
New York, NY 10023

Order number: 102053

Typeset by Mercury Printing Co.,
San Francisco
Printed in the United States
of America
by Levison-McNally,
Reno, Nevada
Production: Planned Production
Cover: Thomas W. Benton

To Sandy, who endured almost a year of grim exile in Washington, D.C. while this book was being written.
—HST

Between the Idea and the Reality . . . . Falls the Shadow.
—T. S. Eliot

Contents

Contents

Author's Note

DAWN IS COMING UP in San Francisco now: 6:09 A.M. I can hear the rumble of early morning buses under my window at the Seal Rock Inn . . . out here at the far end of Geary Street: this is the end of the line, for buses and everything else, the western edge of America. From my desk I can see the dark jagged hump of "Seal Rock" looming out of the ocean in the grey morning light. About two hundred seals have been barking out there most of the night. Staying in this place with the windows open is like living next to a dog pound. Last night we had a huge paranoid poodle up here in the room, and the dumb bastard went totally out of control when the seals started barking—racing around the room like a chicken hearing a pack of wolves outside the window, howling & whining, leaping up on the bed & scattering my book-galley pages all over the floor, knocking the phone off the hook, upsetting the gin bottles, trashing my carefully organized stacks of campaign photographs . . . off to the right of this typewriter, on the floor between the beds, I can see an 8x10 print of Frank Mankiewicz yelling into a telephone at the Democratic Convention in Miami; but that one will never be used, because the goddamn hound put five big claw-holes in the middle of Frank's chest.

That dog will not enter this room again. He came in with the book-editor, who went away about six hours ago with thirteen finished chapters—the bloody product of fifty-five consecutive hours of sleepless, foodless, high-speed editing. But there was no other way to get the thing done. I am not an easy person to work with, in terms of deadlines. When I arrived in San Francisco to put this book together, they had a work-hole set up for me downtown at the *Rolling Stone* office . . . but I have a powerful aversion to working in offices, and when I didn't show up for three or four days they decided to do the only logical thing: move the office out here to the Seal Rock Inn.

One afternoon about three days ago they showed up at my

door, with no warning, and loaded about forty pounds of supplies into the room: two cases of Mexican beer, four quarts of gin, a dozen grapefruits, and enough speed to alter the outcome of six Super Bowls. There was also a big Selectric typewriter, two reams of paper, a face-cord of oak firewood and three tape recorders— in case the situation got so desperate that I might finally have to resort to verbal composition.

We came to this point sometime around the thirty-third hour, when I developed an insoluble Writer's Block and began dictating big chunks of the book straight into the microphone—pacing around the room at the end of an eighteen-foot cord and saying anything that came into my head. When we reached the end of a tape the editor would jerk it out of the machine and drop it into a satchel . . . and every twelve hours or so a messenger would stop by to pick up the tape satchel and take it downtown to the office, where unknown persons transcribed it onto manuscript paper and sent it straight to the printer in Reno.

There is a comfortable kind of consistency in this kind of finish, because that's the way all the rest of the book was written. From December '71 to January '73—in airport bars, all-nite coffee shops and dreary hotel rooms all over the country—there is hardly a paragraph in this jangled saga that wasn't produced in a last-minute, teeth-grinding frenzy. There was never enough time. Every deadline was a crisis. All around me were experienced professional journalists meeting deadlines far more frequent than mine, but I was never able to learn from their example. Reporters like Bill Greider from the Washington *Post* and Jim Naughton of the New York *Times,* for instance, had to file long, detailed, and relatively complex stories *every day*—while my own deadline fell every two weeks—but neither one of them ever seemed in a hurry about getting their work done, and from time to time they would try to console me about the terrible pressure I always seemed to be laboring under.

Any $100-an-hour psychiatrist could probably explain this problem to me, in thirteen or fourteen sessions, but I don't have time for that. No doubt it has something to do with a deep-seated personality defect, or maybe a kink in whatever blood vessel leads into the pineal gland . . . . On the other hand, it might easily be something as simple & basically perverse as whatever instinct it is that causes a jackrabbit to wait until the last possible second to dart across the road in front of a speeding car.

People who claim to know jackrabbits will tell you they are primarily motivated by Fear, Stupidity, and Craziness. But I have spent enough time in jackrabbit country to know that most of them lead pretty dull lives; they are bored with their daily routines: eat, fuck, sleep, hop around a bush now & then . . . . No wonder some of them drift over the line into cheap thrills once in a while; there has to be a powerful adrenalin rush in crouching by the side of a road, waiting for the next set of headlights to come along, then streaking out of the bushes with split-second timing and making it across to the other side just inches in front of the speeding front wheels.

Why not? Anything that gets the adrenalin moving like a 440 volt blast in a copper bathtub is good for the reflexes and keeps the veins free of cholesterol . . . but too many adrenalin rushes in any given time-span has the same bad effect on the nervous system as too many electro-shock treatments are said to have on the brain: after a while you start burning out the circuits.

When a jackrabbit gets addicted to road-running, it is only a matter of time before he gets smashed—and when a journalist turns into a politics junkie he will sooner or later start raving and babbling in print about things that only a person who has Been There can possibly understand.

Some of the scenes in this book will not make much sense to anybody except the people who were involved in them. Politics has its own language, which is often so complex that it borders on being a code, and the main trick in political journalism is learning how to translate—to make sense of the partisan bullshit that even your friends will lay on you—without crippling your access to the kind of information that allows you to keep functioning. Covering a presidential campaign is not a hell of a lot different from getting a long-term assignment to cover a newly elected District Attorney who made a campaign promise to "crack down on Organized Crime." In both cases, you find unexpected friends on both sides, and in order to protect them—and to keep them as sources of private information—you wind up knowing a lot of things you can't print, or which you can only say without even hinting at where they came from.

This was one of the traditional barriers I tried to ignore when I moved to Washington and began covering the '72 presidential campaign. As far as I was concerned, there was no such thing as "off the record." The most consistent and ultimately damaging failure of political journalism in America has its roots in the clubby/cocktail personal relationships that inevitably develop between politicians and journalists—in Washington or anywhere else where they meet on a day-to-day basis. When professional antagonists become after-hours drinking buddies, they are not likely to turn each other in . . . especially not for "minor infractions" of rules that neither side takes seriously; and on the rare occasions when Minor infractions suddenly become Major, there is panic on both ends.

A classic example of this syndrome was the disastrous "Eagleton Affair." Half of the political journalists in St. Louis and at least a dozen in the Washington press corps knew Eagleton was a serious boozer with a history of mental breakdowns—but none of them had ever written about it, and the few who were known to have mentioned it privately clammed up 1000 percent when McGovern's harried staffers began making inquiries on that fateful Thursday afternoon in Miami. Any Washington political reporter who blows a Senator's chance for the vice-presidency might as well start looking for another beat to cover—because his name will be instant Mud on Capitol Hill.

When I went to Washington I was determined to avoid this kind of trap. Unlike most other correspondents, I could afford to burn all my bridges behind me—because I was only there for a year, and the last thing I cared about was establishing long-term connections on Capitol Hill. I went there for two reasons: (1) to learn as much as possible about the mechanics and realities of a presidential campaign, and (2) to write about it the same way I'd write about anything else—as close to the bone as I could get, and to hell with the consequences.

It was a fine idea, and on balance I think it worked out pretty well—but in retrospect I see two serious problems in that kind of merciless, ball-busting approach. The most obvious and least serious of these was the fact that even the few people I considered my friends in Washington treated me like a walking bomb; some were reluctant to even drink with me, for fear that their tongues might get loose and utter words that would almost certainly turn up on the newsstands two weeks later. The other, more complex, problem had to do with my natural out-front bias in favor of the McGovern candidacy—which was not a problem at first, when George was such a hopeless underdog that his staffers saw no harm in talking frankly with any journalist who seemed friendly and interested—but when he miraculously emerged as the front-runner I found myself in a very uncomfortable position. Some of the friends I'd made earlier, during the months when the idea of McGovern winning the Democratic nomination seemed almost as weird as the appearance of a full-time *Rolling Stone* correspondent on the campaign trail, were no longer just a handful of hopeless idealists I'd been hanging around with for entirely personal reasons, but key people in a fast-rising movement that suddenly seemed capable not only of winning the party nomination but driving Nixon out of the White House.

McGovern's success in the primaries had a lasting effect on my relationship with the people who were running his campaign—especially those who had come to know me well enough to sense that my contempt for the time-honored double standard in political journalism might not be entirely compatible with the increasingly pragmatic style of politics that George was getting into. And their apprehension increased measurably as it became obvious that dope fiends, anarchists, and Big-Beat dropouts were not the only people who read the political coverage in *Rolling Stone*. Not long after McGovern's breakthrough victory in the Wisconsin primary, arch-establishment mouthpiece Stewart Alsop went out of his way to quote some of my more venomous comments on Muskie and Humphrey in his *Newsweek* column, thus raising me to the level of at least neo-respectability at about the same time McGovern began to look like a winner.

Things were never the same after that. A cloud of hellish intensity had come down on the McGovern campaign by the time it rolled into California. Mandates came down from the top, warning staffers to beware of the press. The only exceptions were reporters who were known to have a decent respect for things said "in confidence," and I didn't fit that description.

And so much for all that. The point I meant to make here—before we wandered off on that tangent about jackrabbits—is that everything in this book except the footnotes was written under savage deadline pressure in the traveling vortex of a campaign so confusing and unpredictable that not even the participants claimed to know what was happening.

I had never covered a presidential campaign before I got into this one, but I quickly got so hooked on it that I began betting on the outcome of each primary—and, by combining aggressive ignorance with a natural instinct to mock the conventional wisdom, I managed to win all but two of the fifty or sixty bets I made between February and November. My first loss came in New Hampshire, where I felt guilty for taking advantage of one of McGovern's staffers who wanted to bet that George would get more than 35 percent of the vote; and I lost when he wound up with 37.5 percent. But from that point on, I won steadily—until November 7, when I made the invariably fatal mistake of betting my emotions instead of my instinct.

The final result was embarrassing, but what the hell? I blew that one, along with a lot of other people who should have known better, and since I haven't changed anything else in this mass of first-draft screeds that I wrote during the campaign, I can't find any excuse for changing my final prediction. Any re-writing now would cheat the basic concept of the book, which—in addition to the publisher's desperate idea that it might sell enough copies to cover the fantastic expense bills I ran up in the course of those twelve frantic months—was to lash the whole thing together and essentially *record the reality of an incredibly volatile presidential campaign while it was happening:* from an eye in the eye of the hurricane, as it were, and there is no way to do that without rejecting the luxury of hindsight.

So this is more a jangled campaign diary than a record or reasoned analysis of the '72 presidential campaign. Whatever I wrote in the midnight hours on rented typewriters in all those cluttered hotel rooms along the campaign trail—from the Wayfarer Inn outside Manchester to the Neil House in Columbus to the Wilshire Hyatt House in L.A. and the Fontainebleau in Miami

—is no different now than it was back in March and May and July when I was cranking it out of the typewriter one page at a time and feeding it into the plastic maw of that goddamn Mojo Wire to some hash-addled freak of an editor at the *Rolling Stone* news-desk in San Francisco.

What I would like to preserve here is a kind of high-speed cinematic reel-record of what the campaign was like *at the time,* not what the whole thing boiled down to or how it fits into history. There will be no shortage of books covering that end. The last count I got was just before Christmas in '72, when ex-McGovern speech writer Sandy Berger said at least nineteen people who'd been involved in the campaign were writing books about it—so we'll eventually get the whole story, for good or ill.

Meanwhile, my room at the Seal Rock Inn is filling up with people who seem on the verge of hysteria at the sight of me still sitting here wasting time on a rambling introduction, with the final chapter still unwritten and the presses scheduled to start rolling in twenty-four hours . . . . but unless somebody shows up pretty soon with extremely powerful speed, there might not *be* any Final Chapter. About four fingers of king-hell Crank would do the trick, but I am not optimistic. There is a definite scarcity of genuine, high-voltage Crank on the market these days—and according to recent statements by official spokesmen for the Justice Department in Washington, that's solid evidence of progress in Our War Against Dangerous Drugs.

Well . . . thank Jesus for that. I was beginning to think we were never going to put the arm on that crowd. But the people in Washington say we're finally making progress. And if anybody should know, it's them. So maybe this country's about to get back on the Right Track.

—HST
Sunday, January 28, 1973
San Francisco, Seal Rock Inn

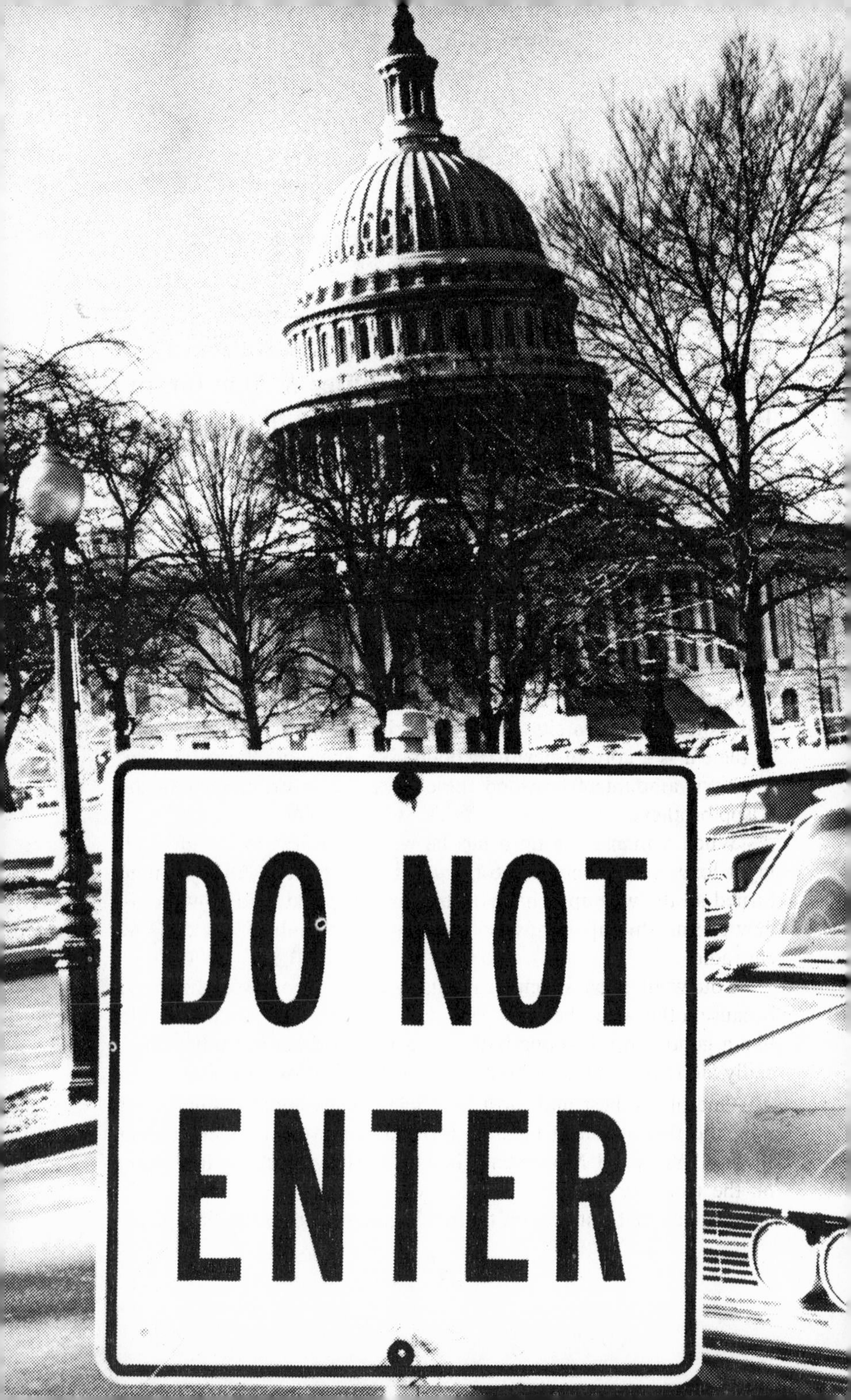
DO NOT
ENTER

December 1971

Is This Trip Necessary? . . . Strategic Retreat into National Politics . . . Two Minutes & One Gram Before Midnight on the Pennsylvania Turnpike . . . Setting Up the National Affairs Desk . . . Can Georgetown Survive the Black Menace? . . . Fear and Loathing in Washington . . .

OUTSIDE MY NEW FRONT DOOR the street is full of leaves. My lawn slopes down to the sidewalk; the grass is still green, but the life is going out of it. Red berries wither on the tree beside my white colonial stoop. In the driveway my Volvo with blue leather seats and Colorado plates sits facing the brick garage. And right next to the car is a cord of new firewood: pine, elm, and cherry. I burn a vicious amount of firewood these days . . . even more than the Alsop brothers.

When a man gives up drugs he wants big fires in his life—all night long, every night, huge flames in the fireplace & the volume turned all the way up. I have ordered more speakers to go with my new McIntosh amp—and also a fifty watt "boombox" for the FM car radio.

You want good strong seatbelts with the boombox, they say, because otherwise the bass riffs will bounce you around inside like a goddamn ping-pong ball . . . a very bad act in traffic; especially along these elegant boulevards of Our Nation's Capital.

One of the best and most beneficial things about coming East now and then is that it tends to provoke a powerful understanding of the "Westward Movement" in U.S. history. After a few years on the Coast or even in Colorado you tend to forget just exactly what it was that put you on the road, going west, in the first place.

You live in L.A. a while and before long you start cursing traffic jams on the freeways in the warm Pacific dusk . . . and you tend to forget that in New York City you can't even *park;* forget about driving.

Even in Washington, which is still a relatively loose and open city in terms of traffic, it costs me about $1.50 an hour every time I park downtown . . . which is nasty: but the shock is not so much the money-cost as the rude understanding that it is no longer considered either sane or natural to *park* on the city streets. If you happen to find a spot beside an open parking meter you don't dare use it, because the odds are better than even that somebody will come along and either steal your car or reduce it to twisted rubble because you haven't left the keys in it.

There is nothing unusual, they tell me, about coming back to your car and finding the radio aerial torn off, the windshield wipers bent up in the air like spaghetti and all the windows smashed . . . for no particular reason except to make sure you know just exactly where it's at these days.

Where indeed?

At 5:30 in the morning I can walk outside to piss casually off my stoop and watch the lawn dying slowly from a white glaze of frost . . . Nothing moving out here tonight; not since that evil nigger hurled a three-pound Washington *Post* through the shattered glass coachlight at the top of my stone front steps. He offered to pay for it, but my Dobermans were already on him.

Life runs fast & mean in this town. It's like living in an armed camp, a condition of constant fear. Washington is about 72 percent black; the shrinking white population has backed itself into an elegant-looking ghetto in the Northwest quadrant of town—which seems to have made things a lot easier for the black marauders who have turned places like chic Georgetown and once-stylish Capitol Hill into hellishly paranoid Fear Zones.

Washington *Post* columnist Nicholas Von Hoffman recently pointed out that the Nixon/Mitchell administration—seemingly obsessed with restoring Law and Order in the land, at almost any cost

24

—seems totally unconcerned that Washington, D.C. has become the "Rape Capital of the World."

One of the most dangerous areas in town is the once-fashionable district known as Capitol Hill. This is the section immediately surrounding the Senate/Congress office buildings, a very convenient place to live for the thousands of young clerks, aides and secretaries who work up there at the pinnacle. The peaceful, tree-shaded streets on Capitol Hill look anything but menacing: brick colonial townhouses with cut-glass doors and tall windows looking out on the Library of Congress and the Washington Monument . . . When I came here to look for a house or apartment, about a month ago, I checked around town and figured Capitol Hill was the logical place to locate.

"Good *God,* man!" said my friend from the liberal New York *Post.* "You can't live *there!* It's a goddamn jungle!"

Crime figures for "The District" are so heinous that they embarrass even J. Edgar Hoover.[1] Rape is said to be up 80 percent this year over 1970, and a recent rash of murders (averaging about one every day) has mashed the morale of the local police to a new low. Of the two hundred and fifty murders this year, only thirty-six have been solved . . . and the Washington *Post* says the cops are about to give up.

Meanwhile, things like burglaries, street muggings and random assaults are so common that they are no longer considered news. The Washington *Evening Star,* one of the city's three dailies, is located in the Southeast District—a few blocks from the Capitol—in a windowless building that looks like the vault at Fort Knox. Getting into the *Star* to see somebody is almost as difficult as getting into the White House. Visitors are scrutinized by hired cops and ordered to fill out forms that double as "hall passes." So many *Star* reporters have been mugged, raped and menaced that they come & go in fast taxis, like people running the gauntlet—fearful, with good reason, of every sudden footfall between the street and the bright-lit safety of the newsroom guard station.

This kind of attitude is hard for a stranger to cope with. For

1. Hoover died in the spring of 1972. Figures released later in the year showed that the national crime rate declined for the first time in the last decade.

the past few years I have lived in a place where I never even bothered to take the keys out of my car, much less try to lock up the house. Locks were more a symbol than a reality, and if things ever got serious there was always the .44 magnum. But in Washington you get the impression—if you believe what you hear from even the most "liberal" insiders—that just about everybody you see on the street is holding at least a .38 Special, and maybe worse.

Not that it matters a hell of a lot at ten feet . . . but it makes you a trifle nervous to hear that nobody in his or her right mind would dare to walk alone from the Capitol Building to a car in the parking lot without fear of later on having to crawl, naked and bleeding, to the nearest police station.

All this sounds incredible—and that was *my* reaction at first: "Come on! It can't be *that* bad!"

"You wait and see," they said. "And meanwhile, keep your doors locked." I immediately called Colorado and had another Doberman shipped in. If this is what's happening in this town, I felt, the thing to do was get right on top of it . . . but paranoia gets very heavy when there's no more humor in it; and it occurs to me now that maybe this is what has happened to whatever remains of the "liberal power structure" in Washington. Getting beaten in Congress is one thing—even if you get beaten a *lot*—but when you slink out of the Senate chamber with your tail between your legs and *then* have to worry about getting mugged, stomped, or raped in the Capitol parking lot by a trio of renegade Black Panthers . . . well, it tends to bring you down a bit, and warp your Liberal Instincts.

There is no way to avoid "racist undertones" here. The simple heavy truth is that Washington is mainly a Black City, and that most of the violent crime is therefore committed by blacks—not always against whites, but often enough to make the relatively wealthy white population very nervous about random social contacts with their black fellow citizens. After only ten days in this town I have noticed the Fear Syndrome clouding even my own mind: I find myself ignoring black hitchhikers, and every time I do it I wonder, "Why the fuck did you do that?" And I tell myself, "Well, I'll pick up the next one I see." And sometimes I do, but not always . . .

26

My arrival in town was not mentioned by any of the society columnists. It was shortly after dawn, as I recall, when I straggled into Washington just ahead of the rush-hour, government-worker car-pool traffic boiling up from the Maryland suburbs . . . humping along in the slow lane on U.S. Interstate 70S like a crippled steel piss-ant; dragging a massive orange U-haul trailer full of books and "important papers" . . . feeling painfully slow & helpless because the Volvo was never made for this kind of work.

It's a quick little beast and one of the best ever built for rough-road, mud & snow driving . . . but not even this new, six-cylinder super-Volvo is up to hauling 2000 pounds of heavy swill across the country from Woody Creek, Colorado to Washington, D.C. The odometer read 2155 when I crossed the Maryland line as the sun came up over Hagerstown . . . still confused after getting lost in a hamlet called Breezewood in Pennsylvania; I'd stopped there to ponder the drug question with two freaks I met on the Turnpike.

They had blown a tire east of Everett, but nobody would stop to lend them a jack. They had a spare tire—and a jack, too, for that matter—but no jack-*handle;* no way to crank the car up and put the spare on. They had gone out to Cleveland, from Baltimore —to take advantage of the brutally depressed used-car market in the vast urban web around Detroit . . . and they'd picked up this '66 Ford Fairlane for $150.

I was impressed.

"Shit," they said. "You can pick up a goddamn *new Thunderbird* out there for seven-fifty. All you need is *cash,* man; people are desperate! There's *no work* out there, man; they're selling everything! It's down to a dime on the dollar. Shit, I can sell any car I can get my hands on around Detroit for *twice* the money in Baltimore."

I said I would talk to some people with capital and maybe get into that business, if things were as good as they said. They assured me that I could make a natural fortune if I could drum up enough cash to set up a steady shuttle between the Detroit-Toledo-Cleveland area and places like Baltimore, Philly and Washington. "All you need," they said, "is some dollars in front and some guys to drive the cars."

"Right," I said. "And some jack-handles."

"What?"

"Jack-handles—for scenes like these."

They laughed. Yeah, a jack-handle or so might save a lot of trouble. They'd been waving frantically at traffic for about three hours before I came by . . . and in truth I only stopped because I couldn't quite believe what I thought I'd just seen. Here I was all alone on the Pennsylvania Turnpike on a fast downhill grade —running easily, for a change—when suddenly out of the darkness in a corner of my right eye I glimpsed what appeared to be a white gorilla running towards the road.

I hit the brakes and pulled over. What the fuck was *that?* I had noticed a disabled car as I crested the hill, but the turnpikes & freeways are full of abandoned junkers these days . . . and you don't really notice them, in your brain, until you start to zoom past one and suddenly have to swerve left to avoid killing a big furry white animal, lunging into the road on its hind legs.

A white bear? *Agnew's other son?*

At this time of the morning I was bored from bad noise on the radio and half-drunk from doing off a quart of Wild Turkey between Chicago and the Altoona exit so I figured, Why Not? Check it out.

But I was moving along about seventy at the time and I forgot about the trailer . . . so by the time I got my whole act stopped I was five hundred yards down the Turnpike and I couldn't back up.

But I was still curious. So I set the blinker lights flashing on the Volvo and started walking back up the road, in pitch darkness, with a big flashlight in one hand and a .357 magnum in the other. No point getting stomped & fucked over, I thought—by wild beasts or anything else. My instincts were purely humanitarian— but what about that Thing I was going back to look for? You read about these people in the *Reader's Digest:* blood-crazy dope fiends who crouch beside the highway and prey on innocent travelers.

Maybe Manson, or the ghost of Charley Starkweather. You never know . . . and that warning works both ways. Here were these two poor freaks, broke & hopelessly stoned, shot down beside the highway for lack of nothing more than a ninety-cent jack-handle

. . . and now, after three hours of trying to flag down a helping hand, they finally catch the attention of a drunken lunatic who rolls a good quarter-mile or so before stopping and then creeps back toward them in the darkness with a .357 magnum in his hand.

A vision like this is enough to make a man wonder about the wisdom of calling for help. For all they knew I was half-mad on PCP and eager to fill my empty Wild Turkey jug with enough fresh blood to make the last leg of the trip into Washington and apply for White House press credentials . . . nothing like a big hit of red corpuscles to give a man the right lift for a rush into politics.

But this time things worked out—as they usually do when you go with your instincts—and when I finally got back to the derailed junker I found these two half-frozen heads with a blowout . . . and the "white bear" rushing into the road had been nothing more than Jerry, wrapped up in a furry white blanket from a Goodwill Store in Baltimore, finally getting so desperate that he decided to do anything necessary to make somebody stop. At least a hundred cars & trucks had zipped past, he said: "I *know* they could see me, because most of them swerved out into the passing lane—even a Cop Car; this is the first time in my goddamn life that I really wanted a cop to stop for me . . . shit, they're supposed to *help* people, right . . . ?"

Lester, his friend, was too twisted to even get out of the car until we started cranking it up. The Volvo jack wouldn't work, but I had a huge screwdriver that we managed to use as a jack-handle.

When Lester finally got out he didn't say much; but finally his head seemed to clear and he helped put the tire on. Then he looked up at me while Jerry tightened the bolts and said: "Say, man, you have anything to smoke?"

"Smoke?" I said. "Do I look like the kind of person who'd be carrying marrywanna?"

Lester eyed me for a moment, then shook his head. "Well, shit," he said. "Let's smoke some of ours."

"Not here," I said. "Those blue lights about a hundred yards from where my car's parked is a State Police barracks. Let's get some coffee down in Breezewood; there's bound to be a truckstop."

Jerry nodded. "It's cold as a bastard out here. If we want to get loaded, let's go someplace where it's warm."

They gave me a ride down to the Volvo, then followed me into Breezewood to a giant truckstop.

"This is *terrible* shit," Lester muttered, handing the joint to Jerry. "There's *nothin'* worth a damn for sale these days. It's got so the only thing you can get off on is smack."

Jerry nodded. The waitress appeared with more coffee. "You boys are sure laughin' a lot," she said. "What's so *funny* at this hour of the morning?"

Lester fixed her with a front-toothless smile and two glittering eyes that might have seemed dangerous if he hadn't been in such a mellow mood. "You know," he said, "I used to be a male whore, and I'm laughin' because I'm so happy that I finally found Jesus."

The waitress smiled nervously as she filled our cups and then hurried back to her perch behind the counter. We drank off the coffee and traded a few more stories about the horrors of the latter-day drug market. Then Jerry said they would have to get moving. "We're heading for Baltimore," he said. "What about you?"

"Washington," I said.

"What for?" Lester asked. "Why the fuck would anybody want to go *there?*"

I shrugged. We were standing in the parking lot while my Doberman pissed on the wheel of a big Hard Brothers poultry truck. "Well . . . it's a weird sort of trip," I said finally. "What happened is that I finally got a job, after twelve years."

"Jesus!" said Lester. "That's heavy. Twelve years on the dole! Man, you must of been really strung out!"

I smiled. "Yeah . . . yeah, I guess you could say that."

"What *kind* of a job?" Jerry asked.

Now the Doberman had the driver of the Hard Brothers truck backed up against his cab, screeching hysterically at the dog and kicking out with his metal-toed Army boots. We watched with

vague amusement as the Doberman—puzzled by this crazy outburst
—backed off and growled a warning.

"O God Jesus," screamed the trucker. "Somebody help me!" It
was clear that he felt he was about to be chewed up and killed,
for no reason at all, by some vicious animal that had come out of
the darkness to pin him against his own truck.

"OK, Benjy!" I shouted. "Don't fool with that man—he's nervous." The trucker shook his fist at me and yelled something about
getting my license number.

"Get out of here, you asshole!" Lester screamed. "It's pigs like
you that give Dobermans a bad name."

Jerry laughed as the trucker drove off. "You won't last long
on the job with a dog like that," he said. "Seriously—what kind of
work do you do?"

"It's a political gig," I said. "I'm going to Washington to cover
the '72 presidential campaign for *Rolling Stone.*"

"Jesus Christ!" Jerry muttered. "That's weird! The Stone is
into politics?"

I stared down at the asphalt, not sure of what to say. Was "The
Stone" into politics? Or was it just *me?* I had never really wondered
about it . . . but suddenly on the outskirts of Washington, in the
cold grey dawn of this truckstop near Breezewood just north of
the Maryland line, it suddenly occurred to me that I couldn't really
say what I *was* doing there—except heading for D.C. with an orange
pig-shaped trailer and a Doberman Pinscher with bad bowels after
too many days on the road.

"It sounds like a stinking goddamn way to get back into work,"
said Lester. "Why don't you hang up that bullshit and we'll put
something together with that car shuttle Jerry told you about?"

I shook my head. "No, I want to at least *try* this trip," I said.

Lester stared at me for a moment, then shrugged. "God damn!"
he said. "What a bummer. Why would *anybody* want to get hung
up in a pile of shit like Politics?"

"Well . . ." I said, wondering if there was any sane answer
to a question like that: "It's mainly a personal trip, a very hard
thing to explain."

Jerry smiled. "You talk like you've *tried it,*" he said. "Like
maybe you *got off on it.*"

"Not as far as I meant to," I said, "but definitely high."

Lester was watching me now with new interest. "I always *thought* that about politicians," he said. "Just a gang of goddamn power junkies, gone off on their own strange trips."

"Come on now," said Jerry. "Some of those guys are OK."

"Who?" Lester asked.

"That's why I'm going to Washington," I said. "To check out the people and find out if they're *all* swine."

"Don't worry," said Lester. "They are. You might as well go looking for cherries in a Baltimore whorehouse."

"OK," I said. "I'll see you when I make it over to Baltimore." I stuck out my hand and Jerry took it in a quick conventional handshake—but Lester had his thumb up, so I had to adjust for the Revolutionary Drug Brothers grip, or whatever that goddamn thing is supposed to mean. When you move across the country these days you have to learn about nineteen different handshakes between Berkeley and Boston.

"He's right," said Jerry. "Those bastards wouldn't even *be* there if they weren't rotten." He shook his head without looking at us, staring balefully across the parking lot. The grey light of dawn was getting brighter now; Thursday night was dying and the highway at the other end of the parking lot was humming with cars full of people going to work on Friday morning.

WELCOME TO WASHINGTON, D.C. That's what the sign says. It's about twenty feet wide & ten feet tall—a huge stone plaque lit up by spotlights at the head of Sixteenth Street, just in from the Maryland line. The street is five lanes wide, with fat green trees on both sides and about 1,300 out-of-phase stoplights between here and the White House.

It is not considered fashionable to live in "The District" itself unless you can find a place in Georgetown, an aged brick townhouse with barred windows, for $700 or so a month. Georgetown is Washington's lame answer to Greenwich Village. But not really. It's more like the Old Town section of Chicago, where the leading citizens are half-bright Playboy editors, smoking tailor-made joints.

32

The same people, in Georgetown, are trendy young lawyers, journalists and bureaucrats who frequent a handful of pine-paneled bars and "singles only" discotheques where drinks cost $1.75 and there's No Cover Charge for girls wearing hotpants.

I live on the "black side" of Rock Creek park, in what my journalistic friends call "a marginal neighborhood." Almost everybody else I know or have any professional contact with lives either in the green Virginia suburbs or over on the "white side" of the park, towards Chevy Chase and Bethesda, in Maryland.

The Underculture is scattered into various far-flung bastions, and the only thing even approximating a crossroads is the area around Dupont Circle, downtown. The only people I know who live down there are Nicholas Von Hoffman and Jim Flug, Teddy Kennedy's hyper-active Legislative Assistant. But Von Hoffman seems to have had a belly-full of Washington and now talks about moving out to the Coast, to San Francisco . . . and Flug, like everybody else even vaguely connected with Kennedy, is gearing down for a very heavy year: like maybe twenty hours a day on the telephone, and the other four on planes.

With December winding down, there is a fast-swelling undercurrent of political angst in the air around Washington, a sense of almost boiling desperation about getting Nixon and his cronies out of power before they can finish the seizure that began three years ago.

Jim Flug says he'd rather not talk about Kennedy running for President—at least not until he has to, and that time seems to be coming up fast. Teddy is apparently sincere about not planning to run, but it is hard for him or anyone else not to notice that almost everybody who "matters" in Washington is fascinated by the recent series of Gallup Polls showing Kennedy creeping ever closer to Nixon—almost even with him now, and this rising tide has cast a very long shadow on the other Democratic candidates.

There is a sense of muted desperation in Democratic ranks at the prospect of getting stuck—and beaten once again—with some tried and half-true hack like Humphrey, Jackson, or Muskie . . . and George McGovern, the only candidate in either party worth voting for, is hung in a frustrated limbo created mainly by the gross cynicism of the Washington Press Corps. "He'd be a fine

President," they say, "but of course he can't possibly win."

Why not?

Well . . . the wizards haven't bothered to explain that, but their reasoning appears to be rooted in the hazy idea that the people who could make McGovern President—that huge & confused coalition of students, freaks, blacks, anti-war activists & dazed dropouts—won't even bother to register, much less drag themselves to the polls on election day.

Maybe so . . . but it is hard to recall many candidates, in recent history, who failed to move what is now called "The McGovern Vote" to the polls if they *actually represented it.*

It sure as hell wasn't the AFL/CIO that ran LBJ out of the White House in 1968; and it wasn't Gene McCarthy either. It was the people who *voted* for McCarthy in New Hampshire that beat Johnson . . . and it wasn't George Meany who got shot with Bobby Kennedy in Los Angeles; it was a renegade "radical" organizer from the UAW.

It wasn't the big-time "Democratic bosses" who won the California primary for Bobby—but thousands of Niggers and Spics and white Peace Freaks who were tired of being gassed for not agreeing with The Man in the White House. Nobody had to drag them to the polls in California, and nobody would have had to drag them to the polls in November to beat Nixon.

But there was, of course, The Murder—and then the Convention in Chicago, and finally a turnip called Humphrey. He appealed to "respectable" Democrats, then and now—and if Humphrey or any of his greasy ilk runs in '72, it will be another debacle like the Eisenhower/Stevenson wipeout in 1956.

The people who turned out for Bobby are still around—along with several million others who'll be voting for the first time—but they won't turn out for Humphrey, or Jackson, or Muskie, or any other neo-Nixon hack. They will not even come out for McGovern if the national press wizards keep calling him a Noble Loser . . .

According to the Gallup Polls, however, the Underculture vote is building up a fearful head of steam behind Ted Kennedy; and this drift has begun to cause genuine alarm among Bigwigs and "pros" in both parties. The mere mention of Kennedy's name is said to give Nixon bad cramps all over his body, such as it is. His thugs are already starting to lash Kennedy with vicious denunciations—calling him a "liar" and a "coward" and a "cheater."

And this is only December of 1971; the election is still ten months away.

The only person more nervous than Nixon about Kennedy's recent surge in the polls seems to be Kennedy himself. He won't even admit that it's happening—at least not for the record—and his top-level staffers, like Jim Flug, find themselves walking a public tightrope. They can see the thing coming—too soon, perhaps, but there's nothing they can do about that either. With the boss hunkered down, insisting he's not a candidate, his lieutenants try to keep their minds off the storm by working feverishly on Projects.

When I called Flug the other night at the office he was working late on a doomed effort to prevent Earl Butz from being confirmed by the Senate as Nixon's new Secretary of Agriculture.

"To hell with Butz," I said, "what about Rehnquist? Are they actually going to put a swine like that on the Supreme Court?"

"They have the votes," he replied.

"Jesus," I muttered, "is he as bad as all the rotten stuff I've read about him?"

"Worse," Flug said. "But I think he's in. We tried, but we can't get the votes."

Jim Flug and I are not close friends in any long-standing personal sense. I met him a few years ago when I went to Washington to do a lot of complicated research for an article about Gun Control Laws for *Esquire*—an article that finally died in a blaze of niggling between me and the editors about how to cut my "final version" down from 30,000 words to a size that would fit in the magazine.

Flug had gone far out of his way to help me with that research. We talked in the dreary cafeteria in the Old Senate Office Building where we sat down elbow to elbow with Senator Roman Hruska, the statesman from Nebraska, and various other heavies whose names I forget now.

We idled through the line with our trays and then took our plastic-wrapped tunafish sandwiches and coffee in styrofoam cups over to a small formica table. Flug talked about the problems he was having with the Gun Control Bill—trying to put it into some form that might possibly pass the Senate. I listened, glancing up now and then toward the food-bar, half-expecting to see somebody like Robert Kennedy pushing his tray through the line . . . until I suddenly remembered that Robert Kennedy was dead.

Meanwhile, Flug was outlining every angle and aspect of the Gun Control argument with the buzz-saw precision of a trial lawyer. He was totally *into* it: crouched there in his seat, wearing a blue pin-striped suit with a vest and oxblood cordovans—a swarthy, bright-eyed little man about thirty years old, mercilessly shredding every argument the National Rifle Association had ever mounted against federal gun laws. Later, when I learned he really *was* a lawyer, it occurred to me that I would never under any circumstances want to tangle with a person like Flug in a courtroom . . . and I was careful not to tell him, even in jest, about my .44 magnum fetish.

After lunch that day we went back to his office and he gave me an armload of fact sheets and statistics to back up his arguments. Then I left, feeling very much impressed with Flug's trip— and I was not surprised, a year later, when I heard he had been the prime mover behind the seemingly impossible challenge to the Carswell Supreme Court nomination, one of the most impressive long-shot political victories since McCarthy sent Lyndon back to the ranch in 1968.

Coming on the heels of Judge Haynesworth's rejection by the Senate, Carswell had seemed like a shoo-in . . . but a hard-core group of Senate staffers, led by Flug and Birch Bayh's assistants, had managed to dump Carswell, too.

Now, with Nixon trying to fill two *more* Court vacancies, Flug said there was not a chance in hell of beating either one of them.

"Not even Rehnquist?" I asked. "Christ, that's like Lyndon

Johnson trying to put Bobby Baker on the Court."

"I know," said Flug. "Next time you want to think about appealing a case to the U.S. Supreme Court, just remember who'll be up there."

"You mean *down* there," I said. "Along with all the rest of us," I laughed. "Well, there's always smack. . . ."

Flug didn't laugh. He and a lot of others have worked too hard for the past three years to derail the kind of nightmare that the Nixon/Mitchell team is ready to ram down our throats. There is not much satisfaction in beating Haynesworth & Carswell, then having to swallow a third-rate yoyo like Powell and a vengeful geek like Rehnquist. What Nixon and Mitchell have done in three years—despite the best efforts of the sharpest and meanest young turks the Democratic opposition can call on—is reduce the U.S. Supreme Court to the level of a piss-poor bowling team in Memphis—and this disastrous, nazi-bent shift of the federal government's Final-Decision-making powers won't even *begin* to take effect until the spring of '72.

The effects of this takeover are potentially so disastrous—in terms of personal freedom and police power—that there is no point even speculating on the fate of some poor, misguided geek who might want to take his "Illegal Search & Seizure" case all the way up to the top.

A helpful hint, however, might be found in the case of the Tallahassee newspaper reporter who went to Canada in 1967 to avoid the draft—and returned to find that he was no longer a citizen of the United States, and now he has ninety days to leave the country. He appealed his case to the Supreme Court, but they refused to even hear it.

So now he has to go, but of course he has no passport—and international travel is not real easy without a passport. The federal immigration officials understand this, but—backed up by the Supreme Court—they have given him an ultimatum to vacate, anyway. They don't care where he goes; just get out—and meanwhile Chief Justice Burger has taken to answering his doorbell at night with a big six-shooter in his hand. You never know, he says, who might come crashing in.

Indeed. Maybe Rehnquist—far gone with an overdose of raw

sowbelly and crazy for terminal vengeance on the first house he comes to.

This world is full of dangerous beasts—but none quite as ugly and uncontrollable as a lawyer who has finally flipped off the tracks of Reason. He will run completely amok—like a Priest into sex, or a narc-squad cop who suddenly decides to start sampling his contraband.

Yes . . . and . . . uh, where were we? I have a bad tendency to rush off on mad tangents and pursue them for fifty or sixty pages that get so out of control that I end up burning them, for my own good. One of the few exceptions to this rule occurred very recently, when I slipped up and let about two hundred pages go into print . . . which caused me a lot of trouble with the tax man, among others, and it taught me a lesson I hope I'll never forget.

Live steady. Don't fuck around. Give anything weird a wide berth—including people. It's not worth it. I learned this the hard way, through brutal overindulgence.

And it's also a nasty fact that I have to catch a plane for Chicago in three hours—to attend some kind of national Emergency Conference for New Voters, which looks like the opening shot in this year's version of the McCarthy/Kennedy uprising in '68—and since the conference starts at six o'clock tonight, I *must* make that plane . . .

. . . Back to Chicago; it's never dull out there. You never know exactly what kind of terrible shit is going to come down on you in that town, but you can always count on *something*. Every time I go to Chicago I come away with scars.

January

The Million Pound Shithammer . . . Pros Scorn
the Youth Vote . . . Fresh Meat for the Boys in
the Back Room . . . "The Death of Hope" & A
Withering of Expectation . . . Another McCarthy
Crusade? . . . John Lindsay? . . . The Rancid
Resurrection of Hubert Humphrey . . . Violence in
the Press Box & Mano a Mano on TWA . . .
Who Is Big Ed & Why Is Everybody Sucking
Up to Him? . . .

*"There are issues enough. What is gone is the popular passion
for them. Possibly, hope is gone. The failure of hope would be
a terrible event; the blacks have never been cynical about America.
But conversation you hear among the young now, on the South
Side of Chicago, up in Harlem or in Bedford-Stuyvesant, certainly
suggests the birth of a new cynicism. In the light of what government is doing, you might well expect young blacks to lose hope
in the power elites, but this is something different—a cold personal indifference, a separation of man from man. What you hear
and see is not rage, but injury, a withering of expectations."*
                                    —D.J.R. Bruckner, 1/6/72 in the L.A. *Times*

BRUCKNER'S ARTICLE WAS FOCUSED on the mood of Young Blacks,
but unless you were reading very closely, the distinction was easy to
miss. Because the mood among Young Whites is not much different
—despite a lot of well-financed publicity about the potentially
massive "youth vote."

   These are the 25 million or so new voters between 18 and
25—going, maybe, to the polls for the first time—who supposedly

hold the fate of the nation in the palms of their eager young hands. According to the people who claim to speak for it, this "youth vote" has the power to zap Nixon out of office with a flick of its wrist. Hubert Humphrey lost in '68 by 499,704 votes—a miniscule percentage of what the so-called "youth vote" could turn out in 1972.

But there are not many people in Washington who take this notion of the "youth vote" very seriously. Not even the candidates. The thinking here is that the young people who vote for the first time in '72 will split more or less along the same old lines as their parents, and that the addition of 25 million new (potential) voters means just another sudden mass that will have to be absorbed into the same old patterns . . . just another big wave of new immigrants who don't know the score yet, but who will learn it soon enough, so why worry?

Why indeed? The scumbags behind this thinking are probably right, once again—but it might be worth pondering, this time, if perhaps they might be right for the wrong reasons. Almost all the politicians and press wizards who denigrate the "so-called youth vote" as a factor in the '72 elections have justified their thinking with a sort of melancholy judgment on "the kids" themselves.

"How many will even register?" they ask. "And even then—even assuming a third of the *possibles* might register, how many of those will actually get out and vote?"

The implication, every time, is that the "youth vote" menace is just a noisy paper tiger. Sure, *some* of these kids will vote, they say, but the way things look now, it won't be more than ten percent. That's the colleges; the other ninety percent are either military types, on the dole, or working people—on salary, just married, hired into their first jobs. Man, these people are already *locked down,* the same as their parents.

That's the argument . . . and it's probably safe to say, right now, that there is not a single presidential candidate, media guru, or backstairs politics wizard in Washington who honestly believes the "youth vote" will have more than a marginal, splinter-vote effect on the final outcome of the 1972 presidential campaign.

These kids are turned off from politics, they say. Most of 'em don't even want to hear about it. All they want to do these days is lie around on waterbeds and smoke that goddamn marrywanna . . . yeah, and just between you and me, Fred, I think it's probably all for the best.

Among the half-dozen high-powered organizations in Washington who claim to speak for the "youth vote," the only one with any real muscle at this point is the National Association of Student Governments, which recently—after putting together an "Emergency Conference for New Voters" in Chicago last month—brought its leadership back to D.C. and called a press conference in the Old Senate office building to announce the formation of a "National Youth Caucus."

The idea, said 26-year-old Duane Draper—the main organizer —was to get student-type activists into power on the local level in every state where they might be able to influence the drift of the '72 election. The press conference was well attended. Edward P. Morgan of PBS was there, dressed in a snappy London Fog raincoat and twirling a black umbrella; the New York *Times* sent a woman, the Washington *Post* was represented by a human pencil, and the rest of the national press sent the same people they send to everything else that happens, officially, in this doomed sinkhole of a city.

As always, the "print people" stood or sat in a timid half circle behind the network TV cameras—while Draper and his mentor, Senator Fred Harris of Oklahoma, sat together at the front table and explained that the success of the Chicago rally had gotten the "youth vote" off to a running start. Harris didn't say much; he just sat there looking like Johnny Cash while Draper, a former student body president at the University of Oklahoma, explained to the jaded press that the "youth vote" would be an important and perhaps decisive factor in this year's election.

I came in about ten minutes late, and when question time came around I asked the same one I'd asked Allard Lowenstein at a similar press conference in Chicago: Would the Youth Caucus support Hubert Humphrey if he won the Democratic nomination?

Lowenstein had refused to answer that question in Chicago, saying, "We'll cross that bridge if we come to it." But in Washington Draper said "Yes," the Youth Vote could get behind Hubert if he said the right things—"if he takes the right positions."

41

"How about Jackson?" I asked.

This made for a pause . . . but finally Draper said the National Youth Caucus might support Jackson, too, "if he comes around."

"Around to what?" I asked. And by this time I was feeling very naked and conspicuous. My garb and general demeanor is not considered normal by Washington standards. Levis don't make it in this town; if you show up wearing Levis they figure you're either a servant or a messenger. This is particularly true at high-level press conferences, where any deviation from standard journalistic dress is considered rude and perhaps even dangerous.

In Washington all journalists dress like bank tellers—and those who don't have problems. Mister Nixon's press handlers, for instance, have made it ominously clear that I shall *not* be given White House press credentials. The first time I called, they said they'd never heard of *Rolling Stone*. "Rolling what?" said the woman.

"You'd better ask somebody a little younger," I said.

"Thank you," she hissed. "I'll do that." But the next obstacle up the line was the deputy White House press secretary, a faceless voice called Gerald Warren, who said Rolling Whatever didn't *need* White House press credentials—despite the fact they had been issued in the past, without any hassle, to all manner of strange and obscure publications, including student papers like the George Washington University *Hatchet*.

The only people who seem genuinely interested in the '72 elections are the actual participants—the various candidates, their paid staff people, the thousands of journalists, cameramen & other media-connected hustlers who will spend most of this year humping the campaign along . . . and of course all the *sponsors,* called "fat cats" in the language of Now-Politics, who stand to gain hugely for at least the next four years if they can muscle their man down the homestretch just a hair ahead of the others.

The fat-cat action is still one of the most dramatic aspects of a presidential campaign, but even in this colorful area the tension is leaking away—primarily because most of the really serious fat cats figured out, a few years back, that they could beat the whole rap—along with the onus of going down the tube with some desperate loser—by "helping" two candidates, instead of just one.

A good example of this, in 1972, will probably be Mrs. Rella Factor—ex-wife of "Jake the Barber" and the largest single contributor to Hubert Humphrey's campaign in '68. She didn't get a hell of a lot of return for her investment last time around. But this year, using the new method, she can buy the total friendship of two, three, or perhaps even four presidential candidates, for the same price . . . by splitting up the nut, as discreetly as possible, between Hubert, Nixon, and maybe—just for the natural randy hell of it —a chunk to Gene McCarthy, who appears to be cranking up a genuinely weird campaign this time.

I have a peculiar affection for McCarthy; nothing serious or personal, but I recall standing next to him in the snow outside the "exit" door of a shoe factory in Manchester, New Hampshire, in February of 1968 when the five o'clock whistle blew and he had to stand there in the midst of those workers rushing out to the parking lot. I will never forget the pain in McCarthy's face as he stood there with his hand out, saying over and over again: "Shake hands with Senator McCarthy . . . shake hands with Senator McCarthy . . . shake hands with Senator McCarthy . . . ," a tense plastic smile on his face, stepping nervously toward anything friendly, "Shake hands with Senator McCarthy" . . . but most of the crowd ignored him, refusing to even acknowledge his outstretched hand, staring straight ahead as they hurried out to their cars.

There was at least one network TV camera on hand that afternoon, but the scene was never aired. It was painful enough, just being there, but to have put that scene on national TV would have been an act of genuine cruelty. McCarthy was obviously suffering; not so much because nine out of ten people refused to shake his hand, but because he really hated being there in the first place. But his managers had told him it was necessary, and maybe it was . . .

Eugene McCarthy.

Later, when his outlandish success in New Hampshire shocked Johnson into retirement, I half-expected McCarthy to quit the race himself, rather than suffer all the way to Chicago (like Castro in Cuba—after Batista fled) . . . and God only knows what kind of vengeful energy is driving him this time, but a lot of people who said he was suffering from brain bubbles when he first mentioned that he might run again in '72 are beginning to take him seriously: not as a Democratic contender, but as an increasingly possible Fourth Party candidate with the power to put a candidate like Muskie through terrible changes between August and November.

To Democratic chairman Larry O'Brien, the specter of a McCarthy candidacy in '72 must be something like hearing the Hound of the Baskervilles sniffing and pissing around on your porch every night. A left-bent Fourth Party candidate with a few serious grudges on his mind could easily take enough left/radical votes away from either Muskie or Humphrey to make the Democratic nomination all but worthless to either one of them.

Nobody seems to know what McCarthy has in mind this year, but the possibilities are ominous, and anybody who thought he was kidding got snapped around fast last week when McCarthy launched a brutish attack on Muskie within hours after the Maine Senator made his candidacy official.

The front page of the Washington *Post* carried photos of both men, along with a prominent headline and McCarthy's harsh warning that he was going to hold Muskie "accountable" for his hawkish stance on the war in Vietnam prior to 1968. McCarthy also accused Muskie of being "the most active representative of Johnson administration policy at the 1968 Convention."

Muskie seemed genuinely shaken by this attack. He immediately called a press conference to admit that he'd been wrong about Vietnam in the past, but that now "I've had reason to change my mind." His new position was an awkward thing to explain, but after admitting his "past mistakes" he said that he now favored "as close to an immediate withdrawal from Vietnam as possible."

McCarthy merely shrugged. He had done his gig for the day, and Muskie was jolted. The Senator focused all his efforts on the question of his altered Vietnam stance, but he was probably far more disturbed by McCarthy's ugly revenge-tainted reference to Muskie's role in the '68 Democratic Convention. This was obviously the main bone in McCarthy's throat, but Muskie ignored it and nobody asked Gene what he really meant by the charge . . . probably because there is no way to understand what happened to McCarthy in Chicago unless you were there and saw it yourself.

I have never read anything that comes anywhere close to explaining the shock and intensity I felt at that convention . . . and although I was right in the middle of it the whole time, I have never been able to write about it myself. For two weeks afterwards, back in Colorado, I couldn't even talk about it without starting to cry—for reasons I think I finally understand now, but I still can't explain.

I went there as a journalist, with no real emotional attachment to any of the candidates and only the barest of illusions about the outcome . . . I was not personally involved in the thing, so there is no point in presuming to understand what kind of hellish effect Chicago must have had on Gene McCarthy.

I remember seeing him cross Michigan Avenue on Thursday night—several hours after Humphrey had made his acceptance speech out at the Stockyards—and then wandering into the crowd in Grant Park like a defeated general trying to mingle with his troops just after the Surrender. But McCarthy couldn't mingle. He could barely talk. He acted like a man in deep shock. There was not much to say. The campaign was over.

McCarthy's gig was finished. He had knocked off the President and then strung himself out on a fantastic six-month campaign that had seen the murder of Martin Luther King, the murder of

Bobby Kennedy, and finally a bloody assault on his own campaign workers by Mayor Daley's police, who burst into McCarthy's private convention headquarters at the Chicago Hilton and began breaking heads. At dawn on Friday morning, his campaign manager, a seasoned old pro named Blair Clark, was still pacing up and down Michigan Avenue in front of the Hilton in a state so close to hysteria that his friends were afraid to talk to him because every time he tried to say something his eyes would fill with tears and he would have to start pacing again.

Perhaps McCarthy has placed that whole scene in its proper historical and poetic perspective, but if he has I didn't read it . . . or maybe he's been hanging onto the manuscript until he can find a right ending. McCarthy has a sharp sense of drama, along with his kinky instinct for timing. . . . but nobody appears to have noticed, until now, that he might also have a bull-sized taste for revenge.

Maybe not. In terms of classic journalism, this kind of wandering, unfounded speculation will have a nasty effect on that asshole from Ireland who sent word across The Waters to nail me for bad language and lack of objectivity. There have been numerous complaints, in fact, about the publisher allowing me to get away with calling our new Supreme Court Justice William Rehnquist a "swine."

Well . . . shit, what can I say? Objective Journalism is a hard thing to come by these days. We all yearn for it, but who can point the way? The only man who comes to mind, right offhand, is my good friend and colleague on the Sports Desk, Raoul Duke. Most journalists only *talk* about objectivity, but Dr. Duke grabs it straight by the fucking throat. You will be hard pressed to find any argument, among professionals, on the question of Dr. Duke's Objectivity.

As for mine . . . well, my doctor says it swole up and busted

47

about ten years ago. The only thing I ever saw that came close to Objective Journalism was a closed-circuit TV setup that watched shoplifters in the General Store at Woody Creek, Colorado. I always admired that machine, but I noticed that nobody paid much attention to it until one of those known, heavy, out-front shoplifters came into the place . . . but when that happened, everybody got so excited that the thief had to do something quick, like buy a green popsicle or a can of Coors and get out of the place immediately.

So much for Objective Journalism. Don't bother to look for it here—not under any byline of mine; or anyone else I can think of. With the possible exception of things like box scores, race results, and stock market tabulations, there is no such thing as Objective Journalism. The phrase itself is a pompous contradiction in terms.

And so much for all that, too. There was at least one more thing I wanted to get into here, before trying to wind this down and get into something human. Like sleep, or that 550‵watt Humm Box they have up there in the Ree-Lax Parlor at Silver Spring. Some people say they should outlaw the Humm Box, but I disagree.

Meanwhile, all that venomous speculation about what McCarthy is up to these days leaves a crucial question hanging: The odd truth that almost everybody in Washington who is paid to analyze & predict the behavior of Vote Blocs seems to feel that the much-publicized "youth vote" will not be a Major Factor in the '72 presidential campaign would be a hell of a lot easier to accept if it weren't for the actual figures. . . .

What the experts appear to be saying is that the sudden addition of 25 million new voters between the ages of 18 and 25 will not make much difference in the power-structure of American politics. No *candidate* will say this, of course. For the record, they are all very solicitous of the "youth vote." In a close election even ten percent of that bloc would mean 2.5 million votes—a very serious figure when you stack it up against Nixon's thin margin over Humphrey in 1968.

Think of it: Only *ten percent!* Two and a half million.

Enough—even according to Nixon's own wizards—to swing almost *any* election. There is a general assumption, based on the outcome of recent presidential elections, that it takes something genuinely vile and terrifying to cause either one of the major party candidates to come away with less than 40 percent of the vote. Goldwater managed to do this in '64, but not by much. Even after allowing Johnson's TV sappers to cast him as a stupid, bloodthirsty ghoul who had every intention of blowing the whole world off its axis the moment he got his hands on "the button," Goldwater still got 27,176,799 votes, or 38 percent.

The prevailing wisdom today is that *any* candidate in a standard-brand, two-party election will get about 40 percent of the vote. The root assumption here is that neither party would nominate a man more than 20 percent different from the type of person most Americans consider basically right and acceptable. Which almost always happens. There is no potentially serious candidate in either major party this year who couldn't pass for the executive vice-president for mortgage loans in any hometown bank from Bangor to San Diego.

We are talking about a purely physical-image gig here, but even if you let the candidates jabber like magpies about anything that comes to their minds, not even a dangerous dingbat like Sam Yorty would be likely to alienate more than 45 percent or 50 percent of the electorate.

And even that far-left radical bastard, George McGovern—babbling a maddening litany of his most Far Out ideas—would be hard pressed to crank up any more than a 30 percent animosity quotient.

On balance, they are a pretty bland lot. Even Spiro Agnew—if you catch him between screeds—is not more than 20 percent different from Humphrey or Lindsay or Scoop Jackson. Four years ago, in fact, John Lindsay dug Agnew so much that he seconded his nomination for the vice-presidency. There are a lot of people who say we should forget about that this year "because John has already said he made a mistake about Agnew," but there

are a lot of others who take Lindsay's "Agnew Mistake" seriously—
because they assume he would do the same thing again next week
or next month, if he thought it would do him any good.

Nobody seems very worried about Lindsay right now; they are
waiting to see what kind of action he can generate in Florida, a
state full of transient and old transplanted New Yorkers. If he can't
make it there, he's done for. Which is just as well. But if he scores
big in Florida, we will probably have to start taking him seriously—
particularly if Muskie looks convincing in New Hampshire.

A Muskie-Lindsay ticket could be one of those "naturals," a
marriage made in heaven and consummated by Larry O'Brien . . .
Which gets us back to one of the main reasons why the political
wizards aren't counting on much of a "youth vote" this year. It is
hard to imagine even a zealot like Allard Lowenstein going out
on the trail, once again, to whip up a campus-based firestorm for
Muskie and Lindsay . . . particularly with Gene McCarthy lurking
around, with that ugly mouth of his, and all those deep-bleeding
grudges.

Another nightmare we might as well start coming to grips with
is the probability that Hubert Humphrey will be a candidate for
the Democratic nomination this year . . . And . . . there is probably some interesting talk going down around Humphrey headquarters these days:

"Say . . . ah, Hube, baby. I guess you heard what your old
buddy Gene did to Muskie the other day, right? Yeah, and we
always thought they were *friends,* didn't we?(Long pause, no reply
from the candidate . . .)

"So . . . ah . . . Hube? You still with me? Jesus Christ! Where's
that sunlamp? We gotta get more of a tan on you, baby. You look
grey. (Long pause, no reply from the candidate . . .) Well, Hube,
we might just as well face this thing. We're comin' up fast on what
just might be a real nasty little problem for you . . . let's not try to
kid ourselves, Hube, he's a really *mean* sonofabitch. (Long pause,
etc. . . .) You're gonna have to be *ready,* Hube. You announce
next Thursday at noon, right? So we might as well figure that crazy

Hubert Humphrey.

Big Ed.

fucker is gonna come down on you like a million pound shit-hammer that same afternoon. He'll probably stage a big scene at the Press Club—and we know who's gonna be there, don't we Hube? Yeah, every bastard in the business. Are you ready for that, Hube Baby? Can you handle it? (Long pause, no reply, etc. —heavy breathing.) OK, Hube, tell me this: What does the bastard know? What's the worst he can spring on you?"

What indeed? Was McCarthy just honing up his act on Ed Muskie? Or does he really believe that Muskie—rather than Humphrey—was the main agent of Johnsonian policy at the '68 Convention?

Is that possible? Was Muskie the man behind all that treachery and bloodletting? Is McCarthy prepared to blow the whole lid off? Whose head does he really want? And how far will he go to get it? Does the man have a price?

This may be the only interesting question of the campaign until the big whistle blows in New Hampshire on March 7th. With Mc-Carthy skulking around, Muskie can't afford anything but a thump-ing win over McGovern in that primary. But Mad Sam is up there too, and even Muskie's local handlers concede Yorty at least 15 percent of the Democratic vote, due to his freakish alliance with the neo-Nazi publisher of New Hampshire's only big newspaper, the Manchester *Union-Leader*.

The Mayor of Los Angeles has never bothered to explain the twisted reasoning behind his candidacy in New Hampshire, but every vote he gets there will come off Muskie's pile, not McGovern's. Which means that McGovern, already sitting on 20 to 25 percent of the vote, could zap Muskie's whole trip by picking up another 10 to 15 percent in a last-minute rush.

Muskie took a headcount in September and found himself lead-ing with about 40 percent—but he will need at least 50 percent to look good for the fence-sitters in Florida, who will go to the polls a week later . . . and in Florida, Muskie will have to beat back the show-biz charisma of John Lindsay on the Left, more or less, and also deal with Scoop Jackson, Hubert Humphrey, and George Wal-lace on the Right.

Jesus! This gibberish could run on forever and even now I can see myself falling into the old trap that plagues every writer who gets sucked into this rotten business. You find yourself getting fascinated by the drifts and strange quirks of the game. Even now, before I've even finished this article, I can already feel the compulsion to start handicapping politics and primaries like it was all just another fat Sunday of pro football: Pick Pittsburgh by six points in the early game, get Dallas even with San Francisco later on . . . win one, lose one . . . then flip the dial and try to get ahead by conning somebody into taking Green Bay even against the Redskins.

After several weeks of this you no longer give a flying fuck who actually wins; the only thing that matters is the point-spread. You find yourself scratching crazily at the screen, pleading for somebody to rip the lungs out of that junkie bastard who just threw an interception and then didn't even *pretend* to tackle the pig who ran it back for six points to beat the spread.

There is something perverse and perverted about dealing with life on this level. But on the other hand, it gets harder and harder to convince yourself, once you start thinking about it, that it could possibly make any real difference if the 49ers win or lose . . . although every once in a while you stumble into a situation where you find yourself really *wanting* some team to get stomped all over the field, severely beaten and humiliated . . .

This happened to me on the last Sunday of the regular NFL season when two slobbering drunk sportswriters from the Alexandria *Gazette* got me thrown out of the press box at the Robert F. Kennedy stadium in Washington. I was there as a special guest of Dave Burgin, sports editor of the Washington *Star* . . . but when Burgin tried to force a bit of dignity on the scene, they ejected *him* too.

We were halfway down the ramp to the parking lot before

I understood what had happened. "That gin-soaked little Nazi from the *Gazette* got pissed off when you didn't doff your hat for the national anthem," Burgin explained. "He kept bitching about you to the guy in charge of the press box, then he got that asshole who works for him all cranked up and they started talking about having you arrested."

"Jesus creeping shit," I muttered. "Now I know why I got out of sportswriting. Christ, I had no idea what was happening. You should have warned me."

"I was afraid you'd run amok," he said. "We'd have been in bad trouble. All those guys from things like the Norfolk *Ledger* and the Army-Navy *Times*. They would have stomped us like rats in a closet."

I couldn't understand it. "Hell, I'd have taken the goddamn hat off, if I thought it was causing trouble. I barely even *remember* the national anthem. Usually, I don't even stand up."

"I didn't think you were going to," he said. "I didn't want to say anything, but I knew we were doomed."

"But I *did* stand," I said. "I figured, hell, I'm Dave's guest—why not stand and make it easy for him? But I never even thought about my goddamn hat."

Actually, I was happy to get out of that place. The Redskins were losing, which pleased me, and we were thrown out just in time to get back to Burgin's house for the 49er game on TV. If they won this one, they would go against the Redskins next Sunday in the playoffs—and by the end of the third quarter I had worked myself into a genuine hate frenzy; I was howling like a butcher when the 49ers pulled it out in the final moments with a series of desperate maneuvers, and the moment the gun sounded I was on the phone to TWA, securing a seat on the Christmas Nite Special to San Francisco. It was extremely important, I felt, to go out there and do everything possible to make sure the Redskins got the mortal piss beaten out of them.

Which worked out. Not only did the 49ers stomp the jingo bastards and knock them out of the playoffs, but my seat companion for the flight from Washington to San Francisco was Edward Bennett Williams, the legendary trial lawyer, who is also president of the Washington Redskins.

"Heavy duty for you people tomorrow," I warned him. "Get braced for a serious beating. Nothing personal, you understand. Those poor bastards couldn't have known what they were doing when they croaked a Doctor of Journalism out of the press box."

He nodded heavily and called for another scotch & soda. "It's a goddamn shame," he muttered. "But what can you really expect? You lie down with pigs and they'll call you a swine every time."

"What? Did you call me a *swine?*"

"Not me," he said. "But this world is full of slander."

We spent the rest of the flight arguing politics. He is backing Muskie, and as he talked I got the feeling that he thought he was already at a point where, sooner or later, we would all be. "Ed's a good man," he said. "He's honest. I respect the guy." Then he stabbed the padded seat arm between us two or three times with his forefinger. "But the *main* reason I'm working for him," he said, "is that he's the only guy we have who can beat Nixon." He stabbed the arm again. "If Nixon wins again, we're in real trouble." He picked up his drink, then saw it was empty and put it down again. "That's the real issue this time," he said. "Beating Nixon. It's hard to even guess how much damage those bastards will do if they get in for another four years."[1]

I nodded. The argument was familiar. I had even made it myself, here and there, but I was beginning to sense something very depressing about it. How many more of these goddamn elec-

---

1. As it turned out, another rabid Redskins fan that year was Richard Nixon, despite his political differences with the management. His unsolicited advice to Coach George Allen resulted in a disastrous interception ending the Redskins' last hopes for a come-from-behind victory in the 1971 play-offs. They lost—the final score was 24 to 20. Two weeks later Nixon announced he was backing Miami against Dallas in the Super Bowl. This time he went so far as to send in a play which once again backfired disastrously. Miami lost 24 to 3. The Nixon jinx continued to plague the Redskins again in the 1973 Super Bowl, despite quarterback Bill Kilmer's widely-quoted statement that this time he would just as soon do without the President's tactical advice. The Redskins were three-point favorites against the Dolphins this time around, but with Nixon on their side they got blown out of the stadium and wound up on the sick end of a deceptively one-sided 14 to 7 defeat.

tions are we going to have to write off as lame but "regrettably necessary" holding actions? And how many more of these stinking, double-downer sideshows will we have to go through before we can get ourselves straight enough to put together some kind of national election that will give me and the at least 20 million people I tend to agree with a chance to vote *for* something, instead of always being faced with that old familiar choice between the lesser of two evils?

I have been through three presidential elections, now, but it has been twelve years since I could look at a ballot and see a name I wanted to vote *for*. In 1964, I refused to vote at all, and in '68 I spent half a morning in the county courthouse getting an absentee ballot so I could vote, out of spite, for Dick Gregory.

Now, with another one of these big bogus showdowns looming down on us, I can already pick up the stench of another bummer. I understand, along with a lot of other people, that the big thing, this year, is Beating Nixon. But that was also the big thing, as I recall, twelve years ago in 1960—and as far as I can tell, we've gone from bad to worse to rotten since then, and the outlook is for more of the same.

Not even James Reston, the swinging Calvinist, claims to see any light at the end of the tunnel in '72. Reston's first big shot of the year dealt mainly with a grim "memo" by former JFK strategist, Fred Dutton, who is now a Washington lawyer.

There are hints of hope in the Reston/Dutton prognosis, but not for the next four years. Here is the rancid nut of it: "The 1972 election probably is fated to be a dated, weakening election, an historical curio, belonging more to the past than to the new national three or four-party trend of the future."

Reston either ignored or overlooked, for some reason, the probability that Gene McCarthy appears to be gearing up almost exactly the kind of "independent third force in American politics" that both Reston and Dutton see as a wave of the future.

An even grimmer note comes with Reston's offhand dismissal of Ed Muskie, the only man—according to E. B. Williams—who can possibly save us from more years of Nixon. And as if poor Muskie didn't already have enough evil shit on his neck, the eminently reasonable, fine old liberal journal, the Washington *Post,* called Muskie's official "new beginning/I am now a candidate" speech on national TV a meaningless rehash of old bullshit and stale cliches raked up from old speeches by . . . yes . . . Himself, Richard Milhous Nixon.

In other words, the weight of the evidence filtering down from the high brain-rooms of both the New York *Times* and the Washington *Post* seems to say we're all fucked. Muskie is a bonehead who steals his best lines from old Nixon speeches. McGovern is doomed because everybody who knows him has so much respect for the man that they can't bring themselves to degrade the poor bastard by making him run for President . . . John Lindsay is a dunce, Gene McCarthy is crazy, Humphrey is doomed and useless, Jackson should have stayed in bed . . . and, well, that just about wraps up the trip, right?

Not entirely, but I feel The Fear coming on, and the only cure for that is to chew up a fat black wad of blood-opium about the size of a young meatball and then call a cab for a fast run down to that strip of X-film houses on 14th Street . . . peel back the the brain, let the opium take hold, and get locked into serious pornography.

As for politics, I think Art Buchwald said it all last month in his "Fan letter to Nixon."

"I always wanted to get into politics, but I was never light enough to make the team."

February

Fear & Loathing in New Hampshire . . . Back on
the Campaign Trail in Manchester, Keene & The
Booth Fish Hatcheries . . . Harold Hughes Is
Your Friend . . . Weird Memories of '68: A
Private Conversation with Richard Nixon . . . Will
Dope Doom the Cowboys? . . . A First, Massive
& Reluctantly Final Judgment on the Reality of
George McGovern . . . Small Hope for the
Hammer & No Hope At All for the
Press Wizards . . .

IT WAS JUST BEFORE MIDNIGHT when I left Cambridge and headed
north on U.S. 93 toward Manchester—driving one of those big
green rented Auto/Stick Cougars that gets rubber for about twenty-
nine seconds in Drive, and spits hot black divots all over the road
in First or Second . . . a terrible screeching and fishtailing through
the outskirts of Boston heading north to New Hampshire, back on
the Campaign Trail . . . running late, as usual: left hand on the
wheel and the other on the radio dial, seeking music, and a glass
of iced Wild Turkey spilling into my crotch on every turn.

Not much of a moon tonight, but a sky full of very bright
stars. Freezing cold outside; patches of ice on the road and snow
on the sidehills . . . running about seventy-five or eighty through
a landscape of stark naked trees and stone fences; the highway
is empty and no lights in the roadside farmhouses. People go
to bed early in New England

Four years ago I ran this road in a different Mercury, but I
wasn't driving then. It was a big yellow sedan with a civvy-clothes

cop at the wheel. Sitting next to the cop, up front, were two of Nixon's top speechwriters: Ray Price and Pat Buchannan.

There were only two of us in back: just me and Richard Nixon, and we were talking football in a very serious way. It was late—almost midnight then, too—and the cop was holding the big Merc at exactly sixty-five as we hissed along the highway for more than an hour between some American Legion hall in a small town somewhere near Nashua where Nixon had just made a speech, to the airport up in Manchester where a Lear Jet was waiting to whisk the candidate and his brain-trust off to Key Biscayne for a Think Session.

It was a very weird trip; probably one of the weirdest things I've ever done, and especially weird because both Nixon and I enjoyed it. We had a good talk, and when we got to the airport, I stood around the Lear Jet with Dick and the others, chatting in a very relaxed way about how successful his swing through New Hampshire had been . . . and as he climbed into the plane it seemed only natural to thank him for the ride and shake hands. . . .

But suddenly I was seized from behind and jerked away from the plane. Good God, I thought as I reeled backwards, Here We Go . . . "Watch Out!" somebody was shouting. "Get the cigarette!" A hand lashed out of the darkness to snatch the cigarette out of my mouth, then other hands kept me from falling and I recognized the voice of Nick Ruwe, Nixon's chief advance man for New Hampshire, saying, "God damnit, Hunter, you almost blew up the plane!"

I shrugged. He was right. I'd been leaning over the fuel tank with a burning butt in my mouth. Nixon smiled and reached out to shake hands again, while Ruwe muttered darkly and the others stared down at the asphalt.

The plane took off and I rode back to the Holiday Inn with Nick Ruwe. We laughed about the cigarette scare, but he was still brooding. "What worries me," he said, "is that nobody else noticed it. Christ, those guys get paid to *protect* the Boss . . ."

"Very bad show," I said, "especially when you remember that I did about three king-size Marlboros while we were standing there. Hell, I was flicking the butts away, lighting new ones . . . you people are lucky I'm a sane, responsible journalist; otherwise

I might have hurled my flaming Zippo into the fuel tank."

"Not you," he said. "Egomaniacs don't do that kind of thing." He smiled. "You wouldn't do anything you couldn't live to write about, would you?"

"You're probably right," I said. "Kamikaze is not my style. I much prefer subtleties, the low-key approach—because I am, after all, a professional."

"We know. That's why you're along."

Actually, the reason was very different: I was the only one in the press corps that evening who claimed to be as seriously addicted to pro football as Nixon himself. I was also the only out-front, openly hostile Peace Freak; the only one wearing old Levis and a ski jacket, the only one (no, there was *one* other) who'd smoked grass on Nixon's big Greyhound press bus, and certainly the only one who habitually referred to the candidate as "the Dingbat."

So I still had to credit the bastard for having the balls to choose *me*—out of the fifteen or twenty straight/heavy press types who'd been pleading for two or three weeks for even a five-minute interview—as the one who should share the back seat with him on this Final Ride through New Hampshire.

But there was, of course, a catch. I had to agree to talk about *nothing except football.* "We want the Boss to relax," Ray Price told me, "but he can't relax if you start yelling about Vietnam, race riots or drugs. He wants to ride with somebody who can talk *football.*" He cast a baleful eye at the dozen or so reporters waiting to board the press bus, then shook his head sadly. "I checked around," he said. "But the others are hopeless—so I guess you're it."

"Wonderful," I said. "Let's do it."

We had a fine time. I enjoyed it—which put me a bit off balance, because I'd figured Nixon didn't know any more about football than he did about ending the war in Vietnam. He had made a lot of allusions to things like "end runs" and "power sweeps" on the stump but it never occurred to me that he actually *knew* anything more about football than he knew about the Grateful Dead.

But I was wrong. Whatever else might be said about Nixon—and there is still serious doubt in my mind that he could pass for Human—he is a goddamn stone fanatic on every facet of pro football. At one point in our conversation, when I was feeling a bit pressed for leverage, I mentioned a down & out pass—in the waning moments of the 1967 Super Bowl mismatch between Green Bay and Oakland—to an obscure, second-string Oakland receiver named Bill Miller that had stuck in my mind because of its pinpoint style & precision.

He hesitated for a moment, lost in thought, then he whacked me on the thigh & laughed: "That's right, by God! The Miami boy!"

I was stunned. He not only remembered the play, but he knew where Miller had played in college.

That was four years ago. LBJ was Our President and there was no real hint, in the winter of '68, that he was about to cash his check. Johnson seemed every bit as tough and invulnerable then as Nixon seems today . . . and it is slightly unnerving to recall that Richard Nixon, at that point in his campaign, appeared to have about as much chance of getting himself elected to the White House as Hubert Humphrey appears to have now, in February of '72.

When Nixon went into New Hampshire, he was viewed by the pros as just another of these stubborn, right-wing waterheads with nothing better to do. The polls showed him comfortably ahead of George Romney, but according to most of the big-time press wizards who were hanging around Manchester at the time, the Nixon-Romney race was only a drill that would end just as soon as Nelson Rockefeller came in to mop up both of them. The bar at the Wayfarer Motor Inn was a sort of unofficial press headquarters, where the press people hovered in nervous anticipation of the Rockefeller announcement that was said to be coming "at any moment."

So I was not entirely overcome at the invitation to spend an hour alone with Richard Nixon. He was, after all, a Born Loser—even if he somehow managed to get the Republican nomination I figured he didn't have a sick goat's chance of beating Lyndon Johnson.

I was as guilty as all the others, that year, of treating the McCarthy campaign as a foredoomed exercise in noble futility. We had talked about it a lot—not only in the Wayfarer bar, but also in the bar of the Holiday Inn where Nixon was staying—and the press consensus was that the only Republican with a chance to beat Johnson was Nelson Rockefeller . . . and the only other possible winner was Bobby Kennedy, who had already made it clear—both publicly and privately—that he would definitely *not* run for President in 1968.

I was remembering all this as I cranked the big green Cougar along U.S. 93 once again, four years later, to cover another one of these flakey New Hampshire primaries. The electorate in this state is notoriously perverse and unpredictable. In 1964, for instance, it was a thumping victory in the New Hampshire primary that got the Henry Cabot Lodge steamroller off to a roaring start . . . and in '68, Gene McCarthy woke up on the morning of election day to read in the newspapers that the last minute polls were nearly unanimous in giving him between six and eight percent of the vote . . . and even McCarthy was stunned, I think, to wake up twenty-four hours later and find himself with 42 percent.

Strange country up here; New Hampshire and Vermont appear to be the East's psychic answer to Colorado and New Mexico—big lonely hills laced with back roads and old houses where people live almost aggressively by themselves. The insularity of the old-timers, nursing their privacy along with their harsh right-wing politics, is oddly similar and even receptive to the insularity of the newcomers, the young dropouts and former left-wing activists—people like Andy Kopkind and Ray Mungo, co-founder of the Liberation News Service—who've been moving into these hills in ever increasing numbers since the end of the Sixties. The hitchhikers you find along these narrow twisting highways look exactly like the people you see on the roads around Boulder and Aspen or Taos.

The girl riding with me tonight is looking for an old boyfriend who moved out of Boston and is now living, she says, in a chicken coop in a sort of informal commune near Greenville, N.H. It is five or six degrees above zero outside and she doesn't even have a blanket, much less a sleeping bag, but this doesn't worry her. "I guess it sounds crazy," she explains. "We don't even sleep together. He's just a friend. But I'm happy when I'm with him because he makes me like myself."

Jesus, I thought. We've raised a generation of stone desperate cripples. She is twenty-two, a journalism grad from Boston University, and now—six months out of college—she talks so lonely and confused that she is eagerly looking forward to spending a few nights in a frozen chicken coop with some poor bastard who doesn't even know she's coming.

The importance of Liking Yourself is a notion that fell heavily out of favor during the coptic, anti-ego frenzy of the Acid Era—but nobody guessed, back then, that the experiment might churn up this kind of hangover: a whole subculture of frightened illiterates with no faith in anything.

The girl was not interested in whatever reasons I might have for going up to Manchester to spend a few days with the McGovern campaign. She had no plans to vote in *any* election, for President or anything else.

She tried to be polite, but it was obvious after two or three minutes of noise that she didn't know what the fuck I was talking about, and cared less. It was boring; just another queer hustle in a world full of bummers that will swarm you every time if you don't keep moving.

Like her ex-boyfriend. At first he was only stoned all the time, but now he was shooting smack and acting very crazy. He would call and say he was on his way over, then not show up for three days—and then he'd be out of his head, screaming at her, not making any sense.

It was too much, she said. She loved him, but he seemed to be drifting away. We stopped at a donut shop in Marlboro and I saw she was crying, which made me feel like a monster because I'd been saying some fairly hard things about "junkies" and "loonies" and "doomfreaks."

63

Once they let you get away with running around for ten years like a king hoodlum, you tend to forget now and then that about half the people you meet live from one day to the next in a state of such fear and uncertainty that about half the time they honestly doubt their own sanity.

These are not the kind of people who really need to get hung up in depressing political trips. They are not ready for it. Their boats are rocking so badly that all they want to do is get level long enough to think straight and avoid the next nightmare.

This girl I was delivering up to the chicken coop was one of those people. She was terrified of almost everything, including me, and this made me very uncomfortable.

We couldn't find the commune. The directions were too vague: "Go far to the dim yellow light, then right at the big tree . . . proceed to the fork and then slow to the place where the road shines. . . ."

After two hours of this I was half crazy. We had been back and forth across the same grid of backroads two or three times, with no luck . . . but finally we found it, a very peaceful-looking place on a cold hill in the woods. She went inside the main building for a while, then came back out to tell me everything was OK.

I shrugged, feeling a little sad because I could tell by the general vibrations that things were not really "OK." I was tempted to take her into Manchester with me, but I knew that would only compound the problem for both of us . . . checking into the Wayfarer at 3:30, then up again at seven for a quick breakfast, and then into the press bus for a long day of watching McGovern shake hands with people at factory gates.

Could she handle that madness? Probably not. And even if she could, why do it? A political campaign is a very narrow ritual, where anything weird is unwelcome. I am trouble enough by myself; they would never tolerate me if I showed up with a nervous blonde nymphet who thought politics was some kind of game played by old people, like bridge.

No, it would never do. But on my way into Manchester, driving like a werewolf, it occurred to me that maybe I was not quite as sane as I'd always thought I was. There is something seriously bent, when you think on it, in the notion that a man with good sense would race out of his peaceful mountain home in Colorado and fly off in a frenzy like some kind of electrified turkey buzzard to spend three or four days being carried around the foulest sections of New England like a piece of meat, to watch another man, who says he wants to be President, embarrassing a lot of people by making them shake his hand outside factory gates at sunrise.

Earlier that night, in Cambridge—over dinner at a bogus Mexican restaurant run by Italian junkies—several people had asked me why I was wasting my time on "this kind of bullshit." McGovern, Muskie, Lindsay, or even Gene McCarthy. I had just come back from a long day at the Massachusetts "Rad/Lib Caucus" in Worchester, billed as a statewide rally to decide which Democratic candidate to support in the Massachusetts primary on April 25th.

The idea, said the organizers, was to *unify* and avoid a disastrous vote-splitting orgy that would splinter the Left between McGovern, Lindsay & McCarthy—thus guaranteeing an easy Muskie win. The Caucus organizers were said to be well-known McCarthy supporters, who'd conceived the gathering as a sort of launching pad for Gene in '72 . . . and McCarthy seemed to agree; he was the only candidate to attend the Caucus in person, and his appearance drew a booming ovation that gave every indication of a pending victory.

The night before, at a crowded student rally in Hogan Student Center at Holy Cross, McCarthy had responded to a questioner who asked if he was "really a serious candidate" by saying: "You'll see how serious I am after tomorrow's Caucus."

The crowd at Holy Cross responded with a rolling cheer. The median age, that night, was somewhere around nineteen and McCarthy was impressively sharp and confident as he drew roar after roar of applause with his quietly vicious attack on Nixon, Humphrey, and Muskie. As I stood there in the doorway of the auditorium, looking across the shoulders of the overflow crowd, it looked like 1968 all over again. There was a definite sense of drama in seeing McCarthy back on the stump, cranking up another crusade.

But that high didn't last long. The site of Saturday's Caucus was the gym at Assumption College, across town, and the crowd over there was very different. The median age at the Caucus was more like thirty-three and the results of the first ballot were a staggering blow to McCarthy's newborn crusade.

McGovern cleaned up, beating McCarthy almost three to one. When the final tally came in, after more than eight hours of infighting, McGovern's quietly efficient grass-roots organizers had locked up 62 percent of the vote—leaving McCarthy to split the rest, more or less equally, with Shirley Chisholm. Both Muskie and Lindsay had tried to ignore the Caucus, claiming it was "stacked" against them, and as a result neither one got enough votes to even mention.

The outcome of the Massachusetts Rad/Lib Caucus was a shock to almost everybody except the busloads of McGovern supporters who had come there to flex their muscle in public for the first time. McCarthy—who had left early to fly back to Washington for an appearance the next day on *Meet the Press*—was seriously jolted by the loss. He showed it the next morning on TV when he looked like a ball of bad nerves caught in a crossfire of hostile questions from Roger Mudd and George Herman. He was clearly off-balance; a nervous shadow of the rising-tide, hammerhead spoiler he had been on Friday night for the rally at Holy Cross.

To make things worse, one of the main organizers of the Rad/Lib Caucus was Jerry Grossman, a wealthy envelope manufacturer from Newton, in the Boston suburbs, and a key McCarthy fundraiser in the '68 campaign . . . but after the Rad/Lib Caucus, Grossman went far out of his way, along with Mudd & Herman, to make sure McCarthy was done for.

He immediately endorsed McGovern, saying it was clear that "Massachusetts liberals no longer believe in McCarthy's leadership quotient." What this meant, according to the unanimous translation by political pros and press wizards, was, "McCarthy won't get any more of Grossman's money."

Grossman ignored the obvious fact that he and other pro-McCarthy heavies had been beaten stupid, on the grass-roots organizing level, by an unheralded "McGovern machine" put together in Massachusetts by John Reuther—a nephew of Walter, late president of the UAW. I spent most of that afternoon wandering around the gym, listening to people talk and watching the action, and it was absolutely clear—once the voting started—that Reuther had everything wired.

Everywhere I went there was a local McGovern floor manager keeping people in line, telling them exactly what was happening and what would probably happen next . . . while the McCarthy forces—led by veteran Kennedy/Camelot field marshal Richard Goodwin—became more and more demoralized, caught in a fast-rising pincers movement between a surprisingly organized McGovern block on their Right, and a wild-eyed Chisholm uprising on the Left.

The Chisholm strength shocked everybody. She was one of twelve names on the ballot—which included almost every conceivable Democratic candidate from Hubert Humphrey to Patsy Mink, Wilbur Mills, and Sam Yorty—but after Muskie and Lindsay dropped out, the Caucus was billed far and wide as a test between McGovern and McCarthy. There was no mention in the press or anywhere else that some unknown black woman from Brooklyn might seriously challenge these famous liberal heavies on their own turf . . . but when the final vote came in, Shirley Chisholm had actually beaten Gene McCarthy, who finished a close third.

The Chisholm challenge was a last-minute idea and only half-organized, on the morning of the Caucus, by a handful of speedy young black politicos and Women's Lib types—but by 6:00 that evening it had developed from a noisy idea into a solid power

Shirley Chisholm

bloc. What began as a symbolic kind of challenge became a serious position after the first ballot—among this overwhelmingly white, liberal, affluent, well-educated, and over-thirty audience—when almost half of them refused to vote for George McGovern because he seemed "too conventional," as one long-haired kid in a ski parka told me.

They had nothing *against* McGovern; they agreed with almost everything he said—but they wanted more; and it is interesting to speculate about what might have happened if the same people who showed up at McCarthy's Holy Cross rally on Friday night had come out to Assumption on Sunday.

There were not many Youth/Freak vote types at the Rad/Lib Caucus; perhaps one out of five, and probably not even that. The bulk of the crowd looked like professors and their wives from Amherst. One of the problems, according to a bushy young radical-talking non-student from Boston, was that you had to pay a "registration fee" of two dollars before you got a vote.

"Shit," he said. "I wouldn't pay it myself, so I can't vote." He shrugged. "But this Caucus doesn't mean anything, anyway. This is just a bunch of old liberals getting their rocks off."

Manchester, New Hampshire, is a broken down mill town on the Merrimack River with an aggressive Chamber of Commerce and America's worst newspaper. There is not much else to say for it, except that Manchester is a welcome change from Washington, D.C.

I checked into the Wayfarer just before dawn and tried to get some music on my high-powered waterproof Sony, but there was nothing worth listening to. Not even out of Boston or Cambridge. So I slept a few hours and then joined the McGovern caravan for a tour of the Booth Fisheries, in Portsmouth.

It was a wonderful experience. We stood near the time clock as the shifts changed & McGovern did his hand-grabbing thing. There was no way to avoid him, so the workers shuffled by and tried to be polite. McGovern was blocking the approach to the drinking fountain, above which hung a sign saying "Dip Hands

69

in Hand Solution Before Returning to Work."

The place was like a big aircraft hangar full of fish, with a strange cold gaseous haze hanging over everything—and a lot of hissing & humming from the fish-packing machines on the assembly line. I have always liked seafood, but after thirty minutes in that place I lost my appetite for it.

The next drill was the official opening of the new McGovern headquarters in Dover, where a large crowd of teenagers and middle-class liberals were gathered to meet the candidate. This age pattern seemed to prevail at every one of McGovern's public appearances: The crowds were always a mix of people either under twenty or over forty. The meaning of this age gap didn't hit me until I looked back on my notes and saw how consistent it was . . . even at the Massachusetts Rad/Lib Caucus, where I guessed the median age to be thirty-three, that figure was a rough mathematical compromise, rather than a physical description. In both Massachusetts and New Hampshire, the McGovern/McCarthy crowds were noticeably barren of people between twenty-five & thirty-five.

After Dover, the next speech was scheduled for the main auditorium at the Exeter Academy for Boys, an exclusive prep school about twenty-five miles up the road. The schedule showed a two-hour break for dinner at the Exeter Inn, where the McGovern press party took over about half the dining room.

I can't recommend the food at that place, because they wouldn't let me eat. The only other person barred from the dining room that night was Tim Crouse, from the *Rolling Stone* bureau in Boston. Neither one of us was acceptably dressed, they said—no ties, no three-button herringbone jackets—so we had to wait in the bar with James J. Kilpatrick, the famous crypto-nazi newspaper columnist. He made no attempt to sit with us, but he made sure that everybody in the room knew exactly who he was. He kept calling the bartender "Jim," which was not his name, and the bartender, becoming more & more nervous, began addressing Kilpatrick as "Mr. Reynolds."

Finally Kilpatrick lost his temper. "My name's not Reynolds, goddamnit! I'm James J. Kilpatrick of the Washington *Evening Star*." Then he hauled his paunch off the chair and reeled out to the lobby.

The Exeter stop was not a happy one for McGovern, because word had just come in from Frank Mankiewicz, his "political director" in Washington, that McGovern's old friend and staunch liberal ally from Iowa—Senator Harold Hughes—had just announced he was endorsing Ed Muskie.

This news hit the campaign caravan like a dung-bomb. Hughes had been one of the few Senators that McGovern was counting on to hang tough. The Hughes/McGovern/Fred Harris (D-Okla.) axis has been the closest thing in the Senate to a Populist power bloc for the past two years. Even the Muskie endorsement-hustlers who were criss-crossing the nation putting pressure on local politicians to come out for Big Ed hadn't bothered with Hughes, because they considered him "un-touchable." If anything, he was thought to be more radical and intransigent than McGovern himself.

Hughes had grown a beard; he didn't mind admitting that he talked to trees now and then—and a few months earlier he had challenged the party hierarchy by forcing a public showdown between himself and Larry O'Brien's personal choice for the chairmanship of the all-important Credentials Committee at the national convention.

Dick Dougherty, a former Los Angeles *Times* newsman who is handling McGovern's national press action in New Hampshire, was so shaken by the news of Hughes' defection that he didn't even try to explain it when reporters began asking Why? Dougherty had just gotten the word when the crowded press limo left Dover for Exeter, and he did his best to fend off our questions until he could talk to the candidate and agree on what to say. But in terms of campaign morale, it was as if somebody had slashed all the tires on every car in the caravan, including the candidate's. When we got to the Exeter Inn I half expected to see a filthy bearded raven perched over the entrance, croaking "Nevermore. . . ."

By chance, I found George downstairs in the Men's Room,

hovering into a urinal and staring straight ahead at the grey marble tiles.

"Say . . . ah . . . I hate to mention this," I said. "But what about this thing with Hughes?"

He flinched and quickly zipped his pants up, shaking his head and mumbling something about "a deal for the vice-presidency." I could see that he didn't want to talk about it, but I wanted to get his reaction before he and Dougherty could put a story together.

"Why do you think he did it?" I said.

He was washing his hands, staring down at the sink. "Well . . . ," he said finally. "I guess I shouldn't say this, Hunter, but I honestly don't know. I'm surprised; we're *all* surprised."

He looked very tired, and I didn't see much point in prodding him to say anything else about what was clearly a painful subject. We walked upstairs together, but I stopped at the desk to get a newspaper while he went into the dining room.

This proved to be my un-doing, because the doorkeeper would no doubt have welcomed me very politely if I'd entered with The Senator . . . but as it happened, I was shunted off to the bar with Crouse & James J. Kilpatrick, who was wearing a vest & a blue pin-stripe suit.

A lot has been written about McGovern's difficulties on the campaign trail, but most of it is far off the point. The career pols and press wizards say he simply lacks "charisma," but that's a cheap and simplistic idea that is more an insult to the electorate than to McGovern. The assholes who run politics in this country have become so mesmerized by the Madison Avenue school of campaigning that they actually believe, now, that all it takes to become a Congressman or a Senator—or even a President—is a nice set of teeth, a big wad of money, and a half-dozen Media Specialists.

McGovern, they say, doesn't make it on this level. Which is probably true. But McCarthy was worse. His '68 campaign had *none* of the surface necessities. He had no money, no press, no endorsements, no camera-presence . . . his only asset was a good eye for the opening, and a good enough ear to pick up the distant rumble of a groundswell with nobody riding it.

★

There is nothing in McGovern's campaign, so far, to suggest that he understands this kind of thing. For all his integrity, he is still talking to the Politics of the Past. He is still naive enough to assume that anybody who is honest & intelligent—with a good voting record on "the issues"—is a natural man for the White House.

But this is stone bullshit. There are only two ways to make it in big-time politics today: One is to come on like a mean dinosaur, with a high-powered machine that scares the shit out of your entrenched opposition (like Daley or Nixon) . . . and the other is to tap the massive, frustrated energies of a mainly young, disillusioned electorate that has long since abandoned the idea that we all have a *duty* to vote. This is like being told you have a *duty* to buy a new car, but you have to choose immediately between a Ford and a Chevy.

McGovern's failure to understand this is what brought people like Lindsay and McCarthy and Shirley Chisholm into the campaign. They all sense an untouched constituency. Chisholm's campaign manager, a sleek young pol from Kansas named Jerry Robinson, calls it the "Sleeping Giant vote."

"Nobody's reaching them," he said. "We got a lot of people out there with nobody they think they can vote for."

Ron Dellums, the black Congressman from Berkeley, called it "the Nigger vote." But he wasn't talking about skin pigment.

"It's time for somebody to lead all of America's Niggers," he said at the Capitol Hill press conference when Shirley Chisholm announced she was running for President. "And by this I mean the Young, the Black, the Brown, the Women, the Poor—all the people who feel left out of the political process. If we can put the Nigger Vote together, we can bring about some real change in this country."

Dellums is probably the only elected official in America who feels politically free enough to stare at the cameras and make a straight-faced pitch to the "Nigger Vote." But he is also enough of a politician to know it's out there . . . maybe not in the Exeter Inn, but the hills north and west of Manchester are teeming with Niggers. They didn't turn out for the speech-making, and they probably won't vote in the primary—but they are there, and there are a hell of a lot of them.

Looking back on that week in New Hampshire, it was mainly a matter of following George McGovern around and watching him do his thing—which was pleasant, or at least vaguely uplifting, but not what you'd call a real jerk-around.

McGovern is not one of your classic fireballs on the stump. His campaign workers in New Hampshire seem vaguely afflicted by a sense of uncertainty about what it all means. They are very *decent* people. They are working hard, they are very sincere, and most of them are young volunteers who get their pay in room & board . . . but they lack something crucial, and that lack is painfully obvious to anybody who remembers the mood of the McCarthy volunteers in 1968.

Those people were *angry*. The other side of that "Clean for Gene" coin was a nervous sense of truce that hung over the New Hampshire campaign. In backroom late night talks at the Wayfarer there was no shortage of McCarthy staffers who said this would probably be their final trip "within the system." There were some who didn't mind admitting that, personally, they'd rather throw firebombs or get heavy into dope—but they were attracted by the drama, the sheer balls, of McCarthy's "hopeless challenge."

McCarthy's national press man at the time was Seymour Hersh, who quit the campaign in Wisconsin and called Gene a closet racist.[1] Two years later, Sy Hersh was back in the public ear with a story about a place called My Lai, in South Vietnam. He was the one who dragged it out in the open.

---

1. Hersh now denies that this is exactly what he said. "I was mad as hell when I quit the McCarthy campaign," he explains. "I might have said almost anything."

McCarthy's state-level press man that year was a hair-freak named Bill Gallagher, who kept his room in the Wayfarer open from midnight to dawn as a sort of all-night refuge for weed fanciers. A year later, when I returned to New Hampshire to write a piece on ski racer Jean-Claude Killy, I got off the cocktail circuit long enough to locate Gallagher in a small Vermont hamlet where he was living as the de facto head of a mini-commune. He had dropped out of politics with a vengeance; his beard was down to his belt and his head was far out of politics. "The McCarthy thing" had been "a bad trip," he explained. He no longer cared who was President.

You don't find people like Hersh and Gallagher around Mc-Govern's headquarters in Manchester this year. They would frighten the staff. McGovern's main man in New Hampshire is a fat young pol named Joe Granmaison, whose personal style hovers somewhere between that of a state trooper and a used-car sales-man.

Granmaison was eager to nail Muskie: "If we elect a President who three years ago said, 'Gee, I made a mistake' . . . well, I think it's about time these people were held *accountable* for those mis-takes."

Indeed. But Granmaison backed away from me like he'd stepped on a rattlesnake when I asked him if it were true that he'd been a *Johnson delegate* to the Chicago convention in '68.

We met at a McGovern cocktail party in a downstate hamlet called Keene. "Let's talk about this word *'accountable,'* I said. I get the feeling you stepped in shit on that one . . ."

"What do you mean?" he snapped. "Just because I was a Johnson delegate doesn't mean anything. *I'm* not running for office."

"Good," I said. We were standing in a short hallway between the kitchen and the living room, where McGovern was saying, "The thing the political bosses want most is for young people to drop out . . . because they know the young people can *change* the system, and the bosses don't *want* any change."

True enough, I thought. But how do you "change the system" by hiring a young fogey like Granmaison to wire up your act in New Hampshire? With a veteran Judas Goat like that in charge of the operation, it's no wonder that McGovern's Manchester head-quarters is full of people who talk like nervous PoliSci students on job-leave.

Joe didn't feel like discussing his gig at the '68 Convention. Which is understandable. If I had done a thing like that, I wouldn't want to talk about it either. I tried to change the subject, but he crammed a handful of potato chips into his mouth and walked away.

Later that night, after the cocktail party, we drove out to the Student Union hall at Keene State College, where McGovern addressed a big and genuinely friendly crowd of almost 3000, jammed into a hall meant for 2000 tops. The advance man had done his work well.

The big question tonight was "Amnesty," and when Mc-Govern said he was for it, the crowd came alive. This was, after all, the first time any active candidate for the presidency had said "Yes" on the Amnesty question—which is beginning to look like a time-bomb with almost as much Spoiler Potential as the busing issue.

They both have long and tangled roots, but it is hard to imagine any question in American politics today that could have more long-range impact than the argument over "Amnesty,"—which is nothing more or less than a proposal to grant presidential pardon to all draft dodgers and U.S. military deserters, on the grounds that history has absolved them. Because if the Vietnam War was *wrong* from the start—as even Nixon has tacitly admitted—then it is hard to avoid the logic of the argument that says the Anti-War Exiles were *right* for refusing to fight it.

There is not much room for politics in the Amnesty argument. It boils down to an official admission that the American Military Establishment—acting in spiritual concert with the White House and the national Business Community—was Wrong.

Almost everybody except Joe Alsop has already admitted this, in private . . . but it is going to be a very painful thing to say in public.

It will be especially painful to the people who got their sons shipped back to them in rubber sacks, and to the thousands of young Vets who got their arms and their legs and balls blown off for what the White House and Ed Muskie now admit was "a mistake."

But 60,000 Americans have died for that "mistake," along with several million Vietnamese . . . and it is only now becoming clear that the "war dead" will also include hundreds of thousands of Cambodians, Laotians, and Thais. When this war goes into the history books, the United States Air Force will rank as the most efficient gang of murderers in the history of man.

Richard Nixon is flatly opposed to a general amnesty for the men who refused to fight this tragic war. Muskie agrees, but he says he might change his mind once the war ends . . . and Lindsay, as usual, is both for and against it.

The only "candidates" in favor of Amnesty are McGovern and Ted Kennedy. I watched McGovern deal with the question when it popped out of that overflow student audience at Keene State. He was talking very sharp, very confident, and when the question of Amnesty came up, he got right on it, saying "Yes, I'm in favor. . . ."

This provoked a nice outburst of cheers and applause. It was a very strong statement, and the students clearly dug it.

Then, moments later, somebody tossed out the fishhook—asking McGovern if he had any plans, pro or con, about supporting Muskie, if Big Ed got the nod in Miami.

McGovern paused, shifted uneasily for a second or so at the podium, then said: "Yes, I'm inclined to that position." I was standing behind him on the stage, looking out at the crowd through a slit in the big velvet curtain, and according to the red-inked speed-scrawl in my notebook, the audience responded with . . . "No cheering, confused silence, the audience seems to *sag.* . . ."

But these were only my notes. Perhaps I was wrong—but even making a certain allowance for my own bias, it still seems perfectly logical to assume that an audience of first-time voters might be at least momentarily confused by a Left/Champion Democratic candidate who says in one breath that his opponent is dead wrong on a very crucial issue . . . and then in the next breath says he plans to support that opponent if he wins the nomination.

I doubt if I was the only person in the hall, at that moment, who thought: "Well, shit . . . if you plan to support him in July, why not support him *now*, and get it over with?"

Moments later, the speech ended and I found myself out on the sidewalk shooting up with Ray Morgan, a veteran political analyst from the Kansas City *Star*. He was on his way to the airport, with McGovern, for a quick flight on the charter plane to Washington, and he urged me to join him.

But I didn't feel up to it. I felt like thinking for a while, running that narrow, icy, little highway back to Manchester just as fast as the Cougar would make it and still hold the road—which was not very fast, so I had plenty of time to brood, and to wonder why I felt so depressed.

I had not come to New Hampshire with any illusions about McGovern or his trip—which was, after all, a longshot underdog challenge that even the people running his campaign said was not much better than 30 to 1.

What depressed me, I think, was that McGovern was the only alternative available this time around, and I was sorry I couldn't get up for it. I agreed with everything he said, but I wished he would say a lot more—or maybe something different.

Ideas? Specifics? Programs? Etc.?

Well . . . that would take a lot of time and space I don't have now, but for openers I think maybe it is no longer enough to have been "against the War in Vietnam since 1963"—especially when your name is not one of the two Senators who voted against the Gulf of Tonkin Resolution in 1964 and when you're talking to people who got their first taste of tear gas at anti-war rallies in places like Berkeley and Cambridge in early '65.

A lot of blood has gone under the bridge since then, and we have all learned a hell of a lot about the realities of Politics in America. Even the politicians have learned—but, as usual, the politicians are much slower than the people they want to lead.

This is an ugly portent for the 25 million or so new voters between 18 and 25 who may or many not vote in 1972. And many

78

of them probably *will* vote. The ones who go to the polls in '72 will be the most committed, the most idealistic, the "best minds of my generation," as Allen Ginsberg said it fourteen years ago in "Howl." There is not much doubt that the hustlers behind the "Youth Vote" will get a lot of people out to the polls in '72. If you give 25 million people a new toy, the odds are pretty good that a lot of them will try it at least once.

But what about next time? Who is going to explain in 1976 that all the people who felt they got burned in '72 should "try again" for another bogus challenger? Four years from now there will be two entire generations—between the ages of 22 and 40— who will not give a hoot in hell about *any* election, and their apathy will be rooted in personal experience. Four years from now it will be very difficult to convince anybody who has gone from Johnson/ Goldwater to Humphrey/Nixon to Nixon/Muskie that there is any possible reason for getting involved in another bullshit election.

This is the gibberish that churned in my head on the drive back from Manchester. Every now and then I would pass a car with New Hampshire plates and the motto "Live Free or Die" inscribed above the numbers.

The highways are full of good mottos. But T. S. Eliot put them all in a sack when he coughed up that line about . . . what was it? Have these Dangerous Drugs fucked my memory? Maybe so. But I think it went something like this:

"Between the Idea and the Reality . . . Falls the Shadow."

The Shadow? I could almost *smell* the bastard behind me when I made the last turn into Manchester. It was late Tuesday night, and tomorrow's schedule was calm. All the candidates had zipped off to Florida—except for Sam Yorty, and I didn't feel ready for that.

The next day, around noon, I drove down to Boston. The only hitchhiker I saw was an 18-year-old kid with long black hair who

Mad Sam and wife touring New Hampshire on the Yortymobile.

was going to Reading—or "Redding," as he said it —but when I asked him who he planned to vote for in the election he looked at me like I'd said something crazy.

"What election?" he asked.

"Never mind," I said. "I was only kidding."

One of the favorite parlor games in Left/Liberal circles from Beverly Hills to Chevy Chase to the Upper East Side and Cambridge has been—for more than a year, now—a sort of guilty, half-public breast-beating whenever George McGovern's name is mentioned. He has become the Willy Loman of the Left; he is liked, but not *well*-Liked, and his failure to make the big charismatic breakthrough has made him the despair of his friends. They can't figure it out.

A few weeks ago I drove over to Chevy Chase—to the "White side" of Rock Creek Park—to have dinner with McGovern and a few of his heavier friends. The idea was to have a small, loose-talking dinner and let George relax after a week on the stump in New Hampshire. He arrived looking tired and depressed. Somebody handed him a drink and he slumped down on the couch, not saying much but listening intently as the talk quickly turned to "the McGovern problem."

For more than a year now, he's been saying all the right things. He has been publicly opposed to the war in Vietnam since 1963; he's for Amnesty Now; his alternative military spending budget would cut Pentagon money back to less than half of what Nixon proposes for 1972. Beyond that, McGovern has had the balls to go into Florida and say that if he gets elected he will probably pull the plug on the $5,000,000,000 Space Shuttle program, thereby croaking thousands of new jobs in the already depressed Cape Kennedy/Central Florida area.

He has refused to modify his stand on the school busing issue, which Nixon/Wallace strategists say will be the number one campaign argument by midsummer—one of those wild-eyed fire and brimstone issues that scares the piss out of politicians because there is no way to dodge it . . . but McGovern went out of his way to make sure people understood he was *for* busing. Not because it's desirable, but because it's "among the prices we are paying for a century of segregation in our housing patterns."

This is not the kind of thing people want to hear in a general election year—especially not if you happen to be an unemployed anti-gravity systems engineer with a deadhead mortgage on a house near Orlando . . . or a Polish millworker in Milwaukee with three kids the federal government wants to haul across town every morning to a school full of *Niggers.*

McGovern is the only major candidate—including Lindsay and Muskie—who invariably gives a straight answer when people raise these questions. He lines out the painful truth, and his reward has been just about the same as that of any other politician who insists on telling the truth: He is mocked, vilified, ignored, and abandoned as a hopeless loser by even his good old buddies like Harold Hughes.

On the face of it, the "McGovern problem" looks like the ultimate proof-positive for the liberal cynics' conviction that there is no room in American politics for an honest man. Which is probably true: if you take it for granted—along with McGovern and most of his backers—that "American politics" is synonymous with the traditional Two Party system: the Democrats and the Republicans, the Ins and the Outs, the Party in Power and The Loyal Opposition.

That's the term National Democratic Party chairman Larry O'Brien has decided to go with this year—and he says he can't for the life of him understand why Demo Party headquarters from coast to coast aren't bursting at the seams with dewy-eyed young voters completely stoned on the latest Party Message.

MESSAGE TO O'BRIEN

Well, Larry . . . I really hate to lay this on you . . . because we used to be buddies, right? That was back in the days when I bought all those white sharkskin suits because I thought I was going to be the next Governor of American Samoa.

You strung me along, Larry; you conned me into buying all those goddamn white suits and kept me hanging around that Holiday

Inn in Pierre, South Dakota, waiting for my confirmation to come through . . . but it never did, Larry; I was never appointed. You bushwhacked me.

But what the hell? I've never been one to hold a grudge any longer than absolutely necessary . . . and I wouldn't want you to think I'd hold that kind of cheap treachery against you, now that you're running the party: The Loyal Opposition, as it were. . . .

You and Hubert, along with Muskie and Jackson. And Mad Sam Yorty, and Wilbur Mills—and, yes, even Lindsay and Mc-Govern. Party loyalty is the name of the game, right? George Meany, Frank Rizzo, Mayor Daley. . . .

Well, shucks. What can I say, Larry? I'm still up for that gig in Samoa; or anywhere else where the sun shines . . . because I still have those stinking white suits, and I'm beginning to think seriously in terms of foreign travel around the end of this year. Maybe November. . . .

Under different circumstances, Larry, I might try to press you on this: maybe lean on you just a trifle for an appointment to the Drugs and Politics desk at our outpost in the Canary Islands. My friend Cardozo, the retired Dean of Gonzo Journalism, just bought a jazz bar out there and he says it's a very weird place.

But shit, Larry; why kid ourselves? You're not going to be in a position to appoint anybody to anything when November comes down on us. You won't even have a job; or if you do it'll be one of those gigs where you'll have to get your half-salary in gold bullion . . . because the way it looks now, the Democratic Party won't be issuing a hell of a lot of certified checks after November Seventh.

Remember the Whigs, Larry? They went belly up, with no warning at all, when a handful of young politicians like Abe Lincoln decided to move out on their own, and fuck the Whigs . . . which worked out very nicely, and when it became almost instantly clear that the Whig hierarchy was just a gang of old impotent windbags with no real power at all, the Party just curled up and died . . . and any politician stupid enough to "stay loyal" went down with the ship.

This is the soft underbelly of the "McGovern problem." He is really just another good Democrat, and the only thing that sets him apart from the others is a hard, almost masochistic kind of honesty that drives him around the country, running up huge bills and turning people off.

We are not a nation of truth-lovers. McGovern understands this, but he keeps on saying these terrible things anyway . . . and after watching him in New Hampshire for a while I found myself wondering—to a point that bordered now and then on quiet anguish —just what the hell it was about the man that left me politically numb, despite the fact that I agreed with everything he said.

I spent about two weeks brooding on this, because I *like* Mc-Govern—which still surprises me, because politicians, like journalists, are pretty hard people to like. The only other group I've ever dealt with who struck me as being essentially meaner than politicians are tight ends in pro football.

There is not much difference in basic temperament between a good tight end and a successful politician. They will both go down in the pit and do whatever has to be done—then come up smiling, and occasionally licking blood off their teeth.

Gene "Big Daddy" Lipscomb was not a tight end, but he had the same instincts. The Baltimore Colts paid Gene to mash quarterbacks—and, failing that, to crack collarbones and make people deaf.

Shortly before he OD'd on smack, Big Daddy explained his technique to a lunchtime crowd of Rotarians. "I always go straight for the head," he explained. "Whoever's across from me, I bash him with the flat part of my hand—nail him square on the ear-hole of his helmet about five straight times. Pretty soon he gets so nervous he can't concentrate. He can't even hear the signals. Once I get him spooked, the rest is easy."

There is a powerful fascination that attaches to this kind of efficiency—and it is worth remembering that Kennedy won the 1960 Democratic nomination not by appealing to the higher and finer consciousness of the delegates, but by laying the stomp & the whipsong on Adlai Stevenson's people when the deal went down in Los Angeles. The "Kennedy machine" was so good that even Mayor Daley came around. A good politician can smell the hammer coming down like an old sailor smells a squall behind the sun.

But Daley is not acting, this year, like a man who smells the hammer. When George McGovern went to pay a "courtesy call" on Daley last month, the Mayor's advice was, "Go out and win an election—then come back and see me."

McGovern and his earnest liberal advisors don't like to talk about that visit; no more than Muskie and his people enjoy talking about Big Ed's "courtesy call" on Supercop Frank Rizzo, the new Mayor of Philadelphia.

But these are the men with the muscle; they can swing a lot of votes. Or at least that's what the Conventional Wisdom says. Daley, Rizzo, George Meany; the good ole boys, the kingmakers.

And there is the flaw in McGovern. When the big whistle blows, he's still a Party Man. Ten years ago the electorate saw nothing wrong with the spectacle of two men fighting savagely for the Party nomination—calling each other "whores" and "traitors" and "thieves" all the way up to balloting time at the convention —and then miraculously Coming Together, letting bygones be bygones, to confront the common foe: The Other Party.

But the electorate has different tastes now, and that kind of honky-tonk bullshit doesn't make it any more. Back in 1960 most Americans still believed that whoever lived in the White House was naturally a righteous and upstanding man. Otherwise he wouldn't be there. . . .

This was after 28 years of Roosevelt and Eisenhower, who were very close to God. Harry Truman, who had lived a little closer to the Devil, was viewed more as an accident than a Real President.[2]

The shittrain began on November 22nd, 1963, in Dallas— when some twisted little geek blew the President's head off . . . and then a year later, LBJ was re-elected as the "Peace Candidate."

---

2. This shoddy estimate was subjected to sudden and almost universal revision immediately after Truman's death shortly after the 1972 election. Whether or not this had any direct connection with the recent Nixon landslide is a matter of speculation—but facing the prospect of Four More Years in the Nixon/Agnew doldrums, a lot of people suddenly decided that Truman looked pretty good, if only in retrospect.

Johnson did a lot of rotten things in those five bloody years, but when the history books are written he will emerge in his proper role as the man who caused an entire generation of Americans to lose all respect for the Presidency, the White House, the Army, and in fact the whole structure of "government."

And then came '68, the year that somehow managed to confirm almost *everybody's* worst fears about the future of the Republic . . . and then, to wrap it all up *another* cheapjack hustler moved into the White House. If Joe McGinnis had written *The Selling of the President* about good old Ike, he'd have been chased through the streets of New York by angry mobs. But when he wrote it about Nixon, people just shrugged and said, "Yeah, it's a goddamn shame, even if it's true, but so what?"

I went to Nixon's Inauguration. Washington was a sea of mud and freezing rain. As the Inaugural Parade neared the corner of 16th and Pennsylvania Avenue, some freak threw a half-gallon wine jug at the convertible carrying the commandant of the Marine Corps . . . and as one-time Presidential candidate George Romney passed by in his new role as Secretary of Health, Education and Welfare, the mob on the sidewalk began chanting "Romney eats shit! Romney eats shit!"

George tried to ignore it. He knew the TV cameras were on him so he curled his mouth up in a hideous smile and kept waving at the crowd—even as they continued to chant "Romney eats shit!"

The mood of the crowd was decidedly ugly. You couldn't walk 50 feet without blundering into a fistfight. The high point of the parade, of course, was the moment when the new President's car passed by.

But it was hard to be sure which one it was. The Secret Service ran a few decoys down the line, from time to time, apparently to confuse the snipers and maybe draw some fire . . . but nothing serious happened: just the normal hail of rocks, beer cans, and wine bottles . . . so they figured it was safe to run the President through.

Nixon came by—according to the TV men—in what appeared to be a sort of huge, hollowed-out cannonball on wheels. It was a very nasty looking armored car, and God only knows who was actually inside it.

I was standing next to a CBS-TV reporter named Joe Benti and I heard him say, "Here comes the President . . . ." "How do you know?" I asked him. It was just barely possible to detect a hint of human movement through the slits that passed for windows.

"The President is waving to the crowd," said Benti into his mike.

"Bullshit!" said Lennox Raphael standing beside me. "That's Neal Cassady in there."

"Who?" said Benti.

"Never mind," I said. "He can't hear you anyway. That car has a vacuum seal."

Benti stared at me, then moved away. Shortly afterward, he quit his job and took his family to Copenhagen.

When the Great Scorer comes to list the main downers of our time, the Nixon Inauguration will have to be ranked Number One. Altamont was a nightmare, Chicago was worse, Kent State was so bad that it's still hard to find the right words for it . . . but there was at least a brief flash of hope in those scenes, a wild kind of momentary high, before the shroud came down.

The Nixon Inauguration is the only public spectacle I've ever dealt with that was a king-hell bummer from start to finish. There was a stench of bedrock finality about it. Standing there on Pennsylvania Avenue, watching our New President roll by in his black/armored hearse, surrounded by a trotting phalanx of Secret Service men with their hands in the air, batting away the garbage thrown out of the crowd. I found myself wondering how Lee felt at Appomattox . . . or the main Jap admiral when they took him out to the battleship Missouri to sign the final papers.

Well . . . it's almost dawn now, and the only thing keeping me sane is the knowledge that just as soon as I finish this gibberish I can zoom off to Florida. I have a credit card that says I can run totally amok, on the tab, at the Colony Hotel in Palm Beach.

Right. Check into the penthouse and have the tailor send up a gallon of rum and ten yards of the best Irish silk. I need a tailor-made free-falling suit, just in case they invite me down to Caracas for the races. Charge it to Clifford Irving . . . and while you're at it, my man, send up a pair of white alligator-neck shoes, and an Arab to polish the windows.

I mean to cover this Florida primary in depth. New Hampshire was . . . well . . . what *was* it? On the plane back from Boston I scanned the New York *Times* and found that James Reston, as always, had his teeth right down on the bone.

"After all," he wrote, *"there are hard and honest differences between the candidates and the parties over the best terms of peace and trade, and the allocation of limited resources to the competing claims of military security abroad and civil order and social security at home. This is really what the presidential campaign is all about."*

Reston is narrow, but he has a good eye when it's focused, and in this case he seems to be right. The '72 presidential campaign is looking more & more like a backroom squabble between Bankers, Generals, and Labor Bosses. There is no indication, at this time, that the outcome will make much difference to anyone else. If the Republicans win, we will immediately declare Limited Nuclear War on all of Indochina and the IRS will start collecting a 20 percent national sales tax on every dollar spent by anybody—for the National Defense Emergency.

But if the Democrats win, Congress will begin a fourteen-year debate on whether or not to declare Massive Conventional War on all of Indochina, and the IRS will begin collecting a 20 percent National Losers' Tax on all incomes under $25,000 per annum—for the National Defense Emergency.

The most recent Gallup Poll says Nixon & Muskie are running Head to Head, but on closer examination the figures had Muskie trailing by a bare one percent—so he quickly resigned his membership in the "Caucasians Only" Congressional Country Club in the horsey suburbs near Cabin John, Maryland. He made this painful move in late January, about the same time he began hammering Nixon's "end the war" proposal.

Watching Muskie on TV that week, I remembered the words of ex-Senator Ernest Gruening (D-Alaska) when he appeared at the Massachusetts Rad/Lib Caucus in his role as the official spokesman for McGovern. Gruening was one of the two Senators who voted against the Gulf of Tonkin Resolution in 1964—the resolution that gave LBJ carte blanche to do Everything Necessary to win the war in Vietnam. (Wayne Morse of Oregon was the only other "nay" vote . . . and both Gruening & Morse were defeated when they ran for re-election in 1966.)

In Worchester, Ernest Gruening approached the stage like a slow-moving golem. He is eighty-five years old, and his legs are not real springy—but when he got behind the podium he spoke like the Grim Reaper.

"I've known Ed Muskie for many years," he said. "I've considered him a friend . . . but I can't help remembering that, for all those years, while we were getting deeper and deeper into that war, and while more and more boys were dying . . . Ed Muskie stayed silent."

Gruening neglected to say where McGovern had been on the day of the Tonkin Gulf vote . . . but I remember somebody saying, up on the press platform near the roof of the Assumption College gym, that "I can forgive McGovern for blowing that Tonkin thing, because the Pentagon lied—but what's his excuse for not voting against that goddamn wire-tapping bill?" (The Omnibus Safe Streets & Crime Control Act of 1968, a genuinely oppressive piece of legislation . . . even Lyndon Johnson was shocked by it, but he couldn't quite bring himself to veto the bugger—for the same reasons cited by the many Senators who called the bill "frightening" while refusing to vote against it because they didn't want to be on record as having voted against "safe streets and crime control." The bare handful of Senators who actually voted against the bill explained themselves in very ominous terms. For details, see *Justice* by Richard Harris.)

I had thought about this, but I had also thought about all the other aspects of this puzzling and depressing campaign—which seemed, a few months ago, to have enough weird and open-ended possibilities that I actually moved from Colorado to Washington for the purpose of "covering the campaign." It struck me as a right thing to do at the time—especially in the wake of the success we'd had with two back-to-back Freak Power runs at the heavily entrenched Money/Politics/Yahoo establishment in Aspen.

But things are different in Washington. It's not that everybody you talk to is aggressively hostile to any idea that might faze their well-ordered lifestyles; they'd just rather not think about it. And there is no sense of life in the Underculture. On the national reality spectrum, Washington's Doper/Left/Rock/Radical community is somewhere between Toledo and Biloxi. "Getting it on" in Washington means killing a pint of Four Roses and then arguing about Foreign Aid, over chicken wings, with somebody's drunken Congressman.

The latest craze on the local high-life front is mixing up six or eight aspirins in a fresh Coca-Cola and doing it all at once. Far more government people are into this stuff than will ever admit to it. What seems like mass paranoia in Washington is really just a sprawling, hyper-tense boredom—and the people who actually live and thrive here in the great web of Government are the first ones to tell you, on the basis of long experience, that the name or even the Party Affiliation of the next President won't make any difference at all, except on the surface.

The leaves change, they say, but the roots stay the same. So just lie back and live with it. To crank up a noisy bad stance out in a place like San Francisco and start yelling about "getting things done in Washington" is like sitting far back in the end zone seats at the Super Bowl and screaming at the Miami linebackers "Stop Duane Thomas!"

That is one aspect of the '72 Super Bowl that nobody has properly dealt with: What was it like for those humorless, godfearing Alger-bent Jesus Freaks to go out on that field in front of 100,000 people in New Orleans and get beaten like gongs by the only certified dope freak in the NFL? Thomas ran through the Dolphins like a mule through corn-stalks.

It was a fine thing to see; and it was no real surprise when the Texas cops busted him, two weeks later, for Possession of Marijuana . . . and the Dallas coach said Yes, he'd just as soon trade Duane Thomas for almost anybody.

They don't get along. Tom Landry, the Cowboys' coach, never misses a chance to get up on the platform with Billy Graham whenever The Crusade plays in Dallas. Duane Thomas calls Landry a "plastic man." He tells reporters that the team's general manager, Tex Schram, is "sick, demented and vicious." Thomas played his whole season, last year, without ever uttering a sentence to anyone on the team: Not the coach, the quarterback, his blockers—nobody; dead silence.

All he did was take the ball and run every time they called his number—which came to be more and more often, and in the Super Bowl Thomas was the whole show. But the season is now over; the purse is safe in the vault; and Duane Thomas is facing two to twenty for possession.

Nobody really expects him to serve time, but nobody seems to think he'll be playing for Dallas next year, either . . . and a few sporting people who claim to know how the NFL works say he won't be playing for *anybody* next year; that the Commissioner is outraged at this mockery of all those Government-sponsored "Beware of Dope" TV shots that dressed up the screen last autumn.

We all enjoyed those spots, but not everyone found them convincing. Here was a White House directive saying several million dollars would be spent to drill dozens of Name Players to stare at the camera and try to stop grinding their teeth long enough to say they hate drugs of any kind . . . and then the best running back in the world turns out to be a goddamn uncontrollable drugsucker.

But not for long. There is not much room for freaks in the National Football League. Joe Namath was saved by the simple blind luck of getting drafted by a team in New York City, a place where social outlaws are not always viewed as criminals. But Namath would have had a very different trip if he'd been drafted by the St. Louis Cardinals.[3]

Which is neither here nor there, for right now. We seem to

---

3. In the summer of 1972 Dallas traded Duane Thomas to the Boston Patriots where he lasted less than a week. The Boston management sent him back to Dallas, citing mysterious "physical problems." Dallas then traded Thomas to the San Diego Chargers, but that didn't work either. After a long salary dispute and widespread speculation on the meaning of his increasingly bizarre public behavior, Thomas dropped out of sight and watched the entire 1972 pro football season on TV at his home in Texas.

have wandered out on another tangent. But why not? Every now and then you have to get away from that ugly Old Politics trip, or it will drive you to kicking the walls and hurling AR3's into the fireplace.

This world is full of downers, but where is the word to describe the feeling you get when you come back tired and crazy from a week on the road to find twenty-eight fat newspapers on the desk: seven Washington *Posts,* seven Washington *Stars,* seven New York *Times,* six *Wall Street Journals,* and one *Suck* . . . to be read, marked, clipped, filed, correlated . . . and then chopped, burned, mashed, and finally hurled out in the street to freak the neighbors.

After two or three weeks of this madness, you begin to feel As One with the man who said, "No news is good news." In twenty-eight papers, only the rarest kind of luck will turn up more than two or three articles of any interest . . . but even then the interest items are usually buried deep around paragraph 16 on the jump (or "Cont. on . . .") page. . . .

The *Post* will have a story about Muskie making a speech in Iowa. The *Star* will say the same thing, and the *Journal* will say nothing at all. But the *Times* might have enough room on the jump page to include a line or so that says something like: "When he finished his speech, Muskie burst into tears and seized his campaign manager by the side of the neck. They grappled briefly, but the struggle was kicked apart by an oriental woman who seemed to be in control."

Now that's good journalism. Totally objective; very active and straight to the point. But we need to know more. *Who* was that woman? *Why* did they fight? *Where* was Muskie taken? *What* was he saying when the microphone broke?

Jesus, what's the other one? Every journalist in America knows the "Five W's." But I can only remember four. "Who, What, Why, Where," . . . and, yes, of course . . . "When!"

But what the hell? An item like that tends to pinch the interest gland . . . so you figure it's time to move out: Pack up the $419 Abercrombie & Fitch elephant skin suitcase; send the phones and the scanner and the tape viewers by Separate Float, load everything else into the weightless Magnesium Kitbag . . . then call for a high-speed cab to the airport; load on and zip off to wherever The Word says it's happening.

The public expects no less. They want a man who can zap around the nation like a goddamn methedrine bat: Racing from airport to airport, from one crisis to another—sucking up the news and then spewing it out by the "Five W's" in a package that makes perfect sense.

Why not? With the truth so dull and depressing, the only working alternative is wild bursts of madness and filigree. Or fly off and write nothing at all; get a room on the edge of Chicago and shoot up for about sixteen straight days—then wander back to Washington with a notebook full of finely-honed insights on "The Mood of the Midwest."

Be warned. The word among wizards is that Muskie will have the Democratic nomination locked up when the votes are counted in Wisconsin . . . and never mind the fact that only 12 percent of the potential voters will go to the polls in that state. (The Arizona pols—using bullhorns, billboards, and fleets of roving Voter Buses —managed to drag out 13 or 14 percent.)

This ugly truth is beginnning to dawn on the big-time Demos. They commandeered a whole network the other night for a TV broadside called "The Loyal Opposition"—featuring Larry O'Brien and all the top managers discussing The Party's prospects for 1972.

It was a terrible bummer. Even though I am paid to watch this kind of atavistic swill, I could barely keep a fix on it. It was like watching a gaggle of Woolworth stockholders, bitching about all the trouble they were having getting the company to hire an executive-level Jew.

Whatever O'Brien and his people had in mind, it didn't come across. They looked and talked like a bunch of surly, burned-out Republicans—still wondering why Hubert Humphrey didn't make it in '68 with his Politics of Joy.

Jesus, what a shock it was! The Hube always seemed like Natural. But something went wrong. . . . What was it?

The Democrats don't seem to know; or if they do they don't want to talk about it. They had a big fund-raising dinner for "the candidates" the other night at a ballroom in downtown Washington, but the people who went said it sucked. No candidates showed up —except Humphrey, and he couldn't stay for dinner. Gene McCarthy was introduced, but he didn't feel like talking. Ted Kennedy stayed for dinner, but nobody mentioned his name . . . and when the party broke up, before midnight, the chairman was still looking for somebody who could *say something meaningful.* But nobody seemed to be ready—or none of the regulars, at least, and when it comes to party affairs, the regulars are the ones who do the talking.

People who went to the party—at $500 a head—said the crowd got strangely restive toward the end of the evening, when it finally became apparent that nobody was going to say anything.

Senator George McGovern with campaign manager Gary Hart.

It was very unsettling, they said—like going to a pep rally with no cheerleaders.

One report said Ted Kennedy "just sat there, looking very uncomfortable."

And so it goes. One of my last political acts, in Colorado, was to check in at the Pitkin County courthouse and change my registration from Democrat to Independent. Under Colorado law, I can vote in either primary, but I doubt if I'll find the time—and it's hard to say, right now, just what kind of mood I'll be in on November 7th.

Meanwhile, I am hunkered down in Washington—waiting for the next plane to anywhere and wondering what in the name of sweet jesus ever brought me here in the first place. This is not what us journalists call a "happy beat."

At first I thought it was *me;* that I was missing all the action because I wasn't plugged in. But then I began reading the press wizards who *are* plugged in, and it didn't take long to figure out that most of them were just filling space because their contracts said they had to write a certain amount of words every week.

At that point I tried talking to some of the people that even the wizards said "were right on top of things." But they all seemed very depressed; not only about the '72 election, but about the whole, long-range future of politics and democracy in America.

Which is not exactly the kind of question we really need to come to grips with right now. The nut of the problem is that covering this presidential campaign is so fucking dull that it's just barely tolerable . . . and the only thing worse than going out on the campaign trail and getting hauled around in a booze-frenzy from one speech to another is having to come back to Washington and write about it.

March

The View from Key Biscayne . . . Enter the Savage Boohoo; Madness & Violence on the "Sunshine Special" . . . Lindsay Runs Amok, Muskie Runs Scared . . . First Flexing of the Big Wallace Muscle; First Signs of Doom for the Democrats . . . Abandon All Hope, Ye Who Enter Here . . . Except Maybe Ted Kennedy . . .

> *"I get the feeling that Muskie is starting to run scared—but not for the same reasons I keep reading about. Sure, he's worried about Humphrey in Florida; he's worried about McGovern with the liberals, and he's worried about Lindsay, but—well, there's the catch: The Muskie people aren't afraid of Lindsay actually winning the nomination. . . . What worries them is that Lindsay might start doing well enough to force Kennedy into this thing."*
> —A Former Campaign Mgr. & Political Strategist

THE GHOST OF KENNEDYS PAST hangs so heavy on this dreary presidential campaign that even the most cynical journalistic veterans of the Jack & Bobby campaigns are beginning to resent it out loud. A few days ago in Jacksonville,[1] creeping through the early morning traffic between the Hilton Hotel and the railroad depot, I was slumped in my seat feeling half-alive and staring morosely at the front page of the Jacksonville *Times-Union* when I caught a few flashes of a conversation from behind my right ear:

---

1. Both the New Hampshire and Florida primaries were scheduled for early March so sometime in late February I left McGovern up in New Hampshire and went down to Florida to check on Muskie and Lindsay. Lindsay had just made a strong showing in the Arizona delegate-selection caucuses, running even with Muskie and beating McGovern almost 2 to 1. All he needed in Florida was 20 percent of the Democratic vote—which

96

". . . getting a little tired of this goddamn ersatz Kennedy campaign . . . now they have Rosey Grier singing 'Let the Sun Shine In' for us. . . . It seems like they'd be embarrassed . . ."

We were going down to the depot to get aboard the "Sunshine Special"—Ed Muskie's chartered train that was about to chug off on a run from Jacksonville to Miami—the whole length of Florida —for a series of "whistlestop" speeches in towns like Deland, Winterhaven, and Sebring.

One of Muskie's Senate aides had told me, as we waited on a downtown streetcorner for the candidate's motorcade to catch up with the press bus, that "nobody has done one of these whistlestop tours since Harry Truman in 1948."

Was he kidding? I looked to be sure, but his face was dead serious. "Well . . ." I said. "Funny you'd say that . . . because I just heard some people on the bus talking about Bobby Kennedy's campaign trains in Indiana and California in 1968." I smiled pleasantly. "They even wrote a song about it: Don't tell me you never heard 'The Ruthless Cannonball'?"

The Muskie man shook his head, not looking at me—staring intently down the street as if he'd suddenly picked up the first distant vibrations from Big Ed's black Cadillac bearing down on us. I looked, but the only vehicle in sight was a rusty pickup truck from "Larry's Plumbing & Welding." It was idling at the stoplight: The driver was wearing a yellow plastic hardhat and nipping at a can of Schlitz. He glanced curiously at the big red/white/blue

---

seemed entirely possible at the time. A Lindsay "win" on Florida would have changed the race entirely. There were twelve candidates in the primary and in February the wizards were saying that no one of them could hope to poll more than 25 or 30 percent of the vote. Muskie was still a front-runner and George Wallace had only recently decided to enter the race as a Democrat, rather than as an American Independent. McGovern was running out of money and had already decided to cut his losses in Florida and go for broke in Wisconsin several weeks later. So if Lindsay had made a strong showing in Florida—even running second or close third to Muskie—he would probably have crippled McGovern's image as a candidate of the Democratic Left. When I arrived in Miami, the consensus of the local pols was that the Democratic primary would probably come down to a relatively close race between Muskie and Lindsay, with Humphrey and Wallace splitting the right-wing vote and McGovern grappling for the booby prize with Shirley Chisholm.

draped Muskie bus, then roared past us when the light changed to green. On the rear window of the cab was a small American flag decal, and a strip on the rear bumper said "President Wallace."

Ed Muskie is a trifle sensitive about putting the Kennedy ghost to his own use, this year. He has ex-L.A. Rams tackle and one-time RFK bodyguard Roosevelt Grier singing songs for him, and one of his main strategists is a former RFK ally named John English . . . but Muskie is far more concerned with the ghost of Kennedy Present.

We were sitting in the lounge car on Muskie's train, rolling through the jackpines of north Florida, when this question came up. I was talking to a dapper gent from Atlanta who was aboard the train as a special guest of Ed Muskie and who said that his PR firm would probably "handle Georgia" for the Democratic candidate, whoever it turned out to be.

"Who would you prefer?" I asked.

"What do you mean by that?" he asked. I could see that the question made him nervous.

"Nothing personal," I explained. "But on a purely professional, objective basis, which one of the Democratic candidates would be the easiest to sell in Georgia?"

He thought for a moment, then shrugged. "No question about it," he said. "Ted Kennedy."

"But he's not a candidate," I said.

He smiled. "I know that. All I did was answer your hypothetical question."

"I understand perfectly," I said. "But why Teddy? Isn't the stuff he's been saying recently a bit heavy for the folks in Georgia?"

"Not for Atlanta," he replied. "Teddy could probably carry The City. Of course he'd lose the rest of the state, but it would be close enough so that a big black vote could make the difference." He sipped his scotch and bent around on the seat to adjust for a new westward lean in the pitch and roll of the train. "That's the key," he said. "Only with a Kennedy can you get a monolithic black turnout."

"What about Lindsay?" I asked.

"Not yet," he said. "But he's just getting started. If he starts building the same kind of power base that Bobby had in '68—that's when you'll see Teddy in the race."

This kind of talk is not uncommon in living rooms around Washington where the candidates, their managers, and various ranking journalists are wont to gather for the purpose of "talking *serious* politics"—as opposed to the careful gibberish they distill for the public prints. The New Kennedy Scenario is beginning to bubble up to the surface. John Lindsay has even said it for the record: Several weeks ago he agreed with a reporter who suggested—at one of those half-serious, after-hours campaign trail drinking sessions— that "the Lindsay campaign might just be successful enough to get Ted Kennedy elected."

This is not the kind of humor that a longshot presidential candidate likes to encourage in his camp when he's spending $10,000 a day on the Campaign Trail. But Lindsay seems almost

John Lindsay.

suicidally frank at times; he will spend two hours on a stage, dutifully haranguing a crowd about whatever topic his speechwriters have laid out for him that day . . . and thirty minutes later he will sit down with a beer and say something that no politician in his right mind would normally dare to say in the presence of journalists.

One of the main marks of success in a career politician is a rooty distrust of The Press—and this cynicism is usually reciprocated, in spades, by most reporters who have covered enough campaigns to command a fat job like chronicling the Big Apple. Fifty years ago H. L. Mencken laid down the dictum that "The only way a reporter should look at a politician is *down*."

This notion is still a very strong factor in the relationship between politicians and the big-time press. On lower levels you find a tendency—among people like "national editors" on papers in Pittsburgh and Omaha—to treat *successful* politicians with a certain amount of awe and respect. But the prevailing attitude among journalists with enough status to work Presidential Campaigns is that all politicians are congenital thieves and liars.

This is usually true. Or at least as valid as the consensus opinion among politicians that The Press is a gang of swine. Both sides will agree that the other might occasionally produce an exception to prove the rule, but the overall bias is rigid . . . and, having been on both sides of that ugly fence in my time, I tend to agree. . . .

Which is neither here nor there, for right now. We seem to have wandered off again, and this time I can't afford the luxury of raving at great length about anything that slides into my head. So, rather than miss another deadline, I want to zip up the nut with a fast and extremely pithy 500 words . . . because that's all the space available, and in two hours I have to lash my rum-soaked red convertible across the Rickenbacker Causeway to downtown Miami and then to the airport—in order to meet John Lindsay in either Tallahassee or Atlanta, depending on which connection I can make: It is nearly impossible to get either in or out of Miami this week. All flights are booked far in advance, and the hotel/motel space is so viciously oversold that crowds of angry tourists are "becoming unruly"—according to the Miami *Herald*—in the lobbies of places that refuse to let them in.

Fortunately, I have my own spacious suite attached to the new

National Affairs office in the Royal Biscayne Hotel.

When things got too heavy in Washington I had no choice but to move the National Affairs desk to a place with better working conditions. Everybody agreed that the move was long overdue. After three months in Washington I felt like I'd spent three years in a mineshaft underneath Butte, Montana. My relations with the White House were extremely negative from the start; my application for press credentials was rejected out of hand. I wouldn't be needing them, they said. Because *Rolling Stone* is a "music magazine," and there is not much music in the White House these days.

And not much on Capitol Hill either, apparently. When I called the Congressional Press Gallery to ask about the application (for press credentials) that I'd filed in early November '71, they said they hadn't got around to making any decision on it yet—but I probably wouldn't be needing that one either. And where the hell did I get the gall to apply for "press" status at the Democratic and Republican National Conventions this summer?

Where indeed? They had me dead to rights. I tried to save face by arguing that political science has never conclusively *proven* that music and politics can't mix—but when they asked for my evidence I said, "Shucks, you're probably right. Why shit in your own nest, eh?"

"What?"

"Nevermind," I said. "I didn't really want the goddamn things anyway."

Which was true. Getting barred from the White House is like being blackballed at the Playboy Club. There are definite advantages to having your name on the Ugly List in places like that.

The move to Key Biscayne had a powerful effect on my humors. My suite in the Royal Biscayne Hotel is in a big palm grove on the beach and less than a mile from the Florida White House. Nixon is on the less desirable Biscayne Bay side of the Key: I face the Atlantic; sitting here at the typewriter on my spacious screen porch I can hear the ocean bashing up against the seawall about two hundred feet away.

Nobody is out there tonight. The spongy green lawn between

here and the beach is empty, except for an occasional wild dog on the putting green. They like the dampness, the good footing, and the high sweet smell of slow-rotting coconuts. I sit here on my yellow lamp-lit porch, swilling rum, and work up a fine gut-level understanding of what it must feel like to be a wild dog.

Not much has been written on this subject, and when I have more time I'll get back to it—but not tonight; we still have to deal with the Lindsay-Kennedy problem.

There is a certain twisted logic in Lindsay's idea that he might succeed beyond his wildest dreams and still accomplish nothing more than carving out a place for himself in history as the Gene McCarthy of 1972. At this stage of the '68 campaign, McCarthy was lucky to crack 5 percent in the Gallup Poll—the same percentage Lindsay is pulling today.

It was not until after New Hampshire—after McCarthy proved that a hell of a lot of people were taking him seriously—that Robert Kennedy changed his mind and decided to run instead of playing things safe and waiting for '72. That was the plan, based on the widespread assumption that LBJ would naturally run again and win a second term—thus clearing the decks for Bobby the next time around.

There is something eerie in the realization that Ted Kennedy is facing almost exactly the same situation today. He would rather not run: The odds are bad; his natural constituency has apparently abandoned politics; Nixon seems to have all the guns, and all he needs to make his life complete is the chance to stomp a Kennedy in his final campaign.

So it is hard to argue with the idea that Teddy would be a fool to run for President now. Nineteen seventy-six is only four years away. Kennedy is only forty-two years old, and when Nixon bows out, the GOP will have to crank up a brand new champion to stave off the Kennedy challenge.

This is the blueprint, and it looks pretty good as long as there's not much chance of any Democrat beating Nixon in '72—and especially not somebody like Lindsay, who would not only put Teddy on ice for the next eight years but also shatter the lingering menace of the "waiting for Kennedy" mystique. With John Lindsay in the White House, Ted Kennedy would no longer be troubled by questions concerning his own plans for the presidency.

Even a Muskie victory would be hard for Kennedy to live with —particularly if Lindsay shows enough strength to make Muskie offer him the vice-presidency. This would make Lindsay the Democratic heir apparent. Unlike Agnew—who has never been taken seriously, even by his enemies, as anything but a sop to the yahoo/ racist vote—Lindsay as vice-president would be so obviously Next in Line that Kennedy would have to back off and admit, with a fine Irish smile, that he blew it . . . the opening was there, but he didn't see it in time: while Lindsay did.

This is a very complicated projection and it needs a bit more thought than I have time to give it right now, because the computer says I have to leave for Atlanta at once—meet Lindsay in the Delta VIP hideout and maybe ponder this question at length on the long run to Los Angeles.

Meanwhile, if you listen to the wizards you will keep a careful eye on John Lindsay's action in the Florida primary . . . because if he looks good down here, and then even better in Wisconsin, the wizards say he can start looking for some very heavy company . . . and that would make things very interesting.

With both Kennedy and Lindsay in the race, a lot of people who weren't figuring on voting this year might change their minds in a hurry. If nothing else it would turn the Democratic National Convention in Miami this July into something like a week-long orgy of sex, violence, and treachery in the Bronx Zoo.

Muskie could never weather a scene like that. God only knows who would finally win the nomination, but the possibilities—along with the guaranteed momentum that a media-spectacle of that magnitude would generate—are enough to make Nixon start thinking about stuffing himself into the White House vegetable shredder.

"The whistle-stops were uneventful until his noon arrival in

Miami, where Yippie activist Jerry Rubin and another man heckled and interrupted him repeatedly. The Senator at one point tried to answer Rubin's charges that he had once been a hawk on (Vietnam) war measures. He acknowledged that he had made a mistake, as did many other senators in those times, but Rubin did not let him finish.

"Muskie ultimately wound up scolding Rubin and fellow heckler Peter Sheridan, who had boarded the train in West Palm Beach with press credentials apparently obtained from Rolling Stone's *Washington correspondent, Dr. Hunter S. Thompson."*

—Miami *Herald,* 2/20/72

This incident has haunted me ever since it smacked me in the eyes one peaceful Sunday morning a few weeks ago as I sat on the balmy screened porch of the National Affairs Suite here in the Royal Biscayne Hotel. I was slicing up grapefruit and sipping a pot of coffee while perusing the political page of the *Herald* when I suddenly saw my name in the middle of a story on Ed Muskie's "Sunshine Special" campaign train from Jacksonville to Miami.

Several quick phone calls confirmed that something ugly had happened on that train, and that I was being blamed for it. A New York reporter assigned to the Muskie camp warned me to "stay clear of this place . . . they're really *hot* about it. They've pulled your pass for good."

"Wonderful," I said. "That's one more bummer that I have an excuse to avoid. But what happened? Why do they blame *me?*"

"Jesus Christ!" he said. "That crazy sonofabitch got on the train wearing *your* press badge and went completely crazy. He drank about ten martinis before the train even got moving, then he started abusing people. He cornered some poor bastard from one of the Washington papers and called him a Greasy Faggot and a Communist Buttfucker . . . then he started pushing him around and saying he was going to throw him off the train at the next bridge . . . we couldn't believe it was happening. He scared one of the network TV guys so bad that he locked himself in a water-closet for the rest of the trip."

"Jesus, I hate to hear this," I said. "But nobody really thought it was *me,* did they?"

"Hell, yes, they did," he replied. "The only people on the train who even know what you look like were me and ———————— and ————————————." (He mentioned several reporters whose names need not be listed here.) "But everybody else just looked at that ID badge he was wearing and pretty soon the word was all the way back to Muskie's car that some thug named Thompson from a thing called *Rolling Stone* was tearing the train apart. They were going to send Rosey Grier up to deal with you, but Dick Stewart [Muskie's press secretary] said it wouldn't look good to have a three-hundred pound bodyguard beating up journalists on the campaign train."

"That's typical Muskie staff-thinking," I said. "They've done everything else wrong; why balk at stomping a reporter?"

He laughed. "Actually," he said, "the rumor was that you'd eaten a lot of LSD and gone wild—that you couldn't control yourself."

"What do you mean *me?*" I said. "I wasn't even *on* that goddamn train. The Muskie people deliberately didn't wake me up in West Palm Beach. They didn't like my attitude from the day before. My friend from the University of Florida newspaper said he heard them talking about it down in the lobby when they were checking off the press list and waking up all the others."

"Yeah, I heard some of that talk," he said. "Somebody said you seemed very negative."

"I was," I said. "That was one of the most degrading political experiences I've ever been subjected to."

"That's what the Muskie people said about your friend," he replied. "Abusing reporters is one thing—hell, we're all used to that—but about halfway to Miami I saw him reach over the bar and grab a whole bottle of gin off the rack. Then he began wandering from car to car, drinking out of the bottle and getting after those poor goddamn girls. That's when it really got bad."

"What girls?" I said.

"The ones in those little red, white, and blue hotpants outfits," he replied. "All those so-called 'Muskie volunteers' from Jacksonville Junior College, or whatever. . . ."

105

"You mean the barmaids? The ones with the straw boaters?"

"Yeah," he said. "The cheerleaders. Well, they went all to goddamn pieces when your friend started manhandling them. Every time he'd come into a car the girls would run out the door at the other end. But every once in a while he'd catch one by an arm or a leg and start yelling stuff like 'Now I gotcha, you little beauty! Come on over here and sit on poppa's face!' "

"Jesus!" I said. "Why didn't they just put him off the train?"

"How? You don't stop a chartered Amtrak train on a main line just because of a drunken passenger. What if Muskie had ordered an emergency stop and we'd been rammed by a freight train? No presidential candidate would risk a thing like that."

I could see the headlines in every paper from Key West to Seattle:

Muskie Campaign Train Collision Kills 34; Demo Candidate Blames "Crazy Journalist"

"Anyway," he said, "we were running late for that big rally at the station in Miami—so the Muskie guys figured it was better to just *endure* the crazy sonofabitch, rather than cause a violent scene on a train full of bored reporters. Christ, the train was *loaded* with network TV crews, all of them bitching about how Muskie wasn't doing anything worth putting on the air. . . ." He laughed. "Hell, yes, we *all* would have loved a big brawl on the train. Personally, I was bored stupid. I didn't get a quote worth filing out of the whole trip." He laughed again. "Actually, Muskie *deserved* that guy. He was a goddamn nightmare to be trapped on a train with, but at least he wasn't *dull*. Nobody was dozing off like they did on Friday. Hell, there was no way to get away from that brute! All you could do was keep moving and hope he wouldn't get hold of you."

Both the Washington *Star* and *Women's Wear Daily* reported essentially the same tale: A genuinely savage person had boarded the train in West Palm Beach, using a fraudulent press pass, then ran amok in the lounge car—getting in "several fistfights" and finally "heckling the Senator unmercifully" when the train pulled into Miami and Muskie went out on the caboose platform to deliver what was supposed to have been the climactic speech of his triumphant whistlestop tour.

It was at this point—according to press reports both published & otherwise—that my alleged friend, calling himself "Peter Sheridan," cranked up his act to a level that caused Senator Muskie to "cut short his remarks."

When the "Sunshine Special" pulled into the station at Miami, "Sheridan" reeled off the train and took a position on the tracks just below Muskie's caboose platform, where he spent the next half hour causing the Senator a hellish amount of grief—along with Jerry Rubin, who also showed up at the station to ask Muskie what had caused him to change his mind about supporting the War in Vietnam.

Rubin had been in Miami for several weeks, making frequent appearances on local TV to warn that "Ten Thousand naked hippies" would be among those attending the Democratic National Convention at Miami Beach in July. "We will march to the Convention Center," he announced, "but there will be no violence —at least not by us."

To questions regarding his presence in Florida, Rubin said he "decided to move down here, because of the climate," and that he was also registered to vote in Florida—as a Republican. Contrary to the rancid suspicions of the Muskie staff people, Sheridan didn't even recognize Rubin and I hadn't seen him since the Counter Inaugural Ball which ran opposite Nixon's inauguration in 1969.

When Rubin showed up at the train station that Saturday afternoon to hassle Muskie, the Senator from Maine was apparently the only person in the crowd (except Sheridan) who didn't know who he was. His first response to Rubin's heckling was, "Shut up, young man—I'm talking."

"You're not a damn bit different from Nixon," Rubin shouted back . . .

. . . And it was at this point, according to compiled press reports and a first-hand account by Monte Chitty of the University of Florida *Alligator,* that Muskie seemed to lose his balance and fall back from the rail.

What happened, according to Chitty, was that "the Boohoo reached up from the track and got hold of Muskie's pants-leg—waving an empty martini glass through the bars around the caboose platform with his other hand and screaming: 'Get your lying ass back inside and make me another drink, you worthless old fart!' "

"It was really embarrassing," Chitty told me later on the phone. "The Boohoo kept reaching up and grabbing Muskie's legs, yelling for more gin . . . Muskie tried to ignore him, but the Boohoo kept after him and after a while it go so bad that even Rubin backed off."

"The Boohoo," of course, was the same vicious drunkard who had terrorized the Muskie train all the way from Palm Beach, and he was still wearing a press badge that said "Hunter S. Thompson—*Rolling Stone.*"

Chitty and I had met him the night before, about 2:30 A.M., in the lobby of the Ramada Inn where the press party was quartered. We were heading out to the street to look for a sandwich shop, feeling a trifle bent & very hungry . . . and as we passed the front desk, here was this huge wild-eyed monster, bellowing at the night-clerk about "All this chickenshit" and "All these pansies around here trying to suck up to Muskie" and "Where the fuck can a man go in this town to have a good time, anyway?"

A scene like that wouldn't normally interest me, but there was something very special about this one—something abnormally crazy in the way he was talking. There was something very familiar about it. I listened for a moment and then recognized the Neal Cassady speed-booze-acid rap—a wild combination of menace, madness, genius, and fragmented coherence that wreaks havoc on the mind of any listener.

This is not the kind of thing you expect to hear in the lobby of a Ramada Inn, and especially not in West Palm Beach—so I knew we had no choice but to take this man along with us.

MARCH

"Don't mind if I do," he said. "At this hour of the night I'll fuck around with just about anybody."

He had just got out of jail, he explained, as we walked five or six blocks through the warm midnight streets to a twenty-four-hour hamburger place called The Copper Penny. Fifteen days for vagrancy, and when he'd hit the bricks today around four he just happened to pick up a newspaper and see that Ed Muskie was in town . . . and since he had this friend who "worked up-top," he said, for Big Ed . . . well, he figured he'd just drift over to the Ramada Inn and say hello.

But he couldn't find his friend. "Just a bunch of pansies from CBS and the New York *Times,* hanging around the bar," he said. "I took a few bites out of that crowd and they faded fast—just ran off like curs. But what the shit can you expect from people like that? Just a bunch of lowlife ass-kissers who get paid for hanging around with politicians."

Well . . . I'd like to run this story all the way out, here, but it's deadline time again and the nuts & bolts people are starting to moan . . . demanding a fast finish and heavy on the *political stuff*. Right. Let's not cheat the readers. We promised them politics, by God, and we'll damn well *give* them politics.

But just for the quick hell of it, I'd like to explain or at least insist—despite massive evidence to the contrary—that this geek we met in the lobby of the Ramada Inn and who scared the shit out of everybody when he got on Muskie's train the next day for the run from Palm Beach to Miami, was in fact an excellent person, with a rare sense of humor that unfortunately failed to mesh, for various reasons, with the prevailing humors on Muskie's "Sunshine Special."

Just how he came to be wearing my press badge is a long and tangled story, but as I recall it had something to do with the fact that "Sheridan" convinced me that he was one of the original ranking Boohoos of the Neo-American Church and also that he was able to rattle off all kinds of obscure and pithy tales about his experiences in places like Millbrook, the Hog Farm, La Honda,

109

and Mike's Pool Hall in San Francisco . . .

. . . Which would not have meant a hell of a lot if he hadn't also been an obvious aristocrat of the Freak Kingdom. There was no doubt about it. This bastard was a serious, king-hell *Crazy*. He had that rare weird electricity about him—that extremely wild & heavy *presence* that you only see in a person who has abandoned all hope of ever behaving "normally."

Monte Chitty and I spent about five hours with "Sheridan" that night in West Palm Beach, and every place we went he caused serious trouble. In a rock club around the corner from The Copper Penny he terrified the manager by merely walking up to the bar and asking if he could check his hat—a mashed-up old Panama that looked like it had come out of the same Goodwill Store where he'd picked up his Levis and his crusty Cuban work shirt.

But when he tried to check his hat, the manager coiled up like a bull-snake—recognizing something in "Sheridan's" tone of voice or maybe just the vibrations that gave him a bad social fear, and I could see in his eyes that he was thinking: "O my God—here it comes. Should we mace him now or later?"

All of which is basic to any understanding of what happened on the Muskie campaign train—and which also explains why his "up-top friend" (later identified in *Women's Wear Daily* as Richie Evans, one of Muskie's chief advance men for Florida) was not immediately available to take care of his old buddy, Pete Sheridan —who was fresh out of jail on a vagrancy rap, with no place to sleep and no transportation down to Miami except the prospect of hanging his thumb out in the road and hoping for a ride.

"To hell with that," I said. "Take the train with *us*. It's the presidential express—a straight shot into Miami and all the free booze you can drink. Why not? Any friend of Richie's is a friend of Ed's, I guess—but since you can't find Evans at this hour of the night, and since the train is leaving in two hours, well, maybe you should borrow this little orange press ticket, just until you get aboard."

"I think you're right," he said.

110

"I am," I replied. "And besides, I paid $30 for the goddamn thing and all it got me was a dozen beers and the dullest day of my life."

He smiled, accepting the card. "Maybe I can put it to better use," he said.

Which was true. He did—and I was subsequently censured very severely, by other members of the campaign press corps, for allowing my "credentials" to fall into foreign hands. There were also ugly rumors to the effect that I had somehow conspired with this monster "Sheridan"—and also with Jerry Rubin—to "sabotage" Muskie's wind-up gig in Miami, and that "Sheridan's" beastly behavior at the train station was the result of a carefully-laid plot by me, Rubin, and the International Yippie Brain-trust.

This theory was apparently concocted by Muskie staffers, who told other reporters that they had known all along that I was up to something rotten—but they tried to give me a break, and now look what I done to 'em: planted a human bomb on the train.

A story like this one is very hard to spike, because people involved in a presidential campaign are so conditioned to devious behavior on all fronts—including the press—that something like that fiasco in the Miami train station is just about impossible for them to understand except in terms of a conspiracy. Why else, after all, would I *give my credentials* to some booze-maddened jailbird?

Well . . . why indeed?

Several reasons come quickly to mind, but the main one could only be understood by somebody who has spent twelve hours on a train with Ed Muskie and his people, doing whistlestop speeches through central Florida.

We left Jacksonville around nine, after Muskie addressed several busloads of black teenagers and some middle-aged ladies from one of the local union halls who came down to the station to hear

Senator Muskie say, "It's time for the *good* people of America to get together behind somebody they can trust—namely me."

Standing next to me on the platform was a kid of about fifteen who looked not entirely fired up by what he was hearing. "Say," I said. "What brings you out here at this hour of the morning, for a thing like this?"

"The bus," he said.

After that, we went down to Deland—about a two-hour run—where Muskie addressed a crowd of about two hundred white teenagers who'd been let out of school to hear the candidate say, "It's about time the good people of America got *together* behind somebody they can trust—namely me."

And then we eased down the tracks to Sebring, where a feverish throng of about a hundred and fifty senior citizens was on hand to greet the Man from Maine and pick up his finely-honed message. As the train rolled into the station, Roosevelt Grier emerged from the caboose and attempted to lead the crowd through a few stanzas of "Let the Sun Shine In."

Then the candidate emerged, acknowledging Grier's applause and smiling for the TV cameramen who had been let off a hundred yards up the track so they could get ahead of the train and set up . . . in order to film Muskie socking it to the crowd about how "It's about time we *good* people, etc., etc. . . . ."

Meanwhile, the Muskie girls—looking very snappy in their tri-colored pre-war bunny suits—were mingling with the folks; saying cheerful things and handing out red, white, and blue buttons that said "Trust Muskie" and "Believe Muskie."

A band was playing somewhere, I think, and the Chief Political Correspondent from some paper in Australia was jabbering into the telephone in the dispatcher's office—feeding Muskie's wisdom straight down to the outback, as it were; direct from the Orange Juice State.

By mid-afternoon a serious morale problem had developed aboard the train. At least half of the national press corps had long since gone over the hump into serious boozing. A few had already filed, but most had scanned the prepared text of Big Ed's "whistle-stop speech" and said to hell with it. Now, as the train headed south again, the Muskie girls were passing out sandwiches and O. B. McClinton, the "Black Irishman of Country Music," was trying to lure people into the lounge car for a "singalong thing."

It took a while, but they finally collected a crowd. Then one of Muskie's college-type staffers took charge: He told the Black Irishman what to play, cued the other staff people, then launched into about nineteen straight choruses of Big Ed's newest campaign song: "He's got the whole state of Florida . . . In his hands . . ."

I left at that point. The scene was pure Nixon—so much like a pep rally at a Young Republican Club that I was reminded of a conversation I'd had earlier with a reporter from Atlanta. "You know," he said. "It's taken me half the goddamn day to figure out what it is that bothers me about these people." He nodded toward a group of clean-cut young Muskie staffers at the other end of the car. "I've covered a lot of Democratic campaigns," he continued, "but I've never felt out of place before—never personally uncomfortable with the people."

"I know what you mean," I said.

"Sure," he said. "It's obvious—and I've finally figured out *why.*" He chuckled and glanced at the Muskie people again. "You know what it is?" he said. "It's because these people act like goddamned Republicans! That's the problem. It took me a while, but I finally figured it out."

There are very few members of the establishment press who will defend the idea that things like aggressive flatulence, forced feedings of swill, or even a barely-muted hostility on the part of the candidate would justify any kind of drastic retaliation by a *professional journalist*—and certainly nothing so drastic as to cause the Democratic front-runner to cut short a major speech because some dangerous freak wearing a press badge was clawing at his legs and

113

screaming for more gin.

I might even agree with this thinking, myself, if the question of "drastic retaliation against a candidate" ever actually confronted me . . . for the same reason that I couldn't crank up enough adrenalin to get myself involved in some low-level conspiracy to heckle a harmless dingbat like Ed Muskie in a Florida railroad station.[2]

Which is not to say that I couldn't get interested in something with a bit of real style to it—like turning 50,000 bats loose in the Convention Center on the night of Hubert Humphrey's nomination. But I don't see much hope for anything that imaginative this time around, and most people capable of putting an Outrage like that together would probably agree with me that giving Hubert the Democratic nomination would be punishment enough in itself.

As for Muskie and his goddamn silly train, my only real feeling about that scene was a desire to get away from it as soon as possible. And I might have flown down to Miami on Friday night if we hadn't got ourselves mixed up with the Boohoo and stayed out until 6:00 A.M. Saturday morning. At that point, all I really cared about was getting myself hauled back to Miami on somebody else's wheels.

The Boohoo agreed, and since the train was leaving in two hours, that was obviously the easiest way to go. But Muskie's press-herders decided that my attitude was so negative that it was probably best to let me sleep—which they did, and there is a certain poetic justice in the results of that decision. By leaving me behind,

---

2. The Boohoo incident haunted me throughout the campaign. First it got me barred from the Muskie camp, then—when investigations of the Watergate Scandal revealed that Nixon staffers had hired people to systematically sabotage the primary campaigns of almost all the serious Democratic contenders—the ex-Muskie lieutenants cited the Boohoo incident as a prime example of CREEP'S dirty work. Ranking Muskie lieutenants told congressional investigators that Sheridan and I had conspired with Donald Segretti and other unnamed saboteurs to humiliate Muskie in the Florida primary. The accusation came as a welcome flash of humor at a time when I was severely depressed at the prospect of another four years with Nixon. This also reinforced my contempt for the waterheads who ran Big Ed's campaign like a gang of junkies trying to send a rocket to the moon to check out rumors that the craters were full of smack.

they unwittingly cut the only person on the train who could have kept the Boohoo under control.

But of course they had no idea that he would be joining them. Nobody even knew the Boohoo existed until he turned up in the lounge car wearing my press badge and calling people like New York *Times* correspondent Johnny Apple an "ugly little wop."

It was just about then, according to another reporter's account, that "people started trying to get out of his way." It was also about then, Monte Chitty recalls, that the Boohoo began ordering things like "triple Gin Bucks, without the Buck." And from then on, things went steadily downhill.

Now, looking back on that tragedy with a certain amount of perspective and another glance at my notes, the Boohoo's behavior on that train seems perfectly logical—or at least as logical as my own less violent but noticeably negative reaction to the same scene a day earlier. It was a very oppressive atmosphere—very tense and guarded, compared to the others I'd covered. I had just finished a swing around central Florida with Lindsay, and before that I'd been up in New Hampshire with McGovern.

Both of those campaigns had been very loose and easy scenes to travel with, which might have been because they were both left-bent underdogs . . . but at that point I didn't really think much about it; the only other presidential candidates I had ever spent any time with were Gene McCarthy and Richard Nixon in 1968. And they were so vastly different—the Left and Right extremes of both parties—that I came into the '72 campaign thinking I would probably never see anything as extreme in either direction as the Nixon & McCarthy campaigns in '68.

So it was a pleasant surprise to find both the McGovern and Lindsay campaigns at least as relaxed and informal as McCarthy's '68 trip; they were nowhere near as intense or exciting, but the difference was more a matter of degree, of style and personal attitudes . . .

In '68 you could drive across Manchester from McCarthy's woodsy headquarters at the Wayfarer to Nixon's grim concrete hole at the Holiday Inn and feel like you'd gone from Berkeley to Pine Bluff, Arkansas.

But then you sort of expected that kind of cheap formica trip from Richard Nixon: all those beefy Midwest detective types in blue sharkskin suits—ex-brokers from Detroit, ex-speculators from Miami, ex gear & sprocket salesmen from Chicago. They ran a very tight ship. Nixon rarely appeared, and when he did nobody in the press corps ever got within ten feet of him, except now and then by special appointment for cautious interviews. Getting assigned to cover Nixon in '68 was like being sentenced to six months in a Holiday Inn.

It never occurred to me that anything could be worse than getting stuck on another Nixon campaign, so it came as a definite shock to find that hanging around Florida with Ed Muskie was even duller and more depressing than traveling with Evil Dick himself.

And it wasn't just me, although the Muskie Downer was admittedly more obvious to reporters who'd been traveling with other candidates than it was to the poor devils who'd been stuck with him from the start. I may have been the rudest "negative attitude" case on the "Sunshine Special," but I was definitely not the *only* one. About halfway through that endless Friday I was standing at the bar when Judy Michaelson, a New York *Post* reporter who had just switched over from the Lindsay campaign, came wandering down the aisle with a pained blank stare on her face, and stopped beside me just long enough to say, "Boy! This is not quite the same as the other one, is it?"

I shook my head, leaning into the turn as the train rounded a bend on the banks of either the Sewanee or the Chatahootchee River. "Cheer up," I said. "It's a privilege to ride the rails with a front-runner."

She smiled wearily and moved on, dragging her notebook behind her. Later that evening, in West Palm Beach, I listened to Dick Stout of *Newsweek* telling a Muskie press aide that his day on the "Sunshine Special" had been "so goddamn disgracefully bad that I don't have the words for it yet."

One of the worst things about the trip was the fact that the candidate spent the whole time sealed off in his private car with a traveling zoo of local Party bigwigs. The New Hampshire primary was still two weeks off, and Muskie was still greedily pursuing his dead-end strategy of piling up endorsements from "powerful Democrats" in every state he visited—presumably on the theory that once he got the Party Bosses signed up, they would automatically deliver the votes. (By the time the deal went down in New Hampshire, Muskie had signed up just about every Democratic politician in the country whose name was well known by more than a hundred people, and it did him about as much good as a notarized endorsement from Martin Bormann.) A week later, when he staggered to a fourth place finish in Florida, a fishmonger in Cairo, Illinois, announced that he and U.S. Senator Harold Hughes of Iowa were forming a corporation to market "Muskie dartboards." Hughes had planned to be present at the ceremony in Cairo, the man said, but the Senator was no longer able to travel from one place to another without the use of custom Weight-Belts.

The New Hampshire results[3] hit the Muskie bandwagon like a front-wheel blowout, but Florida blew the transmission. Big Ed will survive Illinois, whatever the outcome, but he still has to go to Wisconsin—where anything but victory will probably finish him off, and his chances of beating Humphrey up there on The Hube's home court are not good. The latest Gallup Poll, released on the eve of the Illinois primary but based on a nationwide survey taken prior to the vote in New Hampshire, showed Humphrey ahead of Muskie for the first time. In the February poll, Muskie was leading by 35 percent to 32 percent . . . but a month later The Hube had surged up to 35 percent and Muskie had slipped seven points in thirty days down to 28 percent.

According to almost every media wizard in the country, Wisconsin is "the crunch"—especially for Muskie and New York Mayor John Lindsay, who was badly jolted in Florida when his gold-plated Media Blitz apparently had no effect at all on the voters. Lindsay had spent almost a half million dollars in Florida, yet

---

3. Contrary to all predictions and polls except McGovern's, Muskie finished with less than 50 percent of the vote, pulling roughly 46 percent, while McGovern came in with exactly 37.5 percent, a difference of less than ten points. Muskie never recovered from this pyrrhic victory.

limped home fifth with seven percent of the vote—just a point ahead of McGovern, who spent less than $100,000.

Two of the biggest losers in Florida, in fact, were not listed in the election results. They were David Garth, Lindsay's TV-Media guru, and Robert Squier, whose TV campaign for Muskie was such a debacle that some of the Man from Maine's top advisors in Florida began openly denouncing Squier to startled reporters, who barely had time to get their stories into print before Muskie's national headquarters announced that a brand new series of TV spots would begin running yesterday.

But by then the damage was done. I never saw the new ones, but the Squier originals were definitely a bit queer. They depicted Muskie as an extremely slow-spoken man who had probably spent half his life overcoming some kind of dreadful speech impediment, only to find himself totally hooked on a bad Downer habit or maybe even smack. The first time I heard a Muskie radio spot I was zipping along on the Rickenbacker Causeway, coming in from Key Biscayne, and I thought it was a new Cheech & Chong record. It was the voice of a man who had done about twelve Reds on the way to the studio—a very funny ad.

Whatever else the Florida primary might or might not have proved, it put a definite kink in the Media Theory of politics. It may be true, despite what happened to Lindsay and Muskie in Florida, that all you have to do to be President of the U.S.A. is look "attractive" on TV and have enough money to hire a Media Wizard. Only a fool or a linthead would argue with the logic at the root of the theory: If you want to sell yourself to a nation of TV addicts, you obviously can't ignore the medium . . . but the Florida vote at least served to remind a lot of people that the medium is only a tool, not a magic eye. In other words, if you want to be President of the U.S.A. and you're certified "attractive," the only other thing you have to worry about when you lay out all that money for a Media Wizard is whether or not your're hiring a *good* one instead of a bungler . . . and definitely lay off the Reds when you go to the studio.

Later in March

The Banshee Screams in Florida . . . The
Emergence of Mankiewicz . . . Hard Times for
the Man from Maine . . . Redneck Power & Hell
on Wheels for George Wallace . . . The Hube
Slithers out of Obscurity . . . Fear and Loathing
on The Democratic Left . . .

ON MONDAY MORNING, the day before the Florida primary, I flew
down to Miami with Frank Mankiewicz, who runs the McGovern
campaign.

We hit the runway at just over two hundred miles an hour in a
strong crosswind, bouncing first on the left wheel and then—about
a hundred yards down the runway—on the right wheel . . . then
another long bounce, and finally straightening out just in front of
the main terminal at Miami's International Airport.

Nothing serious. But my Bloody Mary was spilled all over
Monday's Washington *Post* on the armrest. I tried to ignore it and
looked over at Mankiewicz sitting next to me . . . but he was still
snoring peacefully. I poked him. "Here we are," I said. "Down
home in Fat City again. What's the schedule?"

Now he was wide awake, checking his watch. "I think I have
to make a speech somewhere," he said. "I also have to meet Shirley MacLaine somewhere. Where's a telephone? I have to make
some calls."

Soon we were shuffling down the corridor toward the big baggage-claim merry-go-round; Mankiewicz had nothing to claim. He
has learned to travel light. His "baggage," as it were, consisted of
one small canvas bag that looked like an oversize shaving kit.

119

My own bundle—two massive leather bags and a Xerox tele-copier strapped into a fiberglass Samsonite suitcase—would be coming down the baggage-claim chute any moment. I tend to travel heavy; not for any good reason, but mainly because I haven't learned the tricks of the trade.

"I have a car waiting," I said. "A fine bronze-gold convertible. Do you need a ride?"

"Maybe," he said. "But I have to make some calls first. You go ahead, get your car and all that goddamn baggage and I'll meet you down by the main door."

I nodded and hurried off. The Avis counter was only about fifty yards away from the wall-phone where Mankiewicz was setting up shop with a handful of dimes and a small notebook. He made at least six calls and a page of notes before my bags arrived . . . and by the time I began arguing with the car-rental woman the expression on Mankiewicz's face indicated that he had everything under control.

I was impressed by this show of efficiency. Here was the one-man organizing vortex, main theorist, and central intelligence behind the McGovern-for-President campaign—a small, rumpled little man who looked like an out-of-work "pre-Owned Car" salesman—putting McGovern's Florida primary action together from a public wall-phone in the Miami airport.

Mankiewicz—a 47-year-old Los Angeles lawyer who was Di-rector of the Peace Corps before he became Bobby Kennedy's press secretary in 1968—has held various job-titles since the McGovern campaign got underway last year. For a while he was the "Press Secretary," then he was called the "Campaign Manager"—but now he appears to feel comfortable with the title of "Political Director." Which hardly matters, because he has become George McGovern's alter ego. There are people filling all the conventional job-slots, but they are essentially front-men. Frank Mankiewicz is to McGovern what John Mitchell is to Nixon—the Man behind the Man.

Two weeks before voting day in New Hampshire, Mankiewicz was telling his friends that he expected McGovern to get 38 percent of the vote. This was long before Ed Muskie's infamous "break-down scene" on that flatbed truck in front of the Manchester *Union-Leader*.

When Frank laid this prediction on his friends in the Washington Journalism Establishment, they figured he was merely doing his job—trying to con the press and hopefully drum up a last minute surge for McGovern, the only candidate in the '72 presidential race who had any real claim on the residual loyalties of the so-called "Kennedy Machine."

Beyond that, Mankiewicz was a political columnist for the Washington *Post* before he quit to run McGovern's campaign—and his former colleagues were not inclined to embarrass him by publicizing his nonsense. Journalists, like The Rich, are inclined to protect Their Own . . . even those who go off on hopeless tangents.

So Frank Mankiewicz ascended to the Instant-Guru level on the morning of March 8th, when the final New Hampshire tally showed McGovern with 37.5 percent of the Democratic primary vote, and "front-runner" Ed Muskie with only 46 percent.

New Hampshire in '72 jolted Muskie just as brutally as New Hampshire in '68 jolted LBJ. He cursed the press and hurried down to Florida, still talking like "the champ," & reminding everybody within reach that he had, after all, *Won* in New Hampshire.

Just like LBJ—who beat McCarthy by almost 20 points and then quit before the next primary four weeks later in Wisconsin.

But Muskie had only *one* week before the deal would go down in Florida, and he was already locked in . . . he came down and hit the streets with what his handlers called a "last minute blitz" . . . shaking many hands and flooding the state with buttons, flyers & handbills saying "Trust Muskie" and "Believe Muskie" and "Muskie Talks Straight" . . .

When Big Ed arrived in Florida for The Blitz, he looked and acted like a man who'd been cracked. Watching him in action, I remembered the nervous sense of impending doom in the face of Floyd Patterson when he weighed in for his championship re-match with Sonny Liston in Las Vegas. Patterson was so obviously crippled, in his head, that I couldn't raise a bet on him—at *any* odds—among the hundred or so veteran sportswriters in the ringside seats on fight night.

Frank Mankiewicz.

Wallace on the stump.

I was sitting next to Rocky Marciano in the first row, and just before the fight began I bought two tall paper cups full of beer, because I didn't want to have to fuck around with drink-vendors after the fight got underway.

"Two?" Marciano asked with a grin.

I shrugged, and drank one off very quickly as Floyd came out of his corner and turned to wax the first time Liston hit him. Then, with a minute still to go in the first round, Liston bashed him again and Patterson went down for the count. The fight was over before I touched my second beer.

Muskie went the same way to Florida—just as Mankiewicz had predicted forty-eight hours earlier in the living room of his suburban Washington home. "Muskie is already finished," he said then. "He had no *base*. Nobody's really *for* Muskie. They're only for the Front-Runner, the man who says he's the only one who can beat Nixon—but not even Muskie himself believes that anymore; he couldn't even win a majority of the Democratic vote in New Hampshire, on his own turf."

The next morning, on the plane from Washington to Miami, I tried for a firmer insight on Mankiewicz's wisdom by offering to bet $100 that Muskie would finish worse than second. I saw him running third, not much ahead of Jackson—with The Hube not far behind Wallace and Lindsay beating McGovern with something like 11 percent to 9 percent. (This was before I watched both McGovern's and Lindsay's final lame shots on Monday night; McGovern at the University of Miami and Lindsay with Charles Evers at a black church in North Miami. By late Monday, seven hours before the polls opened, I thought both of them might finish behind Shirley Chisholm . . . which almost happened: Lindsay finished with something around 7 percent, McGovern with roughly 6 percent, and Chisholm with 4 percent—while George Wallace rolled home with 42 percent, followed in the distance by Humphrey with 18.5 percent, Jackson with 12.5 percent . . . and Muskie with 9 percent.

FEAR AND LOATHING

"Remember when you go out to vote tomorrow that the eyes of America are upon you, all the live-long day. The eyes of America are upon you, they will not go away."

—Senator George McGovern at a rally at the University of Miami the night before the Florida primary.

Cazart! . . . this fantastic rain outside: a sudden cloudburst, drenching everything. The sound of rain smacking down on my concrete patio about ten feet away from the typewriter, rain beating down on the surface of the big aqua-lighted pool out there across the lawn . . . rain blowing into the porch and whipping the palm fronds around in the warm night air.

Behind me, on the bed, my waterproof Sony says, "It's 5:28 right now in Miami . . ." Then Rod Stewart's hoarse screech: *"Mother don't you recognize your son . . . ?"*

Beyond the rain I can hear the sea rolling in on the beach. This atmosphere is getting very high, full of strange memory flashes. . . .

"Mother don't you recognize me now . . . ?"

Wind, rain, surf. Palm trees leaning in the wind, hard funk/ blues on the radio, a flagon of Wild Turkey on the sideboard . . . are those footsteps outside? High heels running in the rain?

Keep on typing . . . but my mind is not really on it. I keep expecting to hear the screen door bang open and then turn around to see Sadie Thompson standing behind me, soaked to the skin . . . smiling, leaning over my shoulder to see what I'm cranking out tonight . . . then laughing softly, leaning closer; wet nipples against my neck, perfume around my head . . . and now on the radio: *"Wild Horses . . . We'll ride them some day . . ."*

Perfect. Get it on. Don't turn around. Keep this fantasy rolling and try not to notice that the sky is getting light outside. Dawn is coming up and I have to fly to Mazatlan in five hours to deal with a drug-fugitive. Life is getting very complicated. After Mazatlan I have to rush back to San Francisco and get this gibberish ready for the printer . . . and then on to Wisconsin to chronicle the next act in this saga of Downers and Treachery called "The Campaign Trail."

Wisconsin is the site of the next Democratic primary. Six serious candidates in this one—racing around the state in chartered jets, spending Ten Grand a day for the privilege of laying a series of terrible bummers on the natives. Dull speeches for breakfast, duller speeches for lunch, then bullshit with gravy for dinner.

How long, O Lord . . . How long? Where will it end? The only possible good that can come of this wretched campaign is the ever-increasing likelihood that it will cause the Democratic Party to self-destruct.

A lot of people are seriously worried about this, but I am not one of them. I have never been much of a Party Man myself . . . and the more I learn about the realities of national politics, the more I'm convinced that the Democratic Party is an atavistic endeavor—more an Obstacle than a Vehicle—and that there is really no hope of accomplishing anything genuinely new or different in American politics until the Democratic Party is done away with.

It is a bogus alternative to the politics of Nixon: A gang of senile leeches like George Meany, Hubert Humphrey, and Mayor Daley . . . Scoop Jackson, Ed Muskie, and Frank Rizzo, the super-cop Mayor of Philadelphia.

George McGovern is also a Democrat, and I suppose I have to sympathize in some guilt-stricken way with whatever demented obsession makes him think he can somehow cause this herd of venal pigs to see the light and make him their leader . . . but after watching McGovern perform in two primaries I think he should stay in the Senate, where his painfully earnest style is not only more appreciated but also far more effective than it is on the nationwide stump.

His surprising neo-victory in New Hampshire was less a triumph than a spin-off from Muskie's incredible bungling. But, up close, he is a very likeable and convincing person—in total contrast to Big Ed, who seems okay on TV or at the other end of a crowded auditorium, but who turns off almost everybody who has the misfortune of having to deal with him personally.

Another key factor in New Hampshire was that McGovern only needed 33,007 votes to achieve the psychological "upset" that came with his 37 percent figure versus Muskie's 46 percent. This was possible because McGovern was able, in New Hampshire, to campaign in the low-key, town-meeting, person-to-person style in which he is most effective . . . but which will be physically impossible in big, delegate-heavy states like California, Pennsylvania, Illinois, or even Wisconsin. (Chicago alone will send eighty delegates to the Democratic Convention, compared to only twenty for the whole state of New Hampshire . . . and in Florida, McGovern managed to reach more than 75,000 voters, but wound up in sixth place with a depressing six percent of the state's total.)

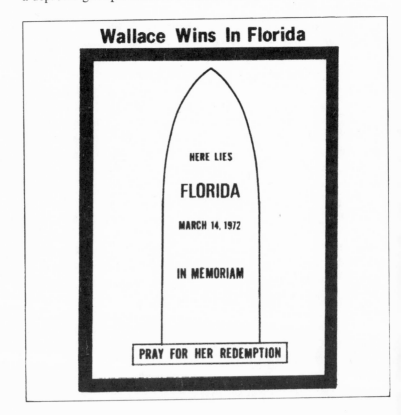

The New Hampshire primary is perhaps the only important national election where a candidate like McGovern can be truly effective. Crowds seem to turn him *off*, instead of on. He lacks that sense of drama—that instinct for timing and orchestration that is the real secret of success in American politics.

Frank Mankiewicz seems to have it—and that helps, but probably not enough. In a political situation where it is almost mathematically impossible to win *anything* unless you can make the sap rise in a crowd, a presidential candidate like McGovern—who simply lacks the chemistry—is at a fatal disadvantage in mass-vote scenes where a ho-ho verbal counterpunch, at the right moment, can be worth four dozen carefully reasoned position papers.

The main problem in any democracy is that crowd-pleasers are generally brainless swine who can go out on a stage and whup their supporters into an orgiastic frenzy—then go back to the office and sell every one of the poor bastards down the tube for a nickel apiece. Probably the rarest form of life in American politics is the man who can turn on a crowd and still keep his head straight— assuming it was straight in the first place.

Which harks back to McGovern's problem. He is probably the most honest big-time politician in America; Robert Kennedy, several years before he was murdered, called George McGovern "the most decent man in the Senate." Which is not quite the same thing as being the best candidate for President of the United States. For that, McGovern would need at least one dark kinky streak of Mick Jagger in his soul. . . .

Not much, and perhaps not even enough so people would notice at lunch in the Capitol Hill Hotel or walking down the hallway of the Senate Office Building—but just enough to drift out on the stage in front of a big crowd and let the spectacle turn *him* on.

That may be the handle. Maybe the whole secret of turning a crowd on is getting turned on yourself by the crowd. The only candidate running for the presidency today who seems to understand this is George Wallace . . . which might at least partially explain why Bobby Kennedy was the only candidate who could take votes away from Wallace in '68. Kennedy, like Wallace, was able to connect with people on some kind of visceral, instinctive level that is probably both above and below "rational politics."

McGovern does not appear to have this instinct. He does not *project* real well, and his sense of humor is so dry that a lot of people insist on calling it "withered."

Maybe so—and that may be the root of the reason why I can't feel entirely comfortable around George . . . and he would probably not agree with my conviction that a sense of humor is the main measure of sanity.

But who can say for sure? Humor is a very private thing. One night about five years ago in Idaho, Mike Solheim and I were sitting in his house talking about Lenny Bruce in a fairly serious vein, when he suddenly got up and put on a record that I still remember as one of the most hysterical classics of satire I'd ever heard in my life. I laughed for twenty minutes. Every line was perfect. "What's the name of that album?" I said. "I thought I'd heard all of his stuff, but this one is incredible."

"You're right," he said. "But it's not Lenny Bruce."

"Bullshit," I said. "Let's see the jacket."

He smiled and tossed it across the room to me. It was General Douglas MacArthur's famous "farewell speech" to Congress in '52.

Remember that one? The "old soldiers never die" number? My friend Raoul Duke calls it "one of the ten best mescaline records ever cut."

I am still a little sick about that episode. Solheim and I are still friends, but not in the same way. That record is not for everybody. I wouldn't recommend it to a general audience . . . But then I wouldn't recommend it to George McGovern either.

Jesus! The only small point I meant to make when I jack-knifed into this trip was that McGovern is unusual, for a politician, in that he is less impressive on TV than he is in person.

One of Muskie's main problems, thus far, has been that not even his own hired staff people really like him. The older ones try to explain this problem away by saying, "Ed's under a lot of pressure these days, but he's really a fine guy, *underneath.*"

The younger staff members have apparently never had much contact with "the real Muskie." With very few exceptions, they justify their strained allegiance to the man by saying, "I wouldn't be working for him except that he's the only Democrat who can beat Nixon."

Or at least that's what they said before the polls closed in Florida. After that—when it quickly became apparent that Muskie couldn't even be .t Scoop Jackson, much less Hubert Humphrey or George Wallace—he was faced with a virtual election-night mutiny among the younger staff people, and even the veterans were so alarmed that they convened an emergency conference in Muskie headquarters at Miami's Dupont Plaza Hotel and decided that the candidate would have to drastically *change his image.*

For months they'd been trying to sell "the Man from Maine" as a comfortable, mushmouth, middle-of-the-road compromiser who wouldn't dream of offending anybody—the ideal "centrist" candidate, who would be all things to all men.

But the voters were not quite that stupid. Muskie bombed in New Hampshire, on what even the candidate admitted was his own turf—and then he came down to Florida and got stomped so badly that his campaign staffers were weeping uncontrollably in front of TV cameras in the ballroom that had been advertised all day—on the Dupont Plaza billboard—as the scene of "Muskie's Victory Party."

I got there just after he had come down from his upstairs hideaway to console the crowd and denounce George Wallace on network TV as "a demagogue of the worst sort" and "a threat to the country's underlying values of humanism, of decency, of progress."

This outburst was immediately interpreted, by local politicians, as a slur on the people of Florida—calling 42 percent of the electorate Dupes and Racist Pigs because they voted for George Wallace.

U.S. Senator Ed Gurney (R-Fla.) demanded an apology, but Muskie ignored him and went back upstairs to the smoke-filled room where his wizards had already decided that his only hope was a fast turn to the Left. No more of that "centrist" bullshit. They looked both ways and—seeing the Right very crowded —convinced each other that Muskie's "new image" would be "The Liberal Alternative to Hubert Humphrey."

And besides, neither McGovern nor Lindsay were showing much strength out there in Left Field, so Big Ed would probably fare a hell of a lot better by picking a fight with those two than he would by moving Right and tangling with Humphrey and Jackson.

Robert Squier, Muskie's national media advisor, emerged from the meeting and said, "We're going to erase that yellow stripe in the middle of the road." Another one of the brain-trusters tried to put a better face on it: "The irony of this defeat," he said, "is that it will make Muskie what we all wanted him to be all along . . . the only question is whether it's too late."

In the final analysis, as it were, this painful think session was "summed up" for the New York *Times* by a nameless "key aide/advisor" who explained: "The reason people didn't vote for Ed Muskie here is that they didn't have any reason to."

Zang! The candidate's reaction to this ultimate nut of wisdom was not recorded, but we can only assume he was pleased to see signs that at least one of his ranking advisors was finally beginning to function well enough on the basic motor-skill/signal-recognition level that he might soon learn to tie his own shoes.

If I were running for the presidency of the United States and heard a thing like that from somebody I was paying a thousand dollars a week I would have the bastard dropped down an elevator shaft.

But Muskie has apparently grown accustomed to this kind of waterhead talk from his staff. They are not an impressive group, on the evidence. One of the first things you notice around any Muskie headquarters, local or national, is that many of the people in charge are extremely fat. Not just chubby or paunchy or flabby, but serious glandular cases. They require assistance getting in and out of cars, or even elevators.

Under normal circumstances I wouldn't mention this kind of thing—for all the obvious reasons: general humanity, good taste, relevance, etc.—but in the context of what has happened to Ed

130

Muskie in the first two primaries, it's hard to avoid the idea that there may be some ominous connection between the total failure of his campaign and the people who are running it.

As late as February 15th, Ed Muskie was generally conceded —even by his political opponents—to be within an eyelash or two of having the Democratic nomination so skillfully locked up that the primaries wouldn't even be necessary. He had the public endorsements of almost every Big Name in the party, including some who said they were only backing him because he was so far ahead that nobody else had a chance . . . which was just as well, they said, because it is very important to get the Party machinery into high gear, early on, behind a *consensus candidate*. And Ed Muskie, they all agreed, was the only Democrat who could beat Nixon in November.

The word went out early, long before Christmas, and by January it had already filtered down to low-level fringe groups like the National Association of Student Governments and other "youth vote" organizers, who were suddenly faced with the choice of either "getting your people behind Muskie" or "crippling the party with another one of those goddamn protest movements that'll end up like all the others and not accomplish anything except to guarantee Nixon's re-election."

A lot of people bought this—particularly the "youth leader" types who saw themselves playing key roles in a high-powered, issue-oriented Muskie campaign that would not only dump Nixon but put a certified "good guy" in the White House.

In retrospect, the "Sunshine Special" looks far more like an ill-conceived disaster than it did at the time, when Rubin and the Boohoo made such a shambles of Muskie's arrival in Miami that the local news media devoted almost as much time and space to the Senator's clash with "anti-war hecklers" at the train station as it did to the whole four hundred-mile, thirty-six-hour Whistlestop Tour that covered the length of the state and produced what the candidate's headquarters said were "five major statements in five cities."

It probably cost the Muskie campaign almost $40,000—almost $7,500 of that for rental of the five car train from Amtrak. Staff salaries and special expenses for the trip (thirty advance men spending two weeks each in towns along the route to make sure Big Ed would draw crowds for the TV cameras; payment to musicians, Rosey Grier, etc.) . . . a list of *all* expenses would probably drive the cost of the spectacle up closer to $50,000.

For all this money, time, and effort, Muskie's combined whistle-stop crowds totaled less than three thousand, including the disastrous climax that not only botched news coverage in Miami, the state, and the whole country—but also came close to shattering the Senator's nerves. In addition to all that, his "major statements" along the way were contemptuously dismissed as "oatmeal" by most of the press and the network TV news editors in New York & Washington.

In a word, the "Sunshine Special" *bombed.* The Miami *Herald* reported—in the same article dominated by the Rubin/Boohoo incident—that Muskie's trip into "the politics of the past" was considered a failure even by the Senator's own staff.

Meanwhile, in that same issue of the *Herald,* right next to the ugly saga of the "Sunshine Special," was a photograph of a grinning George Wallace chatting with national champion stock car racer Richard Petty at the Daytona 500, where 98,600 racing fans were treated to "a few informal remarks" by The Governor, who said he had only come to watch the races and check up on his old friend, Dick Petty—who enjoys the same kind of superhero status in the South that Jean-Claude Killy has in ski country.

That appearance at the Daytona 500 didn't cost Wallace a dime, and the AP wire-photo of him and Petty that went to every daily and Sunday newspaper in Florida was worth more to Wallace than his own weight in pure gold . . . and there was also the weight of the 98,600 racing fans, who figure that any friend of Richard Petty's must sit on both shoulders of God in his spare time. . . .

The Florida primary is over now. George Wallace stomped everybody, with 42 percent of the vote in a field of eleven. Ed Muskie, the erstwhile National Front-runner, finished a sick fourth, with only 9 percent . . . and then he went on all the TV networks to snarl about how this horrible thing would never have happened except that Wallace is a Beast and a Bigot.

Which is at least half true, but it doesn't have much to do with why Muskie got beaten like a gong in Florida. The real reason is that The Man From Maine, who got the nod many months ago as the choice of the Democratic Party's ruling establishment, is running one of the stupidest and most incompetent political campaigns since Tom Dewey took his dive and elected Truman in 1948.

If I had any vested interest in the Democratic Party I would do everything possible to have Muskie committed at once. Another disaster at the polls might put him around the bend. And unless all the other Democratic candidates are killed in a stone-blizzard between now and April 4, Muskie is going to absorb another serious beating in Wisconsin.

I am probably not the only person who has already decided to be almost anywhere except in Big Ed's Milwaukee headquarters when the polls close on election night. The place will probably be dead empty, and all the windows taped . . . TV crews hunkered down behind overturned ping-pong tables, hoping to film the ex-Front-runner from a safe distance when he comes crashing into the place to blame his sixth-place finish on some kind of unholy alliance between Ti-Grace Atkinson and Judge Crater. Nor is there any reason to believe he will refrain from physical violence at that time. With his dream and his nerves completely shot, he might start laying hands on people.

Hopefully, some of his friends will be there to restrain the wiggy bastard. All we can be sure of, however, is the list of those who will *not* be there, under any pretense at all . . . Senator Harold Hughes will not be there, for instance, and neither will Senator John Tunney . . . Nor will any of the other Senators, Governors, Mayors, Congressmen, Labor Leaders, Liberal Pundits, Fascist Lawyers, Fixers from ITT, and extremely powerful Democratic National Committeewomen, who are already on the record as full-bore committed to stand behind Big Ed.

None of those people will be there when Muskie sees the first

133

returns from Wisconsin and feels the first rush of pus into his brain. At that point he will have to depend on his friends, because that suitcase full of endorsements he's been dragging around won't be worth the price of checking it into a local bus station locker.

Except perhaps for Birch Bayh. There is something that doesn't quite meet the eye connected with this one. It makes no sense at all, on its face. Why would one of Ted Kennedy's closest friends and allies in the Senate suddenly decide to jump on the Muskie bandwagon when everybody else is struggling to get off gracefully?

Maybe Birch is just basically a nice guy—one of those down-home, warm-hearted Hoosiers you hear so much about. Maybe he and Big Ed are lifelong buddies. But if that were so, you'd think Bayh might have offered to fix Muskie up with some high-life political talent back then when it might have made a difference.

But times are tricky now, and you never know when even one of your best friends might slap a ruinous lawsuit on you for some twisted reason that nobody understands. Almost everybody you meet these days is nervous about the nasty drift of things.

It is becoming increasingly possible, for instance, that Hubert Humphrey will be the Democratic presidential nominee this year—which would cause another Nixon-Humphrey campaign. And a thing like that would probably have a serious effect on my nerves. I'd prefer no election at all to another Humphrey nightmare. Six months ago it seemed out of the question. But no longer.

Frank Mankiewicz was right. For months he's been telling anybody who asked him that the Democratic race would boil down, after the first few primaries, to a Humphrey/McGovern battle. But nobody took him seriously. We all assumed he was just talking up Humphrey's chances in order to slow Muskie down and thus keep McGovern viable.

But apparently he was serious all along. Humphrey is the bookies' choice in Wisconsin, which would finish Muskie and make Hubert the high rider all the way to the Oregon and California primaries in early June.

The "other" race in Wisconsin is between McGovern and Lindsay, which might strike a lot more sparks than it has so far if anybody really believed the boneheads who run the Democratic

Party would conceivably nominate either one of them. But there is a definite possibility that the Democratic Convention this year might erupt into something beyond the control of anybody; the new delegate-selection rules make it virtually impossible for old-style bosses like Mayor Daley to treat delegates like sheep hauled in to be dipped.

A candidate like Lindsay or McGovern might be able to raise serious hell in a deadlocked convention, but the odds are better than even that Hubert will peddle his ass to almost anybody who wants a chunk of it, then arrive in Miami with the nomination sewed up and Nixon waiting to pounce on him the instant he comes out of his scumbag.

Another Nixon/Humphrey horror would almost certainly cause a "Fourth Party" uprising and guarantee Nixon's re-election—which might bring the hounds of hell down on a lot of people for the next four very long years.

But personally I think I'd be inclined to take that risk. Hubert Humphrey is a treacherous, gutless old ward-heeler who should be put in a goddamn bottle and sent out with the Japanese Current. The idea of Humphrey running for President again makes a mockery out of things that it would take me too long to explain or even list here. And Hubert Humphrey wouldn't understand what I was talking about anyway. He was a swine in '68 and he's worse now. If the Democratic Party nominates Humphrey again in '72, the Party will get exactly what it deserves.

April

Stunning Upset in Wisconsin . . . McGovern
Juggernaut Croaks Muskie . . . Humphrey Falters;
Wallace Rolls On . . . Big Ed Exposed as Ibogaine
Addict . . . McGovern Accosts the Sheriff . . .
Bad News from Bleak House: Mojo Madness in
Milwaukee; or How Nazis Broke My Spirit on
Election Night . . . Mankiewicz Predicts First
Ballot Victory in Miami . . .

EASTER MORNING IN MILWAUKEE; ten minutes before five. Dawn
is struggling up through the polluted mist on Lake Michigan to the
east. I can sense the sunrise, but I can't see it—because just outside my window on the twenty-first floor of the (ITT-owned) Sheraton-Schroeder Hotel a huge red neon CITGO sign blocks my view
of everything except the PABST BREWING CO. sign just off to
the right, which is next to four massive pink letters saying YMCA.

The lake is out there somewhere: A giant body of water full
of poison. You can still find a few places that serve "fresh seafood"
in Milwaukee, but they have to fly it in from Maine and Bermuda,
packed in dry ice.

People still fish in Lake Michigan, but you don't want to eat
what you catch. Fish that feed on garbage, human shit, and raw
industrial poisons tend to taste a little strange.

So beef and pork are very big here; prepared in the German
Manner, with sauerkraut. Milwaukee is owned by old Germans
who moved out to the suburbs about thirty years ago and hired
Polaks to run the city for them. The German presence is very
heavy here; the pace is very orderly. Even on totally empty downtown streets, nobody crosses against the Red Light.

136

Yesterday I was grabbed for "jay-walking" outside the hotel. I was standing in a crowd on the corner of Second and Wisconsin— impatient to get across the street to my illegally parked Mustang and zip out to the South Side for a Wallace rally—and after two full minutes of standing on the curb and looking at the empty street I thought "fuck this," and started to cross.

Suddenly a whistle blew and a cop was yelling. "What the hell do you think you're *doing?*"

I kept moving, but glanced around me out of a general curiosity to see who was about to get busted—and I realized at once it was me. I was the only violator . . . so I shrugged and moved back to the curb, enduring the stares of about two dozen Responsible, Law-Abiding Citizens who clearly disapproved of my outburst . . . To first *break the law,* then to be screamed at in public by a *trooper;* this is not the sort of thing you want to call down on yourself in Milwaukee. There is no room in the good German mind for flashes of personal anarchy . . .

(Suddenly the FM radio switches off from the music and starts howling: "Rejoice and be Glad! He is Risen!" Then a thunder of hymns and chanting.)

Of course. Easter morning. Somewhere in Syria the junkies are rolling the rock away. All over the world they are celebrating, once again, the symbolic release of The Church—two thousand years of vengeance.

Wonderful. Vengeance is a hard thing to knock, on principle— but right now I am not especially interested in Principle. I want some decent music, in order to keep working. Time is a factor, here. In forty-eight hours the voters of Wisconsin will go to the polls, and the morning after that the *Rolling Stone* presses will start cranking out No. 107 for newsstand sale in New York & San Francisco Tuesday—Thursday in Boston, Washington, L.A. . . .

So things are getting tense up here in Milwaukee right now, and all this wild screaming about Jesus on the radio is not soothing my head. (Now we have a sermon on the box; it sounds like something out of the Church of the Final Thunder in Swamptown, Mississippi—"This woman Mary Magdalene walked to the tomb, and found it *empty!"*—then a groan of organs and cries of "Amen" in the background . . .)

137

What? . . . What?

"I came to the Senate to fight for human rights! President Kennedy worked with me . . . we broke the filibuster . . ."

There is no avoiding Hubert Humphrey in Wisconsin this week. The bastard is everywhere: on the tube, on the box, in the streets with his sound trucks . . . and now the bastard is even breaking into Easter morning *sermons* with his gibberish.

It didn't last long. The sermon is rolling again—un-fazed by that harsh thirty-second interruption—and I know in my heart that The Hube is not as sleepless as his media schedule would have us think. It is only the miracle of tape that brings us the cracked screeching of Hubert Humphrey's voice at this hour on Easter morning.

Because I know, for an absolute fact, that he is sleeping less than fifty yards away from this typewriter. He is upstairs in Room 2350, about thirty seconds from here, as the raven flies—but for me the journey would be a lot longer. I could make the first forty yards with no trouble, but when I emerged from the Exit next to the ice

The Secret Service arrives in Wisconsin.

machine on the twenty-third floor I would instantly get put in a hammerlock by the SS men.

The arrival of Secret Service personnel has changed the campaign drastically. Each candidate has ten or twelve SS men surrounding him at all times—

(Now, with no warning, another voice cuts into the sermon. Four minutes after seven on Easter morning . . . and this one is a McGovern spot, talking about "courage" . . . but the voice has a definite flash quality to it:

Bobby Kennedy, come back to haunt us in the midst of this low-level campaign that would never have been necessary except for Sirhan Sirhan's twisted little hand . . . so now we have the taped voice of Robert Kennedy, long before he took a bullet in the brain, endorsing George McGovern on the radio in Milwaukee on Easter morning, four years later . . .)

There is not much talk about this around the McGovern campaign. It was Frank Mankiewicz's idea to use the thing, and Mankiewicz was very close to Bobby. He was the one who had to pull himself together on that grim morning in Los Angeles and go out to make The Announcement to a hospital lobby full of stunned reporters: "Senator Kennedy died tonight . . ."

So the sound of his voice being used as a Paid Political Commercial is just a hair unsettling to some people—even to those who might agree with the McGovern/Mankiewicz presumption that Robert would have wanted it this way.

Maybe so. It's a hard thing to argue, and the odds are far better than even that Robert Kennedy would find McGovern preferable to any other candidate for the Democratic nomination at this time. He never had much of a stomach for Hubert, except as the lesser of evils, and it probably never occurred to him that dim hacks like Muskie and Jackson would ever be taken seriously.

So it is probably fair to assume that if Bobby Kennedy were alive today—and somehow retired from politics—he would agree with almost everything McGovern says and stands for. If only because almost everything McGovern says and stands for is a cautious extension of what Bobby Kennedy was trying to put together in the aborted campaign of 1968.

But in another sense the 1972 Democratic Campaign mocks the

memory of everything Bobby Kennedy represented in '68. It is hard to imagine that he would be pleased to see that—four years after his murder—the Democratic Party would be so crippled and bankrupt on all fronts that even the best of its candidates would be fighting for life by trying to put a good face on positions essentially dictated by Nixon & George Wallace.

In purely pragmatic terms, the Kennedy voice tapes will probably be effective in this dreary '72 campaign; and in the end we might all agree that it was Right and Wise to use them[1] . . . but in the meantime there will be a few bad losers here and there, like me, who feel a very powerful sense of loss and depression every time we hear that voice—that speedy, nasal Irish twang that nailed the ear like a shot of *Let It Bleed* suddenly cutting through the doldrums of a dull Sunday morning on a plastic FM station.

There is a strange psychic connection between Bobby Kennedy's voice and the sound of the Rolling Stones. They were part of the same trip, that wild sense of breakthrough in the late Sixties when almost anything seemed possible.

The whole era peaked on March 31, 1968, when LBJ went on national TV to announce that he wouldn't run for re-election—that everything he stood for was fucked, and by quitting he made himself the symbolic ex-champ of the Old Order.

It was like driving an evil King off the throne. Nobody knew exactly what would come next, but we all understood that whatever happened would somehow be a product of the "New Consciousness." By May it was clear that the next President would be either Gene McCarthy or Bobby Kennedy, and The War would be over by Christmas . . . .

---

1. I had a talk with Mankiewicz about this shortly after the Wisconsin primary. I don't recall what town we were in, but it might have been Columbus—or maybe Cleveland. It was sometime after midnight in a ratty hotel room and my memory of the conversation is hazy, due to massive ingestion of booze, fatback, and forty cc's of adrenochrome. In any case the Bobby Kennedy voice tapes were never used again. By mid-May, however, when it was obvious that Hubert Humphrey was the only remaining obstacle between George and the nomination, there were other Kennedy voices supporting McGovern. The whole clan was actively campaigning for him and even Teddy was saying that he would do everything he could for George except run on the same ticket with him.

What happened after that, between April and November of 1968, plunged a whole generation of hyper-political young Americans into a terminal stupor. Nixon blamed it on communist drugs and said he had The Cure, but what he never understood was that the simple stark fact of President Nixon *was* the problem, or at least the main symbol. It is hard to even remember precisely—much less explain—just what a terrible bummer the last half of '68 turned into.

Actually, it took less than three months. Martin Luther King was murdered in April, Bobby Kennedy in June . . . then Nixon was nominated in July, and in August the Democrats went to Chicago for the final act.

By Labor Day it was all over: "The Movement" was finished, except for the trials, and somebody else was dealing. The choice between Nixon & Humphrey was no choice at all—not in the context of what had already gone down, between Selma and Chicago. To be offered Hubert Humphrey as a sort of withered booby prize for all those bloody failures seemed more like a deliberate insult than a choice.

McGovern Wins;
Strong Wallace Vote Edges
Humphrey; Fourth Place Finish
Staggers Ex-Frontrunner Muskie;
Lindsay Quits Race

—Milwaukee *Journal,* April 4, 1972

FAILURE COMES EASY at a time like this. After eight days in this fantastic dungeon of a hotel, the idea of failing totally and miserably in my work seems absolutely logical. It is a fitting end to this gig—not only for me, but for everyone else who got trapped here, especially journalists.

The Wisconsin primary is over now. It came to a shocking climax a few hours ago when George McGovern and George Wallace ran a blitz on everybody.

The results were such a jolt to the Conventional Wisdom that now—with a cold grey dawn bloating up out of Lake Michigan and Hubert Humphrey still howling in his sleep despite the sedatives in his room directly above us—there is nobody in Milwaukee this morning, including me, who can even pretend to explain what really went down last night. The McGovern brain-trust will deny this, but the truth of the matter is that less than twenty-four hours ago it was impossible to get an even-money bet in McGovern headquarters that their man would finish first. Not even Warren Beatty, who is blossoming fast in his new role as one of McGovern's most valuable and enthusiastic organizers, really believed George would finish better than a close second.

A week earlier it would have been considered a sign of madness, among those who knew the score, to bet McGovern any better than a respectable third—but toward the end of the final week the word went out that George had picked up a wave and was showing surprising strength in some of the blue-collar hardhat wards that had been more or less conceded to either Humphrey or Muskie. David Broder of the Washington *Post* is generally acknowledged to be the ranking wizard on the campaign trail this year, and five days before the election he caused serious shock waves by offering to bet— with me at least—that McGovern would get more than 30 percent, and Wallace less than 10.

He lost both ends of that bet, as it turned out—and I mean to hunt the bastard down and rip his teeth out if he tries to welsh— but the simple fact that Broder had that kind of confidence in McGovern's strength was seen as a main signal by the professional pols and newsmen who'd been saying all along that the Wisconsin primary was so hopelessly confused that nobody in his right mind would try to predict the outcome.

The consensus outlook, however, had Humphrey winning with almost 30 percent, McGovern just barely edging Muskie out of second with just under 25 percent, and fourth going to either Jackson or Wallace at roughly 10 percent.

My own bets had Humphrey hanging on to beat McGovern just barely, by something like 27 to 26 percent, Wallace a strong third with about 20 percent, and poor Muskie crawling in a sick fourth with about 10 percent to Jackson's 9 percent. I was sorely tempted to pickup some easy money from Tom Morgan, Lindsay's press secretary, who emptied his pockets one afternoon in the Schroeder hotel bar and came up with $102 to back his conviction that Lindsay would get between 10 and 15 percent—but I had to back off because I had come to like Lindsay; he struck me as the most interesting of all the Democratic candidates in the sense that he seemed open to almost any kind of idea . . . so I regretfully declined Morgan's bet on the grounds that I would feel uncomfortable by profiting from Lindsay's misfortune. (As it turned out, he got only 7 percent and dropped out . . .)

But this was not the story I meant to write—or avoid writing—here; the idea was to say only that we suffered a terrible disaster on election night. All our finely laid plans were blasted into offal by the TV network computers before the night even got into first gear.

When the polls closed at eight, Tim Crouse and I were still sitting idly around the T-shaped bar and desk in our National Affairs Suite at the Sheraton-Shroeder Hotel, laying detailed plans for what we assumed would be the next five or six hours of hellish suspense while the votes were being counted. It would be at least midnight, we felt, before the results would begin to take shape . . . and if it looked at all close we were prepared to work straight through until dawn or even noon, if necessary.

The lead article in Sunday's Washington *Post* echoed the unanimous conviction of all the five or six hundred big-time press/politics wizards who were gathered here for what they all called "the crunch"—the showdown, the first of the national primaries that would finally separate the sheep from the goats, as it were.

After a month of intense research by some of the best political journalists in America, the *Post* had finally concluded that (1) "The Wisconsin primary election seems likely to make dramatic changes in the battle for the 1972 presidential nomination" . . . and (2) that "an unusually high degree of uncertainty remains as the contest nears its climax."

In other words, nobody had the vaguest idea what would happen here, except that some people were going to get hurt—and the smart-money consensus had Muskie and Lindsay as the most likely losers. The fact that Lindsay was almost totally out of money made him a pretty safe bet to do badly in Wisconsin, but Muskie—coming off a convincing victory in Illinois[2] at least partially redeemed his disastrous failure in Florida—looked pretty good in Wisconsin, on paper . . . but there was still something weak and malignant in the spine of the Muskie campaign. There was a smell of death about it. He talked like a farmer with terminal cancer trying to borrow money on next year's crop.

Two weeks before the election the polls had Muskie running more or less even with Humphrey and well ahead of McGovern—but not even his staffers believed it; they kept smiling, but their morale had been cracked beyond repair in Florida, when Muskie called a meeting the day after the primary to announce that he was quitting the race. They had managed to talk him out of it, agreeing to work without pay until after Wisconsin, but when word of the candidate's aborted withdrawal leaked out to the press . . . well, that was that. Nobody published it, nobody mentioned it on TV or radio—but from that point on, the only thing that kept the Muskie campaign alive was a grim political version of the old vaudeville idea that "the show must go on."

Midway in the final week of the campaign even Muskie himself began dropping hints that he knew he was doomed. At one point, during a whistlestop tour of small towns in the Fox River Valley near Green Bay, he fell into a public funk and began muttering about "needing a miracle" . . . and then, when the sense of depres-

2. Actually Muskie's win in Illinois was not that convincing. As expected, he won a clear majority of the delegates at the state Democratic convention but all it did was give him a breather between his disasters in Florida and Wisconsin.

David Broder of the Washington **Post,** one of the few press wizards to predict a McGovern victory in Wisconsin.

Jane Muskie mashing a chunk of Big Ed's birthday cake into the face of **Newsweek** reporter Dick Stout.

sion began spreading like a piss-puddle on concrete, he invited the campaign-press regulars to help him celebrate his fifty-eighth birthday at a small hotel on a snowy night in Green Bay. But the party turned sour when his wife mashed a piece of the birthday cake in the face of *Newsweek* reporter Dick Stout, saying, "One good turn deserves another, eh Dick?"[3]

The Morning News

Finally the True Wisdom arrives. I have been waiting for it all night. Nothing else has been available since Walter Cronkite signed off last night at ten, with McGovern already certified the clear winner and George Wallace a certain strong third.

Nelson Benton on CBS is interviewing Wallace, saying, "Is it true that you've decided to clean up your act?"

Wallace gives him a puzzled grin. He has never felt any need to cultivate the media.

Humphrey comes on, "I think we did well here and I'm looking forward to the next primaries—Indiana, Ohio, and Pennsylvania."

Muskie is heading for Chicago and a painful meeting with his money men—to decide if he'll stay in the race. He has already spent a million & a half dollars on a total disaster.

But the news is no help. Frank McGee on NBC is acting like a wino: "We have the big winner in Wisconsin here with us this morning—Senator Proxmire, and also his lovely wife." (pause) "Did I say Proxmire? I meant McGovern . . . of course . . . We have Senator McGovern here with us this morning, and his wife is with him . . ."

Sometime around seven on Friday night—three days before the

---

3. Both Muskie and his wife had been stewing privately for months over a *Newsweek* story—quoting *Women's Wear Daily*—to the effect that Mrs. Muskie drank heavily and told dirty jokes on the press bus. Stout insisted, however, that Mrs. Muskie mashed the cake in his face as "a joke." Others at the party saw it differently: Some took it as a tip-off that Muskie knew it was all over.

Wisconsin primary—I left my dreary suite in the Sheraton-Schroeder Hotel and drove across town to McGovern headquarters at the Milwaukee Inn, a comfortably obscure sort of motor hotel in a residential neighborhood near Lake Michigan. The streets were still icy from a snowstorm earlier in the week, and my rented purple Mustang had no snow tires.

The car was extremely unstable—one of those Detroit classics, apparently assembled by junkies to teach the rest of us a lesson. I had already been forced to remove the air filter, in order to manipulate the automatic choke by hand, but there was no way to cure the unnerving accelerator delay. It was totally unpredictable. At some stoplights the car would move out normally, but at others it would try to stall, seeming to want more gas—and then suddenly leap ahead like a mule gone amok from a bee sting.

Every red light was a potential disaster. Sometimes I would take off slowly, with the rest of the traffic . . . but at about every third light the goddamn worthless machine would hang back for a second or so, as if to give the others a head start, and then come thundering off the line at top speed with no traction at all and the rear end fishtailing all over the street about halfway to the next corner.

By the time I got to the Milwaukee Inn I had all three lanes of State Street to myself. Anybody who couldn't get safely ahead of me was lagging safely behind. I wondered if anyone had taken my license number in order to turn me in as a dangerous drunk or a dope addict. It was entirely possible that by the time I got back to the car every cop in Milwaukee would be alerted to grab me on sight.

I was brooding on this as I entered the dining room and spotted Frank Mankiewicz at a table near the rear. As I approached the table he looked up with a nasty grin and said, "Ah ha, it's you; I'm surprised you have the nerve to show up over here—after what you wrote about me."

I stared at him, trying to get my brain back in focus. Conversation ceased at every table within ten feet of us, but the only one that really concerned me was a knot of four Secret Service men who suddenly shifted into Deadly Pounce position at their table just behind Mankiewicz and whoever else he was eating with.

I had come down the aisle very fast, in my normal fashion, not thinking about much of anything except what I wanted to ask Mankiewicz—but his loud accusation about me having "the nerve to show up" gave me a definite jolt. Which might have passed in a flash if I hadn't realized, at almost the same instant, that four thugs with wires in their ears were so alarmed at my high-speed appearance that they were about to beat me into a coma on pure instinct, and ask questions later.

This was my first confrontation with the Secret Service. They had not been around in any of the other primaries, until Wisconsin, and I was not accustomed to working in a situation where any sudden move around a candidate could mean a broken arm. Their orders are to *protect the candidate,* period, and they are trained like high-strung guard dogs to react with Total Force at the first sign of danger. Never hesitate. First crack the wrist, then go for the floating rib . . . and if the "assassin" turns out to be just an oddly dressed journalist—well, that's what the SS boys call "tough titty." Memories of Sirhan Sirhan are still too fresh, and there is no reliable profile on potential assassins . . . so *everybody* is suspect, including journalists.

All this flashed through my head in a split second. I saw it all happening, but my brain had gone limp from too much tension. First the car, now this . . . and perhaps the most unsettling thing of all was the fact that I'd never seen Mankiewicz even *smile.*

But now he was actually laughing, and the SS guards relaxed. I tried to smile and say something, but my head was still locked in neutral.

"You better stay away from my house from now on," Mankiewicz was saying. "My wife hates your guts."

Jesus, I thought. What's happening here? Somewhere behind me I could hear a voice saying, "Hey, Sheriff! Hello there! Sheriff!"

I glanced over my shoulder to see who was calling, but all I saw was a sea of unfamiliar faces, all staring at me . . . so I turned quickly back to Mankiewicz, who was still laughing.

"What the hell are you talking about?" I said. "What did I do to your wife?"

He paused long enough to carve a bite out of what looked like a five or six pound Prime Rib on his plate, then he looked up again. "You called me a rumpled little man," he said. "You came over to my house and drank my liquor and then you said I was a rumpled little man who looked like a used car salesman."

"Sheriff! Sheriff!" That goddamn voice again; it seemed vaguely familiar, but I didn't want to turn around and find all those people staring at me.

Then the fog began to lift. I suddenly understood that Mankiewicz was *joking*—which struck me as perhaps the most shocking and peculiar development of the entire '72 campaign. The idea that anybody connected with the McGovern campaign might actually laugh in public was almost beyond my ken. In New Hampshire nobody had ever even smiled, and in Florida the mood was so down that I felt guilty even hanging around.

Even Mankiewicz, in Florida, was acting like a man about to take the bastinado . . . so I was puzzled and even a little nervous to find him grinning like this in Milwaukee.

Was he stoned? Had it come down to that?

"Sheriff! Sheriff!"

I spun around quickly, feeling a sudden flash of anger at some asshole mocking me in these rude and confusing circumstances. By this time I'd forgotten what I'd wanted to ask Mankiewicz in the first place. The night was turning into something out of Kafka.

"Sheriff!"

I glared at the table behind me, but nobody blinked. Then I felt a hand on my belt, poking at me . . . and my first quick instinct was to knock the hand away with a full-stroke hammer-shot from about ear level; really crack the bastard . . . and then immediately apologize: "Oh! Pardon *me,* old sport! I guess my nerves are shot, eh?"

Which they almost were, about thirty seconds later, when I realized that the hand on my belt—and the voice that had been yelling "Sheriff"—belonged to George McGovern. He was sitting right behind me, an arm's length away, having dinner with his wife and some of the campaign staffers.

Now I understood the Secret Service presence. I'd been standing so close to McGovern that every time I turned around to see who was yelling "Sheriff!" I saw almost every face in the room except the one right next to me.

He twisted around in his chair to shake hands, and the smile on his face was the smile of a man who has just cranked off a really wonderful joke.

"God damn!" I blurted, "it's you!" I tried to smile back at him, but my face had turned to rubber and I heard myself babbling: "Well . . . ah . . . how does it look?" Then quickly: "Excellent, eh? Yeah, I guess so. It certainly does look . . . ah . . . but what the hell, I guess you know all this . . ."

He said a few things that I never really absorbed, but there was nothing he could have said at that moment as eloquent or as meaningful as that incredible smile on his face.

The most common known source of Ibogaine is from the roots of Tabernanthe Iboga, a shrub indigenous to West Africa. As early as 1869, roots of T.I. were reported effective in combating sleep or fatigue and in maintaining alertness when ingested by African natives. Extracts of T.I. are used by natives while stalking game; it enables them to remain motionless for as long as two days while retaining mental alertness. It has been used for centuries by natives of Africa, Asia and South America in conjunction with fetishistic and mythical ceremonies. In 1905 the gross effects of chewing large quantities of T.I. roots were described . . . "Soon his nerves get tense in an extraordinary way; an epileptic-like madness comes over him, during which he becomes unconscious and pronounces words which are interpreted by the older members of the group as having a prophetic meaning and to prove that the fetish has entered him."

At the turn of the century, iboga extracts were used as stimulants, aphrodisiacs and inebriants. They have been available in European drugstores for over 30 years. Much of the research with Ibogaine has been done with animals. In the cat, for example,

2-10 mg./kg. given intravenously caused marked excitation, dilated pupils, salivation, and tremors leading to a picture of rage. There was an alerting reaction; obvious apprehension and fear, and attempts to escape . . . In human studies, at a dose of 300 mg. given orally, the subject experiences visions, changes in perception of the environment and delusions or alterations of thinking. Visual imagery became more vivid, with animals often appearing. Ibogaine produces a state of drowsiness in which the subject does not wish to move, open his eyes, or be aware of his environment. Since there appears to be an inverse relationship between the presence of physical symptoms and the richness of the psychological experience, the choice of environment is an important consideration. Many are disturbed by lights or noises . . . Dr. Claudio Naranjo, a psychotherapist, is responsible for most current knowledge regarding Ibogaine effects in humans. He states: "I have been more impressed by the enduring effects resulting from Ibogaine than by those from sessions conducted with any other drug."
—From a study by PharmChem Laboratories, Palo Alto, California

Not much has been written about The Ibogaine Effect as a serious factor in the Presidential Campaign, but toward the end of the Wisconsin primary race—about a week before the vote—word leaked out that some of Muskie's top advisors had called in a Brazilian doctor who was said to be treating the candidate with "some kind of strange drug" that nobody in the press corps had ever heard of.

It had been common knowledge for many weeks that Humphrey was using an exotic brand of speed known as *Wallot* . . . and it had long been whispered that Muskie was into something very heavy, but it was hard to take the talk seriously until I heard about the appearance of a mysterious Brazilian doctor. That was the key.

I immediately recognized The Ibogaine Effect—from Muskie's tearful breakdown on the flatbed truck in New Hampshire, the delusions and altered thinking that characterized his campaign in Florida, and finally the condition of "total rage" that gripped him in Wisconsin.

There was no doubt about it: The Man from Maine had turned to massive doses of Ibogaine as a last resort. The only remaining question was "when did he start?" But nobody could answer this one, and I was not able to press the candidate himself for an answer because I was permanently barred from the Muskie campaign after that incident on the "Sunshine Special" in Florida . . . and that scene makes far more sense now than it did at the time.

Muskie has always taken pride in his ability to deal with hecklers; he has frequently challenged them, calling them up to the stage in front of big crowds and then forcing the poor bastards to debate with him in a blaze of TV lights.

But there was none of that in Florida. When the Boohoo began grabbing at his legs and screaming for more gin, Big Ed went all to pieces . . . which gave rise to speculation, among reporters familiar with his campaign style in '68 and '70, that Muskie was not himself. It was noted, among other things, that he had developed a tendency to roll his eyes wildly during TV interviews, that his thought patterns had become strangely fragmented, and that not even his closest advisors could predict when he might suddenly spiral off into babbling rages, or neo-comatose funks.

In restrospect, however, it is easy to see why Muskie fell apart on that caboose platform in the Miami train station. There he was —far gone in a bad Ibogaine frenzy—suddenly shoved out in a rainstorm to face a sullen crowd and some kind of snarling lunatic going for his legs while he tried to explain why he was "the only Democrat who can beat Nixon."

It is entirely conceivable—given the known effects of Ibogaine —that Muskie's brain was almost paralyzed by hallucinations at the time; that he looked out at that crowd and saw gila monsters instead of people, and that his mind snapped completely when he felt something large and apparently vicious clawing at his legs.

We can only speculate on this, because those in a position to know have flatly refused to comment on rumors concerning the Senator's disastrous experiments with Ibogaine. I tried to find the Brazilian doctor on election night in Milwaukee, but by the time the polls closed he was long gone. One of the hired bimbos in Muskie's Holiday Inn headquarters said a man with fresh welts on his head had been dragged out the side door and put on a bus

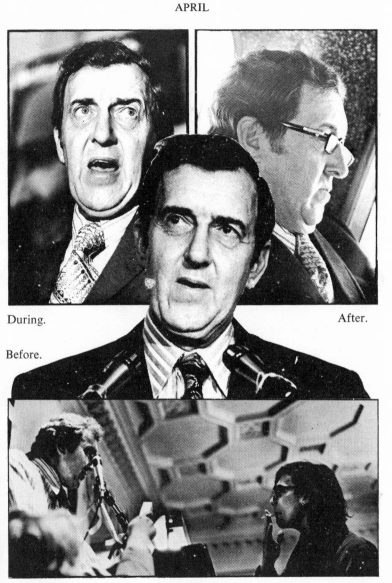

During.

After.

Before.

Big Ed discussed the marijuana question for the dope-smoking students in Madison, Wisconsin, moments before refusing to take a toke himself. Later in the campaign, however, it was reported that Senator Muskie was a known user of a powerful drug called Ibogaine.

153

to Chicago, but we were never able to confirm this.

The final straw, for Muskie, was the result of an unpublished but carefully leaked poll, taken by Oliver Quayle at the behest of Senator Jackson and the local AFL-CIO, that showed Muskie losing 70 percent of his support in Wisconsin in a period of two weeks. According to the Quayle poll, the onetime front-runner slipped from 39 percent to 13 percent, while McGovern was virtually doubling *his* figure from 12 percent to 23 percent in the same period—which put McGovern ahead of Humphrey, who had dropped about five points to 19 percent.

The same poll showed George Wallace with 12 percent, which convinced liberal Democratic Governor Pat Lucey and the moguls of Organized Labor that it would not be necessary to mount a serious effort to short-circuit the Wallace threat. Both the Governor and the state Labor Bosses had been worried about Wallace stomping into Wisconsin and embarrassing everybody by pulling off another one of those ugly, Florida-style upsets.

It is still hard to understand how the polls and the pols, and especially a wizard like Broder, could have so drastically underestimated the Wallace vote. Perhaps the threat of an anti-Wallace backlash by organized labor led the visiting press to think the other George was safely boxed in. Wisconsin's Big Labor braintrust had come up with a theory that Wallace got a huge boost in Florida when the liberal opposition got so hysterical about him that he got twice as many votes as he would have if the other candidates had simply ignored him and done their own things.

So they decided to turn the other cheek in Wisconsin. They ignored the Wallace rallies that, night after night, packed halls in every corner of the state. That was all Wallace did—except for a few TV spots—and every one of his rallies attracted more people than the halls could hold.

I went to one at a place called Serb Hall on the South Side of

Wallace fans listening to the candidate at a rally in Racine.

Milwaukee—a neighborhood the pols said was locked up for Muskie. Serb Hall is a big yellow-brick place that looks like an abandoned gymnasium, across the street from Sentry Supermarket on Oklahoma Street about five miles from downtown Milwaukee. One half of the hall is a "Lounge & Bowling Alley," and the other half is a fair-sized auditorium with a capacity of about 300.

The Serb Hall rally was a last-minute addition to the Wallace schedule. His main rally that night was scheduled for 7:30 at a much bigger hall in Racine, about fifty miles south . . . but one of his handlers apparently decided to get him warmed up with a 5:00 gig at Serb Hall, despite the obvious risk involved in holding a political rally at that hour of the evening in a neighborhood full of Polish factory-workers just getting off work.

I got there at 4:30, thinking to get in ahead of the crowd and maybe chat a bit with some of the early arrivals at the bar . . . but at 4:30 the hall was already packed and the bar was so crowded I could barely reach in to get a beer. When I reached in again, to pay for it, somebody pushed my hand back and a voice said, "It's already taken care of, fella—you're a *guest* here."

For the next two hours I was locked in a friendly, free-wheeling conversation with about six of my hosts who didn't mind telling me they were there because George Wallace was the most important man in America. "This guy is the real thing," one of them said. "I never cared anything about politics before, but Wallace ain't the same as the others. He don't sneak around the bush. He just comes right out and *says* it."

It was the first time I'd ever seen Wallace in person. There were no seats in the hall; everybody was standing. The air was electric even before he started talking, and by the time he was five or six minutes into his spiel I had a sense that the bastard had somehow levitated himself and was hovering over us. It reminded me of a Janis Joplin concert. Anybody who doubts the Wallace appeal should go out and catch his act sometime. He jerked this crowd in Serb Hall around like he had them all on wires. They were laughing, shouting, whacking each other on the back . . . it was a flat-out fire & brimstone *performance*.

156

Humphrey's addiction to *Wallot* has not stirred any controversy so far. He has always campaigned like a rat in heat, and the only difference now is that he is able to do it eighteen hours a day instead of ten. The main change in his public style, since '68, is that he no longer seems aware that his gibberish is not taken seriously by anyone except Labor Leaders and middle-class blacks.

Humphrey's style on the stump was described with embarrassing accuracy by Donald Pfarrer in the Milwaukee *Journal:*

"When Humphrey addresses a crowd he does two things at once. First he makes promises; not 'a promise a day,' as Senator Muskie has charged, but more like a promise every three minutes, with one or two for everybody within reach of his voice. He claims that his promises are the expressions of a program for social change that he'll fight for.

"Second and more important, he tries to weld a bond between himself and the audience. And he succeeds so well that 'audience' is usually the wrong word. His groups are more like meetings of people who want to get something done.

"If you're from Wisconsin, he's your neighbor from Minnesota and he tells you so. If you're old, he has an aging mother living in a nursing home in Huron, S.D. If you're a farmer, he grew up among people like you. If you're a union man, he carries a union card and defended the unions when few others would. If you're black, he fought for civil rights. If you're young, he was a teacher, and he was young once himself. If you're from the city, he was a mayor. If you're poor, he was poor once himself and he had to quit school.

"Then he goes through the crowd, shaking hands, signing autographs and talking. Sometimes he even listens. He spends some time with each person, looks him in the eye and asks for his help."

Pfarrer was trying to be objective, so he stopped short of saying that at least half the reporters assigned to the Humphrey campaign are convinced that he's senile. When he ran for President four years ago he was a hack and a fool, but at least he was consistent.

Now he talks like an eighty-year-old woman who just discovered speed. He will call a press conference to announce that if elected he will "have all our boys out of Vietnam within ninety days"—then rush across town, weeping and jabbering the whole way, to appear on a network TV show and make a fist-shaking emotional appeal for every American to stand behind the President and "applaud" his recent decision to resume heavy bombing in North Vietnam.

Humphrey will go into a black neighborhood in Milwaukee and drench the streets with tears while deploring "the enduring tragedy" that life in Nixon's America has visited on "these beautiful little children"—and then act hurt and dismayed when a reporter who covered his Florida campaign reminds him that "In Miami you were talking just a shade to the Left of George Wallace and somewhere to the Right of Mussolini."

Hubert seems genuinely puzzled by the fast-rising tide of evidence that many once-sympathetic voters no longer believe anything he says. He can't understand why people snicker when he talks about "the politics of joy" and "punishing welfare chiselers" in almost the same breath . . . and God only knows what must have gone through his head when he picked up the current issue of *Newsweek* and found Stewart Alsop quoting *Rolling Stone* to the effect that "Hubert Humphrey is a treacherous, gutless old ward-heeler who should be put in a goddamn bottle and sent out with the Japanese current."

Alsop made it clear that he was not pleased with that kind of language. He called it "brutal"—then wound up his column by dismissing the Humphrey candidacy in terms more polite than mine, but no less final. Both Stewart and his demented brother, Joseph, have apparently concluded—along with almost all the other "prominent & influential" Gentleman Journalists in Washington—that the Democratic primaries have disintegrated into a series of meaningless brawls not worth covering. On the "opinion-shaping" level of the journalism Establishment in both Washington and New York there is virtually unanimous agreement that Nixon's opponent in '72 will be Ted Kennedy.

McGovern's solid victory in Wisconsin was dismissed, by most of the press wizards, as further evidence that the Democratic Party

158

has been taken over by "extremists": George McGovern on the Left and George Wallace on the Right, with a sudden dangerous vacuum in what is referred to on editorial pages as "the vital Center."

The root of the problem, of course, is that most of the big-time Opinion Makers decided a long time ago—along with all those Democratic Senators, Congressmen, Governors, Mayors, and other party pros—that the candidate of the "vital Center" in '72 would be none other than that fireball staesman from Maine, Ed Muskie.

Humphrey was briefly considered, then dumped as a sure loser in November. McGovern was not even considered, and at that point George Wallace hadn't told anybody that he planned to run as a Democrat . . . so it boiled down quick to Muskie, who had in fact been Number One ever since his impressive election-eve TV speech in 1970. It came at a time when the party pros were still reeling from the shock of Chappaquidick, which was seen as a fatal blow to any hope of a Kennedy challenge this year, and they were thrashing around desperately for a candidate when the Man from Maine suddenly emerged from the tube as the party's de facto spokesman.

In contrast to Nixon's vengeful screed on TV from the California Cow Palace just a few hours earlier, Ed Muskie came across as a paragon of decency and wisdom—just as he had looked very good in '68, compared to Hubert Humphrey. He was a Real Statesman, they said; a Reassuring Figure. By the summer of '71 the party bosses had convinced themselves that Ed Muskie was the "only Democrat with a chance of beating Nixon."

This was bullshit, of course. Sending Muskie against Nixon would have been like sending a three-toed sloth out to seize turf from a wolverine. Big Ed was an adequate Senator—or at least he'd seemed like one until he started trying to explain his "mistake" on the war in Vietnam—but it was stone madness from the start to ever think about exposing him to the kind of bloodthirsty thugs that Nixon and John Mitchell would sic on him. They would have him screeching on his knees by sundown on Labor Day. If I were running a campaign against Muskie I would arrange for some anonymous creep to buy time on national TV and announce that twenty-two years ago he and Ed spent a summer working as male whores at a Peg House somewhere in the North Woods.

Nothing else would be necessary.

"It's all over, we have it locked up."

"What?"

"Yeah, we have the delegates. All we have to do now is hang on and not make any mistakes."

"Well . . . ah . . . Jesus, Frank, this comes as a bit of a shock. Actually, I was calling to ask if McGovern has made any decision about whether or not he'd support Humphrey—if it comes to that."

"It won't. The question is moot. Put it out of your mind. We'll win on the first ballot."

"Hmmnnn . . . Well, I guess there's no point in asking you about this other thing, either . . ."

"What's that?"

"That thing about McGovern accepting the Vice-Presidency on a ticket with Ted Kennedy."

"What? I never said that!"

"No? Well . . . I guess we were pretty stoned . . ."

"We?"

"Yeah, Wenner was there too. Remember? And he's pretty sure that's what you said." (pause)

"He is, eh?"

"Yeah . . . but of course we could be mistaken." (pause)

"No . . . no . . . wait a minute. I remember the question . . . but hell, I said it was just a guess."

"What?"

"That thing about Kennedy. What I said, I think, was that I couldn't speak for George—but my own personal feeling was that he wouldn't even think about accepting the number two spot . . ."

"With anybody but Kennedy, right?" (pause)

"Well . . . ah . . . yeah, but I was just kind of thinking out loud. As far as the Senator's concerned, there's no point even talking about it." (pause) "Like I said, we have the delegates now. We'll win. I'm sure of it."

"Okay, I hope you're right." (pause) "But if something goes wrong . . . If you can't carry it on the first ballot and the convention turns up deadlocked . . . then, if Kennedy jumps in, McGovern might consider—"

"Yeah, yeah: I guess it's possible . . . but I told you, goddamnit! We have it locked up."

"I know, I know . . . but what the hell? I'm just reaching around for loose ends here and there: just something to fill the space— you know how it is, eh?"

"Yeah. I did it once myself." (pause) "Say, are you feeling any better?"

"What do you mean?"

"Well . . . maybe I shouldn't say this, but you looked pretty bad up there in Wisconsin."

"I was sick, Frank—extremely sick; and besides that I was full of antibiotics. I had doctors coming into the hotel every afternoon to give me shots."

"What kind of shots?"

"Christ, everything they had: Penicillin, B-12, Cortizone, Moss extract . . . the hotel doctor wouldn't go for it, so I called the medical society and told them to go down their list until they found somebody who wouldn't argue. It took half a day, but they finally sent a man around with everything I wanted . . . He kept shaking his head while he filled the needles. 'I don't know why you want me to shoot all this stuff into you fella,' he said. 'It won't do a goddamn thing for your cold—but if you have any parasites in your body, this is sure going to raise hell with *them*.' Then he gave me about nine shots. Cash on the line. No checks, no receipt. I never even found out his name."

"Well . . . maybe you need some rest, Hunter. I get the feeling that you're not very careful about your health."

"You're right. My health is failing rapidly—but I'll make it to Miami. After that . . . well, let's see how it goes. I may want to have myself committed."

—From a telephone conversation with Frank Mankiewicz, 4/15/72

The idea that George McGovern has the Democratic nomination locked up by mid-April will not be an easy thing for most people to accept—especially since it comes from Frank Mankiewicz, the tall and natty "political director" for McGovern's campaign.

Total candor with the press—or anyone else, for that matter—is not one of the traits most presidential candidates find entirely desirable in their key staff people. Skilled professional liars are as much in demand in politics as they are in the advertising business . . . and the main function of any candidate's press secretary is to make sure the press gets nothing but Upbeat news. There is no point, after all, in calling a press conference to announce that nobody on the staff will be paid this month because three or four of your largest financial bankers just called to say they are pulling out and abandoning all hope of victory.

When something like this happens, you quickly lock all the doors and send your press secretary out to start whispering, off the record, that your opponent's California campaign coordinator just called to ask for a job.

This kind of devious bullshit is standard procedure in most campaigns. Everybody is presumed to understand it—even the reporters who can't keep a straight face while they're jotting it all down for page one of the early edition: SEN. MACE DENIES PULLOUT RUMORS; PREDICTS TOTAL VICTORY IN ALL STATES . . . and then the lead:

The man who has been called The Lowest Underdog of Our Time today denied rumors that all but one of his financial backers have stopped payment on checks formerly earmarked for media time and staff salaries in what some observers have called "a hopeless campaign." Sen. Otto "Slim" Mace, under indictment on twelve charges of Tax Fraud, told reporters at a special noon press conference in the lobby of the Ace Hotel that in fact he has "more money than I know what to do with" and that his headquarters phone has been tied up for days with calls from "extremely important people" now working for his opponent who say they plan to

162

quit and come to work for Sen. Mace.

"Needless to say, I am not free at this time to release any names," the Senator explained. "But I expect we will hire quite a few of them and then roll on to victory."

The best example of this kind of coverage in the current campaign has been the stuff coming out of the Muskie camp. In recent weeks the truth has been so painful that some journalists have gone out of their way to give the poor bastards a break and not flay them in print any more than absolutely necessary.

One of the only humorous moments in the Florida primary campaign, for instance, came when one of Muskie's state campaign managers, Chris Hart, showed up at a meeting with representatives of the other candidates to explain why Big Ed was refusing to take part in a TV debate. "My instructions," he said, "are that the Senator should never again be put in a situation where he has to think quickly."

By nightfall of that day every journalist in Miami was laughing at Hart's blunder but *nobody* published it; and none of the TV reporters ever mentioned it on the air. I didn't even use it myself, for some reason, although I heard about it in Washington while I was packing to go back to Florida.

I remember thinking that I should call Hart and ask him if he'd actually said a thing like that, but when I got there I didn't feel up to it. Muskie was obviously in deep trouble, and Hart had been pretty decent to me when I'd showed up at headquarters to sign up for that awful trip on the "Sunshine Special" . . . so I figured what the hell? Let it rest.

The other press people might have had different reasons for not using Hart's quote, but I can't say for sure because I never asked. Looking back on it, I think it must have been so obvious that the Muskie campaign was doomed that nobody felt mean enough to torment the survivors over something that no longer seemed important.

A week or so later there was another ugly story leaking out of the Muskie compound, and this one was never published either— or if it was, I didn't see it.

Shortly after the election-night returns showed Muskie hopelessly mired in fourth place behind Wallace, Humphrey, and Jackson, the Man from Maine called an emergency staff meeting and *announced he was quitting the race.* This stirred up a certain amount of panic and general anger among the staff people, who eventually persuaded Big Ed to at least get himself under control before talking to any reporters. He agreed to go out and play golf the next day, while the top-level staffers got together and tried to find some alternative.

This was the reality behind the story, widely published the next day, that Muskie had decided to "change his whole style" and start talking like the Fighting Liberal he really was at heart. He would move on to Illinois and Wisconsin with new zeal . . . and his staff people were so happy with this decision to finally "take off the gloves" that they had agreed to work without pay until the day after the big Victory Party in Wisconsin.

It took about a week for the story of Muskie's attempt to quit the race to leak out to the press, but it was not an easy thing to confirm. One of the most frustrating realities of this goddamn twisted business is the situation where somebody says, "I'll only answer your question if you promise not to print it."

Everybody I talked to about the Muskie story seemed to know all the details—but there was no point trying to check it out, they said, because it came from "somebody who was at the meeting" and he "obviously can't talk about it."

Of course not. Only a lunatic would risk getting fired from his unsalaried job on the Muskie campaign several days before the crucial Wisconsin primary.

So I let that one slide, too. I saw no point in wasting any more time on the Man from Maine. He was a walking corpse in Wisconsin—where he finished a wretched fourth, once again—and recent reports from Massachusetts and Pennsylvania are so grim that it is hard to avoid the impression that getting on Muskie's press bus these days is like loading yourself in a closet with a mad dog.

After another hellish argument with his staff, he decided to abandon Massachusetts to McGovern and make his last stand in Pennsylvania against Humphrey, who has never won a primary.

But even a blind pig finds an acorn now and then, if he keeps on rooting around, and it's beginning to look like Hubert's time has come. There is a huge black vote in Pennsylvania, and Humphrey will probably get most of it—for reasons I'd rather not even think about right now.

In any case, both the Massachusetts and Pennsylvania primaries are on April 25, which means they'll be over and done with by the time this thing gets on the newsstands. So that's another thing we can let slide.[4]

Whatever that quack shot into me up in Milwaukee seems to have killed more than parasites. The front half of my brain has been numb for ten days and my legs will no longer support me for more than two or three minutes at a time.

So this is probably as good a time as any to say that I'm inclined to think Mankiewicz was not lying when he told me the other day that McGovern will arrive in Miami with enough delegates to win the nomination on the first ballot.

This is an extremely crazy thing to say—and especially to print —at a time when McGovern has only 95 of the 1509 delegate votes he will need to win, and when the latest national Gallup poll shows him still creeping along at five percent behind Humphrey, Muskie, and Wallace . . . but I suspect these figures are meaningless.

Muskie is finished. His only hope now is to do something like take a long vacation in New Zealand until July and get the Ibogaine

---

4. McGovern scored a clean sweep in Massachusetts, running virtually unopposed. Muskie was on the ballot in that state, but several weeks before the primary he decided to abandon Massachusetts to McGovern—who would have won easily anyway—and concentrate all of his resources on a last-ditch effort in Pennsylvania. This also failed: He finished in an unimpressive tie with McGovern for third place. Humphrey kept his hopes alive by winning handily in Pennsylvania; Wallace finished a strong second and McGovern's predictable defeat did little to slow his momentum. His staff wizards had long since decided that there was no hope of winning Pennsylvania anyway so they had assigned it a low priority. For Muskie however it was the spike that sealed the coffin. The day after the Pennsylvania primary vote he announced he was quitting the race.

out of his system so he can show up in Miami and pray for a dead-locked convention. At that point, he can offer himself up for sacrifice as a "compromise candidate," make a deal with George Wallace for the VP slot, then confront the convention with a Muskie/Wallace "unity ticket."

Which might make the nut. If nothing else, it would command a lot of support from people like me who feel that the only way to save the Democratic Party is to destroy it. I have tried to explain this to George McGovern, but it's not one of the subjects he really enjoys talking about. McGovern is very nervous about the possibility of boxing himself into the role of a McCarthy-type "spoiler" candidate, which he was beginning to look like until he somehow won a big chunk of the hardhat vote in New Hampshire and sensed the first strange seed of a coalition that might make him a serious challenger instead of just another martyr.

There was only a hint of it in New Hampshire, but in Wisconsin it came together with a decisiveness that nobody could quite understand in the alcoholic chaos of election night . . . but when the votes were all counted and the numbers broken down by wards, districts, and precincts, all you had to do was scan the tally sheets to see that McGovern had won all across the board. In Green Bay's Ward 12, which the tally sheet says is "mostly paper mill workers," he beat Wallace by 32 to 22 percent. In Sheboygan's Ward 4, another blue-collar, factory-worker neighborhood, he got 40 percent against Humphrey's 26 and Wallace's 9 percent. In Goetz Township, Chippewa County, he mopped up the Lutheran dairy farmer vote by 52 percent to 14 percent each for Humphrey and Wallace.

Two weeks before the election the wizards said McGovern would win only one of the state's nine congressional districts—D2, which is dominated by the aggressively political University of Wisconsin complex in Madison. This was also a district that Lindsay

166

and McCarthy were counting on . . . but the count from Madison's Ward 10, which is not much different from the others, showed Mc-Govern with 73 percent, Lindsay with 7 percent, and McCarthy with less than 1 percent. Muskie picked up about 5 percent of the student vote, and Humphrey had 3 percent.

The only glaring weakness in McGovern's sweep was his failure to break Humphrey's grip on the black wards in Milwaukee—where The Hube had campaigned avidly, greeting all comers with the Revolutionary Drug Brothers handshake. It was like Nixon flashing the peace sign, or Agnew chanting "Right On!" at a minstrel show.

The real shocker, however, came when McGovern carried the Polish south side of Milwaukee, which Muskie had planned on sweeping by at least ten to one. He was, after all, the first Pole to run for the Presidency of the United States, and he had campaigned on the south side under his original Polish name . . . but when the deal went down he might as well have been an Arab, for all they cared in places like Serb Hall.

Which more or less makes the point, I think. And if it doesn't, well . . . political analysis was never my game, anyway. All I do is wander around and make bets with people, and so far I've done pretty well.

As for betting on the chance that Mankiewicz is right and that McGovern will actually win on the first ballot in Miami . . . I think I'd like some odds on that one, and at this stage of the campaign they should be pretty easy to get. McGovern right now is the only one of the Democratic candidates with any chance at all of getting the nomination . . . and if anybody wants to put money on Muskie, Humphrey or Wallace, get in touch with me immediately.

If McGovern wins California and New York—and Mankiewicz says they have both of those already wired—he will go to Miami with enough delegates to come very close to winning on the first ballot. If not . . . well . . . God only knows what kind of treachery and madness will erupt in Miami if they have to start bargaining. Whatever happens at that point will have to include George Wallace

—who has already said he'll take second place on a ticket with any-body who'll let him write the party platform.

A deadlocked convention would be faced with a choice between bargaining with George Wallace or trying to draft Ted Kennedy, in order to save the party. What Kennedy would do under those circumstances is impossible to say right now . . . but it's worth noting that the only one of the candidates who has presumably given any thought to running second on a Kennedy ticket is George Mc-Govern, and McGovern is the only candidate whom Ted Kennedy would be likely to help over the hump prior to Miami Beach.

I am feeling a little desperate about getting out of this hotel. Eight days in the Sheraton-Schroeder is like three months in the Cook County jail. The place is run by old Germans. The whole staff is German. Most of them speak enough English to make themselves understood in a garbled, menacing sort of way . . . and they are especially full of hate this week because the hotel has just been sold and the whole staff seems to think they'll be fired just as soon as the election crowd leaves.

So they are doing everything possible to make sure that nobody unfortunate enough to be trapped here this week will ever forget the experience. The room radiators are uncontrollable, the tubs won't drain, the elevators go haywire every night, the phones ring for no reason at all hours of the night, the coffee shop is almost never open, and about three days before the election the bar ran out of beer. The manager explained that they were "runnig oud ze inventory"—selling off everything in stock, including all the booze and almost every item on the menu except things like cab-bage and sauerbrauten. The first wave of complaints were turned aside with a hiss and a chop of the hand, but after two days and nights of this Prussian madness the manager was apparently caused to know pressure from forces beyond his control. By Friday the bar was stocked with beer again, and it was once more possible to get things like prime rib and sheep's head in the dining room.

But the root *ambience* of the place never changed. Dick Tuck, the legendary Kennedy advance man now working for McGovern, has stayed here several times in the past and calls it "the worst hotel in the world."

Ah yes . . . I can hear the Mojo Wire humming frantically across the room. Crouse is stuffing page after page of gibberish into it. Greg Jackson, the ABC correspondent, had been handling it most of the day and whipping us along like Bear Bryant, but he had to catch a plane for New York and now we are left on our own.

The pressure is building up. The copy no longer makes sense. Huge chunks are either missing or too scrambled to follow from one sentence to another. Crouse just fed two consecutive pages into the machine upside-down, provoking a burst of angry yelling from whoever is operating the receiver out there on the Coast.

And now the bastard is beeping . . . beeping . . . beeping, which means it is hungry for this final page, which means I no longer have time to crank out any real wisdom on the meaning of the Wisconsin primary. But that can wait, I think. We have a three-week rest now before the next one of these goddamn nightmares . . . which gives me a bit of time to think about what happened here. Meanwhile, the only thing we can be absolutely sure of is that George McGovern is no longer the hopelessly decent loser that he has looked like up to now.

The real surprise of this campaign, according to Theodore White on CBS-TV last night, is that "George McGovern has turned out to be one of the great field organizers of American politics."

But Crouse is dealing with that story, and the wire is beeping again. So this page will have to go, for good or ill . . . and the minute it finishes we will flee this hotel like rats from a burning ship.

[Author's Note]

Actually there was nothing mysterious about McGovern's "stunning" victory in Wisconsin. The most surprising thing about it was that the national press wizards, including me, had somehow overlooked the existence of one of the most impressive grass-roots political organizations in the history of American politics. Gene Pokorny, McGovern's twenty-five-year-old national manager for Wisconsin, had seen no special reason to inform the press about it. When the truth finally dawned on us several days before the election, I was too physically and mentally broken to cope with

Gene Pokorny.

anything that intricate. As the deadline hour approached, I spent more and more time locked in the back bathroom of our National Affairs Suite in Bleak House, raving distractedly and yelling at Crouse to call the doctor for more drugs. When it finally became apparent that I was hopelessly out of control, Crouse went out and lashed the story together on his own:

MILWAUKEE, WISC.—The George McGovern field organization has become a legend. Gene Pokorny has been hailed as the "best young political organizer in the history of this country," and people have begun talking about the volunteers in tones usually reserved for the guys who were in the hills with Castro.

A bunch of beautiful, euphoric, slightly drunk, very young McGovern volunteers were having a completely informal victory party in a block-long two-story brick warehouse, formerly used to store toys. They had been living there for two weeks, sleeping on the linoleum floor of the cavernous rooms.

They had all worked in the Fourth District, the Polish South Side of Milwaukee, a section that even the McGovern staff crossed off as the inviolable turf of Muskie, Wallace, and Humphrey. McGovern had not only won the district but beat Wallace by eight thousand votes. At the warehouse at 3:30 in the morning, nine or ten of the volunteers got up from a sleepy poker game and gathered around to talk.

"Tell everybody we really love George McGovern," said a blonde girl.

"I was in charge of the Wauwatosa-West Allis office in the Fourth," said a skinny young man wearing a T-shirt embroidered with a butterfly. "The Downtown office used to send volunteers out to us saying we couldn't win the Fourth, which was a pretty shitty thing to do. They wouldn't give us bumper stickers or buttons, we had to go down there and rip them off. Downtown was fucked. They sat around there and watched TV while we were putting out mailings until two in the morning."

"The district coordinator we had was really great," said a plump black girl. "He'd yell at us. Every time you came back he'd say, 'I know you'll go out one more time.' But he worked later than anybody. And he had a great way of getting little 13-year-old kids to work so they wouldn't just hang around the office."

"I had to pay to come out from Utah," said a girl who was resting her head on a boy's chest. "I want to see Nixon get the hell beaten out of him."

"We came from Springfield, Illinois," said another girl, who was dressed in overalls. "They sent a school bus from Nebraska to bring us up here. The guy in charge was a teacher from Nebraska who just happened to have a bus driver's license and was for McGovern. He kept singing and talking and he drove off the road twice in a snowstorm."

"When we canvassed we thought a lot of people were against us. We got really discouraged, it was freezing cold. You'd get a whole bunch of uncommitteds and then you'd hit three favorables in a row and it was an amazing up. The people were good to us, they were impressed that we were out in the cold and they let us come in to get warm. They were impressed I had come from Michigan to do this."

"A Wallace lady followed me up one block. She picked up all the literature I had left and put hers there," said a thin girl who was nursing a bottle of wine. "So I went back and picked hers up and put ours down."

"Some of these people were weird," said another girl. "I asked one guy, 'What do you think of McGovern?' and he said, 'I'd vote for him if he'd turn Christian.' A couple of them said, 'McGovern? He's for dope.' "

"I got a lady who liked George because she said he knew how to tie his tie right," said the black girl. "Gloria Steinem showed him how to tie it. You should have seen how he tied it before that."

"I think you should know that in our office we had twenty states represented among the volunteers," said the office manager. "All kinds of people haven't slept in a bed and have gone hungry. We had three hundred volunteers here in the warehouse some nights."

"They promised us room and board but they didn't feed us half the time," said one of the girls. The rest of the group shouted her down.

"One lady fed this whole warehouse for two and a half weeks," said an older woman who seemed to be in charge. "She said she and her husband didn't pay their bills for the month so that they could feed us. She would come home from her job as a teacher

172

and start to cook and then bring the food over. That kind of thing makes you feel good."

"When you write your article," said one of the boys, "tell them that we're all young kids and that they need a band at the next victory party. There was no band at the Pfister tonight. And tell them that we want to see George more."

"I have to crash," the girl from Utah said with a long yawn. "But I have to tell you something first. I've been here less than a week and yet I know so many people here *well,* 'cause they're beautiful people. Even if we'd lost, we'd have won so much."

A year and a half ago, George McGovern set out to be President of the United States of America with little money, no media, chronic five percent showing in the polls, and a face that was recognizable to nobody but a handful of liberals and South Dakota farmers. His only prayer was to build a crack political organization. Last week, that organization made him the front-runner in the Democratic primary race. It was indisputably the best organization in the state of Wisconsin, and it moved one McGovern volunteer, a New York Teamsters boss, to marvel: "I'm not kidding. This is better than Tammany Hall."

"This is the old politics," says Joel Swerdlow, the 26-year-old who ran McGovern's operation in the North half of Milwaukee. "We have precinct captains, ward leaders, car captains, the whole bit. That's the only way you win. But instead of patronage bosses and sewer commissioners, we've got young people who work because they're interested in the issues."

Political organization is basically a matter of list-keeping. You canvass a state by foot and by phone to find out who is for you, who is against you, and who is uncommitted. Once you have the list, you cross off the ones against you, barrage the uncommitted with pleas and information, and make sure your supporters get to the polls.

Not so long ago, the Party Organization that kept the best list and had the patronage clout to keep the listees in line could deliver an election. Today even Mayor Daley's fabled machine is showing signs of breakdown, and if a candidate wants an organization he can count on, he has to build it himself.

Muskie has made countless bungles; one of the earliest was his decision to depend entirely on the Party Organization to come through with the vote in the key Democratic city of Manchester, N. H. The local organization turned out to be a group of hacks led by a mayor who had won by only four hundred votes. "I wouldn't run for ward committee with the organization they have up there," said Providence's Mayor Joseph A. Doorley, who was called in at the last moment to rescue votes for Muskie. Meanwhile, McGovern's organization ran a classic operation in Manchester, canvassing almost every precinct two times, and winning ethnic sections that no one believed they could capture. The McGovern organization was superior in both numbers and fervor. The McGovern people canvassed the city so thoroughly that by election night they were able to predict the vote in most Manchester wards with deadly accuracy.

After the excellent showing in low-income districts in Manchester, the McGovern organization generals made a crucial decision; they decided that the main strategic aim of the campaign would be to prove that the bulk of their candidate's support actually came from working men, not from students and suburbanites.

"I've always thought that the blue-collar vote had to be a source of his strength," said Frank Mankiewicz, McGovern's main strategist. "It always seemed to me that McGovern—not as the anti-war candidate but as the 'change' candidate—would appeal more to Middle America than he would to any other group. They're the ones with the most to gain from change and they're the ones who get screwed by the way we do business in this country."

Wisconsin was the perfect state for McGovern's first big bid for blue-collar votes. The major issue was property tax, and McGovern could hammer relentlessly away for tax reform, which is one of his favorite themes. All he needed was a spectacular organization that could tell the working class district who he was.

Last year, McGovern's campaign manager, a young Coloradan named Gary Hart, who looks like a ski instructor and worked for

Bobby Kennedy, was setting up local organizations in key primary states. In November, 1970, he recruited a former McCarthy worker named Gene Pokorny to oversee the Wisconsin operation. Pokorny, who grew up on a feed-grains farm in Nebraska, started at once to line up workers using the old McCarthy lists. "It's tough starting a year and a half in advance," he said. "But just as long as you can find something useful for volunteers to do, you're OK. So we did lists, rummage sales, parties, petition drives, fund-raising. We had county leadership meetings and statewide workshops to show people how to canvass and how to set up storefronts." The lists were all-important. The McGovern workers sent special-interest mailings to every group they could pin down: ecologists, feminists, university faculties, high-school teachers, lawyers, and businessmen. To get at the farm vote they sent McGovern literature to every rural box-holder in the western districts of Wisconsin.

A shy man, Pokorny has adopted a protective official posture; sitting behind his immaculate metal desk, he comes on suspicious and tightlipped as a loan officer. The sight of the press begging for predictions drives him crazy. "I'm a perennial pessimist, gentlemen," he says. "It's a congenital disease of the spirit." However, he has the directness, energy, and conviction that make a good organizer. When the national McGovern staff—the advance men, schedulers, media men, pollsters, and strategists—arrived in Milwaukee two weeks before the election, Pokorny presented them with 10,000 volunteers, 35 local offices, and a clear appraisal of the situation. According to Pokorny, McGovern would probably lose the Third and Seventh Districts—solid farmland on the Minnesota border. In those districts Hubert, with his perfect agricultural record of twenty years' running and his absolute fluency in farm talk, rates as a Third Senator; they would be his preserve. The Fourth District—the heavily Polish South Side of Milwaukee, was the property of Muskie and Wallace. McGovern could do well in the Farm-Labor Ninth, Sixth, and Eighth Districts. The Second, which contains the university town of Madison, was his for the asking. The First and Fifth, both heavy Labor districts, were tossups. As it turned out, Pokorny's estimates were characteristically pessimistic.

The consensus of the staff, national and local, was that McGovern should blitz the Fifth, Milwaukee especially. North Milwaukee looks like Archie Bunker's street drawn out to infinity; a large proportion of Wisconsin's population lives there. (It also encompasses the downtown area, with every big TV station, radio station, and newspaper in the state.) A mixture of carefully segregated blacks and white labor, the district serves as a textbook example of the ' Roosevelt Democratic Coalition. By rights, it should go to that dogeared textbook Democrat, Hubert Humphrey. "If Humphrey doesn't win," said Pokorny, "that means the union can't deliver the rank and file to anybody anymore."

In the McGovern hierarchy, the task of bringing in the Fifth District belonged to Joel Swerdlow. On the Friday morning before the election, he was standing over two high-school girls in his tiny storefront headquarters, explaining how to send out a last-minute mailing. Having forfeited sleep for two nights, he had taken on a faint greenish tint and looked as if he might rise on Easter if not securely moored.

"I'm a political hack," he says. "I'm here because this is where I got the highest bid. Guys like me, we like to think we only go with candidates who can win." Despite his bluff, he is deeply committed to McGovern.

Swerdlow's boxcar-sized storefront headquarters contained the usual depressing welter of folders, envelopes, and brochures—all the standard paraphernalia for pestering apathetic citizens until they crack and agree to vote for your man. Fourteen-year-olds were running around on errands, out-of-state college kids were stuffing envelopes, and a radio was blaring. Swerdlow started on a tour of inspection.

The walls of the office were papered with printout lists of all the voters in the district. "In most states, you'd find a little R or D by each name," said Swerdlow. "Not here—there's no prior registration in this state. So we have to phone or go see them all and about one-fifth are for Nixon, which means a tremendous waste of energy."

Volunteers had reached 60 percent of the voters by phone and filled out an index card for each one—the back wall was stacked to the ceiling with shoe boxes full of index cards telling how each voter felt about McGovern (on a scale of 1 to 5, hot or cold) and listing the issues that interested each voter. "The whole deal was done with

APRIL

no money, no hired staff, and one phone in this whole place—it was all done by citizens out of their own homes," said Swerdlow. Other volunteers had canvassed a quarter of the district door-to-door, bringing back more cards with the same kind of information. Ideally, a district should be phone-canvassed once and foot-canvassed twice, but in 1972 student volunteers are scarce. Swerdlow decided to settle for dropping a piece of literature at the households that hadn't been canvassed.

"Besides the mailings," he said, "we have a nineteen-man phone bank downtown that's calling all the people we identified as uncommitted—and that's about 60 percent of them."

Swerdlow's other operations included:

● Plantgate leaflets, handed out at factories by two groups leaving the office at 5:30 every morning.

● Postcards, with a picture of McGovern and wife fondling a grandchild. Each local volunteer addresses postcards to thirty friends. Prominent members of parishes, Jewish congregations, and bowling leagues send postcards to these groups. Thirty thousand had been mailed by the Friday before the election.

● Palm cards—small sheets of paper which show exactly where McGovern's name appears on the ballot. Two McGovern workers would hand out cards at polling places in each of the city's three hundred precincts. According to Swerdlow, a good palm-card operation can make a ten percent difference in the vote.

● Signs, which have the same effect as palm cards. A totally befuddled voter may look at a Vote for McGovern sign and do just that. McGovern volunteers began putting up signs outside polling places at two in the morning of election day; rival pols had little time to pull them down.

Swerdlow's two week operation was sketchy and primitive, but McGovern's three biggest rivals in the district—Humphrey, Jackson, and Wallace—could not even approach it.

8:10 P.M., *election night:* Ten minutes after the polls closed down, Pat Caddell, resident McGovern pollster, got the early results of a blue-collar, factory precinct in Sheboygan and predicted that McGovern would end up by taking the nearest opposition by at least seven points.

9:40 P.M., *election night:* Frank Mankiewicz announced to a

177

cheering crowd at the Pfister ballroom that McGovern had taken seven out of Wisconsin's nine congressional districts—lacking only the Fifth and the Seventh (farm country on the Minnesota border) for a clean sweep. He called McGovern a "candidate for all the people."

Joel Swerdlow said that this campaign marked the first time McGovern had run strong in a real urban center. He thought McGovern would take the Fifth. He had lost one of his weak precincts to Humphrey by one vote.

2:00 A.M., *the morning after election night:* Out of the thirty-odd reporters who began the evening manning the banks of typewriters there, only one straggler was left, and he, like almost all the rest, was using the phrase "stunning victory" to describe McGovern's performance. Swerdlow and another McGovern worker were on their hands and knees sorting out adding-machine slips on the floral carpet. McGovern was trailing behind Humphrey in the Fifth District, and Swerdlow was adding up the votes to see whether the race was close enough to demand a recount. He showed me a pencil-written analysis of the voting trends. In most black districts, Humphrey was beating McGovern two to one. In the white labor districts, McGovern was easily taking Humphrey. The blacks were clearly the only bloc in the state that had not gone all out for McGovern.

Later Swerdlow sat on a sofa in the lobby and went over the figures for each precinct with Paul Cobb, who looks like a small edition of Isaac Hayes. Cobb is co-directing McGovern's operation in Northern California but he also serves as the resident expert of the black community. "I'm upset about the black vote," said Swerdlow. "I'm upset and *hypertense,*" said Cobb.

"I'm convinced that if we had had two or three black pros in Milwaukee for a month we could have ripped off 40 percent of the black vote," he said. "You could have organized under the soft underbelly of the Baptist Church hierarchy and literally picked out votes one by one and identified them."

10:00 A.M., *the morning after the election:* The press was assembled in the conference room of the Milwaukee Inn. Pat Caddell and Frank Mankiewicz had summoned the press for their analysis of the vote. This was a precautionary measure they had planned weeks ago—to make sure that the press did not go on writing, out

Gary Hart and Warren Beatty.

179

of sheer force of habit, that McGovern's support comes only from students and suburbanites.

Using analyses of selected precincts, Mankiewicz proved with statistics what he had been saying for weeks—that McGovern has the support of blue-collar workers, farmers, old people, young people, students, housewives—in short he is a presidential candidate so statistically proven that no convention could refuse him.

"Do your notes show any weaknesses?" a reporter asked.

"Yes—Mankiewicz!" another reporter shouted.

Mankiewicz admitted that McGovern has not yet cultivated the black vote. Caddell then got up to analyze the blue-collar support. Both McGovern and Wallace, he said, draw on the same pool of extremely alienated blue-collar voters, a group that is constantly getting deeper into bitterness, cynicism, and resentment about the current government.

Mankiewicz added that the "leading edge of labor support is now beginning to come to Senator McGovern. Some of the top labor officers who endorsed Muskie—like Leonard Woodcock—always said that they had great admiration for McGovern, that he was probably the most qualified candidate. But Muskie was the one who could beat Nixon or unite the party or was the clear leader —or any of those other phrases of antiquity."

Gary Hart now took over to explain why Wisconsin had been McGovern's watershed. Their one resource up to now—"aside from a superior candidate"—had been their organization. "We had to lay our plans very carefully," he said, "and we put the best people we could find in this country into these early key states. The tenor of the campaign is changing now. There is not enough time to develop state by state what we had in New Hampshire and in Wisconsin." From now on George McGovern will be using polls, media endorsements, and all the other resources available to a front-runner. His organization may never reach full flower again.

3:00 P.M., *the day after:*   Back at the Pfister lobby, I ran into Dave Aylward, a veteran of both the New Hampshire and Wisconsin campaigns although less than a year out of Dartmouth. The Sixth District, which had been under his direction, had voted strongly for McGovern. Dave was still high on victory. "Jesus," he said, "we won the fucking city of Fond du Lac with thirty high-school kids,

Election Night in Wisconsin.

three-fourths of whom are drug freaks. We only lost three wards and in one of those we lost to Wallace by two votes! And before last summer I had never done anything like this before."

I asked Dave if he had decided to go into politics full time. "Not forever," he said. "Can't take it physically. My hands were shaking yesterday morning. I was straight out for two nights making lists of positives and writing letters to uncommitteds. But we goddamn well *touched* people with those letters and leaflets."

"There's only one thing that worries me about being out front," he said. "The hacks. When McCarthy took Wisconsin in '68, the hacks were getting on board before anyone knew what had happened and they were saying, 'OK, kids, the fun's over, we'll run it from here, get lost.' And the kids had just racked up 56 percent for McCarthy in this state. If it happens again this time, they can have the campaign. I'll just pack my bags and split."

May

Crank Time on the Low Road . . . Fear and
Loathing in Ohio & Nebraska . . . Humphrey
Gets Ugly, McGovern Backs off . . . Delirium
Tremens at the National Affairs Desk . . . Acid,
Amnesty & Abortion . . . Massive Irregularities
on Election Night in Cleveland; Death Watch in
the Situation Room . . . Wallace Gunned Down in
Maryland . . . Showdown Looms in California . . .

ONE OF MY CLEAREST MEMORIES of the Nebraska primary is getting off the elevator on the wrong floor in the Omaha Hilton and
hearing a sudden burst of song from a room down one of the hallways . . . twenty to thirty young voices in ragged harmony, kicking
out the jams as they swung into the final hair-raising chorus of
"The Hound and the Whore."

I had heard it before, in other hallways of other hotels along
the campaign trail—but never this late at night, and never at this
level of howling intensity:

> *O the Hound chased the Whore across the mountains*
> *Boom! Boom! Boom!*
> *O the Hound chased the Whore into the sea. . . .*
> *Boom! Boom! Boom!*

A very frightening song under any circumstances—but especially frightening if you happen to be a politician running for very
high stakes and you know the people singing that song are *not on
your side.* I have never been in that situation, myself, but I imagine

it is something like camping out in the North Woods and suddenly coming awake in your tent around midnight to the horrible snarling and screaming sounds of a Werewolf killing your guard dog somewhere out in the trees beyond the campfire.

I was thinking about this as I stood in the hallway outside the elevator and heard all those people singing "The Hound and the Whore" . . . in a room down the hall that led into a wing of the hotel that I knew had been blocked off for The Candidate's national staff. But there is nothing in my notes to indicate which one of the candidates was quartered in that wing—or even which floor I was on when I first heard the song. All that I remember for sure is that it was one floor either above or below mine, on the eleventh. But the difference is crucial—because McGovern's people were mainly down on the tenth, and the smaller Humphrey contingent was above me on the twelfth.

It was a Monday night, just a few hours before the polls opened on Tuesday morning—and at that point the race seemed so even that both camps were publicly predicting a victory and privately expecting defeat. Even in retrospect there is no way to be certain which staff was doing the singing.[1]

And my own head was so scrambled at the hour that I can't be sure of anything except that I had just come back from a predawn breakfast at the Omaha Toddle House with Jack Nicholson, Julie Christie, Goldie Hawn, Warren Beatty, and Gary Hart, McGovern's national campaign manager who had just picked up a check for roughly $40,000 gross from another one of Beatty's fund-raising spectacles.

This one had been over in Lincoln, the state capital town about sixty miles west of Omaha, where a friendly crowd of some 7500 had packed the local civic center for a concert by Andy Williams and Henry Mancini . . . which apparently did the trick, because twenty-four hours later Lincoln delivered two to one for McGovern and put him over the hump in Nebraska.

I understand the necessity for these things, and as a certified

---

1. McGovern won. See page 203 for details.

member of the national press corps I am keenly aware of my responsibility to keep calm and endure two hours of Andy Williams from time to time—especially since I went over to Lincoln on the press bus and couldn't leave until the concert was over anyway. But I'm beginning to wonder just how much longer I can stand it: this endless nightmare of getting up at the crack of dawn to go out and watch the candidate shake hands with workers coming in for the day shift at the Bilbo Gear & Sprocket factory, then following him across town for another press-the-flesh gig at the local Slaughterhouse . . . then back on the bus and follow the candidate's car through traffic for forty-five minutes to watch him eat lunch and chat casually with the folks at a basement cafeteria table in some high-rise Home for the Aged.

Both Humphrey and McGovern have been doing this kind of thing about eighteen hours a day for the past six months—and one of them will keep doing it eighteen hours a day for five more months until November. According to the political pros, there is no other way to get elected: Go out and meet the voters on their own turf, shake their hands, look them straight in the eye, and introduce yourself . . . there is no other way.

The only one of the candidates this year who has consistently ignored and broken every rule in the Traditional Politicians Handbook is George Wallace. He doesn't do plant gates and coffee klatches. Wallace is a performer, not a mingler. He campaigns like a rock star, working always on the theory that one really *big* crowd is better than forty small ones.

But to hell with these theories. This is about the thirteenth lead I've written for this goddamn mess, and they are getting progressively worse . . . which hardly matters now, because we are down to the deadline again and it will not be long before the Mojo Wire starts beeping and the phones start ringing and those thugs out in San Francisco will be screaming for Copy. Words! Wisdom! Gibberish!

Anything! The presses roll at noon—three hours from now, and the paper is ready to go except for five blank pages in the middle. The "center-spread," a massive feature story. The cover is already printed, and according to the Story List that is lying out there on the floor about ten feet away from this typewriter, the center-spread feature for this issue will be A Definitive Profile of George McGovern and Everything He Stands For—written by me.

Looking at it fills me with guilt. This room reeks of failure, once again. Every two weeks they send me a story list that says I am lashing together some kind of definitive work on a major subject . . . which is true, but these projects are not developing quite as fast as we thought they would. There are still signs of life in a few of them, but not many. Out of twenty-six projects—a year's work—I have abandoned all hope for twenty-four, and the other two are hanging by a thread.[2]

There is no time to explain, now, why this is not a profile of George McGovern. That story blew up on us in Omaha, on the morning of the primary, when George and most of his troupe suddenly decided that Nixon's decision to force a showdown with Hanoi made it imperative for the Senator to fly back to Washington at once.

Nobody could say exactly why, but we all assumed he had something special in mind—some emergency move to get control of Nixon. No time for long mind-probing interviews. Humphrey had already announced that he was flying back to Washington at dawn, and there were two or three cynics in the press corps who suggested that this left McGovern no choice. If Humphrey thought the War Scare was important enough to make him rush back to the Capitol instead of hanging around Omaha on election day, then McGovern should be there too—or Hubert might say his Distinguished Opponent cared more about winning the Nebraska primary than avoiding World War Three.

As it turned out, neither Humphrey nor McGovern did anything dramatic when they got back to Washington—or at least nothing public—and a week or so later the New York *Times* announced

2. At this point in the campaign I was recovering from a severe case of Hutchinson's disease. For a period of sixteen consecutive days I fed myself intravenously. It was during that period that I completed this comparative analysis of the Ohio and Nebraska primaries.

that the mines in Haiphong harbor had been set to de-activate themselves on the day before Nixon's trip to Moscow for the summit meeting.

Maybe I missed something. Perhaps the whole crisis was solved in one of those top-secret confrontations between the Senate and the White House that we will not be able to read about until the official records are opened seventy-five years from now.

But there is no point in haggling any longer with this. The time has come to get full bore into heavy Gonzo Journalism, and this time we have no choice but to push it all the way out to the limit. The phone is ringing again and I can hear Crouse downstairs trying to put them off.

"What the hell are you guys worried about? He's up there cranking out a page every three minutes . . . What? . . . No, it won't make much sense, but I guarantee you we'll have plenty of words. If all else fails we'll start sending press releases and shit like that . . . Sure, why worry? We'll start sending almost immediately."

Only a lunatic would do this kind of work: twenty-three primaries in five months; stone drunk from dawn till dusk and huge speed-blisters all over my head. Where is the meaning? That light at the end of the tunnel?

Crouse is yelling again. They want more copy. He has sent them all of his stuff on the Wallace shooting, and now they want mine. Those halfwit sons of bitches should subscribe to a wire service; get one of those big AP tickers that spits out fifty words a minute, twenty-four hours a day . . . a whole grab-bag of weird news; just rip it off the top and print whatever comes up. Just the other day the AP wire had a story about a man from Arkansas who entered some kind of contest and won a two-week vacation—all expenses paid—wherever he wanted to go. Any place in the world: Mongolia, Easter Island, the Turkish Riviera . . . but his choice was Salt Lake City, and that's where he went.

Is this man a registered voter? Has he come to grips with the issues? Has he bathed in the blood of the lamb?

So much for all that. The noise-level downstairs tells me Crouse will not be able to put them off much longer. So now we will start getting serious: First Columbus, Ohio, and then Omaha. But mainly Columbus, only because this thing began—in *my* head, at least—as a fairly straight and serious account of the Ohio primary.

Then we decided to combine it with the ill-fated "McGovern Profile." So we arranged to meet George in Nebraska. I flew out from Washington and Wenner flew in from the Coast—just in time to shake hands with the candidate on his way to the airport.

No—I want to be fair about it: There was a certain amount of talk, and on the evidence it seems to have worked out.

But not in terms of "The Profile." We still had five blank pages. So I came back to Washington and grappled with it for a few days, Crouse came down from Boston to help beat the thing into shape . . . but nothing worked; no spine, no hope, to hell with it. We decided to bury the bugger and pretend none of that stuff ever happened. Tim flew back to Boston and I went off to New York in a half-crazed condition to explain myself and my wisdom at the Columbia School of Journalism.

Later that day George Wallace was shot at a rally in Maryland about twelve minutes away from my house. It was the biggest political story of the year, and those five goddamn pages were still blank. Crouse flew back immediately from Boston and I straggled back from New York, but by the time we got there it was all over.

What follows, then, is one of the most desperate last-minute hamburger jobs in the history of journalism—including the first known experiment with large-scale Gonzo Journalism—which we accomplished, in this case, by tearing my Ohio primary notebook apart and sending about fifty pages of scribbled shorthand notes straight to the typesetter.

But we had no choice. The fat was in the fire. When the going gets tough, the tough get going. Ed Muskie said that.

My next job—after getting my brother elected President of the United States—will be the political destruction of Hubert Humphrey.

— Robert Kennedy; after the West Virginia primary in 1960

Strange, how a thing like that can stick in the memory. I may have a word or two wrong, but the balls of that quote are intact . . . and now, twelve years later on a rainy grey dawn in Omaha, Nebraska, it comes back to me with a vengeful clarity that makes me wonder once again if my head is entirely healthy.

That was back in Bobby's "ruthless" period . . . which is a pretty good word for the way I'm feeling right now after watching the CBS Morning News and seeing that Hubert just won the West Virginia primary. He beat George Wallace, two to one . . . and now he's moving on to California, for the nut-cutting ceremony on June 6th.

Which is very convenient for me, because I plan to be in California myself around that time: going out to do a road test on the new Vincent Black Shadow . . . and maybe follow Hubert for a while, track him around the state like a golem and record his last act for posterity.

Remember me, Hubert? I'm the one who got smacked in the stomach by a billy club at the corner of Michigan and Balboa on that evil Wednesday night four years ago in Chicago . . . while you looked down from your suite on the twenty-fifth floor of the Hilton, and wept with a snout full of tear gas drifting up from Grant Park.

I have never been one to hold a grudge any longer than absolutely necessary, Hubert, and I get the feeling that we're about to write this one off. Big Ed was first . . . then you . . and after that—the Other One.

Nothing personal. But it's time to balance the books. The Raven is calling your name, Hubert; he says you still owe some dues—payable, in full, on June 6th. In the coin of the realm; no credit this time, no extensions.

My head is not quite straight this morning. These brutal Tuesday nights are ruining my health. Last week at this time I was pacing around my room on the seventh floor of the Neil House Motor Hotel in Columbus, Ohio, pausing now and then to stare out the window at the early morning buses just starting to move down on High Street . . . listening to the Grateful Dead, sipping Wild Turkey, and trying not to identify with a wino slumped in the doorway of Mister Angelo's Wig Salon down there behind the stoplight and beyond the cool green lawn of the state Capitol Building.

Moments earlier I had left Pat Caddell, McGovern's voter-analysis wizard, muttering to himself in the hallway outside the Situation Room—where he and Frank Mankiewicz and about six others had been grappling all night with botched returns from places like Toledo and Youngstown and Cincinnati.

"Goddamnit," he was saying. "I still can't believe it happened! They *stole* it from us!" He shook his head and kicked a tin spittoon next to the elevator. "We *won* this goddamn election! We had a lock on the nomination tonight, we had it nailed down—but the bastards *stole* it from us!"

Which was more or less true. If McGovern had been able to win Ohio with his last-minute, half-organized blitz it would have snapped the psychic spine of the Humphrey campaign . . . because Hubert had been formidably strong in Ohio, squatting tall in the pocket behind his now-familiar screen of Organized Labor and Old Blacks.

By dawn on Wednesday it was still "too close to call," officially —but sometime around five Harold Himmelman, McGovern's national overseer for Ohio, had picked up one of the phones in the Neil House Situation Room and been jolted half out of his chair by the long-awaited tallies from midtown Cleveland. McGovern had already won three of the four Congressional Districts in Cuyahoga County (metropolitan Cleveland), and all he needed to carry the state, now—along with the thirty-eight additional convention delegates reserved for the statewide winner—was a half-respectable showing in the twenty-first, the heartland of the black vote, a crowded urban fiefdom bossed by Congressman Louis Stokes.

Ten seconds after he picked up the phone Himmelman was screaming: "What? Jesus Christ! No! That can't be right!" (pause . . .) Then: "Awww, shit! That's impossible!"

He turned to Mankiewicz: "It's all over. Listen to this . . ." He turned back to the phone: "Give that to me again . . . okay, yeah, I'm ready." He waited until Mankiewicz got a pencil, then began feeding the figures: "A hundred and nine to one! A hundred and twenty-seven to three! . . . Jesus . . ."

Mankiewicz flinched, then wrote down the numbers. Caddell slumped back in his chair and shook both fists at the ceiling. Himmelman kept croaking out the figures: a fantastic beating, unbelievable—the twenty-first district was a total wipeout. "Well . . . ," he said finally. "Thanks for calling, anyway. What? No . . . but we'll damn well do *something*. Yeah, I realize that . . ." (pause) "Goddamnit I know it's not *your* fault! Sure! We're gonna put some people in jail . . . yeah, this is too obvious . . ." (starts to hang up, then pauses again) "Say, how many more votes do they have to count up there?"

"As many as they need," Mankiewicz muttered.

Himmelman glanced at him, grimaced, then hung up.

"What does that project to," Frank asked Caddell. "About thirty thousand to six?"

The wizard shugged. "Who cares? We got raped. We'll never make *that* up—not even with Akron."

At that point the ancient black bell captain entered, bringing a pot of coffee and a small tin box that he said contained the two Alka-Seltzers I'd asked for—but when I opened the box it was full of dirty vaseline.

"What the fuck is *this?*" I said, showing it to him.

He took the box back and examined it carefully for a long time. "Well . . . damn-*nation,*" he said finally. "Where did *this* stuff come from?"

"Probably Nashville," I said. "That's White Rose Petroleum

Jelly, sure as hell."

He nodded slowly. "Yesss . . . meebee so . . ."

"No maybe about it," I said. "I *know* that stuff. WLAC . . . around 1958 . . . Jesus Christ, man! That grease is fourteen years old! What are you *keeping* it for?"

He shrugged and dropped the tin box in the pocket of his white waiter's smock. "Damn if *I* know," he said. "I thought it was Alka-Seltzer."

I signed the tab for the coffee, then helped him load about a dozen stale glasses on his tray . . . but he seemed very agitated and I thought it was because of his blunder: Of course, the poor old bugger was feeling guilty about the dollar I'd given him for the seltzer.

"Don't worry," I said. "You'll find some. Bring it up with the next pot of coffee."

He shook his head and gestured at the big round wooden table where Mankiewicz, Himmelman, and Caddell were brooding over the tally sheets.

"What's wrong?" I asked.

He was jabbing his finger at the half gallon of Early Times, but I was slow to understand . . . so he picked up one of the coffee cups he'd just brought us, and gestured again at the bottle.

"Ah ha!" I said. "Of course." He held the cup with both hands while I filled it to the brim with fresh whiskey . . . feeling grossly out of sync with my surroundings: Here I was in the nerve center of a presidential campaign that even such far-out latent papists as Evans & Novak considered alarmingly *radical,* and at the peak of the crisis I was taking time out to piece off some befuddled old Darkie with a cup full of bourbon . . . then I opened the door for him as he shuffled out into the hallway with his stash, still holding it with both hands and mumbling his thanks.

A very weird scene, I thought as I closed the door. A flashback to *Gone With the Wind* . . . and as I went back to pour myself a cup of coffee I had another flash: *And so we beat on, boats against the current, borne back ceaselessly into the past.*

I was tempted to lay it on Frank, just to see how he'd handle it. The McGovern campaign has been hagridden from the start with unsettling literary references: Mankiewicz apparently sees the whole thing through the eyes of a latter-day Gertrude Stein; Gary Hart, the national manager, is hung up on Tolstoy . . . and Chris Lydon, the resident New York *Times* correspondent, has an ugly habit of relating mundane things like a bomb scare on the press bus or a low turnout in the Polak wards to pithy lines from Virgil. On the morning of election day in Nebraska I was talking to Lydon in the lobby of the Omaha Hilton when he suddenly wrapped off the conversation with: "You know, Virgil wanted to burn *The Aeneid*."

I stared at him, trying to remember if Virgil was maybe one of McGovern's advance men for Scott's Bluff that I hadn't met yet, or . . . "You pointy-head bastard," I said. "Wait till Wallace gets in. He'll kick your ass all over the street with Virgil."

Meanwhile . . . back in Columbus, Ohio, it was 5:05 A.M. on a cool Wednesday morning and Frank Mankiewicz is calling the Secretary of State, getting him out of bed to protest what he gently but repeatedly refers to as "these fantastic irregularities" in the vote-counting procedure. McGovern's slim lead has suddenly fallen apart; the phones are ringing constantly, and every call brings a new horror story.

In Cincinnati the vote-counters have decided to knock off and rest for twelve hours, a flagrant violation of Sec. 350529 of the State Election Code, which says the counting must go on, without interruption, until all the votes are tallied. In Toledo, McGovern is clinging to a precarious eleven-vote lead—but in Toledo and everywhere else the polling places are manned by local (Democratic) party hacks not friendly to McGovern, and any delay in the counting will give them time to . . . ah . . .

Mankiewicz studiously avoids using words like "fraud" or "cheat" or "steal." Earlier that day Pierre Salinger had gone on the air to accuse the Humphrey forces of "vote fraud," but the charge was impossible to substantiate at the time and Humphrey was able to broadcast an embarrassing counterattack while the polls were still open.

In Cleveland, in fact, 127 polling places had remained open until midnight—on the basis of an emergency directive from the state Supreme Court.

At this point we were forced to switch the narrative into the straight Gonzo mode. The rest of the Ohio section comes straight out of the notebook, for good or ill.

12:00—Cronkite comes on—barely able to talk—and says Humphrey has won Indiana 46 to 41 percent over Wallace (Caddell had Wallace at 29 percent) but only 17 percent of the Ohio vote is counted as of now, so far showing Hump. with the same 41 to 36 percent lead he had at 9:45.

. . . wandering around the hotel with Dick Tuck—into Humphrey Hq: "Mr. Banjo . . ." Returns: H—58,000 to M—53,000.

Midnight—NBC-Columbus (polls just closed in Cleveland) ABC has delegates 55-22 in HH Hq just before McGovern speaks. NBC has 41-39, 91,244 to 86,825. Five thousand difference & the polls just closed in Cleveland. Muskie 24,000.

Mankiewicz's speech in the ballroom was a careful downer; speaking out of one side of his mouth for the mob of young McGovern volunteers & out of the other side for the national press— claiming a victory in Ohio, but also saying that even a narrow defeat would be victory enough . . . I was standing with Warren Beatty while Frank spoke. "What does this mean, Hunter?" he asked with his weird hustler's smile.

"It means McGovern will come into Miami with less than enough to win, and it means pure hell on the convention floor."

Meanwhile, CBS has some kind of wild west cowboy drama . . . Jimmy Stewart, Brig. Gen. USAF rolling in the dust under cow hoofs.

Old woman shooting at the feet of a cowhand tempted to jump in with a six-shooter on the Late Show . . .

She fires the 30-30 and warns to "let 'em fight."

"Where you come from, stranger?"

"I come from Laramie and you better get used to me being here."

"I own this town, stranger."

(Like Daley-Meany to McGovern—"I own this town, stranger." But maybe not.

193

Midnight and the polls just closed in Cleveland—41-39 percent.

12:25—Call Mank on the phone in Situation Room No. 258: "Yeah, we'll be up for four to five more hours." (pause) "Yeah, come on down if you want. But you'll have to bring twenty hamburgers. Otherwise, the press is barred, as always . . ."

"Twenty? Who'll pay?"

"Ask Pierre—he has the cash."

12:33—CBS: 91,000 to 86,000—same 5,000 split.

12:35—Hump. says he has a "great victory in Indiana—Mr. Wallace has made this a sort of second Alabama." And adds, "I doubt that anyone is going to come to that convention with enough votes to win on the first ballot."

So the bloodbath looms. Heavy duty in Miami.

12:36—McGov. tense on CBS interview:
Schoumacher: "Do you regret this decision to come into Ohio?"
McG: "Not at all."

2:30—Arrive in Situation Room with twenty hamburgers and receive $20 from Pierre Salinger . . .

2:36—Mank on phone to Washington says "Hell, let's scrub it." (NBC invitation for McGov. appear on *Today Show* at dawn.)
Yancy Martin: "Sheeitt! McGovern says scrub it to *The Today Show*. Man, we're gettin' *big*."

Mank: "Hell, we used to have to fight to get on *Uncle Bob*— or *The Flintstones*."

2:38—Mank: "It looks like we're winning in Districts 23, 20 & 22—Scammon says he thinks we'll come out of Cuyahoga County with a plurality of 60,000."

Mank: "He [Scoop Jackson] went out like he came in—with a lot of class, huh?"

2:52—bad news from 21.

Himm. (on phone): "Come on, don't play games—how much

are we gonna lose by? . . . (pause; jots down figures) "Shit. We're dead if that happens!"

Bitterness about Stokes brothers in Ohio—"When we win this thing they're gonna have to *crawl*, goddamnit."

3:03—The down feeling again. Caddell shrugs: "I don't know, I just feel pessimistic."

What you tend to forget is that two weeks ago McGov. couldn't have pulled twenty percent in Ohio.

Recall quote from Sunday night:

"If we'd only had one more week."

H. Humphrey in '68—"one more month—even two weeks."

But you don't get any overtimes in this game—"there ain't no instant replay in the football game of life" (Mitch Greenhill).

Caddell: "Watching the map is sort of like watching the clock." (snarling)

3:05—Definite funk setting in now/not going to win. But hope forever springs, etc. . . .

Phones slamming—"The goddamn 21st district is what's killing us. We'll probably carry the other three. . . ."

Himm: "Wagner says it's an 8 to 1 loss in the 21st. JESUS CHRIST!"

Yancy Martin answers all phones with eerie: "Good Morning."

3:34—Door opens and John Chancellor wanders in.

Mank: "Hi, Jack—what do you hear?"

Chancellor: "Well we ended up saying you won . . . so I hope you do."

Mank: "You want a drink, Jack?"

"Yeah . . . But the point is not whether you won, but how close you came."

3:51—It comes down to the 21st.

Caddell (staring gloomily at Chancellor, confirming Mank's wisdom): "Yes, if I had to generalize, I'd say it comes down to the 21st."

3:53—phone rings—"But still no news from the 21st . . ."

Weird, even this presidential election comes down to some

student and/or housewife poll watcher. . . .

Himm (yelling at girl): "Goddamnit, I want you to call me on *every* precinct!"

3:59—Delegate count is 55-37, McGovern.

Mank (on phone to lawyers): "What I think is that Stokes is sitting there and waiting to be told how many they need."

4:11—The whole state now hinges on the outcome in the 21st Congressional District, midtown Cleveland.

Returns from only three precincts out of more than 400 in the 21st District.

4:15—Mank: "Well, I'm at the point where I'm ready to start getting judges out of bed."

4:36—Phone rings. Himmelman answers. 21st starts in: "What! *What* was that?" (shouting) Then aside to Mank and Caddell, "Black middle class—109 to 1! Jesus Christ!"

4:48—The hammer falls. Incredible ratios from black precincts in Cleveland.

4:55—Mank holding phone. Turns to Caddell—"Who is this?"
Caddell: "Jim." (shrugs) "I think he's our man in Cincinnati."
Mank: "Jim—what do they want?" (answer from phone, "They want you to consult with your lawyer and get his agreement to stop counting until 6 P.M.")
(Pause)
Mank: "Well, tell 'em you just talked to your lawyer and he says there's no way he can acquiesce in a violation of the law. And your lawyer's name is Frank Mankiewicz—member of the bar in California and the Supreme Court of the United States! . . . No, I simply can't go along with the breaking of the law."

5:16—Mank on phone to Secretary of State Brown: "Mr. Brown, we're profoundly disturbed about this situation in the 21st. We can't get a single result out of there. The polls have been closed for 12 hours. I can't help but think they're lying in the weeds up there."

Weird conversation with Brown, a tired & confused old man who's been jerked out of bed at 5:15. Mank talking very fast, cool, and vaguely menacing. Brown obviously baffled—end of a bad day. It began when Governor John Gilligan said he (Brown) should resign for reasons of gross incompetence.

5:26—Mank on phone 20 minutes to "Socko' Wiethe, Democratic Party boss in Cincinnati—Mank screaming. Wiethe's voice screeching out of the small black phone receiver shatters quiet tension of the room.

Mank: "OK Mr. Wiethe, all I want from you is a clear affirmation that you're going to ignore the law." (Mank pauses) "Wait a minute, I don't want any more abuse, I just want to know if you're going to obey that law!"

5:31—Mank on phone to lawyer: "Jesus, I think we gotta go in there and get those ballots! Impound 'em! Every damn one!"

5:35—All phones ringing now, the swing shift has shot the gap—now the others are waking up.

Mank: "They're gonna stop the count in Cincinnati in a half hour—and wait 12 hours before starting again. Yeah we're ahead down there, but not by much . . . we can't afford to give 'em time to get their counts documented."

5:43—Mank on phone to "Mary" in Washington; "It now appears quite clear that we'll lead the state—without the 21st."

Mankiewicz has been on the phone now since 11 P.M. with only a few breaks.

Socko Wiethe to Mank: "This is your boss's fault—he should have known—you start *electing* delegates and you get this kind of thing."

Bad note on "party reform."

Night ends, 6:49. Meet in the coffee shop at 7:30; press conference at 10:00.

6:05—Waiting for elevator in Columbus, Ohio, pacing back and forth on the damp red carpet in the second floor hall . . . Pat Caddell is jerking a bundle of legal-sized paper around in his hands and mumbling: "I knew this campaign was too goddamn honest! It was bound to get us in trouble . . . Now I understand why the North Vietnamese wouldn't agree to elections in The South."

Caddell is twenty-one years old. He has never had his face mashed in the dirty realities of American politics. For almost a year now, he has been George McGovern's official numbers wizard. Caddell and his Cambridge Research Associates have been working the streets and suburban neighborhoods in New Hampshire, Wisconsin, and Massachusetts for McGovern, then coming back to headquarters on election nite and calling the results almost down to the percentage point . . .

But tonight was different. The polls closed—officially—at 6:30, but the situation in Cleveland was out of control since early morning . . . And by midnight the outlook was ominous. McGovern's eleventh-hour challenge in Ohio was almost over the hump; he was on the brink of knocking Hubert out of the race, maintaining a razor-thin lead all night long . . . but for some reason there were no results from the black districts in midtown Cleveland.

7:00—*Today Show*: McGee says J. Edgar Hoover died last night and Humphrey won a narrow victory over Wallace in Indiana—but his slim lead over George McGovern in Ohio is by no means certain.

NBC newsman Bill Monroe: "McGov. will wind up with the biggest psychological boost in the Ohio primary—but his pulling power among blue-collar workers still remains uncertain."

Bullshit?

Wallace from Houston: We will definitely be the balance of power in Miami—we've already turned the party in a different direction."

7:30—CBS Morning News:

Scoop Jackson comes on, saying he's dropped out—hoping for a polarization between Wallace and McGovern. (Recall Mank. quote—"class, huh?") "I'm not gonna take sides in this campaign."—Then attacks McGovern again on amnesty, acid, abortion, etc. . . .

CBS John Hart election roundup. No hint of the all-night phone madness and treachery reports in Situation Room. Even reading and watching *all the news,* there is no way to know the truth—except to be there.

Humphrey on CBS says, "If you put Hubert Humphrey and Ed Muskie and Scoop Jackson together—we're pretty much on the same wave length—and we've got the numbers."

McGovern on CBS takes a very gentle line on the "very peculiar things that happened out there in Cleveland." No hint of Mank screaming on the phone at Socko.

McGee on *Today Show* (second hour): "There is still no result in that big Ohio primary—Senator Humphrey is still maintaining his slim lead over Sen. George McGovern."

Suddenly, Kleindienst and Eastland and Thomas Corchoran are on the screen, praising J. Edgar Hoover—Jesus, these are the pigs who *run the country.* Nixon/southerners/Big Business.

10:10—Wednesday morning press conf.—grim faces at head table:

Frank Mankiewicz
Yancy Martin
Gary Hart
Pat Caddell
Harold Himmelman
Bob McCallister

Hart: "We're making no allegations of illegality or fraud—at this point."

An extremely haggard crew; red eyes, hovering on stupor.

"By mid-afternoon massive numbers of people in Youngstown —including the judge up there—were not able to obtain ballots."

Mankiewicz compares yesterday's election in Ohio to the 1969 election of Velasco Ibarra in Ecuador—next to Saigon, perhaps the second most flagrantly crooked election in the history of the democratic process—he needed a team of OAS observers in Guayaquil etc. "In some precincts here, voters were not given the paper ballots unless they asked for them . . ."

Mank: "We have achieved what we set out to do in Ohio— we stood Senator Humphrey at least dead even and probably beat him, as far as the working man's vote is concerned. . . .

"This is Humphrey's peak—from now on there isn't much he can win."

Another Wednesday morning, another hotel room, another grim bout with the TV Morning News . . . and another post-mortem press conference scheduled for 10:00 A.M. Three hours from now. Call room service and demand two whole grapefruits, along with a pot of coffee and four glasses of V-8 juice.

These goddamn Wednesday mornings are ruining my health. Last night I came out of a mild Ibogaine coma just about the time the polls closed at eight. No booze on election day—at least not until the polls close; but they always seem to leave at least one loophole for serious juicers. In Columbus it was the bar at the airport, and in Omaha we had to rent a car and drive across the Missouri River to Council Bluffs, which is also across the state line into Iowa. Every year, on election day, the West End bars in Council Bluffs are jammed with boozers from Omaha.

Which is fine, for normal people, but when you drink all day with a head full of Ibogaine and then have to spend the next ten hours analyzing election returns . . . there will usually be problems.

Last week—at the Neil House Motor Hotel in Columbus, Ohio —some lunatic tried to break into my room at six in the morning. But fortunately I had a strong chain on the door. In every reputable hotel there is a sign above the knob that warns: "For Our Guests'

Protection—Please Use Door Chain at all Times, Before Retiring."

I always use it. During four long months on the campaign trail I have had quite a few bad experiences with people trying to get into my room at strange hours—and in almost every case they object to the music. One out of three will also object to the typewriter, but that hasn't been the case here in Omaha. . . .

(PROPOSED PHOTO CAPTION)

Sen. George McGovern (D-S.D.), shown here campaigning in Nebraska where he has spent 23 hours a day for the past six days denying charges by local Humphrey operatives that he favors the legalization of Marijuana, pauses between denials to shake hands for photographers with his "old friend" Hunter S. Thompson, the National Correspondent for Rolling Stone *and author of* Fear and Loathing in Las Vegas, *who was recently identified by* Newsweek *magazine as a vicious drunkard and known abuser of hard drugs.*

A thing like that would have finished him here in Nebraska. No more of that "Hi, sheriff" bullshit; I am now the resident Puff Adder . . . and the problem is very real. In Ohio, which McGovern eventually lost by a slim 19,000 vote margin, his handlers figure perhaps 10,000 of those were directly attributable to his public association with Warren Beatty, who once told a reporter somewhere that he favored legalizing grass. This was picked up by that worthless asshole Sen. Henry Jackson (D-Wash.) and turned into a major issue.

So it fairly boggles the mind to think what Humphrey's people might do with a photo of McGovern shaking hands with a person who once ran for Sheriff of Aspen on the Freak Power ticket, with a platform embracing the use and frequent enjoyment of Mescaline by the Sheriff and all his Deputies at any hour of the day or night that seemed Right.

No, this would never do. Not for George McGovern—at least not in May of '72, and probably never. He has spent the past week traveling around Nebraska and pausing at every opportunity to explain that he is flatly opposed to the legalization of marijuana. He is also opposed to putting people in prison for mere *possession,* which he thinks should be re-classified as a misdemeanor instead of a felony.

And even *this* went down hard in Nebraska. He came into this state with a comfortable lead, and just barely escaped with a six percentage-point (41 percent to 35) win over Hubert Humphrey—who did everything possible, short of making the accusations on his own, to identify McGovern as a Trojan Horse full of dope dealers and abortionists.

Jackson had raised the same issues in Ohio, but George ignored them—which cost him the state and at least thirty-eight delegates, according to his staff thinkers—so when Hubert laid it on him again, in Nebraska, McGovern decided to "meet them head on." For almost a week, every speech he made led off with an angry denial that he favored either legalized grass or Abortion On Demand . . . and in the dawn hours of Saturday morning, three days before the election, he called his media wizard Charley Guggenheim back from a vacation in the Caribbean to make a Special Film in Nebraska designed—for statewide exposure on Sunday night—to make goddamn sure that The Folks in Nebraska understood that George McGovern was just a regular guy, like them, who would no more tolerate marijuana than send his wife to an abortionist.

And it worked. I watched it in McGovern's Omaha Hilton "press suite" with a handful of reporters and Dick Dougherty, a former L.A. *Times* reporter who writes many of George's major speech/statements, but who is usually kept out of the public eye because of his extremely seedy and unsettling appearance. On Sunday night, however, Dougherty came out of wherever he usually stays to watch The Man on the TV set in the press room. We found him hunkered there with a plastic glass of Old Overholt and a pack of Home Run cigarettes, staring at the tube and saying over and over again: "Jesus, that's fantastic! Christ, look at that camera angle! God damn, this is really a hell of a film, eh?"

I agreed. It was a first-class campaign film: The lighting was fantastic; the sound was as sharp and clear as diamonds bouncing on a magnesium tabletop; the characters and the dialogue made Turgenev seem like a punk. . . . McGovern sat in the round and masterfully de-fused every ugly charge that had ever been leveled at him. He spoke like a combination of Socrates, Clarence Darrow, and God. It was a flat-out masterpiece, both as a film and a performance—and when it ended I joined in the general chorus of praise.

"Beautiful," somebody muttered.

"Damn fine stuff," said somebody else.

Dougherty was grinning heavily. "How about *that?*" he said.

"Wonderful," I replied. "No doubt about it. My only objection is that I disagree with almost everything he said."

"What?"

"Yeah—I'm *for* all those things: Amnesty, Acid, Abortion . . ."

"So what? You're not a candidate for President in the Nebraska primary, are you?"

"No—but if I was—"

Dougherty stood up quickly and backed off a few steps. "Jesus Christ," he snapped. "You're really a goddamn *nit-picker,* aren't you?"

McGovern told a Flint (Mich.) press conference that while "Wallace is entitled to be treated with respect at the convention (in Miami), I don't propose to make any deals with him . . ."

Humphrey (in Michigan) attacked Wallace more personally than McGovern, but when a question about wooing Wallace delegates was thrown at him, Humphrey said, "I will seek support wherever I can get it, if I can convince them to be for me."

—Washington *Post,* May 14, '72

Quotes like this are hard to come by—especially in presidential elections, where most candidates are smart enough to know better than to call a press conference and then announce—on the record —an overweening eagerness to peddle their asses to the highest bidder.

Only Hubert Humphrey would do a thing like that . . . and we can only assume that now, in his lust for the White House—

after suffering for twenty-four years with a case of Political Blue-balls only slightly less severe than Richard Nixon's—that The Hube has finally cracked; and he did it in public.

With the possible exception of Nixon, Hubert Humphrey is the purest and most disgusting example of a Political Animal in American politics today. He has been going at it hammer and tong twenty-five hours a day since the end of World War II—just like Richard Nixon, who launched his own career as a Red-baiting California congressman about the same time Hubert began making headlines as the Red-baiting Mayor of Minneapolis. They are both career anti-Communists: Nixon's gig was financed from the start by Big Business, and Humphrey's by Big Labor . . . and what both of them stand for today is the de facto triumph of a One Party System in American politics.

George Meany, the aging ruler of the AFL-CIO, was one of the first to announce his whole-hearted support of Nixon's decision to lay mines around Haiphong Harbor and celebrate the memory of Guernica with a fresh round of saturation bombing in North Vietnam.

Humphrey disagreed, of course—along with Mayor Daley—but in fact neither one of them had any choice. The war in Vietnam will be a key issue in November, and Senator Henry Jackson of Washington has already demonstrated—with a series of humiliating defeats in the primaries—what fate awaits any Democrat who tries to agree with Nixon on The War.

But Humphrey seems not quite convinced. On the morning before the Wisconsin primary he appeared on *The Today Show,* along with all the other candidates, and when faced with a question involving renewed escalation of the bombing in Vietnam he lined up with Jackson and Wallace—in clear opposition to McGovern and Lindsay, who both said we should get the hell out of Vietnam at once. Big Ed, as usual, couldn't make up his mind.

Since then—after watching Jackson suck wind all over the Midwest—Hubert has apparently decided to stick with Dick Daley on Vietnam. But he has not explained, yet, how he plans to square his late-blooming dovishness with Boss Meany—who could croak Humphrey's last chance for the nomination with a single phone call.

Meany's hired hacks and goon squads are just about all Hubert

"There is no way to grasp what a shallow, contemptible and hopelessly dishonest old hack Hubert Humphrey really is until you've followed him around for a while on the Campaign Trail."

can count on these days, and even his Labor friends are having their problems. Tony Boyle, for instance, is headed for prison on more felony counts than I have space to list here. Boyle, former president of the United Mineworkers Union, was recently cracked out of office by the Justice Department for gross and flagrant "misuse" of the union treasury—which involved, among other things, illegal contributions to Humphrey's presidential campaign in 1968. In addition to all this, Boyle now faces a Conspiracy/Murder rap in connection with the contract-killing of Joseph Yablonski, who made the mistake of challenging him for the union presidency in December, 1969, and paid for it a few months later when hired thugs appeared one night in his bedroom and gunned him down, along with his wife and daughter.

Hubert Humphrey's opinion of Tony Boyle was best expressed when they appeared together at the United Mineworkers Convention in Denver in 1968, and Humphrey referred to Boyle as "My friend, this great American."[3]

For whatever it's worth, the UMW is one of the most powerful political realities in West Virginia, where Humphrey recently won his fourth primary in a row.

This may or may not properly explain Humphrey's startling admission at that press conference in Michigan, which was nothing less than a half-shrouded bargaining overture to George Wallace, who has already gone out of his way to tell the national press corps that "My daughter has a big picture of Hubert Humphrey tacked up on the wall above her bed."

This was very much like Teddy Kennedy telling the press that his wife, his children, and indeed the whole Kennedy blood-clan have decided to vote for McGovern. There is not much doubt, now, that Kennedy is preparing to get seriously and publicly behind McGovern. I haven't talked to him about it. I can't even get through to his goddamn press secretary. The only way to talk to Kennedy these days is to spend a lot of time on the Washington cocktail circuit, which is not my beat—but the society columnists and Gentlemen Journalists who do most of their work in that area

3. Boyle is no longer the President of the United Mine Workers. He was defeated in a bitterly contested special election in November of 1972 by a reform movement headed by Yablonski's sons.

are now convinced that Kennedy is ready to crank his weight behind McGovern any time the Senator asks for it.

The only reporter in Washington who appears to believe that Teddy is marshalling his forces for a last-minute blitz for *his own* candidacy in '72 is Kandy Stroud of *Women's Wear Daily*. She says he is sneaking around the country on weekends, lashing together a very ominous coalition. She broke the story in *WWD* on April 25th, the same day George McGovern swept all 102 delegates in the Massachusetts primary.

"Quietly," she wrote, *"as if it were being pulled by cats, the Kennedy bandwagon has begun rolling.*

"For a couple of days last week, while everyone else was preoccupied with moon shots, primaries and pandas, Sen. Edward Kennedy (D-Mass.) slipped out of town and went to Little Rock, Ark., Columbia, S.C., and Indianapolis, Ind.

"He spoke to the people and his appearances generated the old Kennedy magic. The hands reached out for him, stretching and grasping, seeking just to touch him, and some of them started calling him 'President Kennedy.'

"And while the excitement began to swell, Kennedy quietly solidified relationships with some of the country's most powerful politicians—Rep. Wilbur Mills (D-Ark.), Sen. Ernest 'Fritz' Hollings (D-S.C.) and Sen. Birch Bayh (D-Ind.). Even though he continues to insist he is not a candidate, it is clear to many observers that a campaign of sorts is under way."

Of sorts.

And it may be true. It is hard to imagine anybody flying around the country to visit socially with people like that unless he had some kind of very powerful ulterior motive in mind. The *WWD* article went on to describe Mills as "A conservative who has voted against every major civil rights bill and has never voiced opposition to the war in Southeast Asia . . ." And also: "According to one high-ranking Democratic finance committeeman, it was Rose Kennedy [Teddy's mother] who donated 'most, if not all' of the funds for Mills' New Hampshire primary campaign."

Mills got badly stomped in New Hampshire, running neck in neck for the booby prize with Los Angeles Mayor Sam Yorty and Edward T. Coll, the anti-rat candidate . . . but he refused to comment on the rumor that Rose Kennedy had financed his New Hampshire campaign, and it remained for Mills' brother, Roger, to salvage the story by explaining that "He [Kennedy] is the only Democrat Wallace could support."

This is probably a remark worth remembering. The Democratic Convention in Miami begins on July 10th, and the only major political event between now and then is the California primary on June 6th. If Humphrey loses in California—and he will, I think—his only hope for the nomination will be to make a deal with Wallace, who will come to Miami with something like 350 delegates, and he'll be looking around for somebody to bargain with.

The logical bargainee, as it were, is Hubert Humphrey, who has been running a sort of left-handed, stupid-coy flirtation with Wallace ever since the Florida primary, where he did everything possible to co-opt Wallace's position on busing without actually agreeing with it. Humphrey even went so far as to agree, momentarily, with Nixon on busing—blurting out "Oh, thank goodness!" when he heard of Nixon's proposal for a "moratorium," which amounted to a presidential edict to suspend all busing until the White House could figure out some way to circumvent the U.S. Supreme Court.

When somebody called Hubert's attention to this aspect of the problem and reminded him that he had always been known as a staunch foe of racial segregation, he quickly changed his mind and rushed up to Wisconsin to nail down the Black Vote by denouncing Wallace as a racist demagogue, and Nixon as a cynical opportunist for saying almost exactly the same things about busing that Humphrey himself had been saying in Florida.

There is no way to grasp what a shallow, contemptible, and hopelessly dishonest old hack Hubert Humphrey really is until you've followed him around for a while on the campaign trail. The double-standard realities of campaign journalism, however, make it difficult for even the best of the "straight/objective" reporters to write what they actually think and feel about a candidate.

Hubert Humphrey, for one, would go crazy with rage and attempt to strangle his press secretary if he ever saw in print what most reporters say about him during midnight conversations around barroom tables in all those Hiltons and Sheratons where the candidates make their headquarters when they swoop into places like Cleveland, Pittsburgh, and Indianapolis.

And some of these reporters are stepping out of the closet and beginning to describe Humphrey in print as the bag of PR gimmicks that he is. The other day one of the Washington *Post* regulars nailed him:

"Humphrey has used the campaign slogans of John Kennedy ('let's get this country moving again') and of Wallace ('stand up for America') and some of his literature proclaims that 1972 is 'the year of the people,' a title used by Eugene McCarthy for a book about his 1968 campaign."

Enroute from Columbia to La Guardia airport I stopped off in the midtown *Rolling Stone* office to borrow some money for cabfare and heard that Wallace had just been shot. But the first report was a ten-second radio bulletin, and when I tried to call Washington every news-media phone in the city was busy . . . and by the time the details began coming through on the radio it was 4:30 in Manhattan, the start of the evening Rush Hour. No way to make the airport until 6:00 or maybe 6:30.

Tim Crouse called from Boston, 250 miles north, saying he had a straight shot to Logan airport up there and would probably make it to Washington before I got out of Manhattan.

Which he did, spending most of Monday night and half of Tuesday in the eye of the media-chaos around Holy Cross Hospital in Silver Spring, Maryland—where Wallace had been taken by ambulance for five hours of surgery. While Wallace was under the knife and in the recovery room, Crouse waited with about two hundred reporters to glean tid-bits from announcements by surgeons, police chiefs, and Wallace staffers. The next night, when Wallace had been pronounced out of danger, Crouse changed into a suit and tie and went to the election-night gathering of Maryland Wallace workers at the North Holiday Inn in Baltimore. Wallace was winning big that night in the Maryland primary. Crouse's reports from both places follow:

SILVER SPRING, MD.—In the late night hours after the Wallace shooting, the Press had only one man to interview: Dr. Joseph Schanno, the pale vascular surgeon with bombed-out eyes who had been picking bullets out of George Wallace. The Press, sweltering in the cinderblock gym of the Silver Spring Boys Club, waiting for the doctor, was crazy with hunger for copy.

"Is he a viable candidate?" a reporter kept shouting at Schanno from the middle of the sweating, shoving mass that surrounded the table where he sat.

"He's a very viable *person*," said Schanno.

Schanno was the first one to speak the unspeakable, but a lot of us had already entertained the horrifying possibility that this country might be in for another wheelchair Democrat. The doctor was blithely predicting that Wallace might be going home inside of a week, which meant that he might be on the loose again within the month. When he resumes campaigning, he's going to have a lot going for him: increased coverage, or as one reporter was saying last night, "Jesus, this is the biggest break George ever got."

If Wallace loses the use of the lower half of his body it will make him, in one fell swoop: (a) less of a monster; and (b) more of a superman, the only assassin's target of the last ten years who has been blessed enough and strong enough to survive.

Wallace's handlers were holed up downstairs in the "pastoral services" sector of the hospital, a corridor decorated with plaster madonnas and crucifixes. George Mangum, the tall, boisterous Baptist preacher who warms up the crowds at Wallace rallies ("And now, 'cause we're in Milwaukee, the boys are gonna do their best to play a polka for ya"), was roaming around looking pale and murderous. A skinny woman, straight from a Walker Evans picture, was quietly weeping. A young lean and blond man was uncontrollably sobbing. He was some sort of assistant press officer, wearing a fire-engine red campaign blazer with the WALLACE '72 crest on his breast pocket.

He was being hugged and consoled by . . . I had to look twice, but it *was* a Negro, a huge Pullman porter type, balding with a little grey goatee, and dressed in an elegant blue pinstripe with WALLACE FOR PRESIDENT buttons pinned to each lapel. He was consoling the boy in a beautiful, deep, rolling Paul Robeson bass voice.

I waited a decent interval and then approached him to find out what the hell he was doing on the Wallace campaign. He turned out to be none other than Norman E. Jones, the Chairman of the National Black Citizens for Wallace, Inc., and by conventional Press estimate, the biggest jiveass in all of Campaign '72, a man who can run bullshit circles around even Hubert Humphrey.

"Mr. Wallace is the only hope of the little man," Norman said in a voice so resonant that it set the crucifix trembling. I asked him how many blacks he had signed up for Wallace.

"You want numbers," he replied accusingly. "I have no numbers. As fast as I'm traveling now, I just can't keep up with the thousands of letters coming in every day. The greater majority wish to remain anonymous, for fear of economic and social reprisal."

This is the man who was challenged by the *Wall Street Journal*

Laurel, Maryland, May 16, 1972.

to come up with the name and address of a single Black Citizen for Wallace, and who couldn't do it. He bills himself as a former journalist and public relations man. Now he unwrapped a fat cigar, lit it, and glowered through the smoke. "How's McGovern's Indians getting along?" he challenged me. "How's Humphrey's Indians?"

"What Indians?" I said.

"Why all them Indians that live up in the Dakotas and are starving. There ain't no black that would *live* up there in Dakota." With that he walked away in a huff. Which was too bad, because I wanted to ask him about the reaction of the Wallace crowd at the Laurel Shopping Center. When the five shots spit out, a large part of the crowd had immediately turned its attention to four young blacks who had been heckling Wallace from the rear. One of them sported an Afro and a dashiki. The crowd rounded on them, ready to beat them to shit. They started shouting, "No, no, no, no, it wasn't us, we didn't shoot him!" But the Prince George's County police stepped in between them and the crowd split unscathed. The Wallace crowd was ready for a reflexive lynching.

There were some Wallace supporters, though, who talked like men of peace, and it was easy to feel sympathetic with them. A short, grey-haired county chairman for Wallace in Florida softly asked me why the media had it in for Wallace. I answered that, first of all, it was because Wallace was for segregation.

"You're thinking of the old George Wallace, the man in the schoolhouse door," he said. "He's for integration now, 'cause it's the law of the land, ain't it? He just wants those Northern cities to integrate too." There is no one harder to argue with than a Wallacite who happens to be a Southern gentleman. They'll make you feel hypocritical every time, without one nasty word.

The next afternoon I called up Frank Mankiewicz to find out how the shooting would affect the McGovern campaign. The smart money had McGovern getting beaten in both Maryland and Michigan, but there had been other bets. Ham Davis, the bureau chief of the Providence *Journal,* who has one of the most sensitive political guts in the National Press Building, had felt, for no particular reason, that McGovern had been building a victory in Maryland before the assassination attempt. But that depended largely on one of

McGovern's last minute get-out-the-vote blitzes, which was called off in the wake of the shooting.

"I thought we might have won Michigan," said Mankiewicz. "Our polls there showed us within the range of statistical error. It was within two or three points, so it could have gone either way. But the shooting screws this afternoon's results. I don't think that it hurts McGovern more than anyone else, except that McGovern has traditionally been the second choice of a lot of Wallace voters, and we probably won't get the benefit of that now."

As for Wallace's future effect on the primaries, Mankiewicz said, "Wallace is at his high-water mark right now. He had nowhere to go but home after today anyway. Even if the shooting had never taken place his campaign is over, he has no more delegates to get anywhere. He isn't going to win any in Oregon or California or New York.

"He's got his 300 or 350 delegates and they're indigestible. He just has to go on with the convention around him. Most of his delegates aren't going to break for anybody—that's why I say they're indigestible."

I asked him if he feared for McGovern in California. "I shouldn't allow my peculiarities to prevail," he said, "but I'm very nervous on the West Coast. It's the random violence capital of the world. But there's no way of knowing. They hit Bobby the first time he *didn't* go through a crowd. I always felt very safe in the crowds."

Last night, Senator Ribicoff told a McGovern fund-raising dinner in California that the Wallace incident would help McGovern because it increased people's feeling that they "needed a quiet man."

In Maryland, Wallace's election-night party took place in an oven of a meeting room in the basement of a Baltimore Holiday Inn—long and low-ceilinged, more like a bunker than a ballroom. Wallace parties inevitably take place in Holiday Inns, usually without such standard election-night paraphernalia as blackboards and TV sets, but almost always with a hillbilly band.

But there was no band tonight. The room was too crowded

with TV crews, color TV cameras, a blackboard, and TV sets, over which was coming news of the Wallace landslide. At every fresh set of returns, war whoops.

"Ya wanna hear an Alabama hog call?" asked Zeke Calhoun, who looked like a Kentucky colonel and was a friend of the Wallace family. An Alabaman hog call pierced through the acoustic tiles.

Zeke Calhoun, like most of the men in the room, had on a cheap red silk tie with WALLACE painted on it vertically in white letters. Zeke said he owned a country store that doubled as a Wallace headquarters at Mitchell Springs, Alabama—"just across from Ft. Benning."

"Everytime a soldier is shippin' out for Vietnam or goin' home," Zeke said in his smoked Virginia accent, "I load 'em down with Wallace stickers, and they're glad to take 'em. I was heartsick yesterday after hearin' the news. My wife was afraid I'd have another heart attack. Today I couldn't be still 'til I made a plane up here. The Chief was in trouble and I had to be near him."

Off in a corner three old Wallace workers were having a reunion — a middle-aged rake with a pencil moustache who was "in construction"; a man in glasses and a styrofoam Wallace "straw" hat who was an automobile dealer; and a burly gas-station attendant. "Boys, we been together since May 1, 1964—that's when George Wallace came to the Lord Baltimore Hotel," said the man in construction. "Madeleine Murray's son climbed up a fence and tried to take our flag away from us, remember?"

"And remember, that Commie from New York wrapped himself in a flag and gave you a hard time?" the auto dealer reminisced.

"We might get our country back," said the construction man, stirred. "I feel like I lost it. I feel like I been lost in it all this time."

"I've been lost too," said the gas-station operator. "I've been trying to find somebody I can understand to vote for. This is one of the happiest days of my life."

"One thing puzzling the press is why there weren't more Wallace stickers on cars," the auto dealer told me. "It's fear. Fear of retaliation from blacks. Of getting bricks thrown at your car."

"You didn't have any problems down in that black section did you?" asked the construction man.

215

"A few. Just a few," said the auto dealer.

"I think it's just a small group of black revolutionaries cause the trouble," the construction man said.

Everyone in the room was drunk on victory and quite sure George Wallace was going to win the nomination. Every so often they would cheerfully scoff at a TV commentator who attributed the Wallace victory to a "sympathy vote."

"A sympathy vote? Definitely not. We never had any doubts he was gonna run away with it in Maryland."

"I don't want a sympathy vote for George. I want people to vote for him out of outrage."

Charles Snyder, the National Campaign Manager, was making a statement to the cameras. Snyder, short, neatly groomed, the kind of man who reads *Playboy*. In real life, a general contractor. Which provokes smirks from every political reporter who has ever witnessed that special and beautiful relationship a contractor and a politician can have when highways and public works are involved. "Probably the biggest bagman in the state of Alabama," pronounced a reporter, with absolutely no evidence.

The Governor, said Snyder, had been informed of his two victories. "They got a big smile out of him and a nod of his head."

—Tim Crouse

"I predict regretfully that you in California will see one of the dirtiest campaigns in the history of this state—and you have had some of the dirtiest."

—Sen. Abraham Ribicoff, speaking in San Francisco

No hope for this section. Crouse is caving in downstairs; they have him on two phones at once and even from up here I can hear the conversation turning ugly . . . so there is not much time for anything except maybe a flash roundup on the outlook for California and beyond.

George Wallace himself will not be a factor in the California primary. His handlers are talking about a last-minute write-in campaign, but he has no delegates—and the California ballot doesn't list candidates; only *delegates pledged to candidates*.

216

Wallace is not even likely now to have much bargaining power at the Convention. Even before he was shot—and before he won Michigan and Maryland—his only hope for real leverage in Miami depended on Humphrey coming into the convention with enough delegates of his own (something like seven to eight hundred) to bargain with Wallace *from* strength. But as things stand now, Humphrey and Wallace between them will not have 1000 delegates on the first ballot—and McGovern is a pretty good bet, today, to go down to Miami with almost 1300.

Humphrey's last chance for leverage now is to win California, and although the polls still show him ahead I doubt if even Hubert believes it. Even before his weak showings in Michigan and Maryland, one of Humphrey's main strategists—Kenny O'Donnell—was quietly leaking word to the press that Hubert didn't really *need*

California to get the nomination.

This is an interesting notion—particularly after Humphrey himself had de-emphasized the importance of winning the New York primary a few days earlier. He understood, even then, that there was no point even thinking about New York unless he could win in California.

And that's not going to happen unless something very drastic happens between now and June 6th. Hubert's only hope in California is a savage, all-out attack on McGovern—a desperate smear campaign focused on Grass, Amnesty, Abortion, and even Busing. And to do that he would have to consciously distort McGovern's positions on those issues . . . which is something he would find very hard to do, because Humphrey and McGovern have been close personal friends for many years.

I have said a lot of foul things about Hubert, all deserved, but I think I'd be genuinely surprised to see him crank up a vicious and groundless attack on an old friend. His California managers have already said they will try to do it, with or without his approval—but Hubert knows he could never carry that off. In Ohio he got away with letting Jackson do his dirty work, and in Nebraska he let his supporters smear McGovern in a Catholic newspaper, *The True Voice* . . . but Hubert himself never got down in the ditch; he stayed on what he likes to call "the high road."

But he won't have that option in California. His only hope for winning out there is go flat out on the Low Road.

Maybe he will, but I doubt it. The odds are too long. McGovern would probably win anyway—leaving Humphrey to rot in the history books for generations to come.

June

California: Traditional Politics with a Vengeance
. . . Return of the Vincent Black Shadow . . . The
Juggernaut Roars on; McGovern Troops Ease off
as Polls Predict Sweeping Victory . . . Hubert's
Last Stand: Vicious Attacks, Desperate Appeals,
Strange Tales of Midnight Money from Vegas . . .
Free Booze & Foul Rumors in the Press Room . . .
Ominous Eleventh-Hour Slump Reveals Fistula
in McGovern's Woodpile . . .

> *"In my own country I am in a far-off land.*
> *I am strong but have no force or power*
> *I win all yet remain a loser*
> *At break of day I say goodnight*
> *When I lie down I have a great fear of falling."*
>
> —François Villon

THERE IS PROBABLY some long-standing "rule" among writers, journalists, and other word-mongers that says: "When you start stealing from your own work you're in bad trouble." And it may be true.

I am growing extremely weary of writing constantly about politics. My brain has become a steam-vat; my body is turning to wax and bad flab; impotence looms; my fingernails are growing at a fantastic rate of speed—they are turning into claws; my standard-size clippers will no longer cut the growth, so now I carry a set of huge toe-nail clippers and sneak off every night around dusk, regardless of where I am—in any city, hamlet, or plastic hotel room along the campaign trail—to chop another quarter of an inch or

219

FEAR AND LOATHING

so off of all ten fingers.

People are beginning to notice, I think, but fuck them. I am beginning to notice some of *their* problems, too. Drug dependence is out in the open, now: Some people are getting heavy into downers —Reds, Quaaludes, Valiums—and others are gobbling speed, booze, Maalox, and other strange medications with fearsome regularity. The 1972 presidential campaign is beginning to feel more and more like the second day of a Hell's Angels Labor Day picnic.

And we are only halfway home: Five more months . . . the moment I finish this goddamn thing I have to rush off to New York for the June 20th primary, then back to Washington to get everything packed for the move home to Colorado . . . and after that to Miami for the Democratic Convention, which is shaping up very fast these days as one of the most brutal and degrading animal acts of our time.

After Miami the calendar shows a bit of a rest on the political front—but not for me: I have to come back out to California and ride that goddamn fiendish Vincent Black Shadow again, for the road tests. The original plan was to deal with the beast in my off-hours during the California primary coverage, but serious problems developed.

Ten days before the election—with McGovern apparently so far ahead that most of the press people were looking for ways to *avoid* covering the final week—I drove out to Ventura, a satellite town just north of L.A. in the San Fernando Valley, to pick up the bugger and use it to cover the rest of the primary. Greg Jackson, an ABC correspondent who used to race motorcycles, went along with me. We were both curious about this machine. Chris Bunche, editor of *Choppers* magazine, said it was so fast and terrible that it made the extremely fast Honda 750 seem like a harmless toy.

This proved to be absolutely true. I rode a factory-demo Honda for a while, just to get the feel of being back on a serious road-runner again . . . and it seemed just fine: very quick, very powerful, very easy in the hands, one-touch electric starter. A very civilized machine, in all, and I might even be tempted to buy

220

one if I didn't have the same gut distaste for Hondas that the American Honda management has for *Rolling Stone.* They don't like the image. "You meet the nicest people on a Honda," they say—but according to a letter from American Honda to the *Rolling Stone* ad manager, none of these *nicest people* have much stomach for a magazine like the *Stone.*

Which is probably just as well; because if you're a safe, happy, *nice,* young Republican you probably don't want to read about things like dope, rock music, and politics anyway. You want to stick with *Time,* and for weekend recreation do a bit of the laid-back street-cruising on your big fast Honda 750 . . . maybe burn a Sportster or a Triumph here & there, just for the *fun* of it: But nothing serious, because when you start that kind of thing you don't meet many *nice people.*

Jesus! Another tangent, and right up front, this time—the whole *lead,* in fact, completely fucked.

What can I say? Last week I blew the whole thing. Total failure. Missed the deadline, no article, no wisdom, no excuse . . . Except one: Yes, I was savagely and expertly duped by one of the oldest con trips in politics.

By Frank Mankiewicz, of all people. That scurvy, rumpled, treacherous little bastard . . . If I were running for President I would hire Mankiewicz to handle the press for me, but as a journalist I wouldn't shed a tear if I picked up tomorrow's paper and saw where nine thugs had caught poor Frank in an alley near the Capitol and cut off both of his Big Toes, making it permanently impossible for him to keep his balance for more than five or six feet in any direction.

The image is horrible: Mankiewicz gets a phone call from Houston, saying the Texas delegation is on the verge of selling out to a Humphrey/Wallace coalition . . . he slams down the phone and lunges out of his cubicle in "McGovern for President" headquarters, bouncing off the door-jamb and then grabbing the Coke machine in order to stay upright—then lunging again into Rick Stearns' office to demand a detailed breakdown on the sex lives and bad debts of every member of the Texas delegation . . . then, trying to catch his breath, gasping for air from the terrible exertion, he finally lunges back down the hall to his own cubicle.

221

It is very hard to walk straight with the Big Toes gone; the effect is sort of like taking the keel off a sailboat—it becomes impossibly top-heavy, wallowing crazily in the swells, needing outriggers to hold it upright . . . and the only way a man can walk straight with no Big Toes is to use a very complex tripod mechanism, five or six retractable aluminum rods strapped to each arm, moving around like a spider instead of a person.

Ah . . . this seems to be getting heavy. Very harsh and demented language. I have tried to suppress these feelings for more than a week, but every time I sit down at a typewriter they foam to the surface. So it is probably better—if for no other reason than to get past this ugly hang-up and into the rest of the article —to just blow it all out and take the weight off my spleen, as it were, with a brief explanation.

Morning again in downtown Los Angeles; dawn comes up on this city like a shitmist. Will it burn off before noon? Will the sun eventually poke through? That is the question they'll be asking each other down there on the Pool Terrace below my window a few hours from now. I'm into my eighteenth day as a resident of the Wilshire Hyatt House Hotel, and I am getting to know the dreary routine of this place pretty well.

Outside of that pigsty in Milwaukee, this may be the worst hotel in America. The Sheraton-Schroeder remains in a class of its own: Passive incompetence is one thing, but aggressive nazi hostility on the corporate level is something else again. The only thing these two hotels have in common is that the Sheraton (ITT) chain got rid of them: The Schroeder was sold to a local business magnate, and this grim hulk ended up as a part of the Hyatt House chain.

As far as I know there was no pool in the Schroeder. Maybe a big grease pit or a scum vat of some kind on the roof, but I never saw a pool. There were rumors of a military-style S&M gallery in the basement with maybe an icewater plunge for the survivors, but I never saw that one either. There was no way to deal with management personnel in the Schroeder unless your breath smelled heavily of Sauerbraten . . . and in fact one of the happiest things about my life, these days, is that my memories of life in the Sheraton-Schroeder are becoming mercifully dim. The only open sore that remains from that relationship is the trouble I'm still having with the IBM typewriter-rental service in Milwaukee—with regard to the $600 Selectric Typewriter I left behind the desk when I checked out. It was gone when the IBM man came around to pick it up the next morning, and now they want me to pay for it.

Right. Another contribution to the Thousand Year Reich: "We will march on a road of bones. . . ." Tom Paxton wrote a song about it. And now I get these harsh letters from Milwaukee: "Herr Docktor Thompson—Der Typewriting machine you rented hass disappeared! And you vill of course pay!"

No. Never in hell. Because I have a receipt for that typewriter.[1]

But first things first. We were talking about motorcycles. Jackson and I were out there in Ventura fucking around with a 750 Honda and an experimental prototype of the new Vincent—a 1000-cc brute that proved out to be so awesomely fast that I didn't even have time to get scared of it before I found myself coming up on a highway stoplight at ninety miles an hour and then skidding halfway through the intersection with both wheel-brakes locked.

A genuinely hellish bike. Second gear peaks around 65—cruising speed on the freeways—and third winds out somewhere between 95 and 100. I never got to fourth, which takes you up to 120 or so—and after that you shift into fifth.

Top speed is 140, more or less, depending on how the thing is tuned—but there is nowhere in Los Angeles County to run a bike like that. I managed to get it back from Ventura to McGovern's downtown headquarters hotel, staying mainly in second gear, but the vibration almost fused my wrist bones and boiling oil from the breather pipes turned my right foot completely black. Later, when I tried to start it up for another test-run, the backlash from the kick-starter almost broke my leg. For two days afterward I limped around with a golfball-size blood-bruise in my right arch.

Later in the week I tried the bastard again, but it stalled on a

---

1. That IBM typewriter isn't the only thing that disappeared since this was written. The Sheraton-Schroeder itself no longer exists. Its disastrous reputation caused the new owners to get rid of the name along with most of the staff as soon as they took over. It would hardly be fair at this point to reveal the new name. Give the poor buggers a chance.

The Vincent Black Shadow.

ramp leading up to the Hollywood Freeway and I almost broke my hand when I exploded in a stupid, screaming rage and punched the gas tank. After that, I locked it up and left it in the hotel parking lot—where it sat for many days with a MCGOVERN FOR PRESIDENT tag on the handlebars.

George never mentioned it, and when I suggested to Gary Hart that the Senator might like to take the machine out for a quick test-ride and some photos for the national press, I got almost exactly the same reaction that Mankiewicz laid on me in Florida when I suggested that McGovern could pick up a million or so votes by inviting the wire-service photographers to come out and snap him lounging around on the beach with a can of beer in his hand and wearing my Grateful Dead T-shirt.

Looking back on it, I think that was the moment when my relationship with Mankiewicz turned sour. Twenty-four hours earlier I had showed up at his house in Washington with what John Prine calls "an illegal smile" on my face—and the morning after that visit he found himself sitting next to me on the plane to Florida and listening to some lunatic spiel about how his man should commit political suicide by irreparably identifying himself as the candidate of the Beachbums, Weirdos, and Boozers.

The Villon quote leading into this chapter was lifted from a book I wrote a few years ago on outlaw motorcycle gangs, and at the time it seemed like a very apt little stroke—reaching back into time and French poetry for a reminder that a sense of doomed alienation on your own turf is nothing new.

But why use the same quote to lead off another one of these rambling screeds on American politics in 1972? On the California Democratic primary? The McGovern campaign?

There has to be a reason. And there is, in fact—but I doubt if I'm up to explaining it right now. All I can say for sure is that I walked into the room and stared at the typewriter for a long time . . . knowing I'd just spent seventeen days and $2000 in California lashing together this thirty-three-pound satchel of notes, tapes, clippings, propaganda, etc. . . . and also knowing that somewhere in one of these goddamn drawers is a valid contract that says I have to write a long article, immediately, about whatever happened out there.

How long, O Lord, how long? Where will it end?

All I ever wanted out of this grueling campaign was enough money to get out of the country and live for a year or two in peaceful squalor in a house with a big screen porch looking down on an empty white beach, with a good rich coral reef a few hundred yards out in the surf and *no neighbors*.

Some book reviewer whose name I forget recently called me a "vicious misanthrope" . . . or maybe it was a "cynical misanthrope" . . . but either way, he (or she) was right; and what got me this way was *politics*. Everything that is wrong-headed, cynical & vicious in me today traces straight back to that evil hour in September of '69 when I decided to get heavily involved in the political process . . .

But that is another story. What worries me now—in addition to this still unwritten saga of the California primary—is the strong possibility that my involvement in politics has become so

225

deep and twisted that I can no longer think rationally about that big screen porch above the beach except in terms of an appointment as Governor of American Samoa.

I coveted that post for many years. For a while it was my only ambition. I pursued it relentlessly, and at one point in either 1964 or '65 it seemed within my grasp. Larry O'Brien, now the chairman of the Democratic Party, was the man in charge of pork-barrel/patronage appointments at the time, and he gave me excellent reason to believe my application was on the verge of bearing fruit. I was living at the Holiday Inn in Pierre, South Dakota when the good news arrived. It came on a Wednesday, as a recall, by telegram. The manager of the Inn was ecstatic; he called a cab immediately and sent me downtown to a drygoods store where I bought six white sharkskin suits—using a Sinclair Oil card, which was subsequently revoked and caused me a lot of trouble.

I never learned all the details, but what was finally made clear —in the end, after a bad communications breakdown—was that O'Brien had pulled a fast one on me. As it turned out, he never had any intention of making me Governor of American Samoa, and when I finally realized this it made me very bitter and eventually changed my whole life.

Like George Metesky—the "Mad Bomber" who terrorized New York for fifteen years to get even with Con Edison for overcharging him on his light bill and finally cutting off his electricity— I changed my whole lifestyle and channeled my energies into long-range plotting for vengeance on O'Brien and the Democratic Party. Instead of going into government service in the South Pacific, I fled Pierre, S.D. in a junk Rambler and drove to San Francisco—where I fell in with the Hells Angels and decided to become a writer instead of a diplomat.

Several years later I moved to Colorado and tried to live quietly. But I never forgot O'Brien. In the solitude of the Rockies I nursed a lust for vengeance . . . saying nothing to anyone, until suddenly in the summer of '69 I saw an opportunity to cripple the Democratic Party in Aspen.

This took about fifteen months, and by the time it was done I was hopelessly hooked again on the politics of vengeance. The next step would have to be national. O'Brien was riding high in Washington, commanding a suite of offices in the Watergate and reluctantly gearing up to send a party with no real candidate and a $9 million debt from '68 into a hopeless battle with Nixon—a battle that would not only humiliate the candidate (the Man from Maine, they said), but also destroy the party by plunging it into a state of financial and ideological bankruptcy from which it would never recover.

Wonderful, I thought. I won't even have to *do* anything. Just watch, and write it all down.

That was six months ago. But things are different now—and in the strange calm of those first few days after the votes were counted in California I began to see that George McGovern has scrambled my own carefully laid plans along with all the others, except his own—and that I am suddenly facing the very distinct possibility that I might have to drag myself into a voting booth this November and actually pull the lever for the presidential candidate of the Democratic Party. O'Brien's party. That same gang of corrupt and genocidal bastards who not only burned me for six white sharkskin suits eight years ago in South Dakota and chased me through the streets of Chicago with clubs & tear gas in August of '68, but also forced me to choose for five years between going to prison or chipping in 20 percent of my income to pay for napalm bombs to be dropped on people who never threatened me with anything; and who put my friends in jail for refusing to fight an undeclared war in Asia that even Mayor Daley is now opposed to . . .

Ah . . . careful, careful: That trip has been done. No point getting off on another violent tangent. And besides, now that the Republicans are running The War, the Democrats are against it

. . . or at least *some* of them are against it, including such recent converts as Ed Muskie and Hubert Humphrey. But it is also worth noting that the only Democrat to survive this hellish six-month gauntlet of presidential primaries is the only one of the lot who began as a genuine *anti-war candidate.*

Six months ago George McGovern was dismissed by the press and the pols as a "one-issue candidate." And to a certain extent they were right. He has branched out a bit since then, but The War in Vietnam is still the only issue in McGovern's jumbled arsenal that he never has to explain, defend, or modify. All he has to do is start talking about Vietnam, and the crowd begins cheering and clapping.

For a "one-issue candidate," McGovern has done pretty well. Four years ago Gene McCarthy was another "one-issue candidate"—the same issue poor McGovern is stuck with today—and if McCarthy had somehow managed to put together the kind of political organization that McGovern is riding now, he would be the incumbent President and the '72 campaign would be a very different scene.

Gene Pokorny, one of McGovern's key managers, who also worked for McCarthy in '68, describes the difference between the two campaigns as "the difference between an organization and a happening" . . . Which is probably true, but that "happening" dumped a Democratic President and made McCarthy the front-runner all the way to California, where he lost to Robert Kennedy by only three percentage points. They were still counting the votes when Sirhan Sirhan fired a bullet into Kennedy's head.

What if McCarthy had won California? Would Sirhan have gone after *him,* instead of Kennedy? . . . Like Artie Bremer, who stalked Nixon for a while, then switched to Wallace? Assassins, like politicians and journalists, are not attracted to losers.

Strange speculation . . . and worth pursuing, no doubt, on a day when I have more time. Is the Governor's mansion in American Samoa on a cliff above the beach? Does it have a big screen porch? Sometime soon I will have to speak with Mankiewicz about this. I don't look forward to it, but perhaps we can work something out if we handle the whole thing by telephone.

Some people are easier to deal with at a distance, and Frank is one of them. His whole manner changes when you confront him in person. It is very much like dealing with a gila monster who was only pretending to be asleep when you approached him—but the instant you enter his psychic territory, a radius of about six feet, he will dart off in some unexpected direction and take up a new stance, fixing you with a lazy unblinking stare and apparently trying to make up his mind whether to dart back and sink a fang in your flesh or just sit there and wait till you move on.

This is the way Mankiewicz behaved when I ran across him around midnight, a week or so before election day, in the hallway outside the McGovern press room in the Wilshire Hyatt House Hotel and asked him if he could help me out with some details on a story I'd just picked up in a strip joint called The Losers Club on La Cienega Boulevard—a very strange tale about Hubert Humphrey keeping a private plane on standby at a nearby landing strip, ready to take off at any moment for Vegas and return the same night with a big bag of cash, which would then be rushed to Humphrey headquarters at the Beverly Hilton and used to finance a bare-knuckle media blitz against McGovern during the last days of the campaign.

The story was at least second-hand by the time I heard it, but the source seemed reliable and I was eager to learn more . . . but there was no point in calling Humphrey on a thing like this, so I brooded on it for a while and finally decided—for reasons better left unexplained, at this point—that the only two people even half-likely to know anything about such a bizarre story were Mankiewicz and Dick Tuck.

But a dozen or so phone calls failed to locate either one of them, so I wandered up to the press room to get a free drink and check the bulletin board for a message of some kind from Tim Crouse, who had gone off about six hours earlier to find a bottle of Schnapps and continue his research on How the Press Covers The Campaign. The project had already stirred up a surprising amount of out-spoken resentment among the objects of his study, and now he had gone out to get crazy on German whiskey with a bunch of people who thought he was planning to skewer them in the public prints.

The press room was crowded—two dozen or so ranking media wizards, all wearing little egg-shaped ID tags from the Secret Service: Leo Sauvage/*La Figaro,* Jack Perkins/NBC, R. W. Apple/ N.Y. *Times* . . . the McGovern campaign went big-time, for real, in California. No more of that part-time, secondary coverage. McGovern was suddenly the front-runner, perhaps the next President, and virtually every room in the hotel was filled with either staff or media people . . . twelve new typewriters in the press suite, ten phones, four color TV sets, a well-stocked free bar, even a goddamn Mojo Wire.[2]

The gossip in the press room was heavier than usual that night: Gary Hart was about to be fired as McGovern's campaign manager; Fred Dutton would replace him . . . Humphrey's sister had just been arrested in San Diego on a warrant connected with Hubert's campaign debts . . . Muskie was offering to support McGovern if George would agree to take over $800,000 of his (Muskie's) campaign debt . . . But Crouse was nowhere in sight. I stood around for a while, trying to piece together a few grisly unsubstantiated rumors about "heavy pols preparing to take over the whole McGovern campaign" . . . Several people had chunks of the story, but nobody had a real key; so I left to go back down to my room to work for a while.

That was when I ran into Mankiewicz, picking a handful of thumb-tacked messages off the bulletin board outside the door.

---

2. aka Xerox Telecopier. We have had many inquiries about this. "Mojo Wire" was the name originally given the machine by its inventor, Raoul Duke. But he signed away the patent, in the throes of a drug frenzy, to Xerox board chairman Max Palevsky, who claimed the invention for himself and renamed it the "Xerox Telecopier." Patent royalties now total $100 million annually, but Duke receives none of it. At Palevsky's insistence he remains on the *Rolling Stone* payroll, earning $50 each week, but his "sports column" is rarely printed and he is formally barred by court order, along with a Writ of Permanent Constraint, from Palevsky's house & grounds.

230

"I have a very weird story for you," I said.

He eyed me cautiously. "What is it?"

"Come over here," I said motioning him to follow me down the corridor to a quiet place . . . Then I told him what I had heard about Humphrey's midnight air-courier to Vegas. He stared down at the carpet, not seeming particularly interested—but when I finished he looked up and said, "Where'd you *hear* that?"

I shrugged, sensing definite interest now. "Well, I was talking to some people over at a place called The Losers, and—"

"With Kirby?" he snapped.

"No," I said. "I went over there looking for him, but he wasn't around." Which was true. Earlier that day Kirby Jones, Mc-Govern's press secretary, had told me he planned to stop by The Losers Club later on, because Warren Beatty had recommended it highly . . . but when I stopped by around midnight there was no sign of him.

Mankiewicz was not satisfied. "Who was there?" he asked. "Some of *our* people? Who was it?"

"Nobody you'd know," I said. "But what about this Humphrey story? What can you tell me about it?"

"Nothing," he said, glancing over his shoulder at a burst of yelling from the press room. Then: "When's your next issue coming out?"

"Thursday."

"Before the election?"

"Yeah, and so far I don't have anything worth a shit to write about—but this thing sounds interesting."

He nodded, staring down at the floor again, then shook his head. "Listen," he said. "You could cause a lot of trouble for us by printing a thing like that. They'd know where it came from, and they'd jerk our man right out."

"What man?"

He stared at me, smiling faintly.

At this point the story becomes very slippery, with many loose ends and dark shadows—but the nut was very simple: I had blundered almost completely by accident on a flat-out byzantine spook story. There was nothing timely or particularly newsworthy about it, but when your deadline is every two weeks you don't tend to worry about things like scoops and newsbreaks. If Mankiewicz had broken down and admitted to me that night that he was actually a Red Chinese agent and that McGovern had no pulse, I wouldn't have known how to handle it—and the tension of trying to keep that kind of heinous news to myself for the next four days until *Rolling Stone* went to press would almost certainly have caused me to lock myself in my hotel room with eight quarts of Wild Turkey and all the Ibogaine I could get my hands on.

So this strange tale about Humphery & Vegas was not especially *newsworthy,* by my standards. Its only real value, in fact, was the rare flash of contrast it provided to the insane tedium of the

"I was a Jew once myself."

surface campaign. Important or not, this was something very different: midnight flights to Vegas, mob money funneled in from casinos to pay for Hubert's TV spots; spies, runners, counterspies; cryptic phone calls from airport phone booths . . . Indeed; the dark underbelly of big-time politics. A useless story, no doubt, but it sure beat the hell out of getting back on that goddamn press bus and being hauled out to some shopping center in Gardena and watching McGovern shake hands for two hours with lumpy housewives.

Unfortunately, all I really knew about what I called the U-13 story was the general outline and just enough key points to convince Mankiewicz that I might be irresponsible enough to go ahead and try to write the thing anyway. All I knew—or *thought* I knew—at that point was that somebody very close to the top of the Humphrey campaign had made secret arrangements for a night flight to Vegas in order to pick up a large bundle of money from unidentified persons presumed to be sinister, and that this money would be used by Humphrey's managers to finance another one of Hubert's eleventh-hour fast-finish blitzkriegs.

Even then, a week before the vote, he was thought to be running ten points and maybe more behind McGovern—and since the average daily media expenditure for each candidate in the California primary was roughly $30,000 a day, Humphrey would need at least twice that amount to pay for the orgy of exposure he would need to overcome a ten-point lead. No less than a quick $500,000.

The people in Vegas were apparently willing to spring for it, because the plane was already chartered and ready to go when McGovern's headquarters got word of the flight from their executive-level spy in the Humphrey campaign. His identity remains a mystery—in the public prints, at least—but the handful of people aware of him say he performed invaluable services for many months.

His function in the U-13 gig was merely to call McGovern headquarters and tell them about the Vegas plane. At this point, my second- or third-hand source was not sure what happened next. According to the story, two McGovern operatives were instantly dispatched to keep around-the-clock watch on the plane for the next seventy-two hours, and somebody from McGovern headquarters called Humphrey and warned him that they knew what he was up to.

In any case, the plane never took off and there was no evidence in the last week of the campaign to suggest that Hubert got a last-minute influx of money, from Vegas or anywhere else.

That is as much of the U-13 story as I could piece together without help from somebody who knew the details—and Mankiewicz finally agreed, insisting the whole time that he knew nothing about the story except that he didn't want to see it in print before election day, that if I wanted to hold off until the next issue he would put me in touch with somebody who would tell me the whole story, for good or ill.

"Call Miles Rubin," he said, "and tell him I told you to ask him about this. He'll fill you in."

That was fine, I said. I was in no special hurry for the story, anyway. So I let it ride for a few days, missing my deadline for that issue . . . and on Wednesday I began trying to get hold of Miles Rubin, one of McGovern's top managers for California. All I knew about Rubin before I called was that several days earlier he had thrown Washington *Post* correspondent David Broder out of his office for asking too many questions—less than twenty-four hours before Broder appeared on Rubin's TV screen as one of the three interrogators on the first Humphrey/McGovern debate.

My own experience with Rubin turned out to be just about par for the course. I finally got through to him by telephone on Friday, and explained that Mankiewicz had told me to call him and find out the details of the U-13 story. I started to say we could meet for a beer or two sometime later that afternoon and he could—

"Are you kidding?" he cut in. "That's one story you're never going to hear."

"What?"

"There's no point even talking about it," he said flatly. Then he lanuched into a three-minute spiel about the fantastic honesty and integrity that characterized the McGovern campaign from top to bottom, and why was it that people like me didn't spend more time writing about The Truth and The Decency and The Integrity, instead of picking around the edge for minor things that weren't important anyway?

"Jesus Christ!" I muttered. Why argue? Getting anything but pompous bullshit and gibberish out of Rubin would be like trying to steal meat from a hammerhead shark.

"Thanks," I said, and hung up.

That night I found Mankiewicz in the press room and told him what had happened.

He couldn't understand it, he said. But he would talk to Miles tomorrow and straighten it out.

I was not optimistic; and by that time I was beginning to agree that the U-13 story was not worth the effort. The Big Story in California, after all, was that McGovern was on the brink of locking up a first-ballot nomination in Miami—and that Hubert Humphrey was about to get stomped so badly at the polls that he might have to be carried out of the state in a rubber sack.

The next time I saw Mankiewicz was on the night before the election and he seemed very tense, very strong into the gila monster trip . . . and when I started to ask him about Rubin he began ridiculing the story in a VERY LOUD VOICE, so I figured it was time to forget it.

Several days later I learned the reason for Frank's bad nerves that night. McGovern's fat lead over Humphrey, which had hovered between 14 and 20 percentage points for more than a week, had gone into a sudden and apparently uncontrollable dive in the final days of the campaign. By election eve it had shrunk to five points, and perhaps even less.

The shrinkage crisis was a closely guarded secret among McGovern's top command. Any leak to the press could have led to disastrous headlines on Tuesday morning: Election Day . . . McGOVERN FALTERS; HUMPHREY CLOSING GAP . . . a headline like that in either the Los Angeles *Times* or the San Francisco *Chronicle* might have thrown the election to Humphrey by generating a last minute Sympathy/Underdog turnout and whipping Hubert's field workers into a frenzied "get out the vote" effort.

But the grim word never leaked, and by noon on Tuesday an almost visible wave of relief rolled through the McGovern camp.

The dike would hold, they felt, at roughly five percent.

The coolest man in the whole McGovern entourage on Tuesday was George McGovern himself—who had spent all day Monday on airplanes, racing from one critical situation to another. On Monday morning he flew down to San Diego for a major rally; then to New Mexico for another final-hour rally on the eve of the New Mexico primary (which he won the next day—along with New Jersey and South Dakota) . . . and finally on Monday night to Houston for a brief, unscheduled appearance at the National Governors' Conference, which was rumored to be brewing up a "stop McGovern" movement.

After defusing the crisis in Houston he got a few hours' sleep before racing back to Los Angeles to deal with another emergency: His 22-year-old daughter was having a premature baby and first reports from the hospital hinted at serious complications.

But by noon the crisis had passed, and sometime around one o'clock he arrived with his praetorian guard of eight Secret Service agents at Max Palevsky's house in Bel Air, where he immediately changed into swimming trunks and dove into the pool. The day was grey and cool, no hint of sun, and none of the other guests seemed to feel like swimming.

For a variety of tangled reasons—primarily because my wife was one of the guests in the house that weekend—I was there when McGovern arrived. So we talked for a while, mainly about the possibility of either Muskie or Humphrey dropping out of the race and joining forces with George if the price was right . . . and it occurred to me afterward that it was the first time he'd ever seen me without a beer can in my hand or babbling like a loon about Freak Power, election bets, or some other twisted subject . . . but he was kind enough not to mention this.

It was a very relaxed afternoon. The only tense moment occurred when I noticed a sort of narrow-looking man with a distinctly predatory appearance standing off by himself and glowering down at the white telephone as if he planned to jerk it out by the root if it didn't ring within ten seconds and tell him everything he wanted to know.

236

"Who the hell is *that*?" I asked, pointing across the pool at him.

"That's Miles Rubin," somebody replied.

"Jesus," I said. "I should have guessed."

Moments later my curiosity got the better of me and I walked over to Rubin and introduced myself. "I understand they're going to put you in charge of press relations after Miami," I said as we shook hands.

He said something I didn't understand, then hurried away. For a moment I was tempted to call him back and ask if I could feel his pulse. But the moment passed and I jumped into the pool, instead.[3]

The rest of the day disintegrated into chaos, drunkenness, and the kind of hysterical fatigue that comes from spending too much time racing from one place to another and being shoved around in crowds. McGovern won the Democratic primary by exactly five percent—45 to 40—and Nixon came from behind in the GOP race to nip Ashbrook by 87 to 13.

She was gonna be an actress and I was gonna learn to fly
She took off to find the footlights and I took off to find the sky.
—Taxi by Harry Chapin

George McGovern's queer idea that he could get himself elected President on the Democratic ticket by dancing a muted whipsong on the corpse of the Democratic Party is suddenly beginning to look very sane, and very possible. For the last five or six days in California, McGovern's campaign was covered from dawn to midnight by fifteen or twenty camera crews, seventy-five to a hundred still photographers, and anywhere from fifty to two hundred linear/writing press types.

The media crowd descended on McGovern like a swarm of

---

3. Later in the campaign, when Rubin and I became reasonably good friends, he told me that the true story of the "U-13" was essentially the same as the version I'd pieced together in California. The only thing I didn't know, he said, was that Humphrey eventually got the money anyway. For some reason, the story as I originally wrote it was almost universally dismissed as "just another one of Thompson's Mankiewicz fables".

wild bees, and there was not one of them who doubted that he/she was covering The Winner. The sense of impending victory around the pool at the Wilshire Hyatt House was as sharp and all-pervasive as the gloom and desperation in Hubert Humphrey's national staff headquarters about ten miles west at the far more chic and fashionable Beverly Hilton.

In the McGovern press suite the big-time reporters were playing stud poker—six or eight of them, hunkered down in their shirtsleeves and loose ties around a long white-cloth-covered table with a pile of dollar bills in the middle and the bar about three feet behind Tom Wicker's chair at the far end. At the other end of the room, to Wicker's left, there were three more long white tables, with four identical big typewriters on each one and a pile of white legal-size paper stacked neatly beside each typewriter. At the other end of the room, to Wicker's right, was a comfortable couch and a giant floor-model 24-inch Motorola color TV set . . . the screen was so large that Dick Cavett's head looked almost as big as Wicker's, but the sound was turned off and nobody at the poker table was watching the TV set anyway. Mort Sahl was dominating the screen with a seemingly endless, borderline-hysteria monologue about a bunch of politicians he didn't have much use for—(Muskie, Humphrey, McGovern)—and two others (Shirley Chisholm and former New Orleans DA Jim Garrison) that he liked.

I knew this, because I had just come up the outside stairway from my room one floor below to get some typing paper, and I'd been watching the Cavett show on my own 21-inch Motorola color TV.

I paused at the door for a moment, then edged around to the poker table towards the nearest stack of paper. "Ah, decadence, decadence . . . ," I muttered. "Sooner or later it was bound to come to this."

Kirby Jones looked up and grinned. "What are you bitching about this time, Hunter? Why are you always bitching?"

"Never mind that," I said. "You owe me $20 & I want it now."

"What?" he looked shocked. "Twenty dollars for what?"

I nodded solemnly. "I knew you'd try to welsh. Don't tell me you don't remember that bet."

"What bet?"

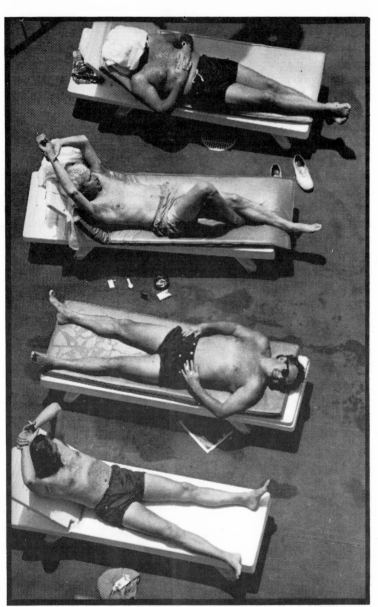

National press wizards covering McGovern in Los Angeles.

"The one we made on the train in Nebraska," I said. "You said Wallace wouldn't get more than 300 delegates . . . But he already has 317, and I want that $20."

He shook his head. "Who *says* he has that many? You've been reading the New York *Times* again." He chuckled and glanced at Wicker, who was dealing. "Let's wait until the convention, Hunter, things might be different then."

"You pig," I muttered, easing toward the door with my paper. "I've been hearing a lot about how the McGovern campaign is finally turning dishonest, but I didn't believe it until now."

He laughed and turned his attention back to the game. "All bets are payable in Miami, Hunter. That's when we'll count the marbles."

I shook my head sadly and left the room. Jesus, I thought, these bastards are getting out of hand. Here we were still a week away from D-day in California, and the McGovern press suite was already beginning to look like some kind of Jefferson-Jackson Day stag dinner. I glanced back at the crowd around the table and realized that not one of them had been in New Hampshire. This was a totally different crowd, for good or ill. Looking back on the first few weeks of the New Hampshire campaign, it seemed so different from what was happening in California that it was hard to adjust to the idea that it was still the same campaign. The difference between a sleek front-runner's act in Los Angeles and the spartan, almost skeletal machinery of an underdog operation in Manchester was almost more than the mind could deal with all at once.[4]

Four months ago on a frozen grey afternoon in New Hampshire the McGovern "press bus" rolled into the empty parking lot of a motel on the outskirts of Portsmouth. It was 3:30 or so, and we had an hour or so to kill before the Senator would arrive by air from Washington and lead us downtown for a hand-shaking gig at the Booth fishworks.

The bar was closed, but one of McGovern's advance men had

4. California was the first primary where the McGovern campaign was obviously well-financed. In Wisconsin, where McGovern's money men had told him privately that they would withdraw their support if he didn't finish first or a very close second, the press had to pay fifty cents a beer in the hospitality suite.

arranged a sort of beer/booze and sandwich meat smorgasbord for the press in a lounge just off the lobby . . . so all six of us climbed out of the bus, which was actually an old three-seater airport limousine, and I went inside to kill time.

Of the six passengers in the "press bus," three were local McGovern volunteers. The other three were Ham Davis from the Providence *Journal,* Tim Crouse from the *Rolling Stone* Boston Bureau, and me. Two more media/press people were already inside: Don Bruckner from the Los Angeles *Times,* and Michelle Clark from CBS.[5]

There was also Dick Dougherty, who had just quit his job as chief of the L.A. *Times* New York bureau to become George McGovern's press secretary, speechwriter, main fixer, advance man, and all-purpose traveling wizard. Dougherty and Bruckner were sitting off by themselves at a corner table when the rest of us straggled into the lounge and filled our plates at the smorgasbord table: olives, carrots, celery stalks, salami, deviled eggs . . . but when I asked for beer, the middle-aged waitress who was also the desk clerk said beer "wasn't included" in "the arrangements," and that if I wanted any I would have to pay cash for it.

"That's fine," I said. "Bring me three Budweisers."

She nodded. "With three glasses?"

"No. One glass."

She hesitated, then wrote the order down and lumbered off toward wherever she kept the beer. I carried my plate over to an empty table and sat down to eat and read the local paper . . . but there was no salt and pepper on the table, so I went back up to the smorgasbord to look for it & bumped into somebody in a tan garbardine suit who was quietly loading his plate with carrots & salami.

"Sorry," I said.

---

5. The New Hampshire primary was Michelle's first assignment in national politics. "I don't have the vaguest idea what I'm doing," she told me. "I think they're just letting me get my feet wet." Three months later, when McGovern miraculously emerged as the front-runner, Michelle was still covering him. By that time her star was rising almost as fast as McGovern's. At the Democratic Convention in Miami, Walter Cronkite announced on the air that she had just been officially named "correspondent." On December 8, 1972 Michelle Clark died in a plane crash at Midway Airport in Chicago —the same plane crash that killed the wife of Watergate defendant Howard Hunt.

"Pardon *me,*" he replied.

I shrugged and went back to my table with the salt and pepper. The only noise in the room was coming from the L.A. *Times* corner. Everybody else was either reading or eating, or both. The only person in the room not sitting down was the man in the tan suit at the smorgasbord table. He was still fumbling with the food, keeping his back to the room. . . .

There was something familiar about him. Nothing special—but enough to make me glance up again from my newspaper; a subliminal recognition-flash of some kind, or maybe just the idle journalistic curiosity that gets to be a habit after a while when you find yourself drifting around in the nervous murk of some story with no apparent meaning or spine to it. I had come up to New Hampshire to write a long thing on the McGovern campaign—but after twelve hours in Manchester I hadn't seen much to indicate that it actually existed, and I was beginning to wonder what the fuck I was going to write about for that issue.

There was no sign of communication in the room. The press people, as usual, were going out of their way to ignore each other's existence. Ham Davis was brooding over the New York *Times,* Crouse was re-arranging the contents of his knapsack, Michelle Clark was staring at her fingernails, Bruckner and Dougherty were trading Sam Yorty jokes . . . and the man in the tan suit was still shuffling back and forth at the smorgasbord table—totally absorbed in it, studying the carrots. . . .

Jesus Christ! I thought. The Candidate! That crouching figure up there at the food table is George McGovern.

But where was his entourage? And why hadn't anybody else noticed him? Was he actually *alone?*

No, that was impossible. I had never seen a presidential candidate moving around in public without at least ten speedy "aides" surrounding him at all times. So I watched him for a while, expecting to see his aides flocking in from the lobby at any moment . . . but it slowly dawned on me that The Candidate was by *himself*: there were no aides, no entourage, and nobody else in the room had even noticed his arrival.

This made me very nervous. McGovern was obviously waiting for somebody to greet him, keeping his back to the room, not even looking around—so there was no way for him to know that nobody in the room even knew he was there.

Finally I got up and walked across to the food table, watching McGovern out of the corner of one eye while I picked up some olives, fetched another beer out of the ice bucket . . . and finally reached over to tap The Candidate on the arm and introduce myself:

"Hello, Senator. We met a few weeks ago at Tom Braden's house in Washington."

He smiled and reached out to shake hands. "Of course, of course," he said. "What are you doing up *here?*"

"Not much, so far," I said. "We've been waiting for *you.*"

He nodded, still poking around with the cold cuts. I felt very uneasy. Our last encounter had been somewhat jangled. He had just come back from New Hampshire, very tired and depressed, and when he arrived at Braden's house we had already finished dinner and I was getting heavily into drink. My memory of that evening is somewhat dim, but even in dimness I recall beating my gums at top speed for about two hours about how he was doing everything wrong and how helpless it was for him to think he could ever accomplish anything with that goddamn albatross of a Democratic Party on his neck, and that if he had any *real* sense he would make drastic alterations in the whole style & tone of his campaign and re-model it along the lines of the Aspen Freak Power Uprising, specifically, along the lines of my own extremely weird and nerve-rattling campaign for Sheriff of Pitkin County, Colorado.

McGovern had listened politely, but two weeks later in New Hampshire there was no evidence to suggest that he had taken my advice very seriously. He was still plodding along in the passive/underdog role, still driving back & forth across the state in his lonely one-car motorcade to talk with small groups of people in rural living rooms. Nothing heavy, nothing wild or electric. All he was offering, he said, was a rare and admittedly longshot opportunity to vote for an honest and intelligent presidential candidate.

A very strange option, in any year—but in mid-February of 1972 there were no visible signs, in New Hampshire, that the citizenry was about to rise up and drive the swine out of the temple. Beyond that, it was absolutely clear—according to the Wizards, Gurus, and Gentlemen Journalists in Washington—that Big Ed Muskie, the Man from Maine, had the Democratic nomination so deep in the bag that it was hardly worth arguing about.

Nobody argued with the things McGovern said. He was right, of course—but nobody took him very seriously, either . . .

7:45 A.M. . . . The sun is fighting through the smog now, a hot grey glow on the street below my window. Friday morning business-worker traffic is beginning to clog Wilshire Boulevard and the Glendale Federal Savings parking lot across the street is filling up with cars. Slump-shouldered girls are scurrying into the big Title Insurance & Trust Company and Crocker National Bank buildings, rushing to punch in on the time clock before 8:00.

I can look down from my window and see the two McGovern press buses loading. Kirby Jones, the press secretary, is standing by the door of the No. 1 bus and herding two groggy CBS cameramen aboard like some kind of latter-day Noah getting goats aboard the ark. Kirby is responsible for keeping the McGovern press/media crowd happy—or at least happy enough to make sure they have the time and facilities to report whatever McGovern, Mankiewicz, and the other Main Boys want to see and read on tonight's TV news and in tomorrow's newspapers. Like any other good press secretary, Kirby doesn't mind admitting—off the record—that his love of Pure Truth is often tempered by circumstance. His job is to convince the press that everything The Candidate says is even now being carved on stone tablets.

The Truth is whatever George says; this is all ye know and all ye need to know. If McGovern says today that the most important issue in the California primary is abolition of the sodomy statutes, Kirby will do everything in his power to convince everybody on the press bus that the sodomy statutes *must* be abolished . . . and if George decides tomorrow that his pro-sodomy gig isn't making it with the voters, Kirby will get behind a quick press release to the effect that "new evidence from previously obscure sources" has convinced the Senator that what he really meant to say was that sodomy itself should be abolished.

This kind of fancy footwork was executed a lot easier back there in the early primaries than it is now. Since Wisconsin, Mc-Govern's words have been watched very carefully. Both his mushrooming media entourage and his dwindling number of op-ponents have pounced on anything even vaguely controversial or potentially damaging in his speeches, press conferences, position papers, or even idle comments.

McGovern is very sensitive about this sort of thing, and for excellent reason. In three of the last four big primaries (Ohio, Nebraska & California) he has spent an alarmingly big chunk of his campaign time *denying* that behind his calm and decent facade he is really a sort of Trojan Horse candidate—coming on in public as a bucolic Jeffersonian Democrat while secretly plotting to seize the reins of power and turn them over at midnight on Inauguration Day to a Red-bent hellbroth of Radicals, Dopers, Traitors, Sex Fiends, Anarchists, Winos, and "extremists" of every description.

The assault began in Ohio, when the Senator from Boeing (Henry Jackson, D-Wash.) began telling everybody his advance man could round up to listen to him that McGovern was not only a Marijuana Sympathizer, but also a Fellow Traveler. . . . Not *exactly* a dope-sucker and a card-carrying Red, but almost.

In Nebraska it was Humphrey, and although he dropped the Fellow Traveler slur, he added Amnesty and Abortion to the Marijuana charge and caused McGovern considerable grief. By election day the situation was so grim in traditionally conservative, Catholic Omaha that it looked like McGovern might actually *lose* the Nebraska primary, one of the kingpins in his overall strategy. Several hours after the polls closed the mood in the Omaha Hilton

Situation Room was extremely glum. The first returns showed Humphrey well ahead, and just before I was thrown out I heard Bill Dougherty—Lt. Gov. of South Dakota and one of McGovern's close friends and personal advisors—saying: "We're gonna get zinged tonight, folks."

It was almost midnight before the out-state returns began offsetting Hubert's big lead in Omaha, and by 2:00 A.M. on Wednesday it was clear that McGovern would win—although the final 6 percent margin was about half of what had been expected ten days earlier, before Humphrey's local allies had fouled the air with alarums about Amnesty, Abortion, and Marijuana.

Sometime around 11:30 I was readmitted to the Situation Room —because they wanted to use my portable radio to get the final results—and I remember seeing Gene Pokorny slumped in a chair with his shoes off and a look of great relief on his face. Pokorny, the architect of McGovern's breakthrough victory in Wisconsin, was also the campaign manager of Nebraska, his home state, and a loss there would have badly affected his future. Earlier that day in the hotel coffee shop I'd heard him asking Gary Hart which state he would be assigned to after Nebraska.

"Well, Gene," Hart replied with a thin smile. "That depends on what happens tonight, doesn't it?" Pokorny stared at him, but said nothing. Like almost all the other key people on the staff, he was eager to move on to California.

"Yeah," Hart continued. "We were planning on sending you out to California from here, but recently I've been thinking more and more about that slot we have open in the Butte, Montana office."

Again, Pokorny said nothing . . . but two weeks later, with Nebraska safely in the bag, he turned up in Fresno and hammered out another McGovern victory in the critically important Central Valley. And that slot in Butte is still open . . .

Which is getting a bit off the point here. Indeed. We are drifting badly—from motorcycles to Mankiewicz to Omaha, Butte, Fresno . . . where will it end?

The point, I think, was that in both the Ohio and Nebraska primaries, back to back, McGovern was confronted for the first time with the politics of the rabbit-punch and the groin shot, and in both states he found himself dangerously vulnerable to this kind of thing. Dirty politics confused him. He was not ready for it— and especially not from his fine old friend and neighbor, Hubert Humphrey. Toward the end of the Nebraska campaign he was spending most of his public time explaining that he was Not for abortion on demand, Not for legalized Marijuana, Not for unconditional amnesty . . . and his staff was becoming more and more concerned that their man had been put completely on the defensive.

This is one of the oldest and most effective tricks in politics. Every hack in the business has used it in times of trouble, and it has even been elevated to the level of political mythology in a story about one of Lyndon Johnson's early campaigns in Texas. The race was close and Johnson was getting worried. Finally he told his campaign manager to start a massive rumor campaign about his opponent's life-long habit of enjoying carnal knowledge of his own barnyard sows.

"Christ, we can't get away with calling him a pig-fucker," the campaign manager protested. "Nobody's going to believe a thing like that."

"I know," Johnson replied. "But let's make the sonofabitch *deny* it."

McGovern has not learned to cope with this tactic yet. Humphrey used it again in California, with different issues, and once again George found himself working overtime to deny wild, baseless charges that he was: (1) Planning to scuttle both the Navy and the Air Force, along with the whole Aerospace industry, and (2) He was a sworn foe of all Jews, and if he ever got to the White House he would immediately cut off all military aid to Israel and sit on his hands while Russian-equipped Arab legions drove the Jews into the sea.

McGovern scoffed at these charges, dismissing them as "ridiculous lies," and repeatedly explained his positions on both issues— but when they counted the votes on election night it was obvious that both the Jews and the Aerospace workers in Southern California had taken Humphrey's bait. All that saved McGovern in California was a long-overdue success among black voters, strong support from chicanos, and a massive pro-McGovern Youth Vote.

This is a very healthy power base, if he can keep it together—but it is not enough to beat Nixon in November unless McGovern can figure out some way to articulate his tax and welfare positions a hell of a lot more effectively than he did in California. Even Hubert Humphrey managed to get McGovern tangled up in his own economic proposals from time to time during their TV debates in California—despite the fact that toward the end of that campaign Humphrey's senile condition was so obvious that even I began feeling sorry for him.

Indeed. Sorry. Senile. Sick. Tangled . . . That's exactly how I'm beginning to feel. All those words and many others, but my brain is too numb to spit them out of the memory bank at this time. No person in my condition has any business talking about Hubert Humphrey's behavior. My brain has slowed down to the point of almost helpless stupor. I no longer even have the energy to grind my own teeth.

So this article is not going to end the way I thought it would . . . and looking back at the lead I see that it didn't even start that way either. As for the middle, I can barely remember it. There was something about making a deal with Mankiewicz and then Seizing Power in American Samoa, but I don't feel ready right now. Maybe later . . .

Way out on the far left corner of this desk I see a note that says "Call Mankiewicz—Miami Hotel rooms."

That's right. He was holding three rooms for us at the convention. Probably I should call him right away and firm that up . . . or maybe not.

But what the hell? These things can wait. Before my arms go numb there were one or two points I wanted to make. This is certainly no time for any heavy speculation or long-range analysis—on any subject at all, but especially not on anything as volatile and complex as the immediate future of George McGovern vis-à-vis the Democratic Party.

Yet it is hard to avoid the idea that McGovern has put the

Hart and Mankiewicz search for clues as Pat Caddell briefs the press on the strange case of the disappearing margin at a press conference the morning after the California primary.

Party through some very drastic changes in the last few months. The Good Ole Boys are not pleased with him. But they can't get a grip on him either—and now, less than three weeks before the convention, he is so close to a first-ballot victory that the old hacks and ward-heelers who thought they had total control of the Party less than six months ago find themselves skulking around like old winos in the side alleys of presidential politics—first stripped of their power to select and control delegations, then rejected as delegates themselves when Big Ed took his overcrowded bandwagon over the high side on the first lap . . . and now, incredible as it still seems to most of them, they will not even be allowed into the Party convention next month.

One of the first people I plan to speak with when I get to Miami is Larry O'Brien: shake both of his hands and extend powerful congratulations to him for the job he has done on the Party. In January of 1968 the Democratic Party was so fat and confident that it looked like they might keep control of the White House, the Congress, and in fact the whole U.S. Government almost indefinitely. Now, four and a half years later, it is a useless bankrupt hulk. Even if McGovern wins the Democratic nomination, the Party machinery won't be of much use to him, except as a vehicle.

"Traditional Politics with a Vengeance" is Gary Hart's phrase —a nutshell concept that pretty well describes the theory behind McGovern's amazingly effective organization.

"The Politics of Vengeance" is a very different thing—an essentially psychotic concept that Hart would probably not go out of his way to endorse.

Vehicle . . . vehicle . . . vehicle—a very strange looking word, if you stare at it for eight or nine minutes . . . "Skulking" is another interesting-looking word.

And so much for that.

The morning news says Wilbur Mills is running for President again. He has scorned all invitations to accept the Number Two spot with anyone else—especially George McGovern. A very depressing bulletin. But Mills must know what he's doing. His name is said to be magic in certain areas. If the Party rejects McGovern, I hope they give it to Mills. That would just about make the nut.

Another depressing news item—out of Miami Beach this time —says an unnatural number of ravens have been seen in the city recently. Tourists have complained of being kept awake all night by "horrible croaking sounds" outside their hotel windows. "At first there were only a few," one local businessman explained. "But more and more keep coming. They're building big nests in the trees along Collins Avenue. They're killing the trees and their droppings smell like dead flesh."

Many residents say they can no longer leave their windows open at night, because of the croaking. "I've always loved birds," said another resident. "But these goddamn ravens are something else!"

Later in June

Mass Burial for Political Bosses in New York . . .
McGovern over the Hump . . . The Death by
Beating of a Six-Foot Blue-Black Serpent . . .
What Next for the Good Ole Boys? . . . Anatomy
of a Fixer . . . Treachery Looms in Miami . . .

It is now clear that this once small devoted band has become a great surging multitude all across this country—and it will not be denied.
—George McGovern, on the night of the New York primary

THE DAY AFTER the New York primary I woke up in a suite on the twenty-fourth floor of Delmonico's Hotel on Park Avenue with a hellish wind tearing both rooms apart and rain coming in through all the open windows . . . and I thought: Yes, wonderful, only a lunatic would get out of bed on a day like this; call room service for grapefruit and coffee, along with a New York *Times* for brain food, and one of those portable brick-dome fireplaces full of oil-soaked sawdust logs that they can roll right into the suite and fire up at the foot of the bed.

Indeed. Get some heat in the room, but keep the windows open —for the sounds of the wind and the rain and the far-off honking of all those taxi horns down on Park Avenue.

Then fill a hot bath and get something like *Memphis Underground* on the tape machine. Relax, relax. Enjoy this fine rainy day, and send the bill to Random House. The budget boys won't like it, but to hell with them. Random House still owes me a lot of

252

money from that time when the night watchman beat my snake to death on the white marble steps leading up to the main reception desk.

I had left it overnight in the editor's office, sealed up in a cardboard box with a sacrificial mouse . . . but the mouse understood what was happening, and terror gave him strength to gnaw a hole straight through the side of the box and escape into the bowels of the building.

The snake followed, of course—through the same hole—and somewhere around dawn, when the night watchman went out to check the main door, he was confronted with a six-foot blue-black serpent slithering rapidly up the stairs, flicking its tongue at him and hissing a warning that he was sure—according to his own account of the incident—was the last sound he would ever hear.

The snake was a harmless Blue Indigo that I'd just brought back from a reptile farm in Florida . . . but the watchman had no way of knowing; he had never seen a snake. Most natives of Manhattan Island are terrified of all animals except cockroaches and poodles . . . so when this poor ignorant bastard of a watchman suddenly found himself menaced by a hissing, six-foot serpent coming fast up the stairs at him from the general direction of Cardinal Spellman's quarters just across the courtyard . . . he said the sight of it made him almost crazy with fear, and at first he was totally paralyzed.

Then, as the snake kept on coming, some primal instinct shocked the man out of his trance and gave him the strength to attack the thing with the first weapon he could get his hands on— which he first described as a "steel broom handle," but which further investigation revealed to have been a metal tube jerked out of a nearby vacuum cleaner.

The battle apparently lasted some twenty minutes: a terrible clanging and screaming in the empty marble entranceway, and finally the watchman prevailed. Both the serpent and the vacuum tube were beaten beyond recognition, and later that morning a copy editor found the watchman slumped on a stool in the basement next to the xerox machine, still gripping the mangled tube and unable to say what was wrong with him except that something horrible had tried to get him, but he finally managed to kill it.

The man has since retired, they say. Cardinal Spellman died and Random House moved to a new building. But the psychic scars remain, a dim memory of corporate guilt that is rarely mentioned except in times of stress or in arguments over money. Every time I start feeling a bit uneasy about running up huge bills on the Random House tab, I think about that snake—and then I call room service again.

State Vote Aids M'Govern:
Senator's Slates Win By Large Margin
In The Suburbs

That was the *Times's* big headline on Wednesday morning. The "3 A's candidate" (Acid, Abortion, Amnesty) had definitely improved his position by carrying the suburbs. The bulk of the political coverage on page one had to do with local races—"Ryan, Badillo, Rangel Win: Coller is in Close Battle" . . . "Delegates Named" . . . "Bingham Defeats Scheuer; Rooney Apparent Winner."

Down at the bottom of the page was a block of wire-photos from the National Mayors' Conference in New Orleans—also on Tuesday—and the choice shot from down there showed a smiling Hubert Humphrey sitting next to Mayor Daley of Chicago with the Mayor of Miami Beach leaning into the scene with one of his arms around Daley and the other around Hubert.

The caption said, "Ex-Mayor Is Hit With Mayors." The "details, Page 28" said Humphrey had definitely emerged as the star of the Mayors' conference. The two losers were shown in smaller photos underneath the Daley/Humphrey thing. Muskie "received polite applause," the caption said, and the camera had apparently caught him somewhere near the beginning o' a delayed Ibogaine rush: his eyes are clouding over, his jaw has gone slack, his hair appears to be combed back in a DA.

The caption under the McGovern photo says, "He, too, received moderate response." But McGovern at least looked human, while the other four looked like they had just been trucked over on short notice from some third-rate wax museum in the French Quarter. The only genuinely ugly face of the five is that of Mayor Daley:

He looks like a potato with mange—it is the face of a man who would see nothing wrong with telling his son to go out and round up a gang of thugs with bullhorns and kick the shit out of anybody stupid enough to challenge the Mayor of Chicago's right to name the next Democratic candidate for President of the United States.

I stared at the front page for a long time; there was something wrong with it, but I couldn't quite fix on the problem until . . . yes . . . I realized that the whole front page of the June 21st New York *Times* could just as easily have been dated March 8th, the day after the New Hampshire primary.

"Pacification" was failing again in Vietnam; Defense Secretary Melvin Laird was demanding more bombers; ITT was beating another illegal stock-sales rap . . . but the most striking similarity was in the overall impression of what was happening in the fight for the Democratic presidential nomination.

Apparently nothing had changed. Muskie looked just as sick and confused as he had on that cold Wednesday morning in Manchester four months ago. McGovern looked like the same tough but hopeless underdog—and there was nothing in the face of either Daley or Humphrey to indicate that either one of those corrupt and vicious old screws had any doubt at all about what was going to happen in Miami in July. They appeared to be very pleased with whatever the Mayor of Miami Beach was saying to them. . . .

An extremely depressing front page, at first glance—almost rancid with a sense of dejá vù. There was even a Kennedy story: Will he or Won't he?

This was the most interesting story on the page, if only because of the timing. Teddy had been out of the campaign news for a few months, but now—according to the *Times's* R. W. Apple Jr.—he was about to make his move:

"City Councilman Matthew J. Troy Jr. will announce today that he is supporting Senator Edward M. Kennedy for the Democratic vice-presidential nomination, informed sources said last night. Mr. Troy, a long-time political ally of the Kennedy family, was one of the earliest supporters of Senator George McGovern for the Presidency. As such, he would be unlikely to propose a running mate for the South Dakotan unless both men had indicated their approval."

Unlikely.

Right. The logic was hard to deny. A McGovern/Kennedy ticket was probably the only sure winner available to the Democrats this year, but beyond that it might solve all of Kennedy's problems with one stroke. It would give him at least four and probably eight years in the spotlight; an unnaturally powerful and popular vice-president with all the advantages of the office and very few of the risks. If McGovern ran wild and called for the abolition of Free Enterprise, for instance, Kennedy could back off and shake his head sadly . . . but if McGovern did everything right and won a second term as the most revered and successful President in the nation's history, Teddy would be right there beside him—the other half of the team; so clearly the heir apparent that he would hardly have to bother about campaigning in public in 1980.

Don't worry, boys, we'll weather this storm of approval and come out as hated as ever.
—Saul Alinsky to his staff shortly before his death, June 1972

The primaries are finally over now: twenty-three of the goddamn things—and the deal is about to go down. New York was the last big spectacle before Miami Beach, and this time McGovern's people really kicked out the jams. They stomped every hack, wardheeler, and "old-line party boss" from Buffalo to Brooklyn. The Democratic Party in New York State was left in a frightened shambles.

Not even the state party leader, Joe Crangle, survived the McGovern blitz. He tried to pass for "uncommitted"—hoping to go down to Miami with at least a small remnant of the big-time bargaining power he'd planned on when he originally backed Muskie—but McGovern's merciless young streetfighters chopped Crangle down with the others. He will watch the convention on TV, along with Brooklyn Party boss Meade Esposito and once-powerful Bronx leader Patrick Cunningham.

Former New York Governor Averell Harriman also wound up on the list of ex-heavies who will not attend the convention. He too was an early Muskie supporter. The last time I saw Averell he was addressing a small crowd in the West Palm Beach railroad station—framed in a halo of spotlights on the caboose platform

The candidate with Senator Abraham Ribicoff pitching for the Jewish vote among the Hasidim.

of Big Ed's "Sunshine Special" . . . and the Man from Maine was standing tall beside him, smiling broadly, looking every inch the winner that all those half-bright party bosses had assured him he was definitely going to be.

It was just about dusk when Harriman began speaking, as I recall, and Muskie might have looked a little less pleased if he'd had any way of knowing that—ten blocks away, while Ave was still talking—a human threshing machine named Peter Sheridan was eagerly hitting the bricks after two weeks in the Palm Beach jail on a vagrancy rap.

Unknown to either Big Ed or Peter, their paths were soon destined to cross. Twelve hours later, Sheridan—the infamous wandering Boohoo for the Neo-American church—would board the "Sunshine Special" for the last leg of the trip into Miami.

That encounter is already legend. I am not especially proud of my role in it—mainly because the nightmare developed entirely by accident—but if I could go back and try it all over again I wouldn't change a note.

At the time I felt a bit guilty about it: having been, however innocently, responsible for putting the Demo front-runner on a collision course with a gin-crazed acid freak—but that was before I realized what kind of a beast I was dealing with.

It was not until his campaign collapsed and his ex-staffers felt free to talk that I learned that working for Big Ed was something like being locked in a rolling boxcar with a vicious 200-pound water rat. Some of his top staff people considered him dangerously unstable. He had several identities, they said, and there was no way to be sure on any given day if they would have to deal with Abe Lincoln, Hamlet, Captain Queeg, or Bobo the Simpleminded . . .

Many strange Muskie stories, but this is not the time for them. Perhaps after the convention, when the pressure lets off a bit—although not even that is certain, now: Things are getting weird.

The only "Muskie story" that interests me right now is the one about how he managed to con those poor bastards into making him the de facto party leader and also the bosses' choice to carry the party colors against Nixon in November. I want to know that story, and if anybody who reads this can fill me in on the details, by all means call at once c/o *Rolling Stone,* San Francisco.

The Muskie nightmare is beginning to look more and more like a major political watershed for the Democratic Party. When Big Ed went down he took about half of the national power structure with him. In one state after another—each time he lost a primary—Muskie crippled and humiliated the local Democratic power-mongers: Governors, Mayors, Senators, Congressmen . . . Big Ed was supposed to be their ticket to Miami, where they planned to do business as usual once again, and keep the party at least livable, if not entirely healthy. All Muskie had to do, they said, was keep his mouth shut and act like Abe Lincoln.

The bosses would do the rest. As for that hare-brained bastard McGovern, he could take those reformist ideas he'd been working on, and jam them straight up his ass. A convention packed wall to wall with Muskie delegates—the rancid cream of the party, as it were—would make short work of McGovern's Boy Scout bullshit.

That was four months ago, before Muskie began crashing around the country in a stupid rage and destroying everything he touched. First it was booze, then Reds, and finally over the brink into Ibogaine . . . and it was right about that time that most of the Good Ole Boys decided to take another long look at Hubert Humphrey. He wasn't much; they all agreed on that—but by May he was all they had left.

Not much, for sure. Any political party that can't cough up anything better than a treacherous brain-damaged old vulture like Hubert Humphrey deserves every beating it gets. They don't hardly make 'em like Hubert any more—but just to be on the safe side, he should be castrated anyway.

Castrated? Jesus! Is nothing sacred? Four years ago Hubert Humphrey ran for President of the United States on the Democratic ticket—and he almost won.

It was a very narrow escape. I voted for Dick Gregory in '68, and if somehow Humphrey manages to slither onto the ticket again this year I will vote for Richard Nixon.

But Humphrey will not be on the ticket this year—at least not on the Democratic ticket. He may end up running with Nixon, but the odds are against him there, too. Not even Nixon could stoop to Hubert's level.

So what will Humphrey do with himself this year? Is there no room at the top for a totally dishonest person? A *United States Senator?* A loyal Party Man?

Well . . . as much as I hate to get away from objective journalism, even briefly, there is no other way to explain what that treacherous bastard appears to be cranking himself up for this time around, except by slipping momentarily into the realm of speculation.

But first, a few realities: (1) George McGovern is so close to a first-ballot nomination in Miami that everybody except Hubert Humphrey, Gene McCarthy, Shirley Chisholm, and Ed Muskie seems ready to accept it as a foregone conclusion . . . (2) The national Democratic Party is no longer controlled by the Old Guard, Boss-style hacks like George Meany and Mayor Daley —or even by the Old Guard liberal-manque types like Larry O'Brien, who thought they had things firmly under control as recently as six months ago . . . (3) McGovern has made it painfully clear that he wants more than just the nomination; he has every intention of tearing the Democratic Party completely apart and re-building it according to his own blueprint . . . (4) If McGovern beats Nixon in November he will be in a position to do anything he wants either to or with the party structure . . . (5) But if McGovern loses in November, control of the Democratic Party will instantly revert to the Ole Boys, and McGovern himself will be labeled "another Goldwater" and stripped of any power in the party.

The pattern is already there, from 1964, when the Nixon/Mitchell brain-trust—already laying plans for 1968—sat back and let the GOP machinery fall into the hands of the Birchers and the right-wing crazies for a few months . . . and when Goldwater got stomped, the Nixon/Mitchell crowd moved in and took over the party with no argument from anybody . . . and four years later Nixon moved into the White House.

There have already been a few rumblings and muted threats along these lines from the Daley/Meany faction. Daley has privately threatened to dump Illinois to Nixon in November if McGovern persists in challenging Daley's eighty-five-man slave delegation to the convention in Miami . . . and Meany is prone to muttering out loud from time to time that maybe Organized Labor would be better off in the long run by enduring another four years under Nixon, rather than running the risk of whatever radical madness he fears McGovern might bring down on him.

The only other person who has said anything about taking a dive for Nixon in November is Hubert Humphrey, who has already threatened in public—at the party's Credentials Committee hearings in Washington last week—to let his friend Joe Alioto, the Mayor of San Francisco, throw the whole state of California to Nixon unless the party gives Hubert 151 California delegates— on the basis of his losing show of strength in that state's winner-take-all primary.

Hubert understood all along that California was all or nothing. He continually referred to it as "The Big One," and "The Super Bowl of the Primaries" . . . but he changed his mind when he lost. One of the finest flashes of TV journalism in many months appeared on the CBS evening news the same day Humphrey formally filed his claim to almost half the California delegation. It was a Walter Cronkite interview with Hubert in California, a week or so prior to election day. Cronkite asked him if he had any objections to the winner-take-all aspect of the California primary, and Humphrey replied that he thought it was absolutely wonderful.

"So even if you lose out here—if you lose all 271 delegates— you wouldn't challenge the winner-take-all rule?" Cronkite asked.

"Oh, my goodness, no," Hubert said. "That would make me sort of a spoilsport, wouldn't it?"

On the face of it, McGovern seems to have everything under control now. Less than twenty-four hours after the New York results were final, chief delegate-meister Rick Stearns announced that George was over the hump. The New York blitz was the clincher, pushing him over the 1350 mark and mashing all but the flimsiest chance that anybody would continue to talk seriously about a "Stop McGovern" movement in Miami. The Humphrey/ Muskie axis had been desperately trying to put something together with aging diehards like Wilbur Mills, George Meany, and Mayor Daley—hoping to stop McGovern just short of 1400—but on the weekend after the New York sweep George picked up another fifty or so from the last of the non-primary state caucuses and by Sun-

The candidate with staff advisor Gordon Weil, author of the ill-fated
"thousand dollar per person" welfare proposal—a sort of McGov-
ernized version of Nixon's own guaranteed income plan—but which
inept presentation transformed almost instantly into a permanent
albatross around the neck of the McGovern campaign. George's apparent inability to explain or even understand his own tax reform
ideas gave first Humphrey, then Nixon a club which they used to
destroy one of McGovern's prime assets: his previously untar-
nished image of "competence."

day, June 25th, he was only a hundred votes away from the 1509 that would zip it all up on the first ballot.

At that point the number of officially "uncommitted" delegates was still hovering around 450, but there had already been some small-scale defections to McGovern, and the others were getting nervous. The whole purpose of getting yourself elected as an Uncommitted delegate is to be able to arrive at the Convention with bargaining power. Ideology has nothing to do with it.

If you're a lawyer from St. Louis, for instance, and you manage to get yourself elected as an Uncommitted delegate for Missouri, you will hustle down to Miami and start scouting around for somebody to make a deal with . . . which won't take long, because every candidate still in the running for anything at all will have dozens of his own personal fixers roaming around the hotel bars and buttonholing Uncommitted delegates to find out what they want.

If your price is a lifetime appointment as a judge on the U.S. Circuit Court, your only hope is to deal with a candidate who is so close to that magic 1509 figure that he can no longer function in public because of uncontrollable drooling. If he is stuck around 1400 you will probably not have much luck getting that bench appointment . . . but if he's already up to 1499 he won't hesitate to offer you the first opening on the U.S. Supreme Court . . . and if you catch him peaked at 1505 or so, you can squeeze him for almost anything you want.

The game will get heavy sometimes. You don't want to go around putting the squeeze on people unless you're absolutely clean. *No skeletons in the closet:* no secret vices . . . because if your vote is important and your price is high, the Fixer-Man will have already checked you out by the time he offers to buy you a drink. If you bribed a traffic-court clerk two years ago to bury a drunk driving charge, the Fixer might suddenly confront you with a photostat of the citation you thought had been burned.

When that happens, you're fucked. Your price just went down to zero, and you are no longer an Uncommitted delegate.

There are several other versions of the Reverse-Squeeze: the fake hit-and-run; glassine bags found in your hotel room by a

263

maid; grabbed off the street by phony cops for statutory rape of a teenage girl you never saw before. . . .

Every once in a while you might hit on something with real style, like this one: On Monday afternoon, the first day of the convention, you—the ambitious young lawyer from St. Louis with no skeletons in the closet and no secret vices worth worrying about —are spending the afternoon by the pool at the Playboy Plaza, soaking up sun and gin/tonics when you hear somebody calling your name. You look up and see a smiling, rotund chap about thirty-five years old coming at you, ready to shake hands.

"Hi there, Virgil," he says. "My name's J. D. Squane. I work for Senator Bilbo and we'd sure like to count on your vote. How about it?"

You smile, but say nothing—waiting for Squane to continue. He will want to know your price.

But Squane is staring out to sea, squinting at something on the horizon . . . then he suddenly turns back to you and starts talking very fast about how he always wanted to be a riverboat pilot on the Mississippi, but politics got in the way. . . . "And now, goddamnit, we *must* get these last few votes. . . ."

You smile again, itching to get serious. But Squane suddenly yells at somebody across the pool, then turns back to you and says: "Jesus, Virgil, I'm really sorry about this, but I have to run. That guy over there is delivering my new Jensen Interceptor." He grins and extends his hand again. Then: "Say, maybe we can talk later on, eh? What room are you in?"

"1909."

He nods. "How about seven, for dinner? Are you free?"

"Sure."

"Wonderful," he replies. "We can take my new Jensen for a run up to Palm Beach . . . It's one of my favorite towns."

"Mine too," you say. "I've heard a lot about it."

He nods. "I spent some time there last February . . . but we had a bad act, dropped about twenty-five grand."

Jesus! Jensen Interceptor; twenty-five grand . . . Squane is definitely big-time.

"See you at seven," he says, moving away.

The knock comes at 7:02—but instead of Squane it's a beau-

264

tiful silver-haired young girl who says J. D. sent her to pick you up. "He's having a business dinner with the Senator and he'll join us later at the Crab House."

"Wonderful, wonderful—shall we have a drink?"

She nods. "Sure, but not here. We'll drive over to North Miami and pick up my girlfriend . . . but let's smoke this before we go."

"Jesus! That looks like a cigar!"

"It is!" she laughs. "And it'll make us both crazy."

Many hours later, 4:30 A.M. Soaking wet, falling into the lobby, begging for help: No wallet, no money, no ID. Blood on both hands and one shoe missing, dragged up to the room by two bellboys. . . .

Breakfast at noon the next day, half sick in the coffee shop— waiting for a Western Union money order from the wife in St. Louis. Very spotty memories from last night.

"Hi there, Virgil."

J. D. Squane, still grinning. "Where were you last night, Virgil? I came by right on the dot, but you weren't in."

"I got mugged—by your girlfriend."

"Oh? Too bad. I wanted to nail down that ugly little vote of yours."

"Ugly? Wait a minute. . . . That girl you sent; we went some-place to *meet you.*"

"Bullshit! You double-crossed me, Virgil! If we weren't on the same team I might be tempted to lean on you."

Rising anger now, painful throbbing in the head. "Fuck you, Squane! I'm on *nobody's* team! If you want my vote you know damn well how to get it—and that goddamn dope-addict girlfriend of yours didn't help any."

Squane smiles heavily. "Tell me, Virgil—what was it you wanted for the vote of yours? A seat on the federal bench?"

"You're goddamn fuckin'-A right! You got me in bad trouble last night, J. D. When I got back here my wallet was gone and there was blood on my hands."

"I know. You beat the shit out of her."

"What?"

"Look at these photographs, Virgil. It's some of the most disgusting stuff I've ever seen."

"Photographs?"

Squane hands them across the table.

"Oh my god!"

"Yeah, that's what *I* said, Virgil."

"No! This can't be *me!* I never saw that girl! Christ, she's only a child!"

"That's why the pictures are so disgusting, Virgil. You're lucky we didn't take them straight to the cops and have you locked up." Pounding the table with his fist. "That's *rape,* Virgil! That's *sodomy!* With a *child!*"

"No!"

"*Yes,* Virgil—and now you're going to pay for it."

"How? What are you talking about?"

Squane smiling again. "Votes, my friend. Yours and five others. Six votes for six negatives. Are you ready?"

Tears of rage in the eyes now. "You evil sonofabitch! You're blackmailing me!"

"Ridiculous, Virgil. Ridiculous. I'm talking about coalition politics."

"I don't even *know* six delegates. Not personally, anyway. And besides, they all *want* something."

Squane shakes his head. "Don't *tell* me about it, Virgil. I'd rather not hear. Just bring me six names off this list by noon tomorrow. If they all vote right, you'll never hear another word about what happened last night."

"What if I can't?"

Squane smiles, then shakes his head sadly. "Your life will take a turn for the worse, Virgil."

Ah, bad craziness . . . a scene like that could run on forever. Sick dialogue comes easy after five months on the campaign trail. A sense of humor is not considered mandatory for those who want to get heavy into presidential politics. Junkies don't laugh much; their gig is too serious—and the politics junkie is not much different on that score than a smack junkie.

266

The High is very real in both worlds, for those who are into it—but anybody who has ever tried to live with a smack junkie will tell you it can't be done without coming to grips with the spike and shooting up, yourself.

Politics is no different. There is a fantastic adrenaline high that comes with total involvement in almost any kind of fast-moving political campaign—especially when you're running against big odds and starting to feel like a winner.

As far as I know, I am the only journalist covering the '72 presidential campaign who has done any time on the other side of that gap—both as a candidate and a backroom pol, on the local level—and despite all the obvious differences between running on the Freak Power ticket for Sheriff of Aspen and running as a well-behaved Democrat for President of the United States, the roots are surprisingly similar . . . and whatever real differences exist are hardly worth talking about, compared to the massive, unbridgeable gap between the cranked-up reality of living day after day in the vortex of a rolling campaign—and the fiendish ratbastard tedium of covering that same campaign as a journalist, from the outside looking in.

For the same reason that nobody who has never come to grips with the spike can ever understand how far away it really is across that gap to the place where the smack junkie lives . . . there is no way for even the best and most talented journalist to know what is really going on inside a political campaign unless he has been there himself.

Very few of the press people assigned to the McGovern campaign, for instance, have anything more than a surface understanding of what is really going on in the vortex . . . or if they do, they don't mention it, in print or on the air: And after spending half a year following this goddamn zoo around the country and watching the machinery at work I'd be willing to bet pretty heavily that not even the most privileged ranking insiders among the campaign press corps are telling much less than they know.

POW!

Ralph STEADman

July

Fear and Loathing in Miami: Old Bulls Meet
the Butcher . . . A Dreary Saga Direct from the
Sunshine State . . . How George McGovern Ran
Wild on the Beach & Stomped Almost Everybody
. . . Flashback to the Famous Lindsay Blueprint &
A Strange Epitaph for the Battle of Chicago . . .
More Notes on the Politics of Vengeance,
Including Massive Technical Advice from Rick
Stearns & the Savage Eye of Ralph Steadman . . .

Do not go gentle into that good night.
Rage! Rage! Against the dying of the light.
—Dylan Thomas

SUNDAY IS NOT A GOOD DAY for traveling in the South. Most
public places are closed—especially the bars and taverns—in order
that the denizens of this steamy, atavistic region will not be dis-
tracted from church. Sunday is the Lord's day, and in the South he
still has clout—or enough, at least, so that most folks won't cross
him in public. And those few who can't make it to church will
likely stay home by the fan, with iced tea, and worship him in their
own way.

This explains why the cocktail lounge in the Atlanta airport is
not open on Sunday night. The Lord wouldn't dig it.

Not even in Atlanta, which the local chamber of commerce
describes as the Enlightened Commercial Capital of the "New
South." Atlanta is an alarmingly liberal city, by Southern standards—known for its "progressive" politicians, nonviolent race re-

269

lations, and a tax structure aggressively favorable to New Business. It is also known for moonshine whiskey, a bad biker/doper community, and a booming new porno-film industry.

Fallen pompon girls and ex-cheerleaders from Auburn, 'Bama, and even Ole Miss come to Atlanta to "get into show business," and those who take the wrong fork wind up being fucked, chewed, and beaten for $100 a day in front of hand-held movie cameras. Donkeys and wolves are $30 extra, and the going rate for gang-bangs is $10 a head, plus "the rate." Connoisseurs of porno-films say you can tell at a glance which ones were made in Atlanta, because of the beautiful girls. There is nowhere else in America, they say, where a fuck-flick producer can hire last year's Sweetheart of Sigma Chi to take on twelve Georgia-style Hell's Angels for $220 & lunch.

So I was not especially surprised when I got off the plane from Miami around midnight and wandered into the airport to find the booze locked up. What the hell? I thought: This is only the *public bar*. At this time of night—in the heart of the bible belt and especially on Sunday—you want to look around for something *private*.

Every airport has a "VIP Lounge." The one in Atlanta is an elegant neo-private spa behind a huge wooden door near Gate 11. Eastern Airlines maintains it for the use of traveling celebrities, politicians, and other conspicuous persons who would rather not be seen drinking in public with the Rabble.

I had been there before, back in February, sipping a midday beer with John Lindsay while we waited for the flight to L.A. He had addressed the Florida state legislature in Tallahassee that morning; the Florida primary was still two weeks away, Muskie was still the front-runner, McGovern was campaigning desperately up in New Hampshire, and Lindsay's managers felt he was doing well enough in Florida that he could afford to take a few days off and zip out to California. They had already circled June 6th on the Mayor's campaign calendar. It was obvious, even then, that the California primary was going to be The Big One: winner-take-all for 271 delegate votes, more than any other state, and the winner in California would almost certainly be the Democratic candidate for President of the United States in 1972.

Nobody argued that. The big problem in February was knowing which two of the twelve candidates would survive until then. If California was going to be the showdown, it was also three months and twenty-three primaries away—a long and grueling struggle before the field would narrow down to only two.

Ed Muskie, of course, would be one of them. In late February —and even in early March—he was such an overwhelming favorite that every press wizard in Washington had already conceded him the nomination. At that point in the campaign, the smart-money scenario had Big Ed winning comfortably in New Hampshire, finishing a strong second to Wallace a week later in Florida, then nailing it down in Wisconsin on April 4th.

New Hampshire would finish McGovern, they said, and Hubert's ill-advised Comeback would die on the vine in Florida. Jackson and Chisholm were fools, McCarthy and Wilbur Mills were doomed tokens . . . and that left only Lindsay, a maverick Republican who had only recently switched parties. But he had already caused a mild shock wave on the Democratic side by beating McGovern badly—and holding Muskie to a stand-off—with an eleventh-hour, "Kennedy-style" campaign in non-primary Arizona, the first state to elect delegates.

Lindsay's lieutenants saw that success in Arizona as the first spark for what would soon be a firestorm. Their blueprint had Lindsay compounding his momentum by finishing a strong third or even second in Florida, then polarizing the party by almost beating Muskie in Wisconsin—which would set the stage for an early Right/Left showdown in Massachusetts, a crucial primary state with 102 delegates and a traditionally liberal electorate.

The key to that strategy was the idea that Muskie could not hold the Center, because he was basically a candidate of the Democratic Right, like Scoop Jackson, and that he would move instinctively in that direction at the first sign of challenge from his Left—which would force him into a position so close to Nixon's that eventually not even the Democratic "centrists" would tolerate him.

There was high ground to be seized on The Left, Lindsay felt, and whoever seized it would fall heir to that far-flung, leaderless army of Kennedy/McCarthy zealots from 1968 . . . along with

25 million new voters who would naturally go 3-1 against Nixon—
unless the Democratic candidate turned out to be Hubert Humphrey
or a Moray Eel. This meant that almost anybody who could strike
sparks with the "new voters" would be working off a huge and
potentially explosive new power base that was worth—on paper,
at least—anywhere between 5 percent and 15 percent of the total
vote. It was a built-in secret weapon for any charismatic Left-bent
underdog who could make the November election even reasonably
close.

Now, walking down a long empty white corridor in the Atlanta
airport on a Sunday night in July, I had a very clear memory of
my last visit to this place—but it seemed like something that had
happened five years ago, instead of only five months. The Lindsay
campaign was a loose, upbeat trip while it lasted, but there is
a merciless kind of "out of sight, out of mind" quality about a
losing presidential campaign . . . and when I saw Lindsay on the
convention floor in Miami, sitting almost unnoticed in the front
row of the New York delegation, it was vaguely unsettling to
recall that less than six months ago he was attracting big crowds
out on Collins Avenue—just one block east of his chair, that night,
in the Miami Beach convention hall—and that every word he said,
back then, was being sucked up by three or four network TV crews
and echoed on the front pages of every major newspaper from
coast to coast.

As it turned out, the Lindsay campaign was fatally flawed from
the start. It was all tip and no iceberg—the exact opposite of the
slow-building McGovern juggernaut—but back in February it
was still considered very shrewd and avant-garde to assume that
the most important factor in a presidential campaign was a good
"media candidate." If he had Star Quality, the rest would take
care of itself.

The Florida primary turned out to be a funeral procession for
would-be "media candidates." Both Lindsay and Muskie went
down in Florida—although not necessarily because they geared
their pitch to TV; the real reason, I think, is that neither one of

272

them understood how to *use* TV . . . or maybe they knew, but just couldn't pull it off. It is hard to be super-convincing on the tube if everything you say reminds the TV audience of a Dick Cavett commercial for Alpo dogfood. George McGovern has been widely ridiculed in the press as "the ideal anti-media candidate." He looks wrong, talks wrong, and even acts wrong—by conventional TV standards. But McGovern has his own ideas about how to use the tube. In the early primaries he kept his TV exposure to a minimum—for a variety of reasons that included a lack of both money and confidence—but by the time he got to California for the showdown with Hubert Humphrey, McGovern's TV campaign was operating on the level of a very specialized art form. His thirty-minute biography—produced by Charley Guggenheim—was so good that even the most cynical veteran journalists said it was the best political film ever made for television . . . and Guggenheim's sixty-second spots were better than the bio film. Unlike the early front-runners, McGovern had taken his time and learned how to use the medium—instead of letting the medium use him.

Sincerity is the important thing on TV. A presidential candidate should at least *seem* to believe what he's saying — even if it's all stone crazy. McGovern learned this from George Wallace in Florida, and it proved to be a very valuable lesson. One of the crucial moments of the '72 primary campaign came on election night in Florida, March 14th, when McGovern—who had finished a dismal sixth, behind even Lindsay and Muskie—refused to follow Big Ed's sour example and blame his poor showing on that Evil Racist Monster, George Wallace, who had just swept every county in the state. Moments after Muskie had appeared on all three networks to denounce the Florida results as tragic proof that at least half the voters were ignorant dupes and nazis, Mc-Govern came on and said that although he couldn't agree with some of the things Wallace said and stood for, he sympathized with the people who'd voted for "The Governor" because they were "angry and fed up" with some of the things that are happening in this country.

"I feel the same way," he added. "But unlike Governor Wallace, I've proposed *constructive solutions* to these problems."

Nobody applauded when he said that. The two hundred or

273

so McGovern campaign workers who were gathered that night in the ballroom of the old Waverly Hotel on Biscayne Boulevard were not in a proper mood to cheer any praise for George Wallace. Their candidate had just been trounced by what they considered a dangerous bigot—and now, at the tail end of the loser's traditional concession statement, McGovern was saying that he and Wallace weren't really that far apart.

It was not what the ballroom crowd wanted to hear at that moment. Not after listening to Muskie denounce Wallace as a cancer in the soul of America . . . but McGovern wasn't talking to the people in that ballroom; he was making a very artful pitch to potential Wallace voters in the other primary states. Wisconsin was three weeks away, then Pennsylvania, Ohio, Michigan—and Wallace would be raising angry hell in every one of them. McGovern's brain-trust, though, had come up with the idea that the Wallace vote was "soft"—that the typical Wallace voter, especially in the North and Midwest, was far less committed to Wallace himself than to his thundering, gut-level appeal to rise up and smash all the "pointy-headed bureaucrats in Washington" who'd been fucking them over for so long.

The root of the Wallace magic was a cynical, showbiz instinct for knowing exactly which issues would whip a hall full of beer-drinking factory workers into a frenzy—and then doing exactly that, by howling down from the podium that he had an instant, overnight cure for all their worst afflictions: Taxes? Nigras? Army worms killing the turnip crop? Whatever it was, Wallace assured his supporters that the solution was actually *real simple,* and that the only reason they had any hassle with the government at all was because those greedy bloodsuckers in Washington didn't *want* the problems solved, so they wouldn't be put out of work.

The ugly truth is that Wallace had never even bothered to *understand* the problems—much less come up with any honest solutions—but "the Fighting Little Judge" has never lost much sleep from guilt feelings about his personal credibility gap. Southern politicians are not made that way. Successful con men are treated with considerable respect in the South. A good slice of the settler population of that region were men who'd been given a choice between being shipped off to the New World in leg-irons and spending the rest of their lives in English prisons. The Crown saw no point in feeding them year after year, and they were far too dangerous to be turned loose on the streets of London—so, rather than overload the public hanging schedule, the King's Minister of Gaol decided to put this scum to work on the other side of the Atlantic, in The Colonies, where cheap labor was much in demand.

Most of these poor bastards wound up in what is now the Deep South because of the wretched climate. No settler with good sense and a few dollars in his pocket would venture south of Richmond. There was plenty of opportunity around Boston, New York, and Philadelphia—and by British standards the climate in places like South Carolina and Georgia was close to Hell on Earth: swamps, alligators, mosquitos, tropical disease . . . all this plus a boiling sun all day long and no way to make money unless you had a land grant from the King . . .

So the South was sparsely settled at first, and the shortage of skilled labor was a serious problem to the scattered aristocracy of would-be cotton barons who'd been granted huge tracts of good land that would make them all rich if they could only get people to work it.

The slave-trade was one answer, but Africa in 1699 was not a fertile breeding ground for middle-management types . . . and the planters said it was damn near impossible for one white man to establish any kind of control over a boatload of black primitives. The bastards couldn't even speak English. How could a man get the crop in, with brutes like that for help?

There would have to be managers, keepers, overseers: white men who spoke the language, and had a sense of purpose in life. But where would they come from? There was no middle class in the South: only masters and slaves . . . and all that rich land lying fallow.

The King was quick to grasp the financial implications of the problem: The crops *must* be planted and harvested, in order to sell them for gold—and if all those lazy bastards needed was a few thousand half-bright English-speaking lackeys in order to bring the crops in . . . hell, that was easy: Clean out the jails, cut back on the Crown's grocery bill, jolt the liberals off balance by announcing a new "Progressive Amnesty" program for hardened criminals. . . .

Wonderful. Dispatch royal messengers to spread the good word in every corner of the kingdom; and after that send out professional pollsters to record an amazing 66 percent jump in the King's popularity . . . then wait a few weeks before announcing the new 10 percent sales tax on ale.

That's how the South got settled. Not the whole story, perhaps, but it goes a long way toward explaining why George Wallace is the Governor of Alabama. He has the same smile as his great-grandfather—a thrice-convicted pig thief from somewhere near Nottingham, who made a small reputation, they say, as a jailhouse lawyer, before he got shipped out.

Indeed. With a bit of imagination you can almost hear the cranky litle bastard haranguing his fellow prisoners in London's infamous Hardcase jail, urging them on to revolt:

"Lissen here, you poor fools! There's not much time! Even now —up there in the tower—they're cookin up some kind of cruel new punishment for us! How much longer will we stand for it? And now they want to ship us across the ocean to work like slaves in a swamp with a bunch of goddamn Hottentots!

"We won't go! It's asinine! We'll tear this place apart before we'll let that thieving old faggot of a king send us off to work *next to Africans!*

"How much more of this misery can we stand, boys? I know you're fed right up to *here* with it. I can see it in your eyes—pure misery! And I'm tellin' you, we don't have to stand for it! We can send the king a message and tell him how we feel! I'll write it up myself, and all you boys can sign it . . . or better still, I'll go talk to the king personally! All you boys have to do is dig me a little tunnel under the wall over there behind the gallows, and I'll. . . ."

Right. That bottom line never changes: "You folks be sure and come to see me in the White House, you hear? There'll be plenty of room for my friends, after I clean house . . . but first I need your vote, folks, and after that I'll. . . ."

George Wallace is one of the worst charlatans in politics, but there is no denying his talent for converting frustration into energy. What McGovern sensed in Florida, however—while Wallace was

stomping him, along with all the others—was the possibility that Wallace appealed instinctively to a lot more people than would actually vote for him. He was stirring up more anger than he knew how to channel. The frustration was there, and it was easy enough to convert it—but what then? If Wallace had taken himself seriously as a presidential candidate—as a Democrat or anything else—he might have put together the kind of organization that would have made him a genuine threat in the primaries, instead of just a spoiler.

McGovern, on the other hand, had put together a fantastic organization—but until he went into Wisconsin he had never tried to tap the kind of energy that seemed to be flowing, perhaps by default, to Wallace. He had given it some thought while campaigning in New Hampshire, but it was only after he beat Muskie in two blue-collar, hardhat wards in the middle of Manchester that he saw the possibility of a really mind-bending coalition: a weird mix of peace freaks and hardhats, farmers and film stars, along with urban blacks, rural chicanos, the "youth vote" . . . a coalition that could elect almost anybody.

Muskie had croaked in Florida, allowing himself to get crowded over on the Right with Wallace, Jackson, and Humphrey—then finishing a slow fourth behind all three of them. At that point in the race, Lindsay's presumptuous blueprint was beginning to look like prophecy. The New Hampshire embarrassment had forced Muskie off center in a mild panic, and now the party was polarized. The road to Wisconsin was suddenly clear in both lanes, fast traffic to the Left and the Right. The only mobile hazard was a slow-moving hulk called "The Muskie Bandwagon," creeping erratically down what his doom-stricken Media Manager called "that yellow stripe in the middle of the road."

The only other bad casualty, at that point, was Lindsay. His Wisconsin managers had discovered a fatal flaw in the blueprint: Nobody had bothered to specify the name of the candidate who would seize all that high ground on the Left, once Muskie got knocked off center. Whoever drew it up had apparently been told that McGovern would not be a factor in the later stages of the race. After absorbing two back-to-back beatings in New Hampshire and Florida, he would run out of money and be dragged off to the nearest glue factory . . . or, failing that, to some cut-rate retirement farm for old liberals with no charisma.

But something went wrong, and when Lindsay arrived in Wisconsin to seize that fine high ground on the Left that he knew, from his blueprint, was waiting for him—he found it already occupied, sealed off, and well-guarded on every perimeter, by a legion of hard-eyed fanatics in the pay of George McGovern.[1]

Gene Pokorny, McGovern's 25-year-old field organizer for Wisconsin, had the whole state completely wired. He had been on the job, full time, since the spring of '71—working off a blueprint remarkably similar to Lindsay's. But they were not quite the same. The main difference was painfully obvious, yet it was clear at a glance that both drawings had been done from the same theory: Muskie would fold early on, because The Center was not only indefensible but probably nonexistent . . . and after that the Democratic race would boil down to a quick civil war, a running death-battle between the Old Guard on the Right and a gang of Young Strangers on the Left.

The name-slots on Lindsay's blueprint were still empty, but the working assumption was that the crunch in California would come down to Muskie on the Right and Lindsay on the Left.

Pokorny's drawing was a year or so older than Lindsay's, and all the names were filled in—all the way to California, where the last two slots said, "McGovern" and "Humphrey." The only other difference between the two was that Lindsay's was unsigned, while Pokorny's had a signature in the bottom right-hand corner: "Hart, Mankiewicz & McGovern—architects."

Even Lindsay's financial backers saw the handwriting on the wall in Wisconsin. By the time he arrived, there was not even any *low ground* on the Left to be seized. The Lindsay campaign had

---

1. Later that summer Tom Morgan, Lindsay's press secretary, came out to Colorado and we spent a few days fishing for garbage eels on the banks of the Roaring Fork River. "We all admired that stuff you wrote about the Lindsay blueprint," he told me. "But there was one thing you didn't know— there was no Lindsay blueprint. There wasn't even any Lindsay strategy. We just winged it all the way from the start."

been keyed from the start on the assumption that Muskie would at least have the strength to retire McGovern before he abandoned the center. It made perfect sense, on paper—but 1972 had not been a vintage year for paper wisdom, and McGovern's breakthrough victory in Wisconsin was written off as "shocking" and "freakish" by a lot of people who should have known better.

Wisconsin was the place where he found a working model for the nervous coalition that made the rest of the primary campaign a downhill run. Wisconsin effectively eliminated every obstacle but the corpse of Hubert Humphrey—who fought like a rabid skunk all the way to the end; cranked up on the best speed George Meany's doctors could provide for him, taking his cash and his orders every midnight from Meany's axe-man Al Barkan; and attacking McGovern savagely, day after day, from every treacherous angle Big Labor's sharpest researchers could even crudely define for him . . .

It was a nasty swansong for Hubert. He'd been signing those IOUs to Big Labor for more than twenty years, and it must have been a terrible shock to him when Meany called them all due at the same time.

But how? George Meany, the 77-year-old quarterback of the "Stop McGovern Movement," is said to be suffering from brain bubbles at this stage of the game. Totally paralyzed. His henchmen have kept him in seclusion ever since he arrived in Florida five days ago with a bad case of The Fear. He came down from AFL-CIO headquarters in Washington by train, but had to be taken off somewhere near Fort Lauderdale and rushed to a plush motel where his condition deteriorated rapidly over the weekend, and finally climaxed on Monday night when he suffered a terrible stroke while watching the Democratic Convention on TV.

The story is still shrouded in mystery, despite the best efforts of the five thousand ranking journalists who came here to catch Meany's last act, but according to a wealthy labor boss who said he was there when it happened, the old man went all to pieces when his creature, Hubert Humphrey, lost the crucial "California challenge."

He raged incoherently at the Tube for eight minutes without drawing a breath, then suddenly his face turned beet red and his head swelled up to twice its normal size. Seconds later—while his henchmen looked on in mute horror—Meany swallowed his tongue, rolled out of his chair like a log, and crawled through a plate glass window.

The confrontations with the Old Guard seldom come in public. There are conversations on the telephone, plans are laid, people are put to work, and it's done quietly. California is a classic. There will never be a case in American politics of such a naked power grab—straight power, no principle, straight opportunism. I wasn't aware of it. I thought it was a purely defensive move to protect themselves against attack. We were naive. It never occurred to me that anybody would challenge California—until the last 36 hours before the credentials committee meeting. Then we really got scared when we saw the ferocity of their attack.

—George McGovern, talking to *LIFE*
reporter Richard Meryman in Miami

What happened in Miami was far too serious for the kind of random indulgence that Gonzo Journalism needs. The Real Business happened, as usual, on secret-numbered telephones or behind closed doors at the other end of long hotel corridors blocked off by sullen guards. There were only two crucial moments in Miami —two potential emergencies that might have changed the outcome —and both of them were dealt with in strict privacy.

The only real question in Miami was whether or not McGovern might be stripped of more than half of the 271 delegates he won in the California primary—and that question was scheduled to come up for a vote by the whole convention on Monday night. If the "ABM Movement" could strip 151 of those delegates away, McGovern might be stopped—because without them he had anywhere from 10 to 50 votes less than the 1509 that would give him the nomination on the first ballot. But if McGovern could hold his 271 California delegates, it was all over.

The "ABM Movement" (Anybody but McGovern) was a coalition of desperate losers, thrown together at the last moment by Big Labor chief George Meany and his axe-man, Al Barkan. Hubert Humphrey was pressed into service as the front man for ABM, and

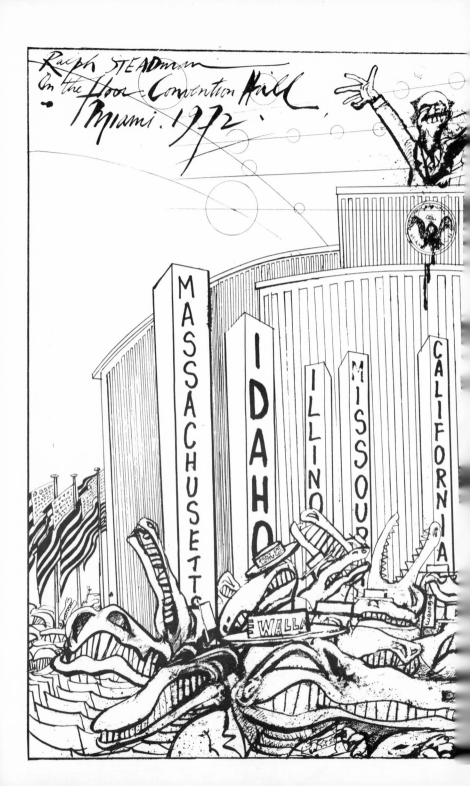

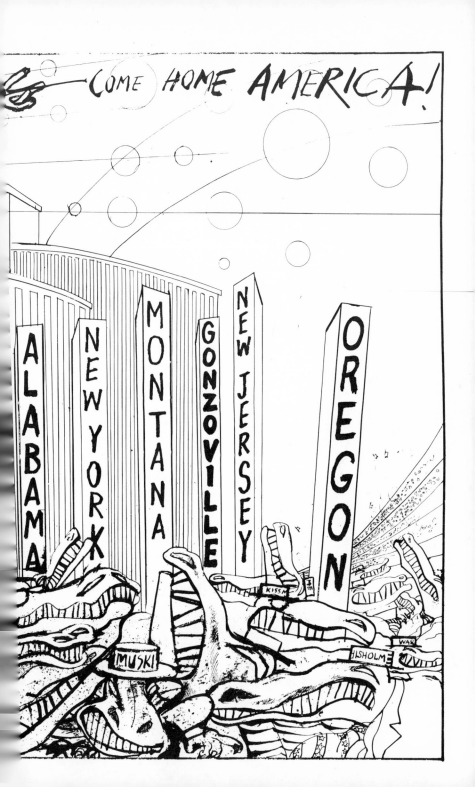

he quickly signed up the others: Big Ed, Scoop Jackson, Terry Sanford, Shirley Chisholm—all the heavies.

The ABM movement came together officially sometime in the middle of the week just before the convention, when it finally became apparent that massive fraud, treachery, or violence was the only way to prevent McGovern from getting the nomination . . . and what followed, once this fact was accepted by all parties involved, will hopefully go down in history as one of the most shameful episodes in the history of the Democratic process.

It was like a scene from the final hours of the Roman Empire: Everywhere you looked, some prominent politician was degrading himself in public. By noon on Sunday both Humphrey and Muskie were so desperate that they came out of their holes and appeared— trailing a mob of photographers and TV crews—in the lobby of the Fontainebleau, the nexus hotel about five hundred yards down the beach from the Doral, racing back and forth from one caucus or press conference to another, trying to make any deal available— on any terms—that might possibly buy enough votes to deny McGovern a first-ballot victory.

The ABM strategy—a very shrewd plan, on paper—was to hold McGovern under the 1500 mark for two ballots, forcing him to peak without winning, then confront the convention with an alternative (ABM) candidate on the third ballot—and if that failed, try *another* ABM candidate on the fourth ballot, then yet another on the fifth, etc. . . . on into infinity, for as many ballots as it would take to nominate somebody acceptable to the Meany/Daley axis.

The name didn't matter. It didn't even make much difference if He, She, or It couldn't possibly beat Nixon in November . . . the only thing that mattered to the Meany/Daley crowd was *keeping control of The Party;* and this meant the nominee would have to be some loyal whore with more debts to Big Labor than he could ever hope to pay . . . somebody like Hubert Humphrey, or a hungry opportunist like Terry Sanford.

Anybody but George McGovern—the only candidate in Miami that week who would be under no obligation to give either Meany or Daley his private number if he ever moved into the White House.

But all that noxious bullshit went by the boards, in the end. The ABM got chewed up like green hamburger on opening night. They were beaten stupid at their own game by a handful of weird-looking kids who never even worked up a sweat. By midnight on Monday it was all over. Once McGovern got a lock on those 271 delegates, there was never any doubt about who would get the nomination on Wednesday.

The blow-by-blow story of how McGovern beat the ABM will become an instant fixture in political science textbooks, regardless of who wins in November—but it's not an easy thing to explain. If a transcript existed, it would read more like an extremely complicated murder trial than the simple, out-front political convention that most people think they watched on TV. Trying to understand the byzantine reality of that convention on TV—or even on the floor, for that matter—was like somebody who's never played chess trying to understand a live telecast of the Fisher/Spassky world championship duel up in Iceland.

The bedrock truths of the McGovern convention were not aired on TV—except once, very briefly on Monday night; but it hardly mattered, because all three networks missed it completely. When the deal went down, Walter Cronkite saw green and called it red, John Chancellor opted for yellow, and ABC was already off the air.

What happened, in a nut, was a surprise parliamentary maneuver—cooked up by over-ambitious strategists in the Women's Caucus—forcing a premature showdown that effectively decided whether or not McGovern would get the nomination. The crisis came early, at a time when most of the TV/Press people were still getting their heads ready to deal with all the intricate possibilities of the vote on the ABM challenge to McGovern's California delegates . . . and when Larry O'Brien announced a pending roll-call vote on whether or not the South Carolina delegation included enough women, very few people on the Floor or anywhere else understood that the result of that roll-call would also be an accurate forecast of how many delegates would later vote for McGovern on the California challenge, and then on the first ballot.

On the evidence, less than a dozen of the five thousand "media" sleuths accredited to the convention knew exactly what was happening, at the time. When McGovern's young strategists *deliberately lost* that vote, almost everybody who'd watched it—including Walter Cronkite—concluded that McGovern didn't have a hope in hell of winning any roll-call vote from that point on: which meant the ABM could beat him on the California challenge, reducing his strength even further, and then stop him cold on the first ballot.

Humphrey's campaign manager, Jack Chestnut, drew the same conclusion—a glaring mistake that almost immediately became the subject of many crude jokes in McGovern's press room at the Doral, where a handful of resident correspondents who'd been attached to the campaign on a live-in basis for many months were watching the action on TV with press secretary Dick Dougherty and a room full of tense staffers—who roared with laughter when Cronkite, far up in his soundproof booth two miles away in the Convention Hall, announced that CBS was about to switch to McGovern headquarters in the Doral, where David Schoumacher was standing by with a firsthand report and at least one painfully candid shot of McGovern workers reacting to the news of this stunning setback.

The next scene showed a room full of laughing, whooping people. Schoumacher was grinning into his microphone, saying: "I don't want to argue with you, Walter—but why are these people cheering?"

Schoumacher then explained that McGovern had actually won the nomination by losing the South Carolina vote. It had been a test of strength, no doubt—but what had never been explained to the press or even to most of McGovern's own delegates on the floor, was that he had the option of "winning" that roll-call by going either up or down . . . and the only way the ABM crowd could have won was by juggling their votes to make sure the South Carolina challenge *almost* won, but not quite. This would have opened the way for a series of potentially disastrous parliamentary moves by the Humphrey-led ABM forces.

"We had to either win decisively or lose decisively," Rick Stearns explained later. "We couldn't afford a close vote."

Stearns, a 28-year-old Rhodes Scholar from Stanford, was McGovern's point man when the crisis came. His job in Miami—working out of a small white trailer full of telephones behind the Convention Hall—was to tell Gary Hart, on the floor, exactly how

many votes McGovern could muster at any given moment, on any question—and it was Stearns who decided, after only ten out of fifty states had voted on the South Carolina challenge, that the final tally might be too close to risk. So he sent word to Hart on the floor, and Gary replied: "Okay, if we can't win big—let's lose it."

The old bulls never quit until the young bulls run them out. The old bulls are dead, but don't forget that the young bulls eventually become old bulls too.

—James H. Rowe, "an old professional
from FDR's days," in *Time* Magazine

The next time I saw Rick Stearns, after he croaked the Humphrey/Meany squeeze play on Monday night, was out on the beach in front of the Doral on Saturday afternoon. He was smoking a cigar and carrying a tall plastic glass of beer—wearing his black and red Stanford tank shirt. I sat with him for a while and we talked as the Coast Guard cutters cruised offshore about a hundred yards from the beach and National Guard helicopters and jets thundered

McGovern strategist Rick Stearns plotting floor strategy with Wisconsin Governor Pat Lucey.

overhead. It was the first time in ten days I'd had a chance to feel any sun and by midnight I was burned, drunk, and unable to get any sleep—waking up every fifteen minutes to rub more grease on my head and shoulders.

What follows is a 98 percent verbatim transcript of my tape recording of that conversation. The other 2 percent was deleted in the editing process for reasons having to do with a journalist's obligation to "protect" his sources—even if it sometimes means protecting them from themselves and their own potentially disastrous indiscretions.

HST: I was reading Haynes Johnson's thing in the Washington *Post* about how you won South Carolina. He mainly had it from Humphrey's side; he cited the fact that it fooled almost everybody. He said only a few McGovern staffers knew.

Stearns: No, that's not true. The guys in the trailer operation knew. The floor leaders, the ones who paid attention, knew; but some of them were just following instructions.

HST: That was it, more or less?

Stearns: That was it, although if you have that many people who know, chances are . . .

HST: Well, I was standing with Tom Morgan, Lindsay's press secretary; I don't know if anybody told him, but he figured it out. Then I went out in the hall and saw Tom Braden, the columnist. He said, "Oh, Jesus! Terrible! A bad defeat." Then I was really confused.

Stearns: Johnny Apple of the New York *Times* rushed out and filed the story which went to [*Times* Managing Editor] Abe Rosenthal. Rosenthal was sitting watching Walter Cronkite sputter on about the great setback the McGovern forces had, you know, the terrible defeat. So he killed Apple's story.

HST: Jesus!

Stearns: Apple got on the phone to Rosenthal and they had a shouting match for thirty minutes that ended with Apple resigning from the N.Y. *Times*.

HST: Cazart!

Stearns: But he was hired back at the end of the next day. They never ran his story, but he was hired back at what I assume was a substantial increase in his salary.

HST: There was a reference in Johnson's story to a private discussion on Sunday. He said you'd explained the strategy twenty-four hours earlier.

Stearns: Let's see. What could that have been? The floor leaders meeting?

HST: He didn't say. You saw it coming that early? Sunday? Or even before that? When did you see the thing coming?

Stearns: It became clear during the maneuvering that went on the week before the Convention when we were trying to define several key parliamentary points.

HST: You'd seen this coming up all the week before during this maneuvering with [Larry] O'Brien and [James G.] O'Hara [the convention parliamentarian]?

Stearns: Well, I'd seen it as of Thursday when we began to get some idea of how O'Brien and O'Hara intended to rule on the two issues, but as early as then we were going over a whole war game of possible parliamentary contingencies. The Humphrey camp would have never turned to procedural chicanery if they'd really had a working majority on the floor. The essential point is that procedure is the last defense of a vanishing majority.

Stearns: First, who could vote, under the rules, on their own challenge? Did the rule which says a delegate can vote on anything but his own challenge mean that the 120 McGovern delegates from California not being challenged would be able to vote? We contended that they could. Eventually the chairman agreed.

The second and most important question was the question of what constituted a majority—whether it was a constitutional majority, or, as we originally contended, a majority of those present-and-voting. The chair's decision on that was a compromise between the two rules—that the majority would be determined by those *eligible* to vote. And he ruled then that since everyone but 153 bogus delegates from California were eligible, the majority on the California question would be 1433. So, in other words, we won the first point on who could vote. On the second point we came up with a compromise which was really to our advantage . . .

HST: What did you lose on that?

Stearns: Well, the only thing we lost was that, if it had been present-and-voting, it would have meant that we could have picked up extra votes by urging people just not to vote: if they were caught between pressures from labor on one hand and us on the other and couldn't find any way out of the dilemma, they could leave, and their absence then would lower the majority.

On the third issue we . . .

[*Helicopter*]

HST: Damn! Fuck! I can't believe those fuckin' helicopters! I'll leave it on the tape just to remind me how bad it was.

Stearns: The LEAA [the Federal Law Enforcement Assistance Act] . . .

HST: Oh, it's one of those pork barrel . . .

Stearns: . . . One thing Jerry and Abbie did for the city of Miami was to beef up the technology of the police department with that grant Miami got to buy all this stuff . . .

Well, the third point—which we lost and which we were arguing obviously because it was in our interest—was that the challenges ought to be considered in the order of the roll-call. This would have put California first and would have avoided the problem entirely, of course. On that, the chair ruled against us, and I think fairly. He followed the precedent of the last Conventions, which was that challenges were to be considered in the order in which the Credentials Committee had discussed them. That meant that we had South Carolina, Alabama, Georgia, and Kentucky—four possible test cases—coming before we got to the California vote.

Stearns: Kentucky we got withdrawn, eliminating one of them. [Dr. John] Cashin's Alabama challenge was the same challenge he brought in '68. It's not a very attractive challenge. A lot of people felt that they had been misled by Cashin in '68, including blacks, and were not disposed to work for him again. He was trying to get Wallace thrown out of the Convention. Wallace's slate had been openly elected. Alabama was one of the first states in the country to comply with the reform rules. Voters happened to choose Wallace delegates. [*Airplane*] So we knew the Alabama challenge would be defeated on a voice vote. On Georgia, Julian [Bond] and Governor Jimmy Carter worked out a compromise. South Carolina was the only possible test vote to come up before the California challenge.

There were two procedural issues that the Humphrey coalition wanted to settle on the South Carolina challenge. The first was that question of *who* could vote. The chair ruled that there were nine South Carolinian women who had not been challenged, who would be entitled to vote on the challenge. It is a thirty-two-member delegation, which meant that there were then twenty-three South Carolinians who were disqualified.

The second area of challenge—and the most troublesome—is what constituted a majority. That was what the Humphrey people went after first. The maneuvering that was going on! There was only one way that the question of what constituted a majority could arise, and that was if either side prevailed in the range of 1497 to 1508 votes. If either side prevailed by more than a constitutional majority, 1509, the question is moot.

It sounds impossible to maneuver a vote into that area, but in fact it's very easy if you have a Humphrey delegation controlled as well as Ohio. Ohio passed and passed and passed. All Frank King, their chairman, had to do was sit there, add correctly, cast the vote accordingly and we would have been in that area.[2] Not only that, we would have been sucked into that area with an *artificial* vote from the Ohio delegation, which means that on the procedural test . . .

[*Helicopter*]

HST: You son of a bitch!

Stearns: If we'd let ourselves be sucked into that trap, I think

---

2. Several months later I was sitting on the pool terrace at the Washington Hilton Hotel, eating honeydew melons with Anthony Lucas. He had just come back from Ohio where he had spent a few days with Frank King in connection with an article he was writing for the New York *Times* magazine section. "You know I think you gave King too much credit," he said. "I asked him about all that byzantine maneuvering Rick Stearns told you was going on in Miami on the South Carolina challenge but he didn't know what I was talking about. I doubt if King ever knew what was really going on that night."

we would have lost both the procedural tests.

HST: I see. They could lend you votes on one roll-call, then take them back on the next one.

Stearns: A bogus count. If you look at the tally on the South Carolina challenge, the Minnesota delegation on which Humphrey had thirty-five hard-core votes went 56-to-8 for the South Carolina challenge, so there were at least thirty-five votes that the Humphrey coalition could have manipulated. In Ohio, Humphrey had as many as eighty votes that could have been cast any way that Humphrey forces chose to cast them . . .

So our problem was to maneuver ourselves around the Ohio delegation in a way that the Ohio votes could not be cast to force us into a test vote on California before we got to the real issue. And remember, to win a procedural test on California, it would only require turning out 1433 votes, but South Carolina would have had to have 1497 votes to win the same procedural question as to who could vote and what constituted a majority.

HST: That's why you wanted to put the showdown off till California?

Stearns: The numbers were much better for us on California than they were on South Carolina.

HST: I was asking [McGovern pollster] Pat Caddell why you didn't just want to get it over with, and he was running back and forth on the floor and just said, "Well, we want to wait for California." But he never explained why.

Stearns: It was the difference in what was the working majority on the floor. Plus, it's much harder to hold delegates on procedural questions since they don't understand the significance of a parliamentary point. Everyone had gotten clear enough instructions on how to handle California that I think they were aware of the procedural problem if it had arisen with the California vote, which it did.

My instructions to our floor leaders and to our delegation chairmen was that on the first twelve tallies we would go all out to win the South Carolina minority report challenges. Perhaps not *all* out. We would go out to win, but not to the extent of jeopardizing votes we had on the California challenge. If there was somebody whose support we knew we had on California, but weren't sure if he would be able to withstand pressure from labor, Humphrey, or whoever else, they were *not* to bother the guy. We didn't want to sacrifice votes on California. But that aside, we went after that challenge. That didn't quite work, because I had a number of passes in the first twelve states that reported, which meant that I put off the decision another eight or nine tallies.

HST: The passes weren't for political reasons, but because they couldn't make up their minds?

Stearns: Well, one for political reasons—that was the Ohio delegation, which was passing so it could put itself in the position of voting *last,* so it could maneuver the vote and throw us into the procedural test. The others, just because it took a long time to get the counting done in the delegation.

HST: What was the women's angle? It was talked about like it was some kind of shameful trip or something.

Stearns: The Women's Caucus was disputing the fact that only nine members of the thirty-two-member delegation were women. The women made the South Carolina Minority Report their test vote to the Convention. I personally don't think they had a terribly good case.

Their case was based on a misunderstanding of the McGovern guidelines. The misunderstanding was thinking that quotas had somehow been established. What the McGovern commission argued was that *quotas would be imposed if the state did not take effective steps to see that women were represented in reasonable proportions.* That is, they had to take down all the barriers to women being elected, but there was no guarantee in the guidelines that because a woman was a woman, she was necessarily going to be elected. The guidelines attempted to give women the same chance of election that men had, removing some of the obstacles that kept them off slates in the past.

It was not a terribly good challenge in the first place, but no credentials challenge has ever really been decided strictly on the justice and merits of the challenge. They all come down to essentially political questions and in that case the Women's Caucus made what was in effect a weak challenge into a political issue. So it had to be treated seriously. This is why we set out at the beginning to try to win it, to try to see if we had the votes to win it the first time around.

HST: You're saying it was sort of forced on you?

Stearns: Well, it was, but I don't think the Women's Caucus really understood the significance of an early test vote. I would have much preferred that they would have picked—well, they had a much better case in Hawaii, for example, because the challenge came up after both the California and Illinois decisions. If we had to have a test vote on a women's issue, I'd rather they had picked a stronger case, Hawaii, which also would have moved the test vote *after California.*

HST: Why did they insist on being first?

Stearns: I'm not sure of the process they went through to pick South Carolina, but they had chosen it, and that made the issue of South Carolina one that we had to respond to as a political question.

HST: But they weren't somehow hooked into the Chisholm/Humphrey/Stop McGovern thing in order to get some bargaining power?

Stearns: I think there may have been some thought of that—the fact that it was to come first would give them some leverage with us that they might otherwise not have had . . . But my intentions were to *win* that California challenge.

[*Also on the beach is Bill Dougherty, Lieutenant Governor of South Dakota, longtime McGovern crony and a key floor leader who worked under Stearns. Forty-two years old, he is wearing trunks and a short-sleeve shirt and staring at the surf.*]

Dougherty: You know, this is the first time I've ever seen the ocean. Oh, I *saw* it out in California, but not like this. Not close up.

HST: Were you over there for the Democratic National Committee meeting yesterday morning [Friday]?

Dougherty: Shit, I never got out of bed all day yesterday. I'm on the national committee. I've got McGovern really pissed at me. I never showed up. I couldn't move. I absolutely couldn't move

McGovern chats with Bella Abzug and Gloria Steinem at the Women's Caucus twenty-four hours before pulling the plug.

McGovern with press secretary Dick Dougherty monitoring Larry O'Brien's handling of the Convention from their penthouse command post at the Doral Beach Hotel.

yesterday. I was sick. I was just sick, physically.

HST: Well, there's a lot of people that are sick . . .

Stearns: I've never been as exhausted as I was on Wednesday night [after McGovern's nomination, but six or so hours *before* the series of staff conferences that led to Eagleton's selection as the VP nominee].

Dougherty: I was going home yesterday, but I couldn't get to the airport. No shit. I didn't sleep at all between Saturday and Wednesday, I think it was . . . and I don't think I ever sat down until yesterday, 'cause I was working hotels.

Stearns: I got two hours of sleep in three days.

HST: This had been the least fun to me of all the things since I've been on this trip. It seems like it would have been at least . . . this is the first time I've been on the beach, except at night or around dawn—when I came down to swim a few times.

[*Tape halts momentarily here, then jumps to preparations for the Convention . . .*]

Stearns: Gary Hart and I came down in May to talk to Southern Bell and outline the communications equipment we wanted for the Convention. See, we ran a two-tier operation. We had 250 whips on the floor, people we'd selected from each delegation to make sure that somebody was talking to the individual delegates. We had one person in every row of the Convention giving instructions somewhere. Then we had our floor leaders, Bill, Pierre Salinger, and so on and then our delegation chairmen. We had two ways to get to them. We had a boiler room here at the hotel, which was plugged into the SCOPE system. You'd call in at whip level.

HST: Which color phone did that come into?

Dougherty: White.

HST: And you had a different color. A red phone?

Dougherty: Blue phone.

Stearns: We had a blue phone for the floor leaders and delegation chairmen.

HST: Who was there in the boiler room at the [Doral Beach/ McGov. Headquarters] hotel?

Stearns: There were ten people. The western director was Barbara McKenzie. Doug Coulter did the Mountain States. Judy Harrington did the Plains States. Scott Lilly did the Central States,

Illinois, Missouri, Kentucky. Gail Channing did Ohio and Michigan. Laura Mizelle did the Pennsylvania, New Jersey, Delaware area. Tony Babb did the New York delegation, Puerto Rico; and Alan Kriegle did the New England States. They were in charge of the whips who were on the floor. They had worked for over a year in Washington as the liaison with regional areas of the campaign, handling the detail work, running to the delegates . . . the group we had in the trailer were the best of our field organizers.

HST: Were the hotel boiler room phones wired right to the floor, or into the trailer?

Stearns: Right to the floor . . . I had a point-to-point line between them and me. Then that red phone in the office, I'd pick that up and it rang automatically at the hotel.

Dougherty: We on the floor could get either place.

HST: Was it completely triangular ?

Stearns: Oh no. We oversaw a full communications system. You could go anywhere with the communications we had.

HST: There wasn't one main nexus where everything had to go through?

Stearns: There was a switchboard here at the Doral. The way instructions went out is that I would stand up in the back of the trailer and shout "NO" and then pick up that red phone which would ring automatically [on the floor & in the Doral "situation room"] and someone would pick it up and I'd say "NO" and then everyone knew that they were to instruct everyone to vote no on that. That way you had two tries at making sure the instructions got through.

Dougherty: David Schoumacher of CBS has a film of you in the trailer with a cigar in your mouth shouting "NO." They're gonna run it Sunday night.

Stearns: When will it be on?

Dougherty: I think *Sixty Minutes.* He said you got a cigar in your mouth. He said, "Boy, Dougherty, does this spoil the grassroots flavor of your campaign." Of course, Schoumacher just loves it.

HST: Let's get back. You came down in May to set up your communications.

Stearns: We had to protect the communications system in the trailer and the communications system in the hotel, so we traced the telephone lines and there were two points where it was vulnerable. In the Convention center it was behind five link fences and pretty well guarded; but you had open manhole covers. The telephone lines here are laid very close to the surface—it's an artificial peninsula and you hit water if you dig any deeper than twelve feet —so anyone who could open a manhole cover could get into any of the telephone lines . . .

HST: If they knew where they were.

Stearns: If you knew where they were. But chances are any manhole cover you pick up in this city you're gonna find telephone lines laid under it. We pointed that out to Southern Bell, and they suggested that we weld the manhole covers down, which we agreed to. The only other vulnerable point was in the hotel itself. There is a switching room at the backside of the hotel behind the room where all the press equipment was set up. That was the other vulnerable spot. So we had an armed guard placed on that. A guy with an axe could have demolished that communications system in thirty seconds.

Dougherty: You can do some of those things at a Convention, 'cause everybody forgets about it five days after it happens. Once the vote goes in, they don't recall any situation even where the crookedest of things may have changed it. There's no protest. There have been terrible things that happen at Conventions.

HST: Yeah, I'm surprised this thing went off as well as it did. You were dealing with a gang of real scum, the kind of people Barkan and Meany & those AFL-CIO people could have brought in . . .

Stearns: Well, they did. They brought them in, but we beat them . . .

HST: I mean people with axes—that kind of thing.

Stearns: Oh, yeah, they wouldn't have hesitated if they'd had the chance.

Dougherty: I'll tell you, one of the things we had going for us: You know how tough it is to keep communications going in *one* camp? The Stop McGovern movement had to keep communications going in *four* camps—try to coordinate all the communications of four camps at a national convention . . .

We could have won the South Carolina challenge if we were absolutely sure of every vote. We were getting votes out of places like Minnesota that we never expected. But we had Ohio waiting with a delegation that Humphrey . . . I mean they had eighty or ninety votes with which they could have done the same thing we did.

HST: Was that Humphrey's accordion delegation—Ohio?

Stearns: Yes. With the eighty or ninety Humphrey delegates, Frank King could have sat up and read any set of figures he wanted. We had a few delegations like that, too, as you saw in the last moments of that challenge.

HST: Oh yeah, but I forget which ones . . .

Stearns: Colorado, Wisconsin, Nebraska, Rhode Island. In the last seven or eight minutes of that challenge we didn't even bother to poll the delegations; I was just reading the numbers that we expected them to cast. That was the best moment of the Convention: when [ex-Governor of Nebraska] Frank Morrison's first instructions were to cut that vote down to 14 and then Bill came rushing up the aisle to take four more.

Dougherty: No, it was 17, and then I changed it to 14. I was whispering right in his ear. They got a shot of that on TV, I guess.

Stearns: I heard.

HST: Was the Humphrey guy standing next to you? When you came up to Morrison, was there somebody there who knew what you were saying to him?

Dougherty: Johnny Apple [New York *Times* reporter] caught me.

HST: Kirby [Jones, McGovern press assistant] said that King was aware that one of your people was on him.

Dougherty: Oh, they were aware of it on the floor.

Stearns: That was Dick Sklar standing next to King. He was

300

our liaison for the Ohio delegation. He and Frank King did not get along.

Dougherty: That South Carolina deal with me, who loves politics, and this is my third Convention, it was so great . . . it was like getting your first piece of ass.

Stearns: [flinching] Bill can describe it better than I can—I mean, I can tell you what it was like sitting in the trailer—but Bill can describe it from working on the floor.

Dougherty: Oh, it was perfect. When I got the word to shave, I had about ten minutes. I couldn't go to the other side after the first night, 'cause I damn near got in a fist fight with the Governor. See, he moved in—you know he moved in a couple of alternates on us, and I wouldn't let him do it. And, God, he got madder 'n hell and he never spoke to me the rest of the Convention. So I had to go way over to the other side because I couldn't use that girl, 'cause she was sittin' right next to the Governor, and I had to lean over him to talk to her. And he was ready to punch me every time I leaned over.

So I ran clear out the other side and got ahold of our whip, then I came back around and got ahold of Mondragon and Ortez, or whatever his name is . . . I told him I wanted to get as many votes as I could get and it wasn't very many.

HST: When did you suddenly decide to start shaving?

Dougherty: Oh, Kansas was the key.

Stearns: Yeah, we counted it down to Kansas and then made the decision at that point that we were not going to win with a working majority of our own.

HST: How far along was that?

Stearns: That was the eleventh or twelfth vote.

Dougherty: But see, you didn't know the real count, because Ohio would pass . . .

Stearns: Right. Ohio would pass, is what screwed us up. So I had to wait for another four or five votes. We had our New York delegation pass.

HST: What number was Ohio?

301

Stearns: Ohio was, I think, eleven.

Dougherty: Kansas was eleven, wasn't it?

Stearns: That's right, Kansas.

Dougherty: Frank King, with his Ohio delegation, has passed on every roll-call since . . .

HST: It's sort of a political habit. You always want to have that leverage at the end, I suppose.

Dougherty: In the legislature you get the same thing, you get guys who pass all the time and wait to see how the vote is.

Stearns: But the question was whether we would throw New York's votes behind the challenge or hold New York out—but when they held out Ohio, I gave instructions to our New York delegates to pass the first time.

HST: That gave you a helluva cushion, right?

Stearns: Yeah, there was a lot to work with there.

Dougherty: Then we started shaving.

Stearns: Then we heard a few more votes just to get a better sense of where things were going, and then the instructions went out to start cutting.

Dougherty: See, we were afraid the Humphrey forces were gonna start going the other way, which, if they were really coordinated, they could have done.

HST: Well, wait a minute. What would have happened then?

Stearns: The game that was going on was to see who could push who over the 1509 mark first. If they'd pushed us up above 1509 with a lot of bogus votes, it would have been very hard to persuade our people to cut back then, 'cause if you think you've won, then the instinct is to go out and fight for every vote you can get your hands on. We tried to hold the obvious switches to the end. We started cutting votes at that point—hold the obvious ones to the end and suddenly throw a lot of votes on them, push them up over 1509, and then at that point the only way they can get out from under that is by abandoning one of their own. Governor West of South Carolina. They would have had to throw him to the wolves at that point.

HST: What do you mean by *they?* You people have been around longer than I have. What do you mean—exactly what would they have done to Governor West?

Dougherty: Well, they'd have to abandon him on the South Carolina challenge by changing their vote.

Stearns: Once they'd gone over 1509, they would have seated Governor West's delegation.

Dougherty: So to get back down under they'd have had to abandon him.

Stearns: When it really came down to it, they had less guts than we had. We were willing to sell out the women, but they weren't willing to sell out a Southern governor.

HST: When did King figure it out?

Stearns: Well, I think we were ahead of them almost from the beginning. It turned out our strategy confused them almost as much as it may have confused our own supporters.

HST: Johnson in the *Post* said it confused Jack Chestnut [Humphrey's campaign manager]. Johnson said the Humphrey people bought it completely; they were sitting there with him watching it on TV.

Stearns: Oh, they did. His aides interpreted it as a great victory. What confused them was the fact that we went out to win it at the beginning. They've been reading the columnists for a month about *undisciplined, unruly McGovern delegates,* and I think once they saw us start to win the South Carolina challenge, I think they relaxed. That was just what they *wanted* us to do. We needed to set out to win for some political reason because we couldn't sell out the women completely. If there was a chance to win it, then we had the obligation to try and win.

Dougherty: What did Chestnut say to Humphrey?

Stearns: He said, "We've given a great setback to McGovern." But Humphrey was smarter: Humphrey said, "No, they ran that deliberately . . . "

HST: Yeah, Humphrey said, "They're pulling it back." There was a TV pool reporter with him at the hotel. I was watching

Humphrey's face, and, Jesus, it just turned to wax. He looked the worst I've ever seen him—which makes me very happy, that son of a bitch. He should be buried with his head down in the sand. I've never been so disgusted with a human being in politics.

Dougherty: One thing, Humphrey isn't dumb. He's got a bunch of dumb guys around him.

Stearns: He's smart—he's been around a long time. He was the only one of that group who knew what was going on.

HST: According to Johnson, they thought they had it locked up until about halfway through—then all of a sudden they realized . . .

Stearns: Yeah, but we really did try to win at first, and I think they relaxed then. But with Ohio coming in, we had thirty bogus votes from Minnesota on that total. Maybe a few others—I have to go over the totals again—but Minnesota was what I caught, and then we had Ohio holding out to the end.

Stearns: King passed twice to make sure that his was the last vote that was cast. At that point I was trying to cut our total down to the point where no matter *how* he cast those votes, no matter how or what they did with those Ohio votes, there was no way they could push us into that area [where the Convention would have been forced to decide *what constituted a majority*—thus imperiling McGovern's chance for a first-ballot victory].

HST: So you just wanted to get as low as you could, once you decided to go down?

Stearns: Well, I didn't want to go as low as I *could,* I wanted a good vote for the women's challenge, but I wanted it just low enough that there was nothing King could do to re-write it.

HST: So it had to be almost 80 votes low.

Stearns: Yeah, I think we came in at about 1420 or 1430. And we were prepared to go lower. The number that I was aiming to get us down to was about 1410 and we had those lined up, but as we started taking the votes off, finally King gave up and went ahead and cast his vote. I think we cut it down to the figure where King couldn't win, and I think he realized that.

HST: When you say dropping it down, now, you mean *changes?*
Dougherty: When we had time, we shaved them and shaved again.
Stearns: Yeah, we cut them as they were cast and we were ready to change them after.

HST: Did you have to go back and do it? I've forgotten.
Stearns: A few of them, we did. We went back to Wisconsin. Wisconsin originally came through at 54, then we cut it down to 37. Oregon came through at 33 and we cut it down to 17 or whatever the figure was. I had Rhode Island ready too, I mean, they would have moved all 22 votes . . .
HST: You were hung between 1410 and a possible 1500?
Stearns: What I was aiming for was the figure at which Ohio could not have made a difference.
HST: Yeah, but the most you could have gotten—if you hadn't had that option of losing, when you saw you might not win—you think it was about 1500?
Stearns: Well, my feeling was that on the issue of the challenge itself we were stuck at around 1500. That was clear from the beginning and it would have been disastrous. To keep them from playing with the vote, we had to show them that we had the discipline on the floor, that there was nothing they could do at that point.
Dougherty: But it got tougher to hold that discipline as it went along.
HST: What Gary Hart was quoted as saying was that you couldn't afford to let them know you had control of the floor. Is that right?
Stearns: No, I think it's just the opposite. We wanted them to think that *we had the control.* Otherwise we would have been shifting votes all night.
HST: How long did that fencing with King go on? Did he fuck you up at any time?
Stearns: No, that was their one attempt at that.
HST: All he did was pass twice?
Stearns: No, Ohio passed three times, but I think they realized

the fourth time they came around that it was hopeless. They knew we had control.

HST: He didn't really make any moves except passing.

Stearns: He kept passing. His strategy was to have Ohio cast their votes last so they could manipulate Ohio votes *in a way that would have thrown us into the procedural test.*

Dougherty: We had some hard votes in Ohio, too—ones they couldn't move.

Stearns: Right, they couldn't move our Ohio votes, and as we began cutting that figure down, we finally got to the point where they realized we'd cut it down to zero if we had to.

HST: So his thing was mainly just waiting.

Stearns: To wait until the truth began to dawn on them, that we controlled the votes on the floor.

Dougherty: What we couldn't afford—hell, it became so obvious —we didn't want to get the women mad at us.

Stearns: Bill's point is very good: It got harder as you went along because the more that vote was pushed to 1509, the more our delegates wanted to go for a majority. That's just what the Humphrey coalition was trying to lure us into, trying to go all out to win the thing, win it with *their* votes which could have been pulled out from under us, and at that point psychologically to get our supporters to change would have almost been impossible.

Dougherty: I was getting nervous, myself.

Stearns: I know, I was getting all those phone calls back, but . . .

Dougherty: The delegates were all bitchin' at me. And I was pissed off.

HST: Why?

Dougherty: I was so worried about our delegates gettin' pissed off, 'cause they're all such a great bunch of nonpolitical professionals. I thought, "Ooh shit!" 'Cause, jeez, they got mad at me when I started shaving votes on some of those delegations. You know, "What are you trying to do?" and all that . . . I didn't have time to explain it. I just had to be hard and say, "Goddamn it! That's the way it's gonna be!"

HST: You mean the delegates themselves didn't know what was going on?

Dougherty: No! Shit, they weren't aware.

Stearns: Well, our whips knew. I held a briefing session with them on Monday, and I spent an hour and a half going over the possible parliamentary contingencies.

Dougherty: But the average delegate didn't know.

Stearns: There were perhaps 250 people on the floor who had a good idea of what was going on. There were another 50 or 60 who had a pretty *complete* idea of what was going on. And then there were about 20 who *knew* what was going on.

HST: Did state-level leaders like Diane White or Dick Perchlick in the Colorado delegation know what was happening?[3]

Stearns: No.

HST: That's amazing. Amazing you could do it. It must have been hell on the floor.

Stearns: It was. That one woman in Nebraska got so damn mad. Oh God, she was mad! But after they saw what it led to in the California vote, then we had a couple of days where we could say almost anything and people realized we weren't trying to . . .

Dougherty: That's when they learned discipline.

HST: Well, Jesus. It was really a helluva gamble then, wasn't it, given the kind of delegates that were there.

Stearns: Yeah, but you had to take it. We had a nomination at stake.

HST: What was the point then in sending Mankiewicz and Salinger and Hart out to call it a terrible defeat on the floor? *After* it was over—not before, but after.

Dougherty: Well, on account of the women.

Stearns: We sure didn't want to get the women angry for us on the California challenge.

Dougherty: The women didn't catch on, though. They still haven't. It's so complicated that they haven't figured it out.

---

3. Diane White disputes this—she says she knew from the start.

Stearns: I felt sort of guilty about what we'd done to the Women's Caucus. Afterwards I went around the trailer saying how bad I felt that we'd done it, but . . .

HST: What was the long-range effect of that, anyway? Was it just a symbolic thing that you'd done?

Dougherty: McGovern never did have that women's meeting yesterday. You know the Women's Caucus called me up and I was in bed. I just hung up. I said, "I can't help it," and I hung up.

Stearns: They called me at 7:30 in the morning after I'd just

Jean Westwood & Frank Mankiewicz stoned on the convention floor

gone to bed, and my response was, "If you really *have* to meet with him, I'll arrange it, but the fact that you want to meet with him at 10:00 when the Democratic National Committee is going to convene and elect its first woman chairman in the history of the party shows us how wrong you've been all along; all you're interested in is the form, not the substance. The substance is going to happen over at the National Committee meeting and if you want to do something meaningful, you should go there at 10:00." So whoever it was hung up. Maybe they went to the committee meeting. Silly.

I mean, they want to meet with McGovern while they're electing their first woman national chairman of the party.

Dougherty: The one that was raisin' all the hell was the delegate from South Dakota.

Stearns: She caught me about 7:00 in the coffee shop as I was finally getting breakfast.

Dougherty: You know what she's done for the Democrats? Nothin', ever. For George McGovern or anything. I really chewed her out on the floor. I said, "Instead of going around startin' all this trouble, you should be goin' around puttin' out the fires."

HTS: What was the loss, then? What did the women suffer?

Dougherty: That wasn't what they complained about. They were complaining that there wasn't enough input from women in the campaign.

HST: Was there any permanent damage done? Any tangible damage?

Dougherty: No, I don't think so.

HST: The networks must have caught on at some point. I remember I went somewhere and came back and saw Mike Wallace saying what a brilliant move it had been.

Dougherty: I went back to that airlines lounge in the hall, and watched TV a little bit and had coffee after I finished all that sweatin'. And Cronkite is on there saying that McGovern forces have suffered a serious setback and all of a sudden they switched him to the Doral Hotel. There's David Schoumacher who says, "Well, I'm sorry Walter, maybe they suffered a serious defeat, but when they lost, everybody in the boiler room cheered."

HST: That probably will go down in the annals of political history. Jesus! What an incredibly byzantine gig! Imagine trying to understand it on TV—not even Machiavelli could have handled *that.*

Stearns: It was the greatest moment in my political career. I'd say I've spent four years studying for the ten mintues on that vote— being able to make the right decision in that circumstance: Learning the names of all those delegates, how they'd been chosen, how the whole thing was put together, what the parliamentary situation might be. . . .

HST: What are the most obvious things that could have gone wrong? In the trailer, on the floor, or at the Doral boiler room . . .?

Stearns: Well, the most obvious thing that could have gone wrong was if we'd lost control of the Convention. The other issue at stake on that South Carolina vote was whether or not we could control our own delegates and whether we could impose the discipline that was going to lead to a working majority that could nominate George McGovern.

HST: Without them even knowing what you were doing.

Stearns: That was the whole question the press was raising right before the Convention. The Humphrey campaign had all this fantastic strategy about how McGovern supporters, because they were ideologically inclined to proportional representation, would desert us on the California issue and then they'd cut us apart from the black caucus by releasing delegates to Chisholm and the women would come running at us in another direction. So the question was whether we could keep *control,* and that was the most important thing that could have gone wrong, just a complete inability . . .

HST: What would have been the first manifestation?

Stearns: Well, South Carolina . . .

HST: No, I mean, even while it was going on. If somebody just stood up and told you to fuck off . . . ?

Stearns: You mean if Bill had gone to Pat Lucy and said, "We want you to cut back to 37 on this" and Pat had turned around to his delegation and said, "I need 20 people to step forward and change their votes." And people said, "Go to hell . . ."

HST: You didn't think that that could have happened?

Stearns: Oh yeah, it could have happened. But we had a bunch of delegates down here that wanted to win . . .

Dougherty: After Tuesday night though, they got . . .

Stearns: They got a little restless. I mean after Monday night, they were willing to follow us anywhere, because they realized what we'd done . . .

HST: On the Daley challenge[4] they didn't. That was Monday night, wasn't it? What caused *that?* Why did some of them desert you on the Daley thing?

Stearns: You mean on the compromise? Our hard-core supporters didn't desert us. We pulled exactly . . .

Dougherty: We needed a two-thirds vote from the whole Convention on that one.

310

Stearns: We pulled *exactly the vote of absolutely loyal support-ers we had.* The people who screwed us on that were the Humphrey and Muskie people who were still convinced that they were gonna win. We got Singer and Jackson to agree to publicly announce the compromise . . .

Dougherty: Let me tell you this story. I was on the floor with John Bailey [Chairman of the Connecticut delegation, and past Chairman of the Democratic National Committee] right when Frank Morrison had the deal in his hand to give it . . .

See, you could divide that motion in two, parliamentary-wise, and I asked Bailey to give it, to make the motion to suspend the rules. If Bailey made the motion for two-thirds to suspend the rules, I think it would have passed. Then I'd have Frank Morrison make the motion to seat both delegations and it only takes a majority to do that.

HST: So if you separated the two motions, you could have got it.

Dougherty: See, if John Bailey had made the motion to suspend the rules . . . I wanted to divide the question: have John Bailey make the motion to suspend the rules, then have Frank Morrison make the motion to have the compromise, and it only would have taken a majority on the compromise, see. And we could let some of our

---

4. Illinois had *two* delegations at the convention. One was Mayor Daley's and the other was a "new politics" delegation led by Chicago alderman Billy Singer and Reverend Jesse Jackson. So before the convention could vote on a nominee, it had to decide which one of the 170 member Illinois delegations was "official." Most people expected a 50-50 compromise—but the convention eventually voted to replace Daley's "regulars" with the "rebel" Singer/Jackson delegation—thus alienating *another* Democratic Party kingpin (along with George Meany) . . . and saddling McGovern with the hellish task of trying to heal The Big Split in the party before he could focus on Nixon. It proved to be a fateful decision. Meany bolted the Democratic Party entirely, taking a big chunk of Organized Labor with him—and Daley stayed in a "neutral" funk until somewhere around mid-October, when he finally realized that a GOP victory in Chicago might take *him* down, along with McGovern/Shriver. But by then it was too late. Chicago "went Democratic," as usual, but not by enough to carry Illinois—or even the state's attorney race, where the Daley-backed incumbent Ed Hanrahan went down to ignominious defeat (despite McGovern's re-luctant endorsement, or perhaps *because* of it) . . . and in the end Mayor Daley came out one of the Big Losers in '72. His *clout* is severely reduced now, both nationally and locally. So the McGovern campaign was not a *total* failure. . .

311

people vote the other way and we still could have won it.

HST: Why didn't Bailey make it?

Dougherty: I was talking to him right on the phone while we were gettin' ready to do it. I was right there on Frank Morrison's phone, and he says, "I won't do it, because the Mayor [Daley] hasn't agreed to it."

And I says, "This is the only chance, John, this is the only chance we've got, otherwise we're gonna kick him right out of the Convention." I pleaded with him, I said to him, "For the good of the Democratic Party." And he wouldn't do it.

Stearns: The Humphrey coalition's last hope at that point was that we would be willing to sell out Singer and Jackson, who came through for us and did everything we asked them to do on that California vote and on the compromise.

HST: Why did Singer and Jackson go for the compromise? Were they just thinking about carrying Illinois in November?

Stearns: They're politicians.

Dougherty: You remember me on the floor. I was mad, because I thought those guys, Jackson and Singer, wouldn't support it either, but they did! See, that just killed any chance Daley had of being seated.

Stearns: That's when I decided to go all out for Jackson. When they kept their word on that, then that's fine with me—we'd keep our word, too.

Dougherty: I'll tell you this. I wanted Daley in that Convention so bad I could taste it.[5]

Stearns: He should have been there.

Dougherty: There's a legal question on it, too. I mean those guys, the Jackson delegation, weren't exactly legally seated, if you really want to be honest about it. I guess they were on the reform

---

5. This view was shared by most of the McGovern staff workers. For wholly pragmatic reasons: To carry Illinois in November they were pro-Daley in Miami. I was sitting in the McGovern press room on Monday night when Daley went down to defeat, and I was the only person in the room who cheered. My only regret was that the bastard hadn't been thrown out *physically,* with mace and cattle prods. The McGovern troops disagreed. "We need him," they said. I shrugged—and in retrospect I think that was the point where I realized that the McGovern campaign was exactly what it had looked like in New Hampshire.

rules, but there was nobody running against them.

Stearns: I agree. The Daley side had a good argument. The Jackson side had a good argument, and the compromise would have settled the whole thing.

The problem at that point was to convince the Humphrey coalition that the compromise was the only way they were going to keep Daley in the Convention. But they wouldn't believe us. Their last hope was that we would not keep that agreement, that we would sell out Singer and Jackson, so that then they could have come back on the majority report, and at that point carry a disaffected Illinois delegation, because whether Daley had been seated or not, at that point the Singer/Jackson delegation would have gone on voting until a majority report had passed.

HST: I don't follow that.

Stearns: Temporary rule votes until you get all through the credential challenges. That is, those 151 unseated delegates from California went on voting right to the end of the evening until the majority report was passed. The same was true of Illinois; the Singer/Jackson delegation would have voted right to the end, regardless of whether Daley had been seated or not. The last hope the Humphrey people had was that we would desert Jackson, that is betray our word on that agreement, and then be able to use that Illinois delegation plus the 151 votes from California to defeat the passage of the majority report on credentials, which would have put us right back at the beginning again. But we kept our word.

HST: I didn't know that. Even the people who had been unseated could vote on the final passage.

Stearns: They would vote on the passage of the final report. And if we did not keep our word—if Jackson had been unseated— he might be angry enough to go out and by that point we would have also offended the women, and would have offended the blacks, and then they could have put together enough of a vote to defeat the passage of the majority report [which would have cost McGovern 151 delegates for "the California challenge"—and probably doomed his chance for the nomination]. But by the time we finished that night, they were so demoralized that they just let it go through on a voice vote. They lost their appetite to fight. On the next morning, Muskie and Humphrey were through.

HST: According to the Haynes Johnson story, they pretty well gave up at the end of the South Carolina roll-call. They knew it.

Stearns: It was obvious. But even as late as the nomination roll-call, I had an AFL-CIO guy come up to me and tell me that we only had 1451 votes for the nomination. What he was telling me was my *own* figure, from our absolutely hard count on the California thing, not realizing we just seated 151 delegates from California to take the total up to 1600.

HST: How important was O'Hara's ruling then? What accounts for the worry over O'Hara's ruling? And the tremendous spread that you got in the end? O'Hara's ruling wouldn't matter, it would appear.

Dougherty: Yeah, it would have. If he'd ruled different, we wouldn't . . . it kinda broke things, and we needed a break at that point.

Stearns: You not only deal with numbers at a Convention, you deal with psychology.

Dougherty: When a train starts leaving the station . . .

Stearns: If people think you're gonna lose, votes can just melt away.

Dougherty: See, just like on the Eagleton vote, there were all kinds of rumors around the floor that we didn't have the votes.

HST: Yeah, I was on the floor. People were trying to leave.

Stearns: We didn't turn it on at that point because we knew we had the votes, and if we turned it on, we would have destroyed the atmosphere for McGovern's presentation.

HST: For good or ill.

Dougherty: It's the first time in the history of this country that the presidential nominating speech was given at three o'clock in the morning.

Stearns: It was one of the best hours in the history of the Democratic Party, that hour. I almost cried.

HST: That was the best speech I've ever heard him give. I've been following the campaign ever since way back in New Hampshire, and that's the best I've ever heard him speak.

Dougherty: He had 126 guys writing his speech for him, but I think he wrote the final draft himself.

HST: Whose idea was it to put in the line about you won't have Nixon to kick around anymore? I thought that was the best part of the . . .

Stearns: That was his. "I want those doors open and that war closed" was also his idea.

HST: That was a good shot at Nixon. I saw it was almost over, so I decided to flee. I was in the cab listening to it on the way back, and the cab driver—a total stranger—just turned around and laughed, as if I understood somehow, too.

HST: Where are you going now?

Stearns: I'm getting my assignments these days from the New York *Times.* There are things that I read about in the *Times* before anybody talked to me. As I understand it from Jim Naughton's latest story, I'm supposed to take the states west of the Mississippi.

HST: Is that in today?

Stearns: It was in the *Times* yesterday. First I ever heard of it. It really pissed me off. I mean, somebody ought to tell me before . . .

Dougherty: That's George McGovern for ya.

Stearns: Yeah, but if you got time to talk to Jim Naughton, you got time . . .

Dougherty: What about Dick Stout's *Newsweek* story?

Stearns: I didn't see that.

Dougherty: Did you see that one Monday? About Dick Dougherty being press secretary and Mankiewicz traveling. Hart being in charge of the campaign.

Stearns: Oh yeah, they had you in there as a seasoned political pro.

Dougherty: Yeah. He got that in Maryland the day I was out there with McGovern. I found out it was gonna be in there. So I went to Dick Stout and I said, "Where in the hell did you get that?" Dick Stout said he ran into Fred Dutton comin' outta the bank in Washington and Fred told him the whole deal. Then Dutton came to me and he said, "I wonder if Cunningham [McGovern's administrative assistant] and those guys know about it." So I said, "I haven't heard anything about it."

When I got in town I got ahold of Dick Dougherty [McGovern's press secretary] and told him the whole deal and he said, "For chrissakes." So he got ahold of Dick Stout and found out exactly how much was gonna be in that story and then I went to Gary and I said, "Here's what's gonna be in *Newsweek* on Monday. I think some of these guys should be aware." Cunningham wasn't even aware, or any of them. But that's typical George McGovern, you know.

[*Garbled conversation. Whistling. Clicks. Airplane.*]

HST: You taking off today?

Stearns: No, I think not. If my luck holds, I'll catch a late flight back to Washington tomorrow. Today I feel like sitting out here on this beach and drinking for awhile.

It was somewhere around eight-thirty or nine on Sunday evening when I dragged myself onto a plane out of Miami—headed for Atlanta and L.A. The '72 Democratic Convention was over.

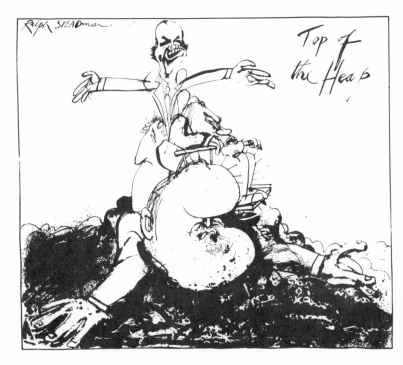

McGovern had wrapped it up just before dawn on Friday, accepting the bloody nomination with an elegant, finely crafted speech that might have had quite an impact on the national TV audience . . . (*Time* correspondent Hugh Sidey called it "perhaps as pure an expression as George McGovern has ever given of his particular moralistic sense of the nation") . . . but the main, middle-American bulk of the national TV audience tends to wither away around midnight, and anybody still glued to the tube at 3:30 A.M. Miami time is probably too stoned or twisted to recognize McGovern anyway.

A few hundred ex-Muskie/Humphrey/Jackson delegates had lingered long enough to cheer Ted Kennedy's bland speech, but they started drifting away when George came on—hurrying out the exits of the air-conditioned hall, into the muggy darkness of the parking lot to fetch up a waiting cab and go back to whichever one of the sixty-five official convention hotels they were staying in . . . hoping to find the tail end of a party or at least one free drink before catching a few hours' sleep and then heading back home on one of the afternoon planes: back to St. Louis, Altoona, Butte . . .

By sundown on Friday the "political hotels" were almost empty. In the Doral Beach—McGovern's ocean-front headquarters hotel —Southern Bell Telephone workers were dragging what looked like about five thousand miles of multicolored wires, junction boxes, and cables out of the empty Press/Operations complex on the mezzanine. Down in the lobby, a Cuban wedding (Martinez-Hernandez: 8:30-10:30) had taken over the vast, ornately sculptured Banquet Room that ten hours earlier had been jammed with hundreds of young, scruffy-looking McGovern volunteers celebrating the end of one of the longest and most unlikely trips in the history of American politics . . . it was a quiet party, by most Convention standards: free beer for the troops, bring your own grass, guitar-minstrels working out here and there; but not much noise, no whooping & shouting, no madness. . . .[6]

---

6. A strange sidelight on the McGovern victory celebration was the showing, in one of the main lounges of the Doral, of the infamous "Zapruder film" from November 22, 1963 in Dallas. I went out of curiosity and despite the angry snarls of many McGovern staffers. The sight of Jack Kennedy's head exploding in a cloud of bloody-pink bone splinters was such a vicious bummer for me that I went up to my room and spent the rest of the night

The atmosphere at the victory party was not much different from the atmosphere of the Convention itself: very cool and efficient, very much under control at all times . . . get the job done, don't fuck around, avoid violence, shoot ten seconds after you see the whites of their eyes.

It was a McGovern party from start to finish. Everything went according to plan—or *almost* everything; as always, there were a few stark exceptions. Minor snarls here and there, but not many big ones. McGovern brought his act into Miami with the same kind of fine-focus precision that carried him all the way from New Hampshire to California . . . and, as usual, it made all the other acts look surprisingly sloppy.

I was trapped in the Doral for ten days, shuttling back & forth

watching TV in a mean-drunk stupor. Sometime near dawn I went down to the beach to swim, ignoring a monsoon-rainstorm that had whipped the surf into nasty six and eight foot swells under a foul black sky, and a wind that was tearing big limbs off the palm trees. Nobody else was on the beach—or even on the pool-patio. From two hundred yards out in the surf I could see people moving around in the dim yellow windows of the McGovern press room on the mezzanine . . . but they couldn't see me, bobbing around in the rain-thrashed surf that I suddenly realized was carrying me out to sea . . .

Indeed, a nasty rip-tide. I can't say for sure how long it took me to get back to the beach, but it seemed like forty years . . . a bad way to die, I kept thinking: thrashing drunkenly in the surf off Miami Beach within sight of the McGovern press room where your friends sat pounding typewriters and glancing out at the sea now and then without seeing you . . . sipping coffee and bloody marys, composing the victory statements.

I kept thinking about this as I clawed desperately in the troughs of the long white-capped waves . . . holding a well-aimed sidestroke to keep my head above the foam and saying constantly to myself: "Don't worry, old sport—you're making fine progress, a human torpedo . . ." until finally I got close enough to dig my heels in the sand and *jump* the last fifty yards, gasping for breath and cursing whatever strange instinct had brought me out here in the first place . . .

When I got to the beach I was on my hands and knees, moving slowly and spasmodically in the style of a wounded crab. I leaned back on the trunk of a coconut palm for about twenty minutes, feeling the rain on my belly and the sand in my teeth, but still too tired to move. . .

It was somewhere around 9:00 A.M., and upstairs in McGovern's penthouse his brain-trust was meeting to select a vice-president. Business as usual . . . and my death by drowning on that ugly Thursday morning would not have changed their decision any more than the rude things I'd already said—to Mankiewicz, Hart, Caddell, on TV—so I limped upstairs to my room on the eighth floor, facing the sea that had almost done me in, and slept for two or three hours.

between the hotel and the Convention Hall by any means available: taxi, my rented green convertible, and occasionally down the canal in the fast white "staff taxi" speedboat that McGovern's people used to get from the Doral to the Hall by water, whenever Collins Avenue was jammed up with sight-seer traffic . . . and in retrospect, I think that boat trip was the only thing I did all week that I actually enjoyed.

There was a lot of talk in the press about "the spontaneous outburst of fun and games" on Thursday night—when the delegates, who had been so deadly serious for the first three sessions, suddenly ran wild on the floor and delayed McGovern's long-awaited acceptance speech until 3:30 A.M. by tying the convention in knots with a long outburst of frivolous squabbling over the vice-presidential nomination. *Newsweek* described it as "a comic interlude, a burst of silliness on the part of the delegates whose taut bonds of decorum and discipline seemed suddenly to snap, now that it didn't make any difference."

There was not much laughter in Miami, on the floor or anywhere else, and from where I stood that famous "comic interlude" on Thursday night looked more like the first scattered signs of mass Fatigue Hysteria, if the goddamn thing didn't end soon. What the press mistook for relaxed levity was actually a mood of ugly restlessness that by 3:00 A.M. on Friday was bordering on rebellion. All over the floor I saw people caving in to the lure of booze, and in the crowded aisle between the California and Wisconsin delegations a smiling freak with a bottle of liquid THC was giving free hits to anybody who still had the strength to stick their tongue out.

After four hours of listening to a seemingly endless parade of shameless dingbats who saw no harm in cadging some free exposure on national TV by nominating each other for vice-president, about half the delegates in the hall were beginning to lose control. On the floor just in front of the New York delegation, leaning against the now-empty VIP box once occupied by Muriel Humphrey, a small blonde girl who once worked for the Lindsay campaign was sharing a nasal inhaler full of crushed amyls with a handful of new-found friends.

Each candidate was entitled to a fifteen-minute nominating

speech and two five-minute seconding speeches. The nightmare dragged on for four hours, and after the first forty minutes there was not one delegate in fifty, on the floor, who either knew or cared who was speaking. No doubt there were flashes of eloquence, now and then: Probably Mike Gravel and Cissy Farentholt said a few things that might have been worth hearing, under different circumstances . . . but on that long Thursday night in Miami, with Senator Tom Eagleton of Missouri waiting nervously in the wings to come out and accept the vice-presidential nomination that McGovern had sealed for him twelve hours earlier, every delegate in the hall understood that whatever these other seven candidates were saying up there on the rostrum, they were saying for reasons that had nothing to do with who was going to be the Democratic candidate for vice-president in November . . . and it was *not* going to be ex-Massachusetts governor "Chub" Peabody, or a grinning dimwit named Stanley Arnold from New York City who said he was The Businessman's Candidate, or some black Step'n'Fetchit-style Wallace delegate from Texas called Clay Smothers.

But these brainless bastards persisted, nonetheless, using up half the night and all the prime time on TV, debasing the whole convention with a blizzard of self-serving gibberish that drove whatever was left of the national TV audience to bed or the *Late Late Show.*

Thursday was not a good day for McGovern. By noon there was not much left of Wednesday night's Triumphant Warrior smile. He spent most of Thursday afternoon grappling with a long list of vice-presidential possibilities and by two, the Doral lobby was foaming with reporters and TV cameras. The name had to be formally submitted by 3:59 P.M., but it was 4:05 when Mankiewicz finally appeared to say McGovern had decided on Senator Thomas Eagleton of Missouri.

There is a very tangled story behind that choice, but I don't feel like writing it now. My immediate reaction was not enthusiastic, and the staff people I talked to seemed vaguely depressed—if only because it was a concession to "the Old Politics," a nice-looking

Catholic boy from Missouri with friends in the Labor Movement. His acceptance speech that night was not memorable—perhaps because it was followed by the long-awaited appearance of Ted Kennedy, who had turned the job down.

Kennedy's speech was not memorable either: "Let us bury the hatchet, etc. . . . and Get Behind the Ticket." There was something hollow about it, and when McGovern came on he made Kennedy sound like an old-timer.

Later that night, at a party on the roof of the Doral, a McGovern

staffer asked me who I would have chosen for VP . . . and finally, after long brooding, I said I would have chosen Ron Dellums, the black congressman from Berkeley.

"Jesus christ!" he said. "That would be suicide!"

I shrugged.

"Why Dellums?" he asked.

"Why not?" I said. "He offered it to Mayor Daley before he called Eagleton."

"No!" he shouted. "Not Daley! That's a lie!"

"I was in the room when he made the call," I said. "Ask anybody who was there—Gary, Frank, Dutton—they weren't happy about it, but they said he'd be good for the ticket."

He stared at me. "What did Daley say?" he asked finally.

I laughed. "Christ, you *believed* that, didn't you?"

He had, for just an instant. After all, there was a lot of talk about "pragmatism" in Miami, and Illinois was a key state . . . I decided to try the Daley rumor on other staff people, to see their reactions.

But I never got around to it, I forgot all about it, in fact, until I flipped through my notebook on the midnight jet from Atlanta. I came across a statement by Ron Dellums. It depressed me, for some reason, but it seems like a good way to end this goddamn thing. Dellums writes pretty good, for a politician. It's part of the statement he distributed when he switched his support from Shirley Chisholm to McGovern:

The great bulk of that coalition committed to change, human freedom and justice in the country has moved actively and power- fully behind the candidacy of Senator McGovern. That coalition of hope, conscience, morality and humanity—of the powerless and the voiceless—that did not exist in 1964, that expressed itself in

outrage and frustration in 1968, and in 1972 began to form and welded itself imperfectly but courageously and lifted a man to the brink of the Democratic nomination for the Presidency of the United States, and within a short but laborious step from the Presidency of the United States. The coalition that has formed behind Senator McGovern has battled the odds, baffled the pollsters, and beat the bosses. It is my conviction that when that total coalition of the victims in this country is ever formed, this potential for change would be unheralded, for it could pose a real alternative to expediency and status quo politics in America.

—Ron Dellums, July 9, 1972

[Postscript]

Friday, Aug. 11
National Broadcasting Company, Inc.
Thirty Rockefeller Plaza
New York, N.Y. 10020
CIRCLE 7-8300

Dear Hunter,

Because we share a fear and loathing for things which aren't true, I point out that it ain't true that I was taken in by the McGoverns on the South Carolina challenge in Miami Beach.

While they were still switching votes, I said on the air that they might be trying to lose it deliberately. We had the floor people try to check this out and they ran into a couple of poolroom liars employed by McGovern who said yas, yas, it was a defeat, etc., but a little while later Doug Kiker got Pat Lucey to tell it all. (Lucey called headquarters for permission, first, as Kiker waited.)

We were pleased that we got it right. Adam Clymer of the Sun called the next day with congratulations. I think the reason most people thought we blew the story is that CBS blew it badly. I guess I should have gone through the night pointing out what happened, but we got involved in the California roll-call and a lot of other stuff, and suddenly it was dawn.

Other than that I enjoyed your convention piece and let's have a double Margarita when we next meet.

J. Chancellor

323

FEAR AND LOATHING

Sept 11 '72
Owl Farm
Woody Creek
Colorado

Dear John. . . . .

You filthy skunk-sucking bastard! What kind of gall would prompt you to write me a letter like that sac of pus dated Aug. 11? I checked your story—about how NBC had the South Carolina trip all figured out—with Mrs. Lucey (Pat wouldn't talk to me, for some reason), and she said both you & Kiker were so fucked up on drugs that you both kept calling it "the South Dakota challenge," despite her attempts to correct you. She was baffled by your behavior, she said, until Mankiewicz told her about you and LSD-25. Then, about an hour later, Bill Daughtery (sp?) found Kiker on his knees in the darkness outside McGovern's command trailer, apparently trying to choke himself with his own hands . . . but, when Bill grabbed him, Kiker said he was trying to un-screw his head from what he called his "neck-pipe," so he could "check the wiring" in his own brain.

But I guess you wouldn't remember that episode, eh? Fuck no, you wouldn't! You dope-addled fascist bastard. I'm heading east in a few days, and I think it's about time we got this evil shit cleared away. Your deal is about to go down, John. You can run, but you can't hide. See you soon. . . .

Hunter S. Thompson

Dark Interlude

IMMEDIATELY AFTER THE DEMOCRATIC CONVENTION, *I flew to Los Angeles and spent several days hanging around the Polo Lounge of the Beverly Hills Hotel on Sunset Boulevard. Then I went back to Woody Creek to prepare for the ordeal of returning to Miami Beach for the Republican Convention in August. Not much seemed to be happening on the political front. That sleepless week in Miami had left the entire McGovern staff in a state of exhaustion. Most of them disappeared in their own directions for a week or so of vacation. The plan was for McGovern's key staff wizards to convene ten days hence for strategy sessions at the Sylvan Lake Lodge outside Custer, South Dakota. Since the press would be barred from these confidential meetings I saw no point in going over there just to hang around and get drunk every night with a bunch of reporters.*

The only people who knew at that point that all hell was about

En route to the press conference where Eagleton's history of mental illness & electric shock was officially revealed.

to break loose at the Sylvan Lake Lodge were Hart, Mankiewicz, and McGovern. When a notice appeared on the bulletin board in the Lodge press room announcing a joint McGovern/Eagleton press conference on Tuesday, it didn't cause much of a stir. But most of the reporters went anyway because there was nothing else to do. On Wednesday every paper in the country carried a story similar to this one below, which appeared on the front page of the Washington Post:

Eagleton Reveals Illness
Hospitalized 3 Times in '60s For 'Fatigue'

By William Greider
Washington Post Staff Writer

CUSTER, ·S.D., July 25—Sen. Thomas Eagleton, the Democratic nominee for Vice President, unexpectedly revealed today that he was hospitalized three times between 1960 and 1966 for psychiatric treatment, suffering from "nervous exhaustion and fatigue."

Under questioning, he said the illness involved "the manifestation of depression" and that twice he received electric shock therapy, which he described as a recognized treatment for that type of ailment.

Sen. George McGovern, the Democratic presidential nominee, promptly expressed full confidence in Eagleton and said he will discourage any talk of dumping Eagleton from the ticket.

Eagleton revealed his medical history after reporters for the Knight Newspapers had confronted McGovern staff members with accounts of it. . . .

I left immediately for Custer, driving at top speed in a rebuilt Hudson Hornet. About four hours later, less than twenty miles from the 12,000-foot summit of Loveland Pass, the Hornet developed a fire in its electrical system and I was forced to abandon it. By that time I had already heard on the radio that Eagleton had left for Hawaii and McGovern had gone into seclusion. So I went back home and followed the Eagleton story for the next few days on television. There was plenty of speculation but not much in the way of hard news. Meanwhile over in Custer the linear press was becoming more and more dismayed at the way McGovern was handling the situation:

326

Vacation Ordeal:
Good Vibrations at Lodge
Jarred by News of Eagleton

By William Greider
Washington Post Staff Writer

CUSTER, S.D., July 28—The people who run George McGovern's campaign for the presidency were all gathered after dinner one night in the pine-paneled lobby of their resort lodge singing folk songs.

"Amazing Grace." "This Land Is Your Land." "Shenandoah." Good vibrations all around.

The candidate stood easily among them, not demanding to be the center of attention like so many politicians. McGovern sang softly himself while his research man, John Holum, played guitar. Even raspy newspaper reporters found themselves leaning into the circle, humming along.

The Rev. Walter Fauntroy, the black preacher-politician from the District of Columbia, sang in his high tenor of that serene biblical promise: "There Is a Balm in Gilead."

They came out here to the Black Hills to plot strategy for the fall campaign, yet they put great store in such moments of personal warmth. "We shall overcome," they sang, as if good feeling among themselves was as crucial as any of those charts about where to find 270 electoral votes.

That was last weekend. Before the Eagleton business. Before the big bad headlines: the alarmed phone calls and telegrams.

Now McGovern dines privately in cabin 22 with his family, no more mingling with the reporters and tourists up at the lodge. The press has his cabin staked out and the Secret Service agents keep them at a distance. What began as a vacation, mixed with political activity, is ending as an ordeal.

The Democratic nominee will be back in Washington Sunday. "He's going to stay home and rest," press secretary Dick Dougherty advised reporters today. "Rest up from his holiday," he added dryly.

The Black Hills in the western end of South Dakota are a proper

327

setting for "Gunsmoke" or "Bonanza," with magnificent pine-covered mountains lined by heroic bluffs of stone and narrow trails which wind among the eroded spires of rock. It doesn't seem right for high political drama, but McGovern is facing it all with the public coolness of a western gunfighter.

McGovern probably chose this spot to help promote the tourist business of his home state and, during the first week of his visit, he cooperated with the ritual appearances.

He went horseback riding, wearing a silk ascot and looking only slightly more at ease than some of the mounted reporters and staff aides who followed him up the trail.

The next day, he airily signed a photograph which showed his profile alongside the four presidential faces carved on Mt. Rushmore —"From George McGovern, the fifth man."

Everyone was loose. The hoard of reporters and TV crews were camped about eight miles away at the Hi Ho Motel in Custer, probably to give the nominee some privacy. But each evening, they would gather at the Sylvan Lake Lodge to mingle freely with the man and his staff, to share the grand view of Harney's Peak and the "hail storms," a pioneer drink served in mason jars.

Then, without any warning, it became the bleak hills. Sen. Thomas Eagleton flew in with his entourage on Tuesday and made his public admission about the past psychiatric problems.

"A gutsy performance," said Fred Dutton, a senior advisor, reserving judgment on the political impact.

"It could turn into a plus," said Bill Dougherty, the lieutenant governor of South Dakota. His hopefulness was not widely shared.

McGovern went to play tennis, shirtless, with his teacher, Washington tennis pro Allie Ritzenberg.

The reporters bombarded everyone with questions. For a day or so, McGovern and Dougherty and the others tried to answer them. No, he was not dumping Eagleton. As of now. Well, did that mean he might? No, it didn't mean that.

Allie Ritzenberg went back to Washington, so did most of the campaign staff. Dutton and Dick Dougherty stayed on to counsel the candidate, but mostly to fend off the reporters. The questions got nastier.

The candidate became more remote, no more interviews, his

press conference cancelled. Finally, when the Eagleton story wouldn't go away, he issued a public notice to his campaign staff, telling them to keep their mouths shut on the subject.

But George McGovern flew a B-24 in World War II and his friends insist that he still does his best thinking when the flak is heavy. At least he remained cool.

When an aide called him yesterday to report that Jack Anderson had added new accusations against Eagleton, the candidate replied: "Do you know how to paddle a canoe?" and invited the aide to join the family in a canoe trip on Sylvan Lake.

That afternoon, he appeared at the movie house in Custer to see a promotional showing of "The Candidate," a movie which depicts an idealistic young man converted to a cosmetic politician, trading ideals for glamour.

There was scattered applause in the Harney Theater when one character exclaimed, "Politics is bullshit." McGovern and his family laughed hardest when a political manager in the film instructed the press secretary: "Get all the reporters on the press bus and drive them over the nearest cliff."

On his last night in South Dakota, McGovern relaxed and chatted again with reporters and agreed that his vacation had been something of a fiasco. "It's not what I had in mind," he said. "What I wanted was a time for reflection."

This morning, good to his word, McGovern showed up for the annual tourist parade which Custer stages to commemorate the discovery of gold in the valley on French Creek nearly one hundred years ago. He and Mrs. McGovern wore buckskin jackets and brown stetsons, but the Secret Service had them ride in a closed car, not on horses.

"Let's just talk about the Discovery Days parade," McGovern told a reporter.

A horse dyed yellow led the line of march, which included blue and red horses too. The security helicopter circling over the tiny town added excitement. The floats followed McGovern. "The Massacre of the Metz Family," by the Custer Lumber Co. "Our Discovery of Gold," by the Young Homemakers Extension Club.

Dutton, wearing a dowdy cowboy hat, cheered the press corps as it puffed by beside McGovern's car. The line of tourists and

Custer citizens complained. "You're spoiling our view," a lady yelled from the curb.

Past the Monster Mansion, past the How the West Was Won Museum. At the Gold Pan Saloon, McGovern got out to shake hands.

"How's your vacation, Mrs. McGovern, hectic?" a girl asked. Eleanor McGovern sighed. "Yes it is."

The parade ended at the east end of Custer in front of Scott's Rock Shop, which sells rocks. The senator and his wife accepted gifts from the mayor, a squirrel and book ends of rose quartz, a local mineral.

"It's been very pleasant for us to be out here," McGovern assured the mayor.

Then the Democratic presidential nominee mingled with tourists from all over Florida, Utah, Illinois, Rhode Island. Rhode Island?

"One of my first visits is going to be to Providence," McGovern told the man from there. "We'll probably be in there next month."

It sounded as if he could hardly wait.

The McGovern Image
Candor of Democratic Nominee Viewed as Chief Casualty of Eagleton Affair
By James M. Naughton
Special to the New York Times

WASHINGTON, JULY 30—The biggest political casualty in the Eagleton affair may prove to be not Senator Thomas F. Eagleton but the man who chose him to seek the Vice Presidency. In the five days since Senator Eagleton disclosed a history of treatment for nervous exhaustion and depression, Senator George McGovern appears to have undone much of his effort over the last 18 months to establish an image as an unusually candid Presidential candidate.

The Democratic nominee declined on Tuesday even to consider Senator Eagleton's offer to withdraw from the ticket, saying that its make-up was irrevocably set. Three days later, he began orchestrating an attempt to persuade Mr. Eagleton to withdraw from the ticket.

McGovern Comments

Having asserted on Tuesday that "there is no one sounder in body, mind and spirit than Tom Eagleton," Mr. McGovern was telling reporters aboard his chartered campaign plane last night that "the one thing we know about Eagleton is that he has been to the hospital three times for [mental] depression."

The Democratic Presidential nominee publically admonished his staff to stop gossiping about what effect Mr. Eagleton's disclosure might have on the Democrats' chances in November. A day later, he contrived through his staff to assemble a group of reporters for a casual discussion on the same subject.

Mr. McGovern appeared, even to disillusioned members of his campaign staff, to be saying one thing and doing another—which was the charge he had been preparing to make in the campaign against President Nixon.

In the Democratic primaries, Senator McGovern managed to convey the impression that he was somehow not a politician in the customary sense—that he was more open, more accessible, more attuned to the issues and more idealistic than other candidates.

Pro-Eagleton Calls

But his reaction to Mr. Eagleton's disclosure may have seriously impaired that image. When newspapers appeared yesterday morning with articles about Senator McGovern's apparent decision to reassess Mr. Eagleton's candidacy, telephone calls began inundating the McGovern headquarters here to back Mr. Eagleton. One McGovern worker said that there were "tons" of pro-Eagleton calls and that the instructions were not to make that information public.

It all seemed to illustrate, as have other events since Mr. McGovern won the Democratic nomination, that he is, after all, a politician.

"Above all else, George McGovern is a very practical, pragmatic man," said George V. Cunningham, deputy campaign manager and a political associate of Mr. McGovern since 1955.

The South Dakota Senator won the nomination with a grass-roots campaign that went around the party professionals, but now he has installed Lawrence F. O'Brien, former chairman of the Democratic National Committee, on the eighth floor of McGovern headquarters and has given Mr. O'Brien the coveted title of campaign chairman.

Daley Is Courted

It was Senator Edmund S. Muskie of Maine who faltered in the primaries by relying on the big names in the Democratic establishment to win the nomination for him. But now it is Mr. McGovern who is energetically courting the big-city machine of Mayor Richard J. Daley in Chicago and implying that the only issue separating him from former President Lyndon B. Johnson is the Vietnam war.

Despite a pledge to give "unequivocal" support to an attempt to put more women on the South Carolina delegation to the Democratic National Convention, Mr. McGovern allowed his operatives to throw some votes against the women's challenge rather than risk a parliamentary showdown that might have imperiled his own nomination. But a McGovern staff study theorizes that, for the first time, wives are equal to husbands in influencing the political attitudes of spouses, and the Senator unabashedly named Mrs. Jean Westwood of Utah to the high visibility post of party chairman.

Closed Door Session

When Mr. McGovern went to Houston last June to meet with disgruntled Democratic Governors, he was pressed to explain why the session would be held behind closed doors. After months of pledging to end secrecy in government, how could he square a secret meeting, Mr. McGovern was asked.

"I can't square it," he replied. "Sometimes I'm just going to have to be inconsistent."

No one could say without absolute certainty today that Mr. Eagleton would be removed from the ticket when he and Mr. McGovern meet tomorrow to consider the question. But while Mr. Eagleton was traveling on the West Coast last week, Mr. McGovern's staff was said to be imploring the Presidential nominee to dump his running mate.

At the time, Mr. McGovern was vacationing in the Blacks Hills of his native South Dakota. On Friday, Mr. McGovern saw a special screening of the recent movie, "The Candidate," in which an idealistic office-seeker is cosmeticized by practical politicians on his staff.

Mr. McGovern did not like the film. It showed, he said, "some of the sicker side of American politics."

The McGovern Course
By William Greider
Washington Post Staff Writer

JULY 31—George McGovern, confronting a political crisis which could destroy his candidacy for the White House, moves like a sailboat headed down the bay.

First, he tacks in one direction, and this is reported. Then he tacks back the other way, and that too is reported. But the reports of these movements do not necessarily reveal where he is ultimately headed.

McGovern apparently wants it that way. Let others seem to speak for you. Hint at your intentions, but don't state them directly. Retreat, move forward. Shave the angle of your words. Keep your objective sufficiently flexible so that, it you must, you can always change it.

In the "old politics," this sort of maneuvering was an accepted technique for approaching tough decisions, euphemistically known as "keeping your options open." The "new politics" of the Mc-Govern campaign, which likes to frown on the old ways, will have to think of something different to call it.

The South Dakota senator has always insisted that he is, above all, a pragmatic politician and his handling of the Eagleton crisis confirms his description. Beneath the exterior of the earnest and open man, there is a cautious tactician, more calculating than either his hard-boiled critics or his starry-eyed admirers have admitted.

He began by embracing his running mate, Sen. Thomas Eagleton, promising full support for the man who had just disclosed to the world that three times earlier in his career he had been hospitalized with psychiatric problems. Never mind, said McGovern, who insisted he would have chosen Eagleton even if he had known.

McGovern held to that heading Tuesday and Wednesday,

both in his own comments and in statements released through his press secretary. But an avalanche of negative comment was building up, both from newspaper editorial writers and from McGovern supporters.

On Thursday, the sailboat turned about—though not so dramatically that one could say McGovern had reversed directions. The senator cancelled a press conference, which meant he did not think it wise to repeat all of his lines about full support for Eagleton.

His staff people, both in Washington and South Dakota, began to speak more freely about the "disaster" confronting them and even the inevitability of Eagleton withdrawing. McGovern issued an order telling the staff people to keep mum.

At that point, the presidential nominee might have been content to keep quiet and let opinions develop naturally over the weekend. Except Eagleton was picking up signals too. As McGovern's staff began raising the possibility of changing horses, Eagleton kept charging forward. He would never step down he said on Friday afternoon.

Never? That is a strong word to use in politics and obviously it needed strong corrective action from McGovern's end of the seesaw. What McGovern did was either very slick or very clumsy. The people who watched still are not quite sure which.

First, his press staff distributed the text of a speech which McGovern would deliver Saturday night before the South Dakota state convention of Democrats. It contained one lukewarm paragraph about Eagleton, revealing that McGovern was now "deliberating" on what he had previously considered a closed question. That would tell the press not to take Eagleton's declarations at face value, but the speech wasn't for release until Saturday evening.

McGovern apparently decided to send a stronger message to his running mate, via the media. It was the last night of the senator's two-week vacation in the Black Hills and, though he had been dining privately with his family, McGovern decided to eat that night at the Sylvan Lake Lodge.

He told his press secretary, Dick Dougherty, to pass the word discreetly to reporters who were staying in Custer, S. D., eight miles away.

Most of the reporters did not get the word, but a lot of them figured on their own it was prudent to dine at the lodge on the last night, just in case he broke his two-day silence. So, with a few tourists thrown in, this group sat in the Dakota Room, eating buffalo steaks and watching one another. Indian pictographs depicting "The Legend of the White Buffalo," surrounded them on the walls.

McGovern ate enthusiastically, as he always does. Then, rather casually, he was standing at the table where The Washington Post, the Chicago Daily News, and United Press International were eating.

"Are you fellas glad to be getting home?" he asked, then sat down for social chit-chat about the Black Hills. The reporters were wondering in their own minds whether it would be offensive to probe the Eagleton thing when McGovern settled it for them. He brought it up.

It had been a terrible business, he said, ruined his vacation, upset the campaign planning. How was he to know the Missouri senator had been in the hospital three times?

McGovern went on to explain that a decision would have to be made and it would mostly be up to Eagleton to withdraw if he realized that public opinion was against him. The tone was more precise than the words—implying that McGovern fully expected Eagleton to withdraw gracefully, rather than imperil the campaign.

He was gone in a few moments. The reporters discussed briefly among themselves the question of whether it was proper to quote a casual dinner conversation. Very briefly. Then they took out notepads and began trying to reconstruct what McGovern had said. Ever so casually, they slipped off to the lobby telephones, no point arousing all those other reporters.

Meanwhile McGovern sat down with CBS and his family and repeated much the same conversation, elaborating on a few points.

At another table, Time Magazine was dining with Newsweek, watching one another on the night before their magazines close for publication. McGovern came over to join them.

Knight Newspapers and the Wall Street Journal were sitting at another table, but they decided to join the circle. So did The New York Times who was eating with McGovern's staff, the one table which McGovern did not visit. Newsweek had a tape recorder hidden on his lap under the table, but when he replayed it later all that could be heard was organ music and the clatter of dishes.

The candidate expanded further on the same theme, adding some negative remarks which made the signal even stronger. When he departed, the reporters at first eyed other newsmen with suspicion, eager to protect what they thought was exclusive. In a moment, they got the picture. It was McGovern who was using the social chatter, not them.

There were only two telephones in the lobby. The New York Times had to race down the mountain eight miles to phone in the story. Meanwhile, the Baltimore Sun was dining in Custer, heard about the table-hopping and raced up the mountain. The Associated Press was with his children at Mt. Rushmore, but another AP man caught up with the story.

All of them filed stories stating with varying degrees of emphasis that McGovern had changed his position and might now abandon Eagleton as a running mate. Only The Los Angeles Times had a stronger story. The L.A. Times had been invited to McGovern's cabin before dinner and emerged with a story which said flatly "it was learned" that McGovern had decided to dump Eagleton.

The next day, McGovern tacked again, though still headed in the same general direction. The question of Eagleton's future, he said in a press statement, needed "a proper period of evaluation."

"Rumors and reports of any decisions having been reached on this question are misleading," he said.

August

Down & Out in the Fontainebleau ... Nixon Sells
Out the Party ... Goldwater on the Comeback
Trail; Agnew in '76 ... Mankiewicz Amok;
Midnight Violence at The Wayfarer ... The
Origins of Eagleton; Death Rattle for the New
Politics ... Can a Bull Elk in the Rut Pass
through the Eye of a Camel? ... A Vicious
Attack on the Demonstrators: "These People
Should Go Back Where They Belong"...

EARLIER TONIGHT I DROVE down the beach to a place called Dixie's
Doll House for two six-packs of Ballantine ale. The place was full
of old winos, middle-aged hookers, and aging young hustlers who
looked like either junkies or Merchant Marine rejects; bearded
geeks in grey T-shirts staggering back and forth along the bar, six
nasty-looking pimps around a blue-lit pool table in the rear, and
right next to me at the bar a ruined platinum-blonde Cuban dazzler
snarling drunkenly at her nervous escort for the night: "Don't
gimme that horseshit, baby! I don't want a goddamn ONE DOL-
LAR dinner! I want a TEN DOLLAR dinner!"

Life gets heavy here on The Beach from time to time. So I paid
$2.70 each for my six-packs and then wheeled my big red Chevy
Impala convertible back home to the Fontainebleau, about forty
blocks north through the balmy southern night to the edge of the
fashionable section.

"Bobo," the master pimp and carmeister who runs what they
call "the front door" here in these showplace beachfront hotels,
eyed me curiously as I got out of the car and started dragging wet
brown bags full of beer bottles out of the back seat. "You gonna

337

need the car again tonight?" he asked.

"Probably," I said.. "But not for a while. I'll be up in the room until about midnight." I looked at my watch. "The Rams-Kansas City game is on in three minutes. After that, I'll work for a while and then go out for something to eat."

He jerked the car door open, sliding fast behind the wheel to take it down to the underground garage. With his hand on the shift lever he looked up at me: "You in the mood for some company?"

"No," I said. "I'm way behind. I'll be up all night with that goddamn typewriter. I shouldn't even take time to watch the game on TV."

He rolled his eyes and looked up at what should have been the sky, but which was actually the gold-glazed portico roof above the entrance driveway: "Jesus, what kind of work do you *do?* Hump typewriters for a living? I thought the convention was over!"

I paused, tucking the wet beer bags under the arm of my crusty brown leather jacket. Inside the lobby door about twenty feet away I could see what looked like a huge movie-set cocktail party for rich Venezuelans and high-style middle-aged Jews: my fellow guests in the Fontainebleau. I was not dressed properly to mingle with them, so my plan was to stride swiftly through the lobby to the elevators and then up to my hide-out in the room.

The Nixon convention had finished on Thursday morning, and by Saturday the hundreds of national press/media people who had swarmed into this pompous monstrosity of a hotel for Convention Week were long gone. A few dozen stragglers had stayed on through Friday, but by Saturday afternoon the style and tone of the place had changed drastically, and on Sunday I felt like the only nigger in the Governor's Box on Kentucky Derby Day.

Bobo had not paid much attention to me during the convention, but now he seemed interested. "I know you're a reporter," he said. "They put 'press' on your house-car tag. But all the rest of those guys took off yesterday. What keeps *you* here?"

I smiled. "Christ, am I the only one left?"

He thought for a moment, then shook his head. "No, there's

you and two others. One guy has that white Lincoln Continental—"

"He's not press," I said quickly. "Probably one of the GOP advance men, getting things settled with the hotel."

He nodded. "Yeah, he acted like he was part of the show. Not like a reporter." He laughed. "You guys are pretty easy to spot, you know that?"

"Balls," I said. "Not me. Everybody else says I look like a cop."

He looked at me for a moment, tapping his foot on the accelerator to keep the engine up. "Yeah," he said. "I guess so. You could pass for a cop as long as you kept your mouth shut."

"I'm usually pretty discreet," I said.

He smiled. "Sure you are. We've all noticed it. That other press guy that's still here asked me who you were the other day, when you were bad-mouthing Nixon . . ."

"What's his name?" I was curious to know who else in the press corps would endure this kind of shame and isolation.

"I can't remember now," Bobo said. "He's a tall guy with grey hair and glasses. He drives a blue Ford station wagon."

I wondered who it could be. It would have to be somebody with a very compelling reason to stay on, in this place. Everybody with good sense or a reasonable excuse had left as soon as possible. Some of the TV network technicians had stayed until Saturday, dismantling the maze of wires and cables they'd set up in the Fontainebleau before the convention started. They were easy to spot because they wore things like Levis and sweatshirts—but by Sunday I was the only guest in the hotel not dressed like a PR man for Hialeah Racetrack on a Saturday night in mid-season.

It is not enough, in the Fontainebleau, to look like some kind of a weird and sinister cop; to fit in here, you want to look like somebody who just paid a scalper $200 for a front row seat at the Johnny Carson show.

Bobo put the car in gear, but kept his foot on the brake pedal and asked: "What are you writing? What did all that bullshit come down to?"

"Jesus," I said. "That's just what I've been trying to put together upstairs. You're asking me to compress about two hundred hours of work into sixty seconds."

He grinned. "You're on *my* time now. Give it a try. Tell me what happened."

I paused in the driveway, shifting the beer bags to my other arm, and thought for a moment. "Okay," I said. "Nixon sold out the party for the next twenty years by setting up an Agnew/Kennedy race in '76, but he knew exactly what he was doing and he did it for the same reason he's done everything else since he first got into politics—to make sure he gets elected."

He stared at me, not grasping it.

I hesitated, trying to put it all in a quick little capsule. "Okay," I said finally, "the reason Nixon put Agnew and the Goldwater freaks in charge of the party this year is that he knows they can't win in '76—but it was a good short-term trade; they have to stay with him this year, which will probably be worth a point or two in November—and that's important to Nixon, because he thinks it's going to be close: Fuck the polls. They always *follow* reality instead of predicting it. . . . But the *real* reason he turned the party over to the Agnew/Goldwater wing is that he knows most of the old-line Democrats who just got stomped by McGovern for the nomination wouldn't mind seeing George get taken out in '72 if they know they can get back in the saddle if they're willing to wait four years."

Bobo laughed, understanding it instantly. Pimps and hustlers have a fine instinct for politics. "What you're saying is that Nixon just cashed his whole check," he said. "He doesn't give a flying fuck what happens once he gets re-elected—because once he wins, it's all over for him anyway, right? He can't run again . . ."

"Yeah," I said, pausing to twist the top off one of the ale bottles I'd been pulling out of the bag. "But the thing you want to understand is that Nixon has such a fine understanding of the way politicians think that he *knew* people like Daley and Meany and Ted Kennedy would go along with him—because it's in *their* interest now to have Nixon get his second term, in exchange for a guaranteed Democratic victory in 1976."

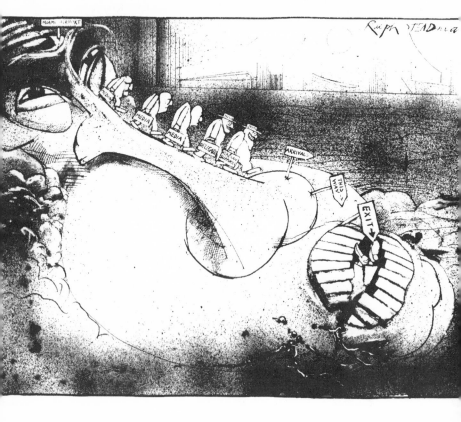

"God damn!" he said. "That's beautiful! They're gonna trade him four years now for eight later, right? Give Nixon his last trip in '72, then Kennedy moves in for eight years in '76. . . . Jesus, that's so rotten I really have to admire it." He chuckled. "Boy, I thought *I* was cynical!"

"That's not cynical," I said. "That's pure, nut-cutting politics. . . . And I advise you to stay out of it; you're too sensitive."

He laughed and hit the accelerator, leaping away with a sharp screech of rubber and just barely missing the tail-light of a long gold Cadillac as he turned down the ramp.

I pushed through the revolving door and crossed the vast lobby to the elevators, still sipping my ale as I thought about what I'd just said. Had Nixon really sold the party down the river? Was it a conscious act, or pure instinct? Had he made a deal with Meany during one of their golf games? Was Daley in on it? Ted Kennedy? Who else?

I finished the ale and dropped the empty bottle into a huge spittoon full of blue gravel. Two elderly women standing next to me looked disgusted, but I ignored them and wandered over to the door of the world-renowned Poodle bar and cocktail lounge. It was almost empty. An imitation Glenn Miller band was playing the Tennessee Waltz, but nobody was dancing. Three nights ago the Poodle had been so crowded that it was difficult to get through the door. Every high-powered, hot-rod journalist in the western world had made the scene here last week. At least that's what Sally Quinn told me, and she knows about things like that.

I went back to the elevators and found one ready to go. The sight of my ale bottle in the spittoon reminded me of Nixon again . . . Who else might be in on that deal? I picked a Miami *Herald* off a stack in the rear of the elevator, then handed the matron a dollar.

"Twenty-five cents," she said briskly, bringing the car to a stop at my floor . . . but before she could hand me the change I stepped out and waved back at her. "Nevermind," I said, "I'm rich." Then I hurried down the hall to my room and bolted the door.

The game had already started, but there was no score. I dumped my ale bottles in the styrofoam cooler, then opened one and sat down to watch the action and brood on Nixon's treachery. But first I concentrated on the game for a while. It is hard to understand how somebody else thinks unless you can get on their wavelength: get in tune with their patterns, their pace, their connections . . . and since Nixon is a known football addict, I decided to get my head totally into the rhythm of this exhibition game between the Rams and Kansas City before attempting the jump into politics.

Very few people understand this kind of logic. I learned it from a Brazilian psychiatrist in the Matto Grosso back in 1963. He called it "Rhythm Logic," in English, because he said I would never be able to pronounce it in the original Jibaro. I tried it once or twice, but the Jibaro language was too much for me—and it didn't make much difference anyway. I seemed to have an instinct for Rhythm Logic, because I picked it up very quickly. But I have never been able to explain it, except in terms of music, and typewriters are totally useless when it comes to that kind of translation.

In any case, by the end of the first quarter I felt ready. By means of intense concentration on *every detail* of the football game, I was able to "derail" my own inner brain waves and re-pattern them temporarily to the inner brain wave rhythms of a serious football fanatic. The next step, then, was to bring my "borrowed" rhythms into focus on a subject quite different from football—such as presidential politics.

In the third and final step, I merely concentrated on a pre-selected problem involving presidential politics, and attempted to solve it subjectively . . . although the word "subjectively," at this point, had a very different true meaning. Because I was no longer reasoning in the rhythms of my own inner brain waves, but in the rhythms of a football addict.

At that point, it became almost unbearably clear to me that Richard Nixon had in fact sold the Republican Party down the tube in Miami. Consciously, perhaps, but never quite verbally. Because the rhythms of his own inner brain waves had convinced his conscious mind that in fact he had no choice. Given the safe assumption that the most important objective in Richard Nixon's life today is minimizing the risk of losing the 1972 election to George McGovern, simple logic decreed that he should bend all his energies to that end, at all costs. All other objectives would have to be subjugated to Number One.

By half time, with the Rams trailing by six, I had established a firm scientific basis for the paranoid gibberish I had uttered, an hour or so earlier, while standing in the hotel driveway and talking with Bobo the night-pimp. At the time, not wanting to seem ignorant or confused, I had answered his question with the first wisdom capsule that popped into my mind. . . . But now it made perfect sense, thanks to Rhythm Logic, and all that remained were two or three secondary questions, none of them serious.

To say that Nixon "sold the Republican Party down the river" in order to minimize his chances of losing this election is probably a bit harsh. Most of the GOP delegates in Miami were eager to make that trip, anyway. All Nixon did was make sure they got safely aboard the raft and into the current. It was no accident that the Nixon convention in Miami looked and sounded like a replay of the Goldwater convention in San Francisco eight years ago. They even brought Goldwater back and treated him like a hero. His opening-night speech was a classic of vengeful ignorance, but the delegates loved it. He was scheduled to speak for ten minutes, but he worked himself into such a fever that it took him half an hour to make sure everybody in the hall—and the TV audience, too—understood what he'd come there to say: That he'd been *eight years ahead of his time* in '64, by God! But now the party had finally caught up with him! At last, they were cheering him again, instead of laughing at him . . . and just in case anybody doubted it, he was here to tell them that the *whole country* was finally catching up with him, too.

No other speaker at that convention was allowed to ignore the time limit laid out for him in the split-second script, but Goldwater was encouraged to rave and snarl at the cameras until he ran out of things to say. His speech set the tone for the whole convention, and his only real competition was Ronald Reagan. Compared to those two, both Agnew and Nixon sounded like bleeding-heart liberals.

The next step, on Tuesday, was a public whipping for GOP "liberals" like Illinois Senator Charles Percy who wanted to change some of the delegate selection rules so the large industrial (and usually more liberal) states would have more of a voice in the 1976 convention. But his proposal lost by a landslide, and the '76 convention—at which Agnew is now expected to be the leading contender —will be dominated as usual by rural conservatives from the South and the West.[1]

At this point, thanks again to Rhythm Logic, a blueprint begins to take shape:

Nixon returned from Miami with a commanding 60-30 lead over McGovern in the public opinion polls—but roughly half of

---

1. JANUARY 7, 1973. *King Features Syndicate.* In the opinion of Republican insiders, Vice President Spiro Agnew is much closer than is generally believed to having the 1976 nomination locked up. As one of them put it to me recently, "If 100 equals the nomination, then Agnew is now at 75, or better."—*Jeffrey Hart*

that margin would disappear overnight if McGovern could somehow get the support of the Old Guard Democrats (the Jewish vote,
the Humphrey vote, AFL-CIO unions still loyal to George Meany)
who lost to McGovern in the primaries and now refuse to support
him.

The reasons they give are generally too vague or unfounded to
argue with: "too radical," "anti-labor," "anti-Semitic," and they
are not worth arguing about anyway; because the real reason why
so many Old Guard Democrats are backing away from McGovern
is a powerful desire to regain their control of the Democratic Party.
The McGovern organization has only a tentative grip on the party
machinery now, but a McGovern victory in November would give
him at least four years to rebuild and revitalize the whole structure
in his own image. To many professional Democrats—particularly
the Big Fish in a Small Pond types who worked overtime for Humphrey or Jackson last spring—the prospect of a McGovern victory
is far more frightening than another four years of Nixon.

Indeed, and Nixon has a keen understanding of these things.
He has been a professional pol all his life, through many ups and
downs. He understands that politics is a rotten, frequently degrading business that corrupts everybody who steps in it, but this knowledge no longer bothers him. Some say it never did, in fact—but that
was the Old Nixon. We have seen many models since then, but now
we are on the brink of coming to grips with The Real Nixon.

This campaign will almost certainly be his last, regardless of
how it turns out. A win would retire him automatically, and a loss
would probably shatter his personality along with his ego. That is
one of the main keys to understanding the Real Nixon Strategy
Analysis. A loss to McGovern would be such a shock to Nixon that
he would probably change his name at once and emigrate to Rho-
desia. Not even a narrow victory would make him happy; this time
he wants to win big, and he intends to.

The intensity of his Big/Sure Win obsession became apparent
to Clark McGregor, his new campaign manager, even before I
picked it up with Rhythm Logic. On the day after the convention,

most of the talk among Nixon's staff members was about "how to avoid complacency." Their Doral Hotel fortress was rank with overconfidence. McGregor, sitting happy on a campaign war chest of "between $35 million and $38 million," had just decided to use some of the cash to fight complacency by organizing Nixon volunteer groups in some of the states. Then he went downstairs to a meeting of the GOP financial committee and was surprised to hear Maurice Stans, Nixon's chief fund-raiser, announce that the presidential campaign budget had just been boosted to $45 million—$15 million more than the 1968 Nixon campaign used in the tight race against Hubert Humphrey.

The President was not immediately available for comment on how he planned to spend his forty-five Big Ones, but Stans said he planned to safeguard the funds personally.

At that point, McGregor cracked Stans upside the head with a Gideon Bible and called him a "thieving little fart." McGregor then began shoving the rest of us out of the room, but when Stans tried to leave, McGregor grabbed him by the neck and jerked him back inside. Then he slammed the door and threw the bolt . . .

Jesus, why do I write things like that? I must be getting sick, or maybe just tired of writing about these greasy Rotarian bastards. I think it's time to move on to something else. But first I guess I should finish off that story about how Nixon sold his party down the river.

It was basically a straight-across trade: Agnew for McGovern. By welcoming all the right-wingers and yahoos back into the front ranks of the party—then watching silently as "liberals" fought vainly for a fair share of the delegate seats in '76—Nixon aimed the party as far towards the Right as he could, while charting his own course straight down the center and opening wide his arms to all those poor homeless Democrats who got driven out of their own party by that jew-baiting, strike-busting, radical bastard George McGovern, "the Goldwater of the Left."

Meanwhile, Barry Goldwater himself is riding high again in the GOP. The party is back in step with him now, and by the time the '76 convention rolls around, Spiro Agnew is likely to find himself hooted off the podium—like Rockefeller in '64—as a useless backsliding liberal. That convention will want to nominate one of their own, and whoever emerges to carry the party colors will almost certainly be doomed from the start and mocked by all the Humphrey/Meany Democrats—who will have gone back home, by then —as "The McGovern of the Right."

Nixon sees his margin of safety on November 7th in the number of anti-McGovern Democrats he can coax across the line to vote for him.[2] Despite his huge lead in the polls, he knows better than to believe he'll be thirty points ahead on election day. Sooner or later, McGovern's top command will get bored with this brainless squabbling among themselves. They've been at it for more than a month now, like a bunch of winos locked in a small closet.

Gary Hart insists the "real work" of the campaign is going along just like it was in New Hampshire, or Wisconsin, or California— "but the press can't see it now, just like they couldn't see it back in the early primaries. Hell, our organizers don't hold press conferences; nobody interviews our canvassers.

"I'd say we're at the same stage now [September 1] that we were back in the third week of February. Stop worrying, Hunter, we're doing fine."

Well . . . maybe so. If it's true, Nixon is going to need all the Humphrey/Meany Democrats he can get. Once his margin starts slipping he'll get nervous, and if that Watergate case ever gets into court he might get *very* nervous.

But he has already bought his insurance policy. The Old Guard anti-McGovern Democrats might not be so willing to dump McGovern if they thought they might lose again in '76. But Nixon appears to have taken care of that problem for them, quietly opening the way for a Kennedy vs. Agnew fiasco four years from now.

---

2. He convinced some 15 million of them by November 7th. It was all he needed.

Compared to the Democratic Convention five weeks earlier, the Nixon celebration was an ugly, low-level trip that hovered somewhere in that grim indefinable limbo between dullness and obscenity—like a bad pornographic film that you want to walk out on, but sit through anyway and then leave the theater feeling depressed and vaguely embarrassed with yourself for ever having taken part in it, even as a spectator.

It was so bad, overall, that it is hard to even work up the energy to write about it. Not even the frenzied efforts of the TV news moguls could make the thing interesting. According to a Miami *Herald* reporter who monitored TV coverage from gavel to gavel, "at any given time, only about 15 percent of New York metropolitan households—where early returns are available—were tuned to network convention coverage."

On the Sunday after the convention, Mike Wallace presided over a CBS-TV roundup "special" on what happened in Miami, and when he summed it all up in the end—after an hour's worth of fantastically expensive film clips—he dismissed the whole thing as a useless bummer. Speaking for the CBS floor reporters, he said, "We labored mightily, and brought forth a mouse."

Most of the linear press people seemed to feel the same way. Every midnight, at the end of each session, the Poodle Lounge in the Fontainebleau filled up with sullen journalists who would spend the next three hours moaning at each other about what a goddamn rotten nightmare it all was. On Tuesday night I was sitting at a table in the Poodle with a clutch of New York heavies— Dick Reeves from *New York Magazine,* Russ Barnard from *Harpers,* Phil Tracy from the *Village Voice,* etc.— and when they started bitching about the music from the bandstand where a 1952 vintage nite-klub saxophone group was fouling the air, I said, "You bastards had better get used to that music; you'll be hearing a hell of a lot of it for the next four years."

Nobody laughed. I finished my double-tequila and went upstairs to my room to get hopelessly stoned by myself and pass out. It was that kind of a convention.

The pervasive sense of gloom among the press/media crowd in Miami was only slightly less obvious than the gung-ho, breast-beating arrogance of the Nixon delegates themselves. That was the real story of the convention: the strident, loutish confidence of the whole GOP machinery, from top to bottom. Looking back on that week, one of my clearest memories is that maddening "FOUR MORE YEARS!" chant from the Nixon Youth gallery in the convention hall. NBC's John Chancellor compared the Nixon Youth cheering section to the Chicago "sewer workers" who were herded into the Stockyards convention hall in Chicago four years ago to cheer for Mayor Daley. The Nixon Youth people were not happy with Chancellor for making that remark on camera. They complained very bitterly about it, saying it was just another example of the "knee-jerk liberal" thinking that dominates the media.

But the truth is that Chancellor was absolutely right. Due to a strange set of circumstances, I spent two very tense hours right in the middle of that Nixon Youth mob on Tuesday night, and it gave me an opportunity to speak at considerable length with quite a few of them. . . .

What happened, in a nut, was that I got lost in a maze of hallways in the back reaches of the convention hall on Tuesday night about an hour or so before the roll-call vote on Nixon's chances of winning the GOP nomination again this year. . . . I had just come off the convention floor, after the Secret Service lads chased me away from the First Family box where I was trying to hear what Charlton Heston was saying to Nelson Rockefeller, and in the nervous wake of an experience like that I felt a great thirst rising . . . so I tried to take a shortcut to the Railroad Lounge, where free beer was available to the press; but I blew it somewhere along the way and ended up in a big room jammed with Nixon Youth workers, getting themselves ready for a "spontaneous demonstration" at the moment of climax out there on the floor. . . . I was just idling around in the hallway, trying to go north for a beer, when I got swept up in a fast-moving mob of about two thousand people heading south at good speed, so instead of fighting the tide I let myself

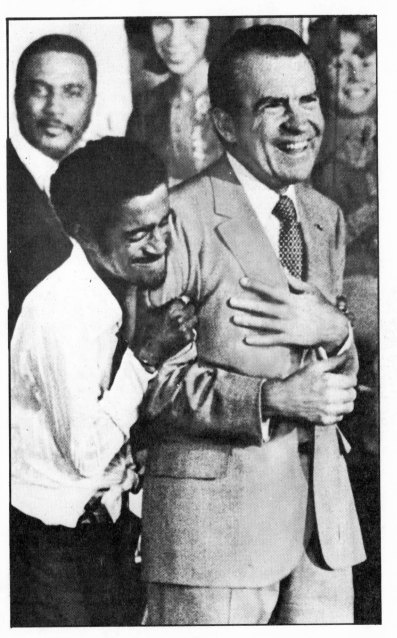

be carried along to wherever they were going. . . .

Which turned out to be the "Ready Room," in a far corner of the hall, where a dozen or so people wearing red hats and looking like small-town high-school football coaches were yelling into bullhorns and trying to whip this herd of screaming sheep into shape for the spontaneous demonstration, scheduled for 10:33 P.M.

It was a very disciplined scene. The red-hatted men with the bullhorns did all the talking. Huge green plastic "refuse" sacks full of helium balloons were distributed, along with handfuls of New Year's Eve party noisemakers and hundreds of big cardboard signs that said things like: "NIXON NOW!" . . . "FOUR MORE YEARS!" . . . "NO COMPROMISE!"

Most of the signs were freshly printed. They looked exactly like the "WE LOVE MAYOR DALEY" signs that Daley distributed to his sewer workers in Chicago in 1968: red and blue ink on a white background . . . but a few, here and there, were hand-lettered, and mine happened to be one of these. It said, "GARBAGE MEN DEMAND EQUAL TIME." I had several choices, but this one seemed right for the occasion.

Actually, there was a long and active time lag between the moment when I was swept into the Ready Room and my decision to carry a sign in the spontaneous demonstration. I have a lot of on-the-spot notes about this, somewhere in my suitcase, but I can't find them now and it's 3:15 A.M. in Miami and I have to catch a plane for Chicago at noon—then change planes for Denver, then change again in Denver for the last plane to Aspen—so I'll try to put some flesh on this scene when I get to Woody Creek and my own typewriter; this one is far too slow for good dialogue or fast-moving behavior.

Just to put a fast and tentative ending on it, however, what happened in that time lag was that they discovered me early on, and tried to throw me out—but I refused to go, and that's when the dialogue started. For the first ten minutes or so I was getting very ominous Hells Angels flashbacks—all alone in a big crowd of hostile, cranked-up geeks in a mood to stomp somebody—but it

354

soon became evident that these Nixon Youth people weren't ready for that kind of madness.

Our first clash erupted when I looked up from where I was sitting on the floor against a wall in the back of the room and saw Ron Rosenbaum from the *Village Voice* coming at me in a knot of shouting Nixon Youth wranglers. "No press allowed!" they were screaming. "Get out of here! You can't stay!"

They had nailed Rosenbaum at the door—but, instead of turning back and giving up, he plunged into the crowded room and made a beeline for the back wall, where he'd already spotted me sitting in peaceful anonymity. By the time he reached me he was gasping for breath and about six fraternity/jock types were clawing at his arms. "They're trying to throw me out!" he shouted.

I looked up and shuddered, knowing my cover was blown. Within seconds, they were screaming at me, too. "You crazy bastard," I shouted at Rosenbaum. "You *fingered* me! Look what you've done!"

"No press!" they were shouting. "OUT! Both of you!"

I stood up quickly and put my back to the wall, still cursing Rosenbaum. "That's right!" I yelled. "Get that bastard out of here! No press allowed!"

Rosenbaum stared at me. There was shock and repugnance in his eyes—as if he had just recognized me as a lineal descendant of Judas Iscariot. As they muscled him away, I began explaining to my accusers that I was really more of a political observer than a journalist. "Have *you* run for office?" I snapped at one of them. "No! I thought not, goddamnit! You don't have the look of a man who's been to the well. I can see it in your face!"

He was taken aback by this charge. His mouth flapped for a few seconds, then he blurted out: "What about *you?* What office did *you* run for?"

I smiled gently. "Sheriff, my friend. I ran for Sheriff, out in Colorado—and I lost by just a hair. Because the *liberals* put the screws to me! Right! Are you surprised?"

He was definitely off balance.

That's why I came here as an *observer*," I continued. "I wanted to see what it was like on the inside of a *winning* campaign."

It was just about then that somebody noticed my "press" tag

was attached to my shirt by a blue and white MᴄGᴏᴠᴇʀɴ button. I'd been wearing it for three days, provoking occasional rude comments from hotheads on the convention floor and in various hotel lobbies—but this was the first time I'd felt called upon to explain myself. It was, after all, the only visible MᴄGᴏᴠᴇʀɴ button in Miami Beach that week—in Flamingo Park or anywhere else—and now I was trying to join a spontaneous Nixon Youth demonstration that was about to spill out onto the floor of the very convention that had just nominated Richard Nixon for re-election, against McGovern.

They seemed to feel I was mocking their efforts in some way . . . and at that point the argument became so complex and disjointed that I can't possibly run it all down here. It is enough, for now, to say that we finally compromised: If I refused to leave without violence, then I was damn well going to have to carry a sign in the spontaneous demonstration—and also wear a plastic red, white, and blue Nixon hat. They never came right out and said it, but I could see they were uncomfortable at the prospect of all three network TV cameras looking down on their spontaneous Nixon Youth demonstration and zeroing in—for their own perverse reasons—on a weird-looking, 35-year-old speed freak with half his hair burned off from overindulgence, wearing a big blue MᴄGᴏᴠᴇʀɴ button on his chest, carrying a tall cup of "Old Milwaukee" and shaking his fist at John Chancellor up in the NBC booth—screaming: "You dirty bastard! You'll *pay* for this, by God! We'll rip your goddamn teeth out! KILL! KILL! Your number just came up, you communist son of a bitch!"

I politely dismissed all suggestions that I remove my MᴄGᴏᴠ-ᴇʀɴ button, but I agreed to carry a sign and wear a plastic hat like everybody else. "Don't worry," I assured them. "You'll be proud of me. There's a lot of bad blood between me and John Chancellor. He put acid in my drink last month at the Democratic Convention, then he tried to humiliate me in public."

"Acid? Golly, that's terrible! What kind of acid?"

"It felt like Sunshine," I said.

"Sunshine?"

"Yeah. He denied it, of course—But hell, he *always* denies it."

"Why?" a girl asked.

"Would *you* admit a thing like that?"

She shook her head emphatically. "But I wouldn't do it either," she said. "You could *kill* somebody by making them drink acid— why would he want to kill *you?*"

I shrugged, "Who knows? He eats a lot of it himself." I paused, sensing confusion. . . . "Actually I doubt if he really wanted to kill me. It was a hell of a dose, but not *that* strong." I smiled. "All I remember is the first rush: It came up my spine like nine taran- tulas . . . drilled me right to the bar stool for two hours; I couldn't speak, couldn't even blink my eyes."

"Boy, what kind of acid does that?" somebody asked.

"Sunshine," I said. "Every time."

By now several others had picked up on the conversation. A bright-looking kid in a blue gabardine suit interrupted: "Sunshine acid? Are you talking about LSD?"

"Right," I said.

Now the others understood. A few laughed, but others mut- tered darkly, "You mean John Chancellor goes around putting LSD in people's drinks? He takes it himself? . . . He's a dope addict . . .?"

"Golly," said the girl. "That explains a lot, doesn't it?"

By this time I was having a hard time keeping a straight face. These poor, ignorant young waterheads. Would they pass this weird revelation on to their parents when they got back home to Middletown, Shaker Heights, and Orange County? Probably so, I thought. And then their parents would write letters to NBC, saying they'd learned from reliable sources that Chancellor was addicted to LSD-25—supplied to him in great quantities, no doubt, by Communist agents—and demanding that he be jerked off the air immediately and locked up.

I was tempted to start babbling crazily about Walter Cronkite: that he was heavy into the white slavery trade—sending agents to South Vietnam to adopt orphan girls, then shipping them back to his farm in Quebec to be lobotomized and sold into brothels up and down the Eastern seaboard. . . .

But before I could get into this one, the men in the red hats began shouting that the magic moment was on us. The Ready Room crackled with tension; we were into the countdown. They divided us into four groups of about five hundred each and gave the final instructions. We were to rush onto the floor and begin chanting, cheering, waving our signs at the TV cameras, and generally whooping it up. Every other person was given a big garbage bag full of twenty-five or thirty helium balloons, which they were instructed to release just as soon as we reached the floor. Our entrance was timed precisely to coincide with the release of the thousands of non-helium balloons from the huge cages attached to the ceiling of the hall . . . so that our balloons would be *rising* while the others were *falling,* creating a sense of mass euphoria and perhaps even weightlessness for the prime-time TV audience.

I was ready for some good clean fun at that point, and by the time we got the signal to start moving I was seized by a giddy conviction that we were all about to participate in a spectacle that would go down, as it were, in history.

They herded us out of the Ready Room and called a ragged kind of cadence while we double-timed it across the wet grass under the guava trees in back of the hall, and finally burst through a well-guarded access door held open for us by Secret Service men just as the balloons were released from the ceiling . . . it was wonderful; I waved happily to the SS man as I raced past him with the herd and then onto the floor. The hall was so full of balloons that I couldn't see anything at first, but then I spotted Chancellor up there in the booth and I let the bastard have it. First I held up my "Garbage Men Demand Equal Time" sign at him. Then, when I was sure he'd noticed the sign, I tucked it under my arm and ripped off my hat, clutching it in the same fist I was shaking angrily at the NBC booth and screaming at the top of my lungs: "You evil scumsucker! You're *through!* You limp-wristed Nazi moron!"

I went deep into the foulest back-waters of my vocabulary for that trip, working myself into a flat-out screeching hate-frenzy for

five or six minutes and drawing smiles of approval from some of
my fellow demonstrators. They were dutifully chanting the slogans
that had been assigned to them in the Ready Room—but I was
really *into it,* and I could see that my zeal impressed them.

But a little bit of that bullshit goes a long way, and I quickly
tired of it. When I realized that my erstwhile buddies were settling
into the FOUR MORE YEARS chant, I figured it was time to
move on.

Which was not easy. By this time, the whole crowd was facing
the TV booths and screaming in unison. People were trampling
each other to get up front and make themselves heard—or at least
to get on camera for the homefolks—and the mood of that crowd
was not receptive to the sight of a MCGOVERN button in their midst,
so I moved against the tide as gently as possible, keeping my
elbows close down on my ribs and shouting "Chancellor to the
Wall!" every thirty seconds or so, to keep myself inconspicuous.

By the time I got to the "periodical press" exit I was almost
overcome with a sense of *deja vu.* I had seen all this before. I
had been right in the middle of it before—but when?

Then it came to me. Yes. In 1964, at the Goldwater convention in San Francisco, when poor Barry unloaded that fateful
line about "Extremism in the defense of liberty is no vice, etc. . . ."
I was on the floor of the Cow Palace when he laid that one on the
crowd, and I remember feeling genuinely frightened at the violent
reaction it provoked. The Goldwater delegates went completely
amok for fifteen or twenty minutes. He hadn't even finished the
sentence before they were on their feet, cheering wildly. Then, as
the human thunder kept building, they mounted their metal chairs
and began howling, shaking their fists at Huntley and Brinkley up
in the NBC booth—and finally they began picking up those chairs
with both hands and bashing them against chairs other delegates
were still standing on.

359

It was a memorable performance, etched every bit as clearly in the grey folds of my brain as the police beatings I saw at the corner of Michigan and Balboa four years later . . . but the Nixon convention in Miami was not even in the same league with Chicago in '68. The blinding stench of tear gas brought back memories, but only on the surface. Around midnight on Wednesday I found myself reeling around completely blind on Washington Avenue in front of the convention hall, bumping against cops wearing black rubber gas masks and running demonstrators clutching wet towels over their faces. Many of the cops were wearing khaki flak jackets and waving three-foot hickory pick-handles . . . but nobody hit me, and despite the gas and the chaos, I never felt in danger. Finally, when the gas got so bad that I no longer knew what direction I was moving in, I staggered across somebody's lawn and began feeling my way along the outside of the house until I came to a water faucet. I sat down on the grass and soaked my handkerchief under the tap, then pressed it on my face, without rubbing, until I was able to see again. When I finally got up, I realized that at least a dozen cops had been standing within twenty feet of me the whole time, watching passively and not offering any help—but not beating me into a bloody, screaming coma, either.

That was the difference between Chicago and Miami. Or at least one of the most significant differences. If the cops in Chicago had found me crawling around in somebody's front yard, wearing a "press" tag and blind from too much gas, they'd have broken half my ribs and then hauled me away in handcuffs for "resisting arrest." I saw it happen so often that I still feel the bile rising when I think about it.

Time Warp: New Hampshire, Aug. 24

We arrived at the Wayfarer sometime around four-thirty or five on Thursday morning, badly twisted—and for a while neither one of us said anything. We just sat there in the driveway and stared straight ahead, with no focus. Somewhere in front of the windshield I thought I could see a long row of sand dunes in the fog and there seemed to be small moving shapes.

"Jesus," I said finally. "Look at all those goddamn sea otters. I thought they were extinct."

"Sea otters?" Crouse muttered, hunching down on the wheel and staring intently into the darkness.

"Straight ahead," I said. "They're hunkered down in the dune grass. Hundreds of the bastards . . . Yeah . . . we're almost to San Luis Obispo."

"What?" he said, still squinting into the darkness.

I noticed he was running through the gears fairly rapidly: First-Second-Third-Fourth . . . Fourth-Third-Second-First. Down and up, up and down; not paying much attention to what he was doing.

"You better slow down," I said. "We'll roll this bastard if we go into the turn with no warning . . . with these goddamn U-joints blown out." I looked over at him. "What the fuck are you doing with the gears?"

He continued to shift aimlessly, not meeting my gaze. The radio was getting louder: some kind of big-beat hillbilly song about truck drivers popping little white pills and driving for six days with no sleep. I could just barely hear him when he started talking.

"I think we came to the motel," he said. "There's a man standing in there behind the desk, trying to watch us."

"Fuck him," I said. "We're okay."

He shook his head. "Not you."

"What?"

"The next thing is to register," he said. "We're here. Mc-Govern headquarters. Manchester, New Hampshire . . . and that man in there might call the police if we sit out here any longer without doing something."

I could see the man staring out at us through the glass doors. "Do we have reservations?" I said finally.

He nodded.

"Okay," I said. "Let's take in the luggage."

He twisted around in his seat and began counting out loud,

very slowly: "One . . . Two . . . Three . . . Four . . . Five . . . Six . . . and two silver ice-buckets." Then he shook his head slowly. "No . . . we can't take it all at once."

"The hell we can't," I snapped. "What the fuck do you want to do—leave it in the car?"

He shrugged.

"Not mine," I said. "Not with these U-joints like they are."

"Bullshit," he muttered. "U-joints, sea otters, sand dunes . . . I think we're about to get busted; let's walk in there and tell him we want to register." He tossed off his seat belt and opened the door. "Let's each take a suitcase and tell him who we are."

"Right," I said, opening my own door and stepping out. "We got here from Boston with no trouble. Why should we have any now?"

He was opening up the back, to get the luggage. It was one of those new Volvo station wagons with a hinge on the whole rear end, like a small garage door. I didn't want to alarm the man inside the motel by moving slowly or erratically, so I planted my left foot firmly on the gravel driveway and moved fast toward the rear of the car.

WHACK!!! A dull sound in my ear, and pain all over my head. I heard myself screech . . . then reeling across the gravel and falling into shrubbery, grasping wildly for a handhold, then hitting a wooden wall with a heavy thump . . . then silence, while I leaned there, holding onto the wall with one hand and my head with the other. I could see Crouse watching me, saying something I couldn't hear. The right half of my skull felt like it had just been blown off by a bazooka. But I felt no blood or bone splinters, and after forty seconds or so I managed to straighten up.

"Jesus god!" I said. "What was *that?*"

He shook his head. "You just suddenly fell away and started yelling," he said. "Christ, you took a real crack on the head—but you were coming so fast I couldn't say anything until . . ."

"Was it Mankiewicz?" I asked.

He hesitated, seeming to think for a moment, then nodded. "I

362

think so," he said quietly. "But he came out of the darkness so fast, I couldn't be sure. Jesus, he never even broke stride. He got a full-stroke running shot on you with that big leather sap he carries . . . then he kept right on going; across the driveway and into those bushes at the end of the building, where the path leads down to the river . . . over there by the gazebo."

I could see the white-domed wooden gazebo out there in the moonlight, squatting peacefully about ten yards offshore in the slow-moving current of the Piscataquog River . . . but now it seemed very ominous-looking, and big enough inside to conceal a dozen men with saps.

Was Mankiewicz out there? How long had he been waiting? And how had he known I was coming? It had been a last-minute decision, precipitated by a snarling argument with the night manager of the Ritz-Carleton in Boston. He'd refused to cash a check for me at 2:00 A.M. . . . but he finally agreed to spring for $10 if I gave the bellboy 10 percent of it for bringing the cash up to the room.

By that time, the bellboy was so rattled that he forgot to take the check. I had to coax him back down the hall and push it into his hands . . . and there was no argument when we checked out moments later, after stripping the room of everything we could haul through the lobby in big laundry bags.

Now, ninety miles away on the outskirts of Manchester, I had to shut one eye in order to focus on Crouse. "Are you sure that was Mankiewicz who hit me?" I asked, trying to look him in the eye.

He nodded.

"How did he know I'd be here tonight?" I snapped. "You *fingered* me, didn't you?"

"Hell no!" he replied. "I didn't even know myself until we had that scene at the Ritz."

I thought for a moment, trying to reconstruct the events that had brought us to this place. "Back there in Boston, you were gone for ten minutes!" I said, "When you went out to get your car . . . yes . . . you carried those ice buckets out, then you disappeared."

I slammed my fist on the raised rear door of the Volvo. " You had time to *call,* didn't you?"

He was pulling our bags out, trying to ignore me.

"Who *else* could have tipped him off?" I shouted.

He glanced nervously at the man behind the desk inside the office. "Okay," he said finally. "I might as well admit it . . . Yeah, I knew Frank was laying for you, so I called him and set it all up."

My head was beginning to swell. "Why?" I groaned. "What was *in* it for you?"

He shrugged, then reached for another suitcase. "Money," he said. "Power. He promised me a job in the White House."

I nodded. "So you set me up, you bastard."

"Why not," he replied. "I've worked with Frank before. We understand each other." He smiled. "How do you think I got this new Volvo wagon?"

"From *Rolling Stone,*" I said. "Hell, they paid for mine."

"What?"

"Sure, we *all* got them."

He stared at me, looking very groggy. "Bullshit," he muttered. "Let's get inside before Mankiewicz decides to come back and finish you off." He nodded toward the gazebo. "I can hear him pacing around out there . . . and if I know Frank, he'll want to finish the job."

I focused my good eye on the gazebo, a moonlit wooden pillbox out in the river . . . Then I picked up my bag. "You're right," I said. "He'll make another try. Let's get inside. I have a can of Mace in that satchel. You think he can handle it?"

"Handle what?"

"Mace. Soak the fucker down with it. Put him right to his knees, stone blind, unable to breathe for forty-five minutes."

Crouse nodded. "Right, it'll be a good lesson for him. That arrogant bastard. This'll teach him to go around cracking responsible journalists in the head."

Checking into the Wayfarer was difficult, but not in the way we expected. The man at the desk ignored our twisted condition and sent us off to a wing so far from the main nexus of the hotel that it took us about forty-five minutes to find our rooms . . . and by then it was almost dawn, so we cranked up the tape machine and got into the Singapore Grey for a while . . . admiring the appointments and congratulating ourselves on having the wisdom to flee the Ritz-Carleton and move to a decent place like the Wayfarer.

In the course of this apparently endless campaign I have set up the National Affairs Desk in some of the worst hotels, motels, and other foul commercial lodging establishments in the western world. Politicians, journalists, and traveling salesmen seem to gravitate to these places—for reasons I'd rather not think about, right now—but the Wayfarer is a rare and constant exception. The one that proves the rule, perhaps . . . but, for whatever reason, it is one of my favorite places: a rambling, woodsy barracks with big rooms, good food, full ice machines, and . . . yes . . . a brief history of pleasant memories.

The Wayfarer was Gene McCarthy's headquarters for the New Hampshire primary in 1968; and it was also McGovern's—unofficially, at least—in the winter of '72. The recent history of the place suggests that it may be something like the Valley Forge of presidential politics. Or maybe the Wayfarer's peculiar mystique has to do with the nature of the New Hampshire primary. There is nothing else quite like it: an intensely personal kind of politics that quickly goes out of style when the field starts narrowing down and the survivors move on to other, larger, and far more complex states.

Which is precisely why both McCarthy and McGovern did so well here. The New Hampshire primary is one of the few situations in presidential politics where the candidates are forced to campaign like human beings, on the same level with the voters. There is no Secret Service presence in New Hampshire, no vast and everpresent staff of hired minions and police escorts . . . the candidates drive around the state in rented Fords, accompanied by a handful of local workers and press people, and they actually walk into people's living rooms and try to explain themselves—taking any and all questions face to face, with no screening, and no place to hide when things get nasty.

It was up in New Hampshire, several weeks before the vote, that I blundered into that now infamous "Men's Room Interview" with McGovern. People have been asking me about it ever since—as if it were some kind of weird journalistic coup, a rare and unnatural accomplishment pulled off by what had to have been a super-inventive or at least super-aggressive pervert.

But in truth it was nothing more than a casual conversation between two people standing at adjoining urinals. I went in there to piss—not to talk to George McGovern—but when I noticed him standing next to me I figured it was only natural to ask him what was happening. If it had been the men's room at the Los Angeles Coliseum during half time at a Rams-49ers game I would probably have cursed John Brodie for throwing "that last interception" . . . but since we were standing in Exeter, New Hampshire, about midway through a presidential primary, I cursed Senator Harold Hughes for siding with Muskie instead of the man I was talking to . . . and if we had just driven through a terrible hailstorm I would probably have cursed the hailstones instead of Hughes.

Which hardly matters. The point is that *anybody* could have walked up to that urinal next to McGovern at that moment, and asked him anything they wanted—and he would have answered, the same way he answered me.

That is the odd magic of the New Hampshire primary, and I didn't really appreciate it until about two months later when I realized that every time McGovern wanted to piss, at least nine Secret Service agents would swoop into the nearest men's room and clear it completely, then cordon off the whole area while the poor bastard went in alone to empty his bladder.

This was only one of the big changes in the style of the McGovern campaign that Crouse and I tried to discuss rationally in the dawn hours of that Friday morning in Manchester. George was scheduled to arrive at the local airport at 10:15, then lead a huge caravan of press, staff, and SS men to the J. F. McElwain Shoe Factory on Silver Street—a symbolic Return to The Roots; his first full-dress campaign appearance since the disastrous "Eagleton affair."

It was the first time since the day after the California primary that we'd had a chance to talk seriously about McGovern. We had covered most of the primaries together, and we had both been in Miami for the convention, but I don't recall uttering a single coherent sentence the whole time I was down there—except perhaps on Thursday afternoon in the basement coffee shop of the Doral Beach Hotel, when I spent an hour or so denouncing McGovern for selecting a "bum" and a "hack" like Eagleton to share the ticket with him. Mankiewicz had not brought the official word down from the penthouse yet, but the name had already leaked and nobody seemed very happy about it.

The lobby of the Doral was jammed with media people, waiting for the announcement, but after milling around up there for a while I went down to the coffee shop with Dave Sugarman, a 22-year-old Dartmouth student from Manchester who had signed on as a volunteer "press aide" in New Hampshire and gone on to handle McGovern's press operations in several other key primary states. He was obviously less than pleased with the Eagleton choice. But he was, after all, on The Staff—so he did his duty and tried to calm me down.

He failed. I had been without sleep for two or three days at the time, and my temper was close to the surface. Beyond that, I had spent the past five or six days brooding angrily over the list of vice-presidential possibilities that McGovern had floated in the New York *Times* several days before the convention even started. I recall telling Mankiewicz in the coffee shop on Friday night that I had never seen so many bums and hacks listed in a single paragraph in any publication for any reason.

Two names that come to mind are Governor Dale Bumpers of Arkansas and Governor Jimmy Carter of Georgia. The others— including Eagleton and Shriver—were almost as bad, I thought. But Frank assured me that my wrath was premature. "Don't worry," he said. "I think you'll be pleasantly surprised."

The clear implication, which made fine sense at the time, was that McGovern was merely tossing a few bones to the demoralized "party bosses" who knew they were about to get steam-rollered. Eagleton was a Muskie man, Shriver was a Kennedy by marriage and a good friend of both Daley and Humphrey, Carter and Bumpers were Good Ole Boys . . . but I had spent enough time around Mankiewicz in the past six months to understand that he was saying all these names were just decoys: that when the deal went down, McGovern would choose his vice-president with the same merciless eye to the New Politics that had characterized his sweep through the primaries.[3]

So there was nothing personal in my loud objections to Eagleton a week later. It struck me as a cheap and unnecessary concession to the pieced-off ward-heeler syndrome that McGovern had been fighting all along. Tom Eagleton was exactly the kind of VP candidate that Muskie or Humphrey would have chosen: a harmless, Catholic, neo-liberal Rotarian nebbish from one of the border states, who presumably wouldn't make waves. A "progressive young centrist" with more ambition than brains: Eagleton would have run with *anybody*. Four years earlier he had seen Hubert lift Muskie out of obscurity and turn him into a national figure, even in defeat. Big Ed had blown it, of course, but his role in the '68 campaign had given him priceless Exposure—the same kind of Exposure that Eagleton knew he would need as a springboard to the White House in '76 or '80, depending on whether McGovern won or lost in '72.

But winning or losing didn't really matter to Eagleton. The important thing was *getting on the ticket*. Exposure. Recognition. No more of this "Tom Who?" bullshit. He was a career politician, and he had driven himself harder than all but a few people knew, to get where he was on that Thursday afternoon in Miami when he heard McGovern's voice on the telephone.

Did he have any "skeletons in his closet?"

Fuck no, he didn't. At least none that either Mankiewicz or Hart were going to locate that afternoon without a king-hell set of bolt-cutters. Eagleton understood—like all the rest of us in Miami that day—that McGovern had to name his choice by 4:00 P.M. or

---

3. As it turned out, Mankiewicz was lying to me—as usual. He had *no idea* on Friday that Tom Eagleton would somehow get the VP nod six days later. Nor did anyone else, including George McGovern—who believed, to the bitter end, that Ted Kennedy would be his running mate.

Ex-Vice-Presidential candidate Thomas Eagleton with James
Naughton of the New York **Times** at right. Below: Sargent Shriver,
Eagleton's replacement.

take his chances with whoever the convention might eventually nominate in what would surely have been a brain-rattling holocaust on Thursday night. It was difficult enough with Eagleton already chosen; God only knows who might have emerged if the *delegates* had actually been forced to name the vice-presidential nominee in an all-night floor fight. Given the nature and mood of the people on that floor, McGovern might have found himself running with Evil Knievel.

So all this gibberish about how many questions Mankiewicz asked Eagleton and how much truth Eagleton avoided telling is beside the point. The deed was done when McGovern made the call. Only a lunatic would have expected Eagleton to start babbling about his "shock treatments" at that point. Shit, all he had to do was *stall* for fifteen minutes; just keep talking . . . it was almost four o'clock, and McGovern was out of options.

Just exactly *why* things came to this desperate pass is still not clear. It is almost impossible now to find anybody remotely associated with McGovern who will admit to having been *for* Eagleton. He "sort of happened," they say, "because none of the others were quite right." Leonard Woodcock, president of the United Auto Workers, was a Catholic, but a fallen one. ("He hasn't been to church in twenty years," said one McGovern aide.) Wisconsin Governor Pat Lucey was Catholic, but his wife was given to tantrums in the Martha Mitchell style . . . and Mayor Kevin White of Boston was not acceptable to Ted Kennedy. At least that's how I heard it from one of McGovern's speech writers. The official public version, however, says White was vetoed by the two kingpins of McGovern's Massachusetts delegation: Harvard Economist John Kenneth Galbraith and Congressman Robert F. Drinan.

One member of the Massachusetts delegation told me Galbraith and Drinan had nothing to do with White's rejection—but when I asked Galbraith about it in Miami, on the first night of the GOP convention, he first refused to say anything at all—but when I persisted he finally said, "Well, I'll tell you this much—it wasn't Teddy." Selah.[4]

---

4. As it turns out, it *was* Teddy He never actually *vetoed* Kevin White,

★

The other vice-presidential finalists were rejected for a variety of reasons that don't really matter much now, because the point of the whole grim story is that McGovern and his brain-trust were determined from the start to use the VP as a peace offering to the Old Politics gang they'd just beaten. It was crucial, they felt, to select somebody acceptable to the Old Guard: The Meany/Daley/Muskie/Humphrey/Truman/LBJ axis — because McGovern *needed* those bastards to beat Nixon.

Which may be true—or at least as true as the hoary wisdom that said a maverick like McGovern couldn't possibly win the Democratic nomination because Ed Muskie began the campaign with a lock on the Party Machinery and all the pols who mattered.

You can't beat City Hall, right?

One of McGovern's closest advisors now is a widely-respected political wizard named Fred Dutton, a 49-year-old Washington lawyer and longtime Kennedy advisor who recently wrote a book called *Changing Sources of Power; American Politics in the 1970's.* Dutton's main theory revolves around the idea that the politics of the Seventies will be drastically different from the politics of the last

---

but he was so vehemently opposed to him as the VP nominee that he first (in a phone talk with McGovern on that fateful Thursday morning) said he might take the Number Two spot himself rather than see it go to White . . . and then, after keeping McGovern dangling for thirty crucial minutes called back to say that a "George & Teddy" ticket was still out of the question—but if it turned out to be "George & Kevin," then he (Kennedy) would just as soon not be included in any plans for the general election campaign. In other words, White was a *good* candidate *but not a great one* —and Kennedys only campaigned for Great Candidates.

McGovern took the hint and scratched White's name off the list without further ado—a fateful move, in retrospect, because after White was dropped the VP selection turned into a desperate grab-bag trip that eventually coughed up Eagleton.

Looking back on it, McGovern would have been better off if he'd stuck with Kevin White. Ted Kennedy wound up "campaigning actively," more or less, for the McGovern/Shriver ticket—which finished with 38.5 percent of the vote, against Nixon's 61.5 percent.

That's a brutal 23-point spread, and it's hard to see how George could have done any worse—with or without Kennedy's help, or even with Charles Manson for a running mate.

thirty or even forty years; that the 1970s will produce a "corner-stone generation" that will bring about a major historical watershed in American politics.

"The politics of the Seventies offer one of those rare chances to rally a new following," he says, "or at least to provoke a different configuration, out of this immense sector of younger voters who are still at an impressionable and responsive stage. If an exciting individual or cause really stirs this generation, it could be activated in numbers that make irrelevant any past indicator of political participation among the young, and it would then become one of the few human waves of historic consequence. If this still unmarshalled mass is allowed to scatter, or a substantial part of it is politically turned off, it will pass by as one of the great lost opportunities in American politics and history."

The book makes more sense—to me, at least—than anything I've read about politics in ten years. It is a cool, scholarly affirmation of the same instinct that plunged me and almost (but not quite) half the population of this Rocky Mountain valley where I live into what came to be known as "The Aspen Freak Power Uprising" of 1969 and '70.

Ah yes . . . but that is a different story. No time for it now.

We were talking about Fred Dutton's book, which reads like a perfect blueprint for everything the McGovern campaign seemed to stand for—until sometime around the middle of the California primary, when Dutton finally agreed to take an active, out-front role, as one of George's main advisors. This was also the fateful point in time when it suddenly became clear to almost every political pro in the country except Hubert Humphrey and his campaign manager that McGovern was going to be the Democratic Party's candidate against Nixon in 1972 . . . and Dutton was not alone when the time came for those who saw the handwriting on the wall, as it were, to come out of their holes and sign on. Senators Frank Church of Idaho, Abe Ribicoff of Connecticut, John Tunney of California: These three and many more scratched all their previous commitments and got going strong behind McGovern. By

June 1—six days before the vote in California—George had more rich and powerful friends than he knew what to do with.

Not everyone agrees that June 1 was also the day—give or take a few—when the McGovern campaign seemed to peak and start losing its energy. There was still enough momentum to edge Hubert in California and to win New York by a landslide against no opposition . . . and enough tactical expertise to croak the ABM (Anybody But McGovern) Movement in Miami. . . .

But once that was done—the moment his troops understood that George had actually *won the nomination*—his act started falling apart.

Another problem in Wisconsin, as elsewhere, is patching things up with old-time Democrats and labor leaders who were strong backers of Senator Humphrey or Senator Muskie. The organization is working on it. Everywhere that an office is opened, the Democratic Party and local candidates are invited to share it. Bumper stickers and signs are being made available to permit candidates to have their names on them with Mr. McGovern. And other efforts are being made. . . .

. . . a move was made a few days ago to try to win favor from Rep. Clement J. Zablocki, a Democrat who has been a strong supporter of the Vietnam war policies of both Democratic and Republican administrations. Mr. Zablocki, whose Fourth (congressional) District includes Milwaukee's working class South Side, is faced with primary opposition Sept. 12, from Grant Waldo, an anti-war candidate.

When the McGovern state organizers found that their Fourth District chairman was running Mr. Waldo's campaign, they squeezed him out abruptly. "We can't possibly win the Fourth without the Zablocki voters," 'Mr. Dixon explained.

—excerpt from a New York *Times* article headlined "Wisconsin McGovern Team Revives Preprimary Faith," by Douglas Kneeland, 8/25/72

There will not be universal agreement at this time on the idea that Nixon is seriously worried about losing to McGovern in November. The September 1 Gallup Poll showed Nixon leading by 61 percent to 30 percent and still climbing . . . while McGovern, on the same day, was appearing on the CBS evening news to deny that his recently hired campaign chairman, former Democratic Party chief Larry O'Brien, was threatening to quit because the campaign is "disorganized" and "uncoordinated." Moments later, O'Brien appeared on the screen to say things weren't really that bad, and that there was no truth to any rumors concerning his inability to stay in the same room for more than forty seconds with Gary Hart, McGovern's campaign manager. . . . Then Hart came on to deny any and all rumors to the effect that he would just as soon feed O'Brien, head-first, into the nearest meat grinder.

This kind of thing is extremely heavy-duty for a presidential candidate. Private power struggles inside a campaign are common enough, but when one of your top three men flips out and starts blowing his bile all over the national press and the TV networks, it means you're in a lot more trouble than you realized . . . and when the howler is a veteran professional pol like O'Brien, you have to start flirting with words like Madness, Treachery, and Doom.

It would have seemed far more logical if Gary Hart had been the one to flip out. After all, he's only thirty-four years old, managing his first presidential campaign, not used to this kind of pressure, etc. . . . but when I called Gary today, almost immediately after catching his strange act on the Cronkite show, he sounded more cheerful and relaxed than I'd ever heard him. It was like calling McGovern headquarters and talking with Alfred E. Neuman . . . "What! *Me* worry?"

But Hart has been talking like that since last Christmas: relentless optimism. There was never any doubt in his mind—at least not in any conversation with me—that McGovern was going to win the Democratic nomination, and then the presidency. One of his central beliefs for the past two years has been that winning the Democratic nomination would be much harder than beating Nixon.

He explained it to me one night in Nebraska, sitting in the bar of the Omaha Hilton on the day before the primary: Nixon was a very vulnerable incumbent, he'd failed to end the war, he'd botched the economy, he was a terrible campaigner, he would crack under pressure, nobody trusted him, etc. . . .

So *any* Democratic candidate could beat Nixon, and all the candidates knew it. That's why they'd been fighting like wolverines for the nomination—especially Humphrey, who was a far more effective campaigner than Nixon, and who had just inherited enough of the "regular" old-line party machinery, money, and connections from the Muskie campaign to make McGovern go into California and take on what amounted to the entire Old Guard of the Democratic Party. . . . California was the key to both the nomination and the White House; a victory on the coast would make all the rest seem easy.

Hart and I agreed on all this, at the time. Nixon was obviously vulnerable, and he was such a rotten campaigner that, four years ago, Humphrey—even without the Youth Vote or the activist Left —had gained something like fifteen points on Nixon in seven weeks, and only lost by an eyelash. So this time around, with even a third of the 25 million potential new voters added to Hubert's '68 power base, anybody who could win the Democratic nomination was almost a cinch to win the presidency.

Now, looking back on that conversation, I can see a few flaws in our thinking. We should have known, for instance, that Nixon had been hoarding his best shots for the '72 stretch drive: The China/Russia trips, pulling the troops out of Vietnam, ram-rodding the economy . . . but none of these things, no matter how successful, would change enough votes to offset the Youth Vote. The day after he won the nomination, McGovern would bank at least five million 18 to 21-year-olds' votes . . . and another five million by mid-October, after massive campus registration drives.

So the minor flaws didn't matter a hell of a lot. It was the Big One—the Humphrey Sidewinder—that blew half the spine out of McGovern's campaign strategy. The one thing that apparently never occurred to either Hart or Frank Mankiewicz—or to me either, for that matter, despite my rancid contempt for the Humphrey/Meany axis and everything it stood for—was the ominous possibility that those evil bastards would refuse to close ranks behind McGovern once he had the nomination. It was almost inconceivable that they would be so bitter in defeat that they would tacitly deliver their own supporters to a conservative Republican incumbent, instead of at least trying to rally them behind the candidate of their own party . . . but this is what they have done, and in doing it they have managed to crack the very foundations of what McGovern had naturally assumed would be the traditional hard core of his Democratic Party power base.

The trademark of the McGovern campaign since it started has been ineptitude which somehow turns into victory.

—unnamed "McGovern topsider," quote in *Newsweek,* 8/14/72

God only knows who actually said that. It sounds like vintage Mankiewicz—from that speedy, free-falling era that ended in California. . . . not on the night of June 6, when the votes were counted, but somewhere prior to June 1, when Frank and all the others were still wallowing crazily in the news from all those polls that said McGovern was going to stomp Humphrey in California by anywhere from fifteen to twenty percentage points.

California was "The Superbowl." Hubert himself had said it; whoever won "on the coast" would get the nod in Miami . . . it was a foregone conclusion, and I doubt if I'll ever forget the sight of Mankiewicz, Hart, and all the other "vets" swaggering through the lobby of the Wilshire Hyatt House Hotel in Los Angeles. It was almost impossible to talk to them. They were "high as a pigeon," in Lord Buckley's words, and the adrenaline level in McGovern headquarters just a few blocks down Wilshire Boulevard was so tall that you could feel it out on the sidewalk. During the day you could almost *hear* the energy humming, and at night the place seemed to glow. One of the lowest underdog trips in American politics was about to explode in a monumental victory celebration at the Hollywood Palladium on Tuesday night, and the people who'd put it together were feeling like champions. . . .

Until somewhere around midnight on election day, when the votes came rolling in and cut McGovern's victory margin down to a nervous five percentage points, instead of fifteen to twenty. On Monday afternoon, Gary Hart had tried to ease the pain of the shock he suddenly realized was coming by announcing that the final margin would be "between eight and ten percent." And just before the polls closed on Tuesday, Mankiewicz cut it again, telling a network TV reporter that he thought McGovern would win California by five points . . . which turned out to be right on the mark, although neither Hart nor Mankiewicz nor any of the embarrassed pollsters could offer any coherent explanation for what looked like a massive swing to Humphrey in the final days of the campaign.

Sometime around 2:00 on Wednesday morning I was standing with Hart in the hall outside the hotel press room when a glum-looking student canvasser grabbed his arm and asked, "What happened?"

"What do you mean, 'What *happened?*' " Gary snapped. "We *won,* goddamnit! What did you expect?"

The young volunteer stared at him, but before he could say anything Hart cut him off: "What are you standing around *here* for? Let's go to New York. We have *work* to do."

The boy hesitated, then flashed a thin smile and darted into the press room, where the beer was flowing free and nobody was hung up on embarrassing questions like "What happened?"

But the question remains, and the answer is too pregnant to be shrugged off with a simple drill-sergeant's comment like "We won." Which was true, and a lot of people called it a Great Victory —which was also true, in a sense—but in the tight little circle of brain-trusters who run the McGovern campaign, the reaction was not euphoric. There was nothing wrong with the victory margin itself. It was "very convincing," they said. "Absolutely decisive."

And besides, it cinched the nomination. California's 271 delegates would send McGovern down to Miami with enough votes to win on the first ballot.

Which he did—although not without some unexpected problems and a few hellish aftereffects—but when the sun loomed out of the ocean to light Miami Beach on the morning of Thursday, July 14, George McGovern was the man in the catbird seat. Despite the savage opposition of Big Labor and "The Bosses," McGovern would carry the party colors against Nixon in November. For better or for worse . . . and to ease the sting on those who figured it was definitely *worse,* McGovern made room in his chariot for a sharp and ambitious young pol from Missouri named Thomas Eagleton; a first-term Senator and a Catholic by birth, known as a friend of Big Labor and also known—even to McGovern—as a man who didn't mind taking thirteen or fourteen tall drinks now and then, and whose only other distinguishing factor at the time was a naked and overweening lust for the Main Chance. Senator Eagleton was one of the two "possibles" on McGovern's list of VP candidates who didn't mind telling anyone who asked that he was ready and willing to spring for it. The other was Ted Kennedy's brother-in-law, Sargent Shriver, a good friend of Mayor Daley's.

McGovern never even considered Shriver in Miami[5] and his personal affinity for Eagleton was close to nil. Which hardly

5. Pierre Salinger, former press secretary to JFK, strategist for Bobby in '68, and a key advisor to McGovern in '72, says Shriver was in fact "the first choice for VP in Miami—but he was in Moscow on business at the time and they couldn't reach him. And it may be true, but I doubt it. Most of the younger national staff people—and McGovern himself, for that matter—considered Sargent Shriver a useless dingbat, not only during the VP selection-nightmare in Miami, but even after he replaced Eagleton on the ticket. On the Shriver press plane he was openly referred to as "Yoyo." ("What's Yoyo's schedule today, Sam?" or "Do we have any copies of Yoyo's speech in Seattle?")

Neither the press nor McGovern's hard-core staffers ever took Shriver seriously—except as a pragmatic necessity and a vaguely embarrassing burden. It was like Nixon's abortive plan to send Jimmy Hoffa to Hanoi to negotiate the release of American prisoners—or sending a used-car salesman from Pasadena into public debate with the Prime Minister of Sweden on mattered—until about six hours before the deadline on Thursday —because up until then George was still convinced that Ted Kennedy would "come around." He had never given much serious thought to alternative candidates, because McGovern and most of his ranking staff people had been interpreting Kennedy's hazy/ negative reaction to the VP offer as a sort of shrewd flirtation that would eventually come up "yes." A McGovern/Kennedy ticket would, after all, put Nixon in deep trouble from the start—and it would also give Teddy a guaranteed launching pad for 1980, when he would still be two years younger than McGovern is today.

Indeed. It made fine sense, on paper, and I recall making that same argument, myself, a few months back—but I'd no sooner sent it on the Mojo Wire than I realized it made no sense at all. There was something finally and chemically wrong with the idea of Ted Kennedy running for *vice*-president; it would be like the Jets trading Joe Namath to the Dallas Cowboys as a sub for Roger Staubach.

Which might make excellent sense, from some angles, but Namath would never consent to it—for the same reasons Kennedy wouldn't put his own presidential ambitions in limbo for eight years, behind McGovern or anyone else. Superstar politicians and superstar quarterbacks have the same kind of delicate egos, and people who live on that level grow accustomed to very thin, rarified air. They have trouble breathing in the lower altitudes; and if they can't breathe right, they can't function.

---

the question of Richard Nixon's moral relationship with the ghost of Adolph Hitler.

Shriver is a proven salesman, but in this case he never understood the product . . . which raises the obvious question: "Who *did?*" But I can't answer that one for now, and I don't know anybody who can.

Not even Mankiewicz. And certainly not McGovern himself. So it is probably not fair to mock Shriver for marching to the beat of a different drummer, as it were . . . because that was a prevailing condition in the McGovern campaign. There were many different drummers—but no real bass-line, and the prospect of unseating *any* incumbent president with that kind of noise is what some people would call "a very hard dollar."

The ego is the crucial factor here, but ego is a hard thing to put on paper—especially on that 3x5 size McGovern recommends. File cards are handy for precinct canvassing, and for people who want to get heavy into the Dewey Decimal System, but they are not much good for cataloguing things like Lust, Ambition, or Madness.

This may explain why McGovern blew his gig with Kennedy. It was a perfectly rational notion—and that was the flaw, because a man on the scent of the White House is rarely rational. He is more like a beast in heat: a bull elk in the rut, crashing blindly through the timber in a fever for something to fuck. Anything! A cow, a calf, a mare—any flesh and blood beast with a hole in it. The bull elk is a very crafty animal for about fifty weeks of the year; his senses are so sharp that only an artful stalker can get within a thousand yards of him . . . but when the rut comes on, in the autumn, any geek with the sense to blow an elk-whistle can lure a bull elk right up to his car in ten minutes if he can drive within hearing range.

The dumb bastards lose all control of themselves when the rut comes on. Their eyes glaze over, their ears pack up with hot wax, and their loins get heavy with blood. Anything that sounds like a cow elk in heat will fuse the central nervous systems of every bull on the mountain. They will race through the timber like huge cannonballs, trampling small trees and scraping off bloody chunks of their own hair on the unyielding bark of the big ones. They behave like sharks in a feeding frenzy, attacking each other with all the demented violence of human drug dealers gone mad on their own wares.

A career politician finally smelling the White House is not much different from a bull elk in the rut. He will stop at nothing, trashing anything that gets in his way; and anything he can't handle personally he will hire out—or, failing that, make a deal. It is a difficult syndrome for most people to understand, because few of us ever come close to the kind of Ultimate Power and Achievement that the White House represents to a career politician.

The presidency is as far as he can go. There *is* no more. The currency of politics is power, and once you've been the Most Powerful Man in the World for four years, everything else is downhill—except four more years on the same trip.

Dozen Protestors Do About-Face

Sgt. Roy Gates, an Army recruiter in Miami Beach, looked out his carpeted and paneled office at a sign in the window saying, "Non-delegates—Help Wanted."

In what must rank as one of the Army's finest recruiting efforts, Gates thought he had convinced 13 non-delegates during the conventions to enlist in the military.

Nine of the protesters, however, failed to pass the Army's intelligence tests.

"Their low education surprised me—around the eighth grade and wanting to change the world," he said. "They said they didn't want to go along with the hard core radicals. It's amazing the different types you find." —Miami *News*, Friday, August 25

On Tuesday afternoon my car disappeared. I left it on the street in front of the hotel while I went in to pick up my swimming trunks, and when I came back out, it was gone.

To hell with it, I thought, it was time to get out of Miami.

I went up to my room and thought for a while, sitting with my back to the typewriter and staring out the window at the big ocean-going yachts and luxury houseboats tied up across the street, at the piers along Indian Creek. Last week they'd been crawling with people, and cocktail parties. Every time the Fontainebleau lobby started buzzing with rumors about another crowd of demonstrators bearing down on the hotel from the direction of Flamingo Park, the boats across Collins Avenue would fill up with laughing Republican delegates wearing striped blazers and cocktail dresses. There was no better place, they said, for watching the street action. As the demonstrators approached the front entrance to the hotel, they found themselves walking a gauntlet of riot-equipped police on one side, and martini-sipping GOP delegates on the other.

One yacht—the Wild Rose, out of Houston—rumbled back and forth, just offshore, at every demonstration. From the middle of Collins Avenue, you could see the guests lounging in deck chairs, observing the action through high-powered field glasses, and reaching around from time to time to accept a fresh drink from crewmen wearing white serving jackets with gold epaulets.

The scene on the foredeck of the Wild Rose was so gross, so flagrantly decadent, that it was hard to avoid comparing it with the kind of bloodthirsty arrogance normally associated with the last days of the Roman Empire: Here was a crowd of rich Texans, floating around on a $100,000 yacht in front of a palatial Miami Beach hotel, giggling with excitement at the prospect of watching their hired gladiators brutalize a mob of howling, half-naked Christians. I half-expected them to start whooping for blood and giving the Thumbs Down signal.

Nobody who was out there on the street with the demonstrators would be naive enough to compare them to "helpless Christians." With the lone exception of the Vietnam Veterans Against the War, the demonstrators in Miami were a useless mob of ignorant, chicken-shit ego-junkies whose only accomplishment was to embarrass the whole tradition of public protest. They were hopelessly disorganized, they had no real purpose in being there, and about half of them were so wasted on grass, wine, and downers that they couldn't say for sure whether they were raising hell in Miami or San Diego.

Five weeks earlier, these same people had been sitting in the lobby of the Doral, calling George McGovern a "lying pig" and a "warmonger." Their target-hotel this time was the Fontainebleau, headquarters for the national press and many TV cameras. If the Rolling Stones came to Miami for a free concert, these assholes would build their own fence around the bandstand—just so they could have something to tear down and then "crash the gates."

The drug action in Flamingo Park, the official campground for "non-delegates" and other would-be "protesters," was so bottom-heavy with downers that it was known as "Quaalude Alley."

Quaalude is a mild sleeping pill, but—consumed in large quantities, along with wine, grass, and adrenaline—it produces the same kind of stupid, mean-drunk effect as Seconal ("Reds"). The Quaalude effect was so obvious in Flamingo Park that the "Last Patrol" caravan of Vietnam Vets—who came here in motorcades from all parts of the country—refused to even set up camp with the other demonstrators. They had serious business in Miami, they explained, and the last thing they needed was a public alliance with a mob of stoned street crazies and screaming teenyboppers.

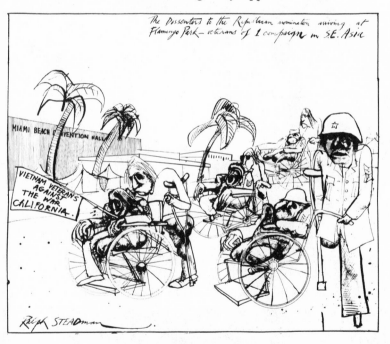

The Vets made their camp in a far corner of the Park, then sealed it off with a network of perimeter guards and checkpoints that made it virtually impossible to enter that area unless you knew somebody inside. There was an ominous sense of dignity

about everything the VVAW did in Miami. They rarely even hinted at violence, but their very presence was menacing—on a level that the Yippies, Zippies, and SDS street crazies never even approached, despite all their yelling and trashing.[6]

The most impressive single performance in Miami during the three days of the GOP convention was the VVAW march on the Fontainebleau on Tuesday afternoon. Most of the press and TV

---

6. Earlier that week, Lucian Truscott from the *Village Voice* and I tried to arrange a brief chat between John "Duke" Wayne and about two dozen Vets from the vanguard of the Last Patrol. They had just arrived in Miami and when they heard Wayne was holding an "open" press conference at Nixon headquarters in the Doral they decided to stop by and pick up on it.

But the GOP security guards wouldn't let them in—so they moved about a half block down Collins Avenue to a public parking lot on the edge of the ocean—where they were quickly surrounded, at a discreet distance, by a cordon of Florida state troopers.

"Say, man," a vet in a wheelchair called out to me after I'd used my press credentials to penetrate the cop-cordon, "Can you get that asshole Wayne out here to talk to us?"

"Why not?" I said. "He's tough as nails, they say. He'd probably *enjoy* coming out here in the sun and abusing you dope-addled communist dupes for a while."

"The Duke fears nothing," Lucian added. "We'll bring him out right after his press conference."

But John Wayne was not eager that day for a chat with the Last Patrol. "What the hell do they want to talk about?" he asked.

"Yeah, *what?*" said his drinking buddy, Glenn Ford. They were standing on the front steps of the Doral waiting for a cab.

"They just want to shoot the bull," said Lucian. "You know, maybe talk about the war . . ."

"*What* war?" Ford snapped.

"The one in Vietnam," Lucian replied. "These guys all fought over there—a lot of them are crippled."

The Duke seemed agitated; he was scanning the street for a cab. Finally, without looking at us, he said: "Naw, not today. I can't see the point in it."

"Why not?" Lucian asked. "They just want to *talk*. They're not looking for trouble. Hell, the place is crawling with cops."

Wayne hesitated, then shook his head again as he suddenly spotted a cab. "So they just want to *talk,* eh?" he said with a thin smile.

I nodded. "Why not. It won't take long."

"Bullshit," Wayne replied. "If they got somethin' to say to me, tell 'em to put it in writing."

Then he waved us away and eased off across the driveway to the waiting cab. "Playboy Plaza," he barked. "Jesus, I need a *drink.*"

people were either down at the Convention Hall, covering the "liberals vs. conservatives" floor-fight over rules for seating delegates in 1976—or standing around in the boiling mid-afternoon sun at Miami International Airport, waiting for Nixon to come swooping out of the sky in Air Force One.

My own plan for that afternoon was to drive far out to the end of Key Biscayne and find an empty part of the beach where I could swim by myself in the ocean, and not have to talk to anybody for a while. I didn't give a fuck about watching the rules fight, a doomed charade that the Nixon brain-trust had already settled in favor of the conservatives . . . and I saw no point in going out to the airport to watch three thousand well-rehearsed "Nixon Youth" robots "welcome the President."

My Great American Dream

I had a dream last night...
I dreamt about 1976.
I dreamt about a country
with incurable brain
damage....
I even dreamt they gave
it a heart transplant
Then I woke up and I
knew it was only a
nightmare—so I
went back to
sleep again.

Given these two depressing options, I figured Tuesday was as good a day as any to get away from politics and act like a human being for a change—or better still, like an animal. Just get off by myself and drift around naked in the sea for a few hours. . . .

But as I drove toward Key Biscayne with the top down, squinting into the sun, I saw the Vets. . . . They were moving up Collins Avenue in dead silence; twelve hundred of them dressed in battle fatigues, helmets, combat boots . . . a few carried full-size plastic M-16s, many peace symbols, girlfriends walking beside vets being pushed along the street in slow-moving wheelchairs, others walking jerkily on crutches. . . . But nobody spoke; all the "stop, start," "fast, slow," "left, right" commands came from "platoon leaders" walking slightly off to the side of the main column and using hand signals.

One look at that eerie procession killed my plan to go swimming that afternoon. I left my car at a parking meter in front of the Cadillac Hotel and joined the march. . . . No, "joined" is the wrong word; that was not the kind of procession you just walked up and "joined." Not without paying some very heavy dues: an arm gone here, a leg there, paralysis, a face full of lumpy scar tissue . . . all staring straight ahead as the long silent column moved between rows of hotel porches full of tight-lipped Senior Citizens, through the heart of Miami Beach.

The silence of the march was contagious, almost threatening. There were hundreds of spectators, but nobody said a word. I walked beside the column for ten blocks, and the only sounds I remember hearing were the soft thump of boot leather on hot asphalt and the occasional rattling of an open canteen top.

The Fontainebleau was already walled off from the street by five hundred heavily armed cops when the front ranks of the Last Patrol arrived, still marching in total silence. Several hours earlier, a noisy mob of Yippie/Zippie/SDS "non-delegates" had shown up in front of the Fontainebleau and been met with jeers and curses from GOP delegates and other partisan spectators, massed behind the police lines. . . . But now there was no jeering. Even the cops seemed deflated. They watched nervously from behind their face-shields as the VVAW platoon leaders, still using hand signals, funneled the column into a tight semicircle that blocked all three northbound lanes of Collins Avenue. During earlier demonstrations—at least six in the past three days—the police had poked people with riot sticks to make sure at least one lane of the street stayed open for local traffic, and on the one occasion when mere prodding didn't work, they had charged the demonstrators and cleared the street completely.

But not now. For the first and only time during the whole convention, the cops were clearly off balance. The Vets could have closed all six lanes of Collins Avenue if they'd wanted to, and nobody would have argued. I have been covering anti-war demonstrations with depressing regularity since the winter of 1964, in cities all over the country, and I have never seen cops so intimidated by demonstrators as they were in front of the Fontainebleau Hotel on that hot Tuesday afternoon in Miami Beach.

There was an awful tension in that silence. Not even that pack of rich sybarites out there on the foredeck of the Wild Rose of Houston could stay in their seats for this show. They were standing up at the rail, looking worried, getting very bad vibrations from whatever was happening over there in the street. Was something *wrong* with their gladiators? Were they spooked? And why was there no noise?

After five more minutes of harsh silence, one of the VVAW platoon leaders suddenly picked up a bullhorn and said: "We want to come inside."

Nobody answered, but an almost visible shudder ran through the crowd. "O my God!" a man standing next to me muttered. I felt a strange tightness coming over me, and I reacted instinctively —for the first time in a long, long while—by slipping my notebook into my belt and reaching down to take off my watch. The first thing to go in a street fight is always your watch, and once you've lost a few, you develop a certain instinct that lets you know when it's time to get the thing off your wrist and into a safe pocket.

I can't say for sure what I would have done if the Last Patrol had tried to crack the police line and seize control of the Fontainebleau—but I have a fair idea, based on instinct and rude experience, so the unexpected appearance of Congressman Pete McCloskey on that scene calmed my nerves considerably. He shoved his way through the police line and talked with a handful of the VVAW spokesmen long enough to convince them, apparently, that a frontal assault on the hotel would be suicidal.

One of the platoon leaders smiled faintly and assured McCloskey that they'd never had any intention of attacking the Fontainebleau. They didn't even *want* to go in. The only reason they asked was to see if the Republicans would turn them away in front of network TV cameras—which they did, but very few cameras were on hand that afternoon to record it. All the network floor crews were down at the Convention Hall, and the ones who would normally have been on standby alert at the Fontainebleau were out at the airport filming Nixon's arrival.

No doubt there were backup crews around somewhere—but I suspect they were up on the roof, using very long lenses; because in those first few moments when the Vets began massing in front of the police line there was no mistaking the potential for real violence . . . and it was easy enough to see, by scanning the faces behind those clear plastic riot masks, that the cream of the Florida State Highway Patrol had no appetite at all for a public crunch with twelve hundred angry Vietnam Veterans.

Whatever the outcome, it was a guaranteed nightmare situation for the police. Defeat would be bad enough, but victory would be intolerable. Every TV screen in the nation would show a small army of heavily armed Florida cops clubbing unarmed veterans— some on crutches and others in wheelchairs—whose only crime was trying to enter Republican convention headquarters in Miami Beach. How could Nixon explain a thing like that? Could he slither out from under it?

Never in hell, I thought—and all it would take to make a thing like that happen, right now, would be for one or two Vets to lose control of themselves and try to crash through the police line; just enough violence to make *one* cop use his riot stick. The rest would take care of itself.

Ah, nightmares, nightmares. . . . Not even Sammy Davis Jr. could stomach that kind of outrage. He would flee the Nixon family compound on Key Biscayne within moments after the first news bulletin, rejecting his newfound soul brother like a suckfish cutting loose from a mortally wounded shark . . . and the next day's Washington *Post* would report that Sammy Davis Jr. had spent most of the previous night trying to ooze through the keyhole of George McGovern's front door in Washington, D.C.

Right . . . but none of this happened. McCloskey's appearance seemed to soothe both the crowd and the cops. The only violent act of the afternoon occurred moments later when a foul-mouthed twenty-year-old blonde girl named Debby Marshal tried to ram her way through the crowd on a 125 Honda. "Get out of my way!" she kept shouting. "This is ridiculous! These people should go back where they belong!"

The Vets ignored her, but about halfway through the crowd

she ran into a nest of press photographers, and that was as far as she went. An hour later she was still sitting there, biting her lips and whining about how "ridiculous" it all was. I was tempted to lean over and set her hair on fire with my Zippo, but by that time the confrontation had settled down to a series of bullhorn speeches by various Vets. Not much of what was said could be heard more than fifteen feet from the bullhorn, however, because of two Army helicopters that suddenly appeared overhead and filled the whole street with their noise. The only Vet speaker who managed to make himself plainly understood above the chopper noise was an ex-Marine Sergeant from San Diego named Ron Kovic, who spoke from a wheelchair because his legs are permanently paralyzed.

I would like to have a transcript or at least a tape of what Kovic said that day, because his words lashed the crowd like a wire whip. If Kovic had been allowed to speak from the convention hall podium, in front of network TV cameras, Nixon wouldn't have had the balls to show up and accept the nomination.

No . . . I suspect that's wishful thinking. Nothing in the realm of human possibility could have prevented Richard Nixon from accepting that nomination. If God himself had showed up in Miami and denounced Nixon from the podium, hired gunsels from the Committee for the Re-Election of the President would have quickly had him arrested for disturbing the peace.

Vietnam veterans like Ron Kovic are not welcome in Nixon's White House. They tried to get in last year, but they could only get close enough to throw their war medals over the fence. That was perhaps the most eloquent anti-war statement ever made in this country, and that Silent March on the Fontainebleau on August 22 had the same ugly sting to it.

There is no anti-war or even anti-establishment group in America today with the psychic leverage of the VVAW. Not even those decadent swine on the foredeck of the Wild Rose can ignore the dues Ron Kovic and his buddies have paid. They are golems, come back to haunt us all—even Richard Nixon, who campaigned for the presidency in 1968 with a promise that he had "a secret plan" to end the war in Vietnam.

Which was true, as it turns out. The plan was to end the war just in time to get himself re-elected in 1972. Four more years.

Fifty years ago

August 23, 1972. Little is known of this picture except that Mr. Nixon (center) suffered from a power complex, a hatred of humanity, near impotence and finally premature senility which resembled Parkinson's disease—or an advanced stage of neuro-syphilis caught during his student days—which has hallucinatory effects on the victim giving him a sense of grandeur. The second possibility has been ruled out on the grounds that at the time Mr. Nixon was a student it would have been socially impossible for him to contract the disease except from a lavatory seat. He died senile in an anti-environment bunker near Camp David, seated before a sun-ray lamp in a deckchair wearing only a pair of oldstyle "jackboots." Miami was subsequently reclaimed in 1982, and became an alligator swamp and tourist attraction during the mid-eighties.

September

Fat City Blues ... Fear and Loathing on the White House Press Plane ... Bad Angst at McGovern Headquarters ... Nixon Tightens the Screws ... "Many Appeared to Be in the Terminal Stages of Campaign Bloat" ...

> *Hear me, people: We have now to deal with another race—small and feeble when our fathers first met them, but now great and overbearing. Strangely enough they have a mind to till the soil and the love of possession is a disease with them. These people have made many rules that the rich may break but the poor may not. They take their tithes from the poor and weak to support the rich and those who rule.*
>
> —Chief Sitting Bull, speaking at the Powder
> River Conference in 1877

IF GEORGE MCGOVERN had a speech writer half as eloquent as Sitting Bull, he would be home free today—instead of twenty-two points behind and racing around the country with both feet in his mouth. The Powder River Conference ended ninety-five years ago, but the old Chief's baleful analysis of the White Man's rape of the American continent was just as accurate then as it would be today if he came back from the dead and said it for the microphones on prime-time TV. The ugly fallout from the American Dream has been coming down on us at a pretty consistent rate since Sitting Bull's time—and the only real difference now, with Election Day '72 only a few weeks away, is that we seem to be on the verge of *ratifying* the fallout and forgetting the Dream itself.

Sitting Bull made no distinction between Democrats and Republicans—which was probably just as well, in 1877 or any other year

—but it's also true that Sitting Bull never knew the degradation of traveling on Richard Nixon's press plane; he never had the bilious pleasure of dealing with Ron Ziegler, and he never met John Mitchell, Nixon's king fixer.

If the old Sioux Chief had ever done these things, I think—despite his angry contempt for the White Man and everything he stands for—he'd be working overtime for George McGovern today.

These past two weeks have been relatively calm ones for me. Immediately after the Republican Convention in Miami, I dragged myself back to the Rockies and tried to forget about politics for a while—just lie naked on the porch in the cool afternoon sun and watch the aspen trees turning gold on the hills around my house; mix up a huge cannister of gin and grapefruit juice, watch the horses nuzzling each other in the pasture across the road, big logs in the fireplace at night; Herbie Mann, John Prine, and Jesse Colin Young booming out of the speakers . . . zip off every once in a while for a fast run into town along a back road above the river: to the health-center gym for some volleyball, then over to Benton's gallery to get caught up on whatever treacheries the local greedheads rammed through while I was gone, watch the late TV news and curse McGovern for poking another hole in his own boat, then stop by the Jerome on the way out of town for a midnight beer with Solheim.

After two weeks on that peaceful human schedule, the last thing I wanted to think about was the grim, inescapable spectre of two more frenzied months on the campaign trail. Especially when it meant coming back here to Washington, to start laying the groundwork for a long and painful autopsy job on the McGovern campaign. What went wrong? Why had it failed? Who was to blame? And, finally, what next?

That was one project. The other was to somehow pass through the fine eye of the White House security camel and go out on the campaign trail with Richard Nixon, to watch him waltz in—if only to get the drift of his thinking, to watch the moves, his eyes. It is a nervous thing to consider: Not just four more years of Nixon, but Nixon's *last four years in politics*—completely unshackled, for the first time in his life, from any need to worry about who might or might not vote for him the next time around.

If he wins in November, he will finally be free to do whatever he wants . . . or maybe "wants" is too strong a word for right now. It conjures up images of Papa Doc, Batista, Somoza; jails full of bewildered "political prisoners" and the constant cold-sweat fear of jackboots suddenly kicking your door off its hinges at four A.M.

There is no point in kidding ourselves about what Richard Nixon really *wants* for America. When he stands at his White House window and looks out on an anti-war demonstration, he doesn't see "dissenters," he sees *criminals*. Dangerous parasites, preparing to strike at the heart of the Great American System that put him where he is today.

There may not be much difference between Democrats and Republicans; I have made that argument myself—with considerable venom, as I recall—over the past ten months. . . . But only a blind geek or a waterhead could miss the difference between McGovern and Richard Nixon. Granted, they are both white men; and both are politicians—but the similarity ends right there, and from that point on the difference is so vast that anybody who can't see it deserves whatever happens to them if Nixon gets re-elected due to apathy, stupidity, and laziness on the part of potential McGovern voters.

The tragedy of this campaign is that McGovern and his staff wizards have not been able to dramatize what is really at stake on November 7th. We are not looking at just another dim rerun of the '68 Nixon/Humphrey trip, or the LBJ/Goldwater fiasco in '64. Those were both useless drills. I voted for Dick Gregory in '68, and for "No" in '64 . . . but this one is different, and since McGovern is so goddamn maddeningly inept with the kind of words he needs to make people understand what he's up to, it will save a lot of time here—and strain on my own weary head— to remember Bobby Kennedy's ultimate characterization of Richard Nixon, in a speech at Vanderbilt University in the spring of 1968, not long before he was murdered.

"Richard Nixon," he said, *"represents the dark side of the American spirit."*

I don't remember what else he said that day. I guess I could look it up in the New York *Times* speech morgue, but why bother? That one line says it all.

Anybody who doubts it should go out and catch The President's act the next time he swoops into the local airport. Watch the big silver-and-blue custom-built 707 come booming down the runway and roll up in front of the small but well-disciplined crowd of Nixon Youth cheerleaders singing the "Nixon Now" song, waving their freshly printed red-white-and-blue RE-ELECT THE PRESIDENT signs and then pausing, in perfect spontaneous unison, before intimidating every TV crew on the runway with the stylish "Four More Years!" chant.

Watch The President emerge from the belly of the plane, holding hands with the aging Barbie doll he calls his wife, and ooze down the rolling VIP stairway while the 105th Division Rolling Thunder Women & Children Classic Napalm U.S. Army Parade Band whips the crowd higher and higher with a big-beat rendition of "God Save the Freaks."

See the Generals strut down from the plane behind The President. Take a long look at the grinning "local dignitaries" who are ushered out, by armed guards, to greet him. See the White House press corps over there about two hundred yards away, herded into that small corral behind heavy ropes stretched around red-white-and-blue painted oil drums. Why are they smiling?

I went out on the campaign trail with Richard Nixon last week . . . Right: After seven straight days of savage in-fighting with the White House press office, the bastards finally caved in and let me join up, if only for a few days, with the Presidential Press Corps.

Cazart! · Vindication! When the magic words of approval finally zipped across the phone line from the White House to my room on the top floor of the Washington Hilton, my brain went limp with pride. "We'll leave from Andrews Air Force Base," said the hard baritone voice of deputy press secretary Gerald Warren. "I don't have the final schedule yet, but if you call me before noon tomorrow I'll tell you exactly when to be there with your bags."

Indeed. My bags. No doubt they would be searched thoroughly, prior to boarding, by extremely sophisticated electronic machinery and a brace of super-sharp Secret Service agents. *When
you travel on the Presidential Press Plane, boy, you do it OUR way.*

Of course. I was ready for it: A total skin-search, if necessary, and perhaps even a lie-detector: *Do you have any violent
thoughts regarding the President?*

Violent? Certainly not. We're old football buddies.

Football buddies?

Right. Richard and I go way back. I was with him long ago,
in the snows of New Hampshire. Things were different then, fella.
Where were *you* in the winter of '68?

I was ready for all the standard-brand Secret Service bullshit.
The only thing that worried me was that maybe some of the SS
boys might have seen the current *Rolling Stone*—which was available that week at newsstands all over Washington. It contained,
along with my calm and well-reasoned analysis of the recent GOP
convention in Miami, some of the most brutal and hateful carica-
tures of Richard Nixon ever committed to print, in this country
or any other.

That crazy bastard Steadman! Why is it that it's always your
friends who cause you to be screwed to the wall? What do you
say when you go across town to the White House to apply for
press credentials to cover the Nixon campaign as the National
Affairs Editor of *Rolling Stone* and the first thing you see when
you walk through the door of the press office is one of Steadman's
unconscionably obscene Nixon/Agnew drawings tacked up on the
bulletin board with a big red circle around Ralph's name?

Well . . . ah . . . yes. Ho ho, eh? My name is . . . ah . . .
Thompson, from *Rolling Stone,* and I'm here to pick up my cre-
dentials to fly around the country with President Nixon on Air
Force One for the next month or so.

Cold stare from the man at the desk. No handshake offered.

"Well . . . Ho ho, eh? I can't help but notice you've been
admiring the work of my friend Ralph Steadman. Ho ho, he

399

sure has an eye for it, eh? Sure does. Good ole Ralph." Sad smile and shrug of the shoulders. "Crazy as a loon, of course. Terminal brain syphilis." Keep smiling, another shrug. "Jesus, what can you do, eh? These goddamn vicious limeys will do anything for money. He was paid *well* for these rotten drawings. My protests were totally ignored. It's a fucking shame, I say. What the hell is the world coming to when the goddamn British can get away with stuff like this?"

Nixon has never made any secret of his feelings about the press. They are still the same gang of "biased bastards" and "cynical sons of bitches" that he called them, backstage, on election day in California ten years ago when he made his now-legendary concession statement after losing the 1962 governor's race to Pat Brown. His aides tried to restrain him, but Nixon would have none of it. Trembling with rage, he confronted a hotel ballroom full of political reporters and snarled: "This is my last press conference! You won't have Richard Nixon to kick around anymore!"

He failed to honor that pledge, but the anger that caused him to utter it still burns in his breast. He rarely holds press conferences, and his personal relationship with the working press is almost nonexistent. In the White House and on the road, he "communicates" with the press corps through his mouthpiece, press secretary Ron Ziegler—an arrogant 33-year-old punk who trained for his current job by working as a PR man for Disneyland, and who treats the White House press corps like a gang of troublesome winos who will only be tolerated as long as they keep out of the boss's hair.

The few reporters who switched off the McGovern campaign to travel with Nixon on this last trip to California were shocked by what they found. The difference between traveling with McGovern and traveling with Nixon is just about like the difference between going on tour with the Grateful Dead & going on tour with the Pope.

My first experience with it came shortly after Nixon's arrival in Oakland. After nervously pressing the flesh with some of the several hundred well-drilled young "supporters" who'd been rounded up to greet him for the TV cameras, Nixon was hustled off in a huge black bulletproof Cadillac for a brief appearance at one of the Bay Area's new rapid-transit stations. The three big press buses followed, taking a different route, and when we arrived at the BART station we were hauled down by freight elevator to a narrow hallway outside a glass-walled control room.

Moments later Nixon emerged from a nearby subway tunnel, waved briefly at the crowd, and was ushered into the control room with a dozen or so local Republican dignitaries. Two certified harmless photographers were allowed inside to take pictures of The President shaking hands and making small talk with the engineers. His pithy remarks were broadcast out to the press mob in the hallway by means of loudspeakers.

After watching for a moment, I turned to Bob Greene, a young Chicago *Sun-Times* reporter who had just dropped off the McGovern campaign. "Jesus," I said. "Is it *always* like this?" '

He laughed. "Hell, this is *accessible!* We can actually *see* him. I spent about twelve hours covering him in New York yesterday, and I never saw him once—except on closed-circuit TV when he made his speech last night. They had us in a separate room, with speakers and TV monitors."

Our next stop was across the Bay in San Francisco, where Nixon was scheduled to address several hundred "Young Republicans" at a $500-a-plate lunch in the ballroom of the (ITT-owned) Sheraton-Palace Hotel. Thousands of anti-war demonstrators milled around in the streets outside, kept off at a safe distance by hundreds of cops carrying twelve-gauge shotguns.

Nixon's "remarks" were piped into the press room, where the cream of American journalism sat down with each other at several long white-cloth-covered banquet tables, to eat a roast beef buffet and take notes while staring intently at two big brown speakers hung on the wall.

I went across the street to the Shields House tavern, where I met a thirty-year-old merchant seaman wearing a tweed sports coat and a tie, who said he and three friends had just "split from that goddamn phony sideshow across the street."

"The Nixon rally?" I asked.

He nodded. "Shit, they tried to make us rehearse cheers! They put us all in a big room and told us to synchronize our watches so we would all start singing that goddamn 'Nixon Now' song at exactly 1:17 P.M., when his car pulled up to the door."

I smiled and ordered a Tuborg. "Why not? You can't sing? You mean you just blew $500 on that lunch, and you didn't even stay to *eat* it?"

He waved me off. "Shit, are you kidding? Do I *look* like one of those Young Republican assholes? You think I'd pay $500 to have lunch with *Nixon?*"

I shrugged.

"Hell no!" he said. "Some guy down at the Maritime Hall just came up and asked us if we wanted to go to a $500-a-plate lunch, for free. We said sure, so he gave us the tickets—but he didn't say anything about cheering and singing songs." He shook his head. "Hell no, not me. When they started that bullshit I just walked out."

"Your friends stayed?" I asked.

He shrugged. "I guess so. They were pretty loaded."

"Loaded?" I said. "Nixon supporters?"

He looked at me. "Nixon? Are you nuts?"

I started to ask him about McGovern, but just then my attorney arrived and we got heavily into business matters until I looked out the window and noticed the press buses beginning to fill up. Moments later we pulled out, with a massive police escort, and joined the Nixon motorcade going back to the Oakland airport, where the press plane was waiting to haul us down to L.A.

Nixon, as always, made the trip in his private compartment aboard Air Force One. Five or six "pool" reporters went with him. Or at least they went on the same plane. The tiny press compartment is far back in the rear, and nobody leaves it in flight except by special permission from Ron Ziegler—who routinely accepts individual requests for brief interviews with Nixon, and just as routinely ignores them.

When we got to L.A. I asked the UPI "pool" man if there was any professional advantage in traveling on Air Force One instead of the press plane.

"Absolutely none," he replied. "We never leave the compartment; just sit in there and play cards. They could all be running around naked up in front, for all we know. We don't even get on and off the plane through the same door Nixon uses. Ours is way back in the tail."

"You never get a chance to talk with him?" I asked. "Never even *see* him?"

He shook his head. "Not usually." He paused. "Oh, every once' in a while he'll ask somebody up front for a few minutes, but it's almost always for *his* reasons, not ours. You know—like if he happens to be writing a speech about hog futures, or something, he might ask Ron if any of the pool guys that day used to be pig farmers . . ."

I shook my head sadly. "Sounds pretty frustrating."

He shrugged. "No, not really. No worse than riding on the press plane."

Which is probably true. The entire White House press corps apparently lives in fear of somehow getting on the wrong side of Ziegler. He is their only human connection with the man they're supposed to be covering—and since they can't possibly get to Nixon on their own, they have to deal with Ron. Every once in a while someone will freak out and start yelling at him, but that involves serious risks. It is just about impossible to stay on the White House beat if Ziegler won't talk to you, and if you push him far enough that's exactly what will happen.

Even king-bee types like the Associated Press correspondent Walter Mears and the New York *Times's* Bob Semple are nervous in Ziegler's presence. The White House beat is one of the most prestigious in American journalism, but Ziegler manages to make it so uncomfortable and potentially humiliating that only the most ambitious reporters still push for it.

The handful of McGovern exiles who traveled with Nixon to California found themselves standing off in little knots by themselves in the press room of Los Angeles' Century Plaza Hotel, and saying things like: "Jesus, this is really incredible! These White House guys are totally broken, they act like sick sheep . . . Christ, McGovern would laugh all night if he could see guys like Mears and Semple whimpering around and kissing Ron Ziegler's ass."

Just for the record, here is the "pool report" from Nixon's New York to California trip. Contrary to popular impression, the press does not ride free. The rate on the chartered planes is First Class plus one third, so to send the two hundred newsmen who went along on this expedition cost, including copy-transmission expenses, approximately a grand apiece.

Pool Report —Waldorf to Oakland airport—Sept. 27

The motorcade departed the Waldorf at 9:28. Fair crowds were out at 50th and Lexington to wave at the President, and knots of people dotted the path. On FDR Drive, small groups of hardhats appeared here and there, waving at the President as he sped by.

Choppers from the Wall Street helipad took a last swing past the Statue of Liberty before reaching Newark. Wheels up was at 9:50.

All was quiet aboard Air Force One until press secretary Ziegler materialized with statements that had already been released aboard the press plane. John Ehrlichman appeared briefly with some added information on BART financing. A total of $219 million in financing has come from the government, out of the total cost of $1.4 billion. Of this new grant of $38 million, $26.6 million goes to work along Market Street. The rest goes to various items such as development of an undercar fire protection system, a fare collection data collecting system, storage buildings, and car washing equipment.

Mr. Ehrlichman also advised that Clark MacGregor has called upon the opposition to "repudiate" demonstrations said to be aborning in San Francisco. Information that demonstrations are being generated "squares with some intelligence that law enforcement agencies had," he said, which shows that "these demonstrations are political rather than of an anti-war nature." Asked if it was possible to make that distinction, Ehrlichman implied that the agencies know what is going on. He did not clarify. He added that the "motorcade seems to be the prime target."

Henry Hubbard, *Newsweek*
Jack Germond, Manchester *Union-Leader*[1]

The worst thing to look like right now is a politician; this is a bad year for them.

—Frank Mankiewicz, April 1972

McGovern was doing better when he was an anti-politician.

—George Gallup, September 1972

You know, I finally figured out why McGovern's gonna get his ass beat this year: He doesn't have half the class of the people who work for him. As a matter of fact, I'm beginning to think George McGovern doesn't have much class at all.

—Jack Germond, correspondent, October 1972

Seldom has the public perception of a major political figure changed so rapidly. George McGovern's political problem stems not from the belief that he is a dangerous radical and unpatriotic American. His trouble lies in the way people feel about him personally. Many who were attracted to him earlier this year because of his freshness and promise now express strong disillusionment."

—Haynes Johnson in the Washington *Post,* October 1972

The mood at McGovern's grim headquarters building at 1910 K Street, NW, in Washington is oddly schizoid these days: a jangled mix of defiance and despair—tempered, now and then,

---

1. Germond actually works for the Gannet chain—this *"Union-Leader"* joke is one he didn't appreciate.

by quick flashes of a lingering conviction that George can still win.

McGovern's young staffers, after all, have *never lost an election they expected to win, at the outset*—and they definitely expected to win this one. They are accustomed to being far behind in the public opinion polls. McGovern has almost always been the underdog, and—except for California—he has usually been able to close the gap with a last-minute stretch run.

Even in the primaries he lost—New Hampshire, Ohio, Pennsylvania—he did well enough to embarrass the pollsters, humiliate the pols, and crank up his staff morale another few notches.

But that boundless blind faith is beginning to fade now. The Curse of Eagleton is beginning to make itself felt in the ranks. And not even Frank Mankiewicz, the Wizard of Chevy Chase, can properly explain why McGovern is now being sneered at from coast to coast as "just another politician." Mankiewicz is still the main drivewheel in this ham-strung campaign; he has been the central intelligence from the very beginning—which was fine all around, while it worked, but there is not a hell of a lot of evidence to suggest that it's working real well these days, and it is hard to avoid the idea that Frank is just as responsible for whatever is happening now as he was six months ago, when McGovern came wheeling out of New Hampshire like the Abominable Snowman on a speed trip.

If George gets stomped in November, it will not be because of anything Richard Nixon did to him. The blame will trace straight back to his brain-trust, to whoever had his ear tight enough to convince him that all that bullshit about "new politics" was fine for the primaries, but it would never work against Nixon—so he would have to abandon his original power base, after Miami, and swiftly move to consolidate the one he'd just shattered: the Meany/Daley/Humphrey/Muskie axis, the senile remnants of the Democratic Party's once-powerful "Roosevelt coalition."

McGovern agreed. He went to Texas and praised LBJ; he revised his economic program to make it more palatable on Wall Street; he went to Chicago and endorsed the whole Daley/Demo-

cratic ticket, including State's Attorney Ed Hanrahan, who is still
under indictment on felony/conspiracy (Obstruction of Justice)
charges for his role in a police raid on local Black Panther headquarters three years ago that resulted in the murder of Fred
Hampton.

False dawn in Chicago: Daley, Kennedy & McGovern whooping it up.

In the speedy weeks between March and July, the atmosphere
in McGovern's cramped headquarters building on Capitol Hill was
so high that you could get bent by just hanging around and watching the human machinery at work.

The headquarters building itself was not much bigger than
McGovern's personal command post in the Senate Office Building,
five blocks away. It was one big room about the size of an Olym-
pic swimming pool—with a grocery store on one side, a liquor
store on the other, and a tree-shaded sidewalk out front. The last
time I was there, about two weeks before the California primary,
I drove my blue Volvo up on the sidewalk and parked right in
front of the door. Crouse went inside to find Mankiewicz while I
picked up some Ballantine ale.

"Is this a charge?" the booze-clerk asked.

"Right," I said. "Charge it to George McGovern."

He nodded, and began to write it down.

"Hey, wait a minute!" I said. "I was just kidding. Here— here's the cash."

He shrugged and accepted the three bills . . . and when I got to Frank's office and told him what had happened, he didn't seem surprised. "Yeah, our credit's pretty good," he said, "in a lot of places where we never even asked for it."

That was back in May, when the tide was still rising. But things are different now, and the credit is not so easy. The new K Street headquarters is an eight-story tomb once occupied by the "Muskie for President" juggernaut. Big Ed abandoned it when he dropped out of the race for the Democratic nomination, and it stood empty for a month or so after that—but when McGovern croaked Humphrey in California and became the nominee-apparent, his wizards decided to get a new and larger headquarters.

The Muskie building was an obvious choice—if only because it was available very cheap, and already wired for the fantastic maze of phone lines necessary for a presidential campaign headquarters. The Man from Maine and his army of big-time backers had already taken care of that aspect; they had plenty of phone lines, along with all those endorsements.

Not everybody on the McGovern staff was happy with the idea of moving out of the original headquarters. The decision was made in California, several days before the primary, and I remember arguing with Gary Hart about it. He insisted the move was necessary, for space reasons . . . and even in retrospect my argument for keeping the original headquarters seems irrational. It was a matter of karma, I said, psychic continuity. And besides, I had spent some time in the Muskie building on the night of the New Hampshire primary, when the atmosphere of the place was strongly reminiscent of Death Row at Sing Sing. So my memories of that building were not pleasant—but my reasons, as usual, had a noticeably mystic flavor to them. And Gary, as usual, was thinking in terms of hard lawyer's logic and political pragmatism.

★

So the McGovern headquarters was moved, after Miami, from the original base between the liquor store and the grocery store on Capitol Hill to the Muskie tomb on K Street, in the fashionable downtown area. It was a central location, they said, with a big parking lot next door. It also had two elevators and sixteen bathrooms.

The original headquarters had only one bathroom, with a cardboard arrow on the door that could be moved, like a one-armed clock, to three different positions: MEN, WOMEN or EMPTY.

There was also a refrigerator. It was small, but somehow there were always a few cans of beer in it, even for visiting journalists. Nobody was in charge of stocking it, but nobody drank the last beer without replacing it, either . . . (or maybe it was all a shuck from the start; maybe they had a huge stash outside the back door, but they only kept two or three cans in the refrigerator, so that anybody who drank one would feel so guilty that he/she would bring six to replace it, the next time they came around . . . but I doubt it; not even that devious Arab bastard Rick Stearns would plot things that carefully).

But what the hell? All that is history now, and after roaming around the new McGovern headquarters building for a week or so, the only refrigerator I found was up in finance director Henry Kimmelman's office on the sixth floor. I went up there with Pat Caddell one afternoon last week to watch the Cronkite/Chancellor TV news (every afternoon at 6:30, all activity in the building is suspended for an hour while the staff people gather around TV sets to watch "the daily bummer," as some of them call it) and Kimmelman has the only accessible color set in the building, so his office is usually crowded for the news hour.

But his set is fucked, unfortunately. One of the color tubes is blown, so everything that appears on the screen has a wet purple tint to it. When McGovern comes on, rapping out lines from a speech that somebody watching one of the headquarters' TV sets just wrote for him a few hours earlier, his face appears on the set in Kimmelman's office as if he were speaking up from the bottom of a swimming pool full of cheap purple dye.

It is not a reassuring thing to see, and most of the staffers prefer to watch the news on the black & white sets downstairs in the political section. . . .

What? We seem to be off the track here. I was talking about my first encounter with the refrigerator in Henry Kimmelman's office—when I was looking for beer, and found none. The only thing in the icebox was a canned martini that tasted like brake fluid.

One canned martini. No beer. A purple TV screen. Both elevators jammed in the basement; fifteen empty bathrooms. Seventy-five cents an hour to park in the lot next door. Chaos and madness in the telephone switchboard. Fear in the back rooms, confusion up front, and a spooky vacuum on top—the eighth floor —where Larry O'Brien is supposed to be holding the gig together . . . what is he doing up there? Nobody knows. They never see him.

"Larry travels a lot," one of the speech writers told me. "He's Number One, you know—and when you're Number One you don't have to try so hard, right?"

The McGovern campaign appears to be fucked at this time. A spectacular Come From Behind win is still possible—on paper and given the right circumstances—but the underlying realities of the campaign itself would seem to preclude this. A cohesive, determined campaign with the same kind of multi-level morale that characterized the McGovern effort in the months preceding the Wisconsin primary might be a good bet to close a twenty-point gap on Nixon in the last month of this grim presidential campaign.

As usual, Nixon has peaked too early—and now he is locked into what is essentially a Holding Action. Which would be di-

sastrous in a close race, but—even by Pat Caddell's partisan estimate—Nixon could blow twenty points off his lead in the next
six weeks and still win. (Caddell's figures seem in general agreement with those of the most recent Gallup Poll, ten days ago,
which showed that Nixon could blow *thirty* points off his lead and
still win.)

My own rude estimate is that McGovern will steadily close
the gap between now and November 7th, but not enough. If I
had to make book right now, I would try to get McGovern with
seven or eight points, but I'd probably go with five or six, if necessary. In other words, my guess at the moment is that McGovern
will lose by a popular vote margin of 5.5 percent—and probably
far worse in the electoral college.[2]

The tragedy of this is that McGovern appeared to have a sure
lock on the White House when the sun came up on Miami
Beach on the morning of Thursday, July 13th. Since then he has
crippled himself with a series of almost unbelievable blunders—
Eagleton, Salinger, O'Brien, etc.—that have understandably convinced huge chunks of the electorate, including at least half of
his own hard-core supporters, that The Candidate is a gibbering
dingbat. His behavior since Miami has made a piecemeal mockery
of everything he seemed to stand for during the primaries.

Possibly I'm wrong on all this. It is still conceivable—to me
at least—that McGovern might actually win. In which case I
won't have to worry about my P.O. Box at the Woody Creek general store getting jammed up with dinner invitations from the
White House. But what the hell? Mr. Nixon never invited me, and
neither did Kennedy or LBJ.

---

2. I was somewhat off on this prediction. The final margin was almost
23%. At this point in the campaign I was no longer functioning with my
usual ruthless objectivity. Back in May and June, when my head was still
clear, I won vast amounts of money with a consistency that baffled the
experts. David Broder still owes me $500 as a result of his ill-advised bet
on Hubert Humphrey in the California primary. But he still refuses to pay
on the grounds that I lost the 500 back to him as a result of a forfeited
foot-race between Jim Naughton and Jack Germond in Miami Beach.

I survived those years of shame, and I'm not especially worried about enduring four more. I have a feeling that my time is getting short, anyway, and I can think of a hell of a lot of things I'd rather find in my mailbox than an invitation to dinner in the Servants' Quarters.

Let those treacherous bastards eat by themselves. They deserve each other.

Ah, Jesus! The situation is out of hand again. The sun is up, the deal is down, and that evil bastard Mankiewicz just jerked the

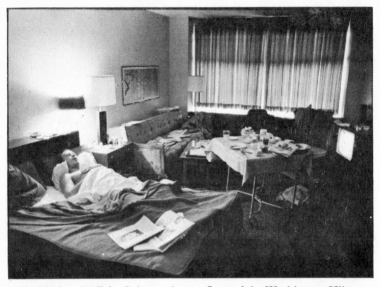

The National Affairs Suite on the top floor of the Washington Hilton.

kingpin out of my finely crafted saga for this issue. My brain has gone numb from this madness. After squatting for thirteen days in this scum-crusted room on the top floor of the Washington Hilton—writing feverishly, night after night, on the home-stretch realities of this goddamn wretched campaign—I am beginning to wonder what in the name of Twisted Jesus ever possessed me to come here in the first place. What kind of madness lured me back to this stinking swamp of a town?

Am I turning into a politics junkie? It is not a happy thought

—particularly when I see what it's done to all the others. After two weeks in Woody Creek, getting back on the press plane was like going back to the cancer ward. Some of the best people in the press corps looked so physically ravaged that it was painful to even see them, much less stand around and make small talk.

Many appeared to be in the terminal stages of Campaign Bloat, a gruesome kind of false-fat condition that is said to be connected somehow with failing adrenal glands. The swelling begins within twenty-four hours of that moment when the victim first begins to suspect that the campaign is essentially meaningless. At that point, the body's entire adrenaline supply is sucked back into the gizzard, and nothing either candidate says, does, or generates will cause it to rise again . . . and without adrenaline, the flesh begins to swell; the eyes fill with blood and grow smaller in the face, the jowls puff out from the cheekbones, the neck-flesh droops, and the belly swells up like a frog's throat. . . . The brain fills with noxious waste fluids, the tongue is rubbed raw on the molars, and the basic perception antennae begin dying like hairs in a bonfire.

I would like to think—or at least *claim* to think, out of charity if nothing else—that Campaign Bloat is at the root of this hellish angst that boils up to obscure my vision every time I try to write anything serious about presidential politics.

But I don't think that's it. The real reason, I suspect, is the problem of coming to grips with the idea that Richard Nixon will almost certainly be re-elected for another four years as President of the United States. If the current polls are reliable—and even if they aren't, the sheer size of the margin makes the numbers themselves unimportant—Nixon will be re-elected by a huge majority of Americans who feel he is not only more honest and more trustworthy than George McGovern, but also more likely to end the war in Vietnam.

The polls also indicate that Nixon will get a comfortable majority of the Youth Vote. And that he might carry all fifty states.

Well . . . maybe so. This may be the year when we finally come face to face with ourselves; finally just lay back and say it—

413

that we are really just a nation of 220 million used car salesmen with all the money we need to buy guns, and no qualms at all about killing anybody else in the world who tries to make us uncomfortable.

The tragedy of all this is that George McGovern, for all his mistakes and all his imprecise talk about "new politics" and "honesty in government," is one of the few men who've run for President of the United States in this century who really understands what a fantastic monument to all the best instincts of the human race this country might have been, if we could have kept it out of the hands of greedy little hustlers like Richard Nixon.

McGovern made some stupid mistakes, but in context they seem almost frivolous compared to the things Richard Nixon does every day of his life, on purpose, as a matter of policy and a perfect expression of everything he stands for.

Jesus! Where will it end? How low do you have to stoop in this country to be President?

October

Ask Not for Whom
the Bell Tolls ...

re-elect
the president

DUE TO CIRCUMSTANCES beyond my control, I would rather not write anything about the 1972 presidential campaign at this time. On Tuesday, November 7th, I will get out of bed long enough to go down to the polling place and vote for George McGovern. Afterwards, I will drive back to the house, lock the front door, get back in bed, and watch television as long as necessary. It will probably be a while before The Angst lifts—but whenever it happens I will get out of bed again and start writing the mean, cold-blooded bummer that I was not quite ready for today. Until then, I think Tom Benton's "re-elect the President" poster (above) says everything that needs to be said right now about this malignant election. In any other year I might be tempted to embellish the Death's Head with a few angry flashes of my own. But not in 1972. At least not in the sullen numbness of these final hours before the deal goes down—because words are no longer important at this stage of the campaign; all the best ones were said a long time ago, and all the right ideas were bouncing around in public long before Labor Day.

That is the one grim truth of this election most likely to come back and haunt us: The options were clearly defined, and all the major candidates except Nixon were publicly grilled, by experts who demanded to know exactly where they stood on every issue from Gun Control and Abortion to the Ad Valorem Tax. By mid-September both candidates had staked out their own separate turfs, and if not everybody could tell you what each candidate stood for *specifically,* almost everyone likely to vote in November understood that Richard Nixon and George McGovern were two very different men: not only in the context of politics, but also in their personalities, temperaments, guiding principles, and even their basic lifestyles . . .

There is almost a Yin/Yang clarity in the difference between the two men, a contrast so stark that it would be hard to find any two better models in the national politics arena for the legendary *duality*—the congenital Split Personality and polarized instincts— that almost everybody except Americans has long since taken for granted as the key to our National Character. This was not what Richard Nixon had in mind when he said, last August, that the 1972 presidential election would offer voters "the clearest choice of this century," but on a level he will never understand he was probably right . . . and it is Nixon himself who represents that dark, venal, and incurably violent side of the American character almost every other country in the world has learned to fear and despise. Our Barbie doll President, with his Barbie doll wife and his box-full of Barbie doll children is also America's answer to the monstrous Mr. Hyde. He speaks for the Werewolf in us; the bully, the predatory shyster who turns into something unspeakable, full of claws and bleeding string-warts, on nights when the moon comes too close. . . .

At the stroke of midnight in Washington, a drooling red-eyed beast with the legs of a man and the head of a giant hyena crawls out of its bedroom window in the South Wing of the White House and leaps fifty feet down to the lawn . . . pauses briefly to strangle the Chow watchdog, then races off into the darkness . . . towards the Watergate, snarling with lust, loping through the alleys behind Pennsylvania Avenue, and trying desperately to remember which one of those four hundred identical balconies is the one outside Martha Mitchell's apartment. . . .

Ah . . . nightmares, nightmares. But I was only kidding. The President of the United States would never act that weird. At least not during football season. But how would the voters react if they knew the President of the United States was presiding over "a complex, far-reaching and sinister operation on the part of White House aides and the Nixon campaign organization . . . involving sabotage, forgery, theft of confidential files, surveillance of Democratic candidates and their families and persistent efforts to lay the basis for possible blackmail and intimidation."

That ugly description of Nixon's staff operations comes from a New York *Times* editorial on Thursday, October 12th. But neither Nixon nor anyone else felt it would have much effect on his steady two-to-one lead over McGovern in all the national polls. Four days later the *Times*/Yankelovich poll showed Nixon ahead by an incredible twenty points (57 percent to 37 percent, with 16 percent undecided) over the man Bobby Kennedy described as "the most decent man in the Senate."

"Ominous" is not quite the right word for a situation where one of the most consistently unpopular politicians in American history suddenly skyrockets to Folk Hero status while his closest advisors are being caught almost daily in nazi-style gigs that would have embarrassed Martin Bormann.

How long will it be before "demented extremists" in Germany, or maybe Japan, start calling us A Nation of Pigs? How would Nixon react? "No comment"? And how would the popularity polls react if he just came right out and admitted it?

November

At the Midnight Hour . . . Stoned on the Zoo
Plane; Stomped in Sioux Falls . . . A Rambling,
Manic/Depressive Screed in Triple-Focus on the
Last Days of the Doomed McGovern Campaign . . .
Then Back to America's Heartland for a Savage
Beating . . . Fear and Loathing at the
Holiday Inn . . .

IT WAS DARK when we took off from Long Beach. I was standing in
the cockpit with a joint in one hand and a glass of Jack Daniels in
the other as we boomed off the runway and up . . . up . . . up . . .
into the cold black emptiness of a Monday night sky three miles
above southern California. "That's San Diego, off there to the
right," said the pilot. We were leaning left now, heading east, and
I hooked an elbow in the cockpit doorway to keep from falling . . .
looking down on the beach cities—Newport, Laguna, San Clemente
—and a thin, sharp white line along the coast that was either U.S.
101 or the Pacific Ocean surf.

"Yeah, that has to be the surf line," I muttered.

"Baja California," the person beside me replied.

I couldn't see who it was. There were five or six of us crowded
into the cockpit, along with the three-man crew. "Here, take this,"
I said, handing him the joint. "I have to get a grip on something."
I seized the back of the navigator's chair as we kept rolling left/east,
and still climbing. Behind us, in the long bright belly of the United
Airlines 727 Whisper Jet—or whatever they call those big three-
engine buggers with the D. B. Cooper door that drops down from
the tail—fifty or sixty drunken journalists were lurching around in
the aisles, spilling drinks on each other and rolling spools of raw
TV film towards the rear of the plane where two smiling steward-

esses were strapped down by their safety belts, according to regulations.

The "Fasten Seat Belts" sign was still on, above every seat, along with the "No Smoking" sign—but the plane was full of smoke and almost nobody was sitting down. Both flight kitchens had long since been converted to bars, stocked with hundreds of those little one-and-a-half ounce flight-size whiskey bottles. We had left New York that morning, with a stop in Philadelphia, and by the time we got to Wichita the scene in the Zoo Plane was like the clubhouse at Churchill Downs on Kentucky Derby Day . . . and now, flying back from L.A. to Sioux Falls, it was beginning to look more and more like the *infield* at Churchill Downs on Kentucky Derby Day.

Ah, jesus . . . here we go again: another flashback . . . the doctors say there's no cure for them; totally unpredictable, like summer lightning in the Rockies or sharks on the Jersey Shore . . . unreeling across your brain like a jumble of half-remembered movies all rolling at once. Yesterday I was sitting on my porch in Woody Creek, reading the sports section of the Denver *Post* and wondering how many points to give on the Rams-49ers game, sipping a beer and looking out on the snow-covered fields from time to time . . . when suddenly my head rolled back and my eyes glazed over and I felt myself sucked into an irresistible time-warp:

I was standing at the bar in the clubhouse at Churchill Downs on Derby Day with Ralph Steadman, and we were drinking Mint Juleps at a pretty good pace, watching the cream of Bluegrass Society getting drunker and drunker out in front of us . . . . It was between races, as I recall: Ralph was sketching and I was making notes ("3:45, Derby Day, standing at clubhouse bar now, just returned from Mens Room / terrible scene / whole place full of Kentucky Colonels vomiting into urinals & drooling bile down their seersucker pants-legs / Remind Ralph to watch for "distinguished-looking" men in pari-mutual lines wearing white-polished shoes with fresh vomit stains on the toes . . . .")

Right. We were standing there at the clubhouse bar, feeling very much on top of that boozy, back-slapping scene . . . when I suddenly glanced up from my notes & saw Frank Mankiewicz and Sonny Barger across the room, both of them wearing Hells Angels costumes and both holding heavy chrome chain-whips . . . and yes, it was clear that they'd spotted us. Barger stared, not blinking, but Mankiewicz smiled his cold lizard's smile and they moved slowly through the drunken crowd to put themselves between us and the doorway.

Ralph was still sketching, muttering to himself in some kind of harsh Gaelic singsong & blissfully unaware of the violence about to come down. I nudged him. "Say . . . ah . . . Ralph, I think maybe you should finish your drink and get that camera strap off your neck real fast."

"What?"

"Don't act nervous, Ralph. Just get that strap off your neck and be ready to run like a bastard when I throw this glass at the mirror."

He stared at me, sensing trouble but not understanding. Over his shoulder I could see Frank and Sonny coming towards us, moving slowly down the length of the long whiskey-wet oaken bar, trying to seem casual as they shoved through the crowd of booze-bent Southern Gentlemen who were crowding the aisle . . . and when I scanned the room I saw others: Tiny, Zorro, Frenchy, Terry the Tramp, Miles Rubin, Dick Dougherty, Freddy The Torch . . . they had us in a bag, and I figured the only way out was a sudden screaming sprint through the clubhouse and up the ramp to the Governor's Box, directly across from the Finish Line & surrounded at all times by State Troopers.

Their reaction to a horde of thugs charging through the crowd towards the Governor's Box would be safely predictable, I felt. They would club the bleeding shit out of anybody who looked even halfway weird, and then make mass arrests . . . . Many innocent people would suffer; the drunk tank of the Jefferson County Jail would be boiling that night with dozens of drink-maddened Blue-bloods who got caught in the Sweep; beaten stupid with truncheons and then hauled off in paddy wagons for no reason at all . . . .

But what the hell? This was certainly acceptable, I felt, and preferable beyond any doubt to the horror of being lashed into hamburger with chain-whips by Mankiewicz and Barger in the Clubhouse Bar . . . .

Indeed, I have spent some time in the Jefferson County Jail, and on balance it's not a bad place—at least not until your nerves go, but when that happens it doesn't really matter which jail you're in. All blood feels the same in the dark—or back in the shower cell, where the guards can't see.

Editor's Note

AT THIS POINT DR. THOMPSON *suffered a series of nervous seizures in his suite at the Seal Rock Inn. It became obvious both by the bizarre quality of his first-draft work and his extremely disorganized lifestyle that the only way the book could be completed was by means of compulsory verbal composition. Despite repeated warnings from Dr. Thompson's personal physician we determined that for esthetic, historical, and contractual reasons The Work would have to be finished at all costs.*

What follows, then, is a transcription of the conversations we had as Dr. Thompson paced around his room—at the end of an eighteen-foot microphone cord—describing the final days of the doomed McGovern campaign.

Ed: Well, Dr. Thompson, if you could explain these references . . . we just left you in the Jefferson County Jail, on a very dark and ominous note which I don't understand. . . . I thought you were on the plane going back to Sioux City and that you were standing . . .

HST: Sioux Falls.

Ed: Sioux Falls, excuse me, and that you were actually standing in the cockpit with a joint in one hand and a glass of Jack Daniels in the other. Were the pilots smoking dope? What was happening on this plane? . . . why was it called the Zoo Plane?

HST: Well, I would have preferred to *write* about this, but under the circumstances, I'll try to explain. There were two planes in the last months of the McGovern campaign. One was the Dakota Queen, actually it was the Dakota Queen II—like "junior"—the Dakota Queen Second. McGovern's bomber in World War II was the original Dakota Queen.

Ed: McGovern's bomber in World War II was named the Dakota Queen?

HST: Right. He was a bomber pilot in World War II.

Dr. Thompson at work.

Ed: Why don't you pull up a chair? Would you stop pacing around??

HST: I'm much more comfortable pacing . . .

Ed: All right. But you'll have to speak into the microphone.

HST: Yes . . . He named his campaign plane the Dakota Queen II, and at first that was enough—just one 727 which he chartered from United Airlines at outrageously inflated rates. They burned him as much as they could. He was doing things like flying back and forth from Washington to New York when he could have stayed in one place and they were running up . . .

Ed: Speak up, please.

HST: They were running up massive bills which were not necessary. I learned this from the United Airlines representative on the plane. But nevertheless, when the campaign began mushrooming around Labor Day, more and more press people came aboard the Dakota Queen, and it was necessary to have two McGovern campaign planes. One of which was divided into three compartments: where McGovern's family, himself and his sort of . . . personal staff sat in front. Like a first-class compartment. The middle of the plane was full of the very serious . . . working press, the New York *Times,* the wire service people, the Washington *Post* . . .

Ed: The New York *Times,* the wires? . . . What else?

HST: The people who had to file every day . . .

Ed: They had some sort of priority?

HST: Right. They were very serious people.

Ed: And they sat in the middle section of the plane?

HST: Yes. In the rear was a bar and a sort of mini press room where there were about five typewriters, a few phones—you could call from the plane to headquarters in Washington—you could call *anywhere* from the plane. But the atmosphere on the Dakota Queen was very . . . ah . . . very . . . *reserved* is the word.

Ed: The atmosphere was reserved? On the day before the election?

HST: Only on the Dakota Queen . . . the atmosphere on the Zoo Plane became crazier and crazier as the atmosphere on the Dakota Queen became more reserved and more somber. The kinkier members of the press tended to drift onto the Zoo Plane. The atmosphere was more comfortable. There were tremendous

424

amounts of cocaine, for instance.

Ed: There was cocaine on the Zoo Plane?

HST: Yes . . . dope.

Ed: Marijuana?

HST: Oh, hell yes . . . lots of marijuana, hash, MDA. . . .

Ed: Was this from the press primarily?

HST: Well, what happened was that the press took over the Zoo Plane—totally.

Ed: There were no McGovern staffers on the Zoo Plane?

HST: A few tried to get on it, but the press people had nailed down their own seats and refused to leave them. Once you got a seat on the Zoo Plane you clung to it. And so people would trade off for different legs of the trip. I recall once when I wanted to talk to McGovern, I traded with John Holum who had a girlfriend on the Zoo Plane. And when I tried to get my seat back, I think it was in Wichita, it was necessary to hint that I might have to use physical force to get Holum out of my seat and back on the Dakota Queen.

Ed: Were the . . . provisions provided on the Zoo Plane brought by the press themselves or were they a part of the hospitality of the McGovern staff?

HST: Well, you have to remember that the press was . . . every member of the press who traveled on either one of the planes, any campaign plane, was billed at the first-class rate plus one-third.

Ed: Why? What was the one-third for?

HST: Well, presumably for the damages . . .

Ed: Damages?

HST: It was a chartered plane, and on charters the stewardesses are more or less at the mercy of the passengers.

Ed: At the *mercy?*

HST: At one point on the Zoo Plane on the way to Sacramento —the pilot, whose name was Paul Prince[1] . . . and he was called Perfect Paul, the Virgin Pilot. . . .

1. Prince, the original pilot of the Zoo Plane, quickly became such a fixture & a favorite with the campaign press corps that he ended up flying more than his normal schedule of flight hours. The mood on the Zoo Plane changed perceptibly for the worse whenever FAA regulations forced Paul

Ed: Perfect Paul, the Virgin Pilot?

HST: Right. He was locked out of the cockpit. . . . And several of the crazier members of the press, who were up front—the cocaine section was up right behind the cockpit—got hold of him . . . and tore all of his clothes off . . . down to his underwear.

Ed: The press people tore off the pilot's clothes??

HST: Well, they sort of helped a woman from, I think it was . . . not *Women's Wear Daily,* but something like that. She was completely drunk and stoned. But, the TV technicians were the worst villains on the plane. . . . They held him while the wild woman tore his clothes off.

Ed: Who was flying the plane at this time?

HST: Well . . . the co-pilot, I guess. . . .

Ed: The co-pilot was flying the plane?

HST: There was a crew aboard—three crew members.

Ed: This was a 727?

HST: Yes, a 727. I think they call them "Whisper Jets." The one with the D. B. Cooper door, you know, the one that drops down out of the tail . . . And the pilot was stripped down to his underwear. Finally he got back into the cockpit, had to land in Sacramento in his underwear with this stoned woman still after him. . . .

Ed: One of the stewardesses?

HST: No, no. It was a woman from . . .

Ed: One of the reporters.

HST: I'd rather not name her.

Ed: Well, let's not mention any names. Certainly not.

HST: That sort of thing happened regularly on the Zoo Plane. All the *sound freaks,* for instance, were on the Zoo Plane. There were speakers up and down the aisle . . . every ten feet there would be a different . . . tape going. There were the Rolling Stones in front, the Grateful Dead in back . . .

Ed: I'd like to interrupt you now to ask what was the prevail-

---

to take time off. None of his temporary replacements had the proper style & élan. Rumblings of angst & general discontent ran up and down the aisle on days when "Perfect Paul, the Virgin Pilot" was not at the helm, as it were. Prince, in his own way, was as much a personal symbol of the McGovern campaign as Frank Mankiewicz.

Perfect Paul, The Virgin Pilot (left) and crewmember.

ing mood of the McGovern staff at this point . . . flying back to Sioux Falls . . . a day before the election, November 6?

HST: We left Long Beach at about 8:30 on Monday night, November 6, and flew directly to Sioux Falls. Long Beach was the last campaign appearance McGovern made except for a . . . sort of . . . homecoming in Sioux Falls at 1:30 at night. And . . . you asked about the mood . . . the mood of the McGovern staff on the Dakota Queen was very, very *quiet.* They had known for a long time what was going to happen. McGovern admitted knowing for at least a week.

Ed: McGovern admitted knowing for a week before the election?

HST: Yeah. I talked to him earlier that day on the way from Wichita to Long Beach and I could tell . . . he loosened up so much that it was clear something happened to him in his head. . . . He was finally relaxed for the first time. This was shortly after he told a heckler in I think it was . . . Grand Rapids, "Kiss my ass." He did it with very . . . considerable élan. . . . He moved up right next to this guy and he said: "I have a secret for you—kiss my ass." Most of the press people missed it. He put his arm around him and whispered, sort of quietly in his ear. McGovern didn't know anyone had heard him. Only two people heard him— one was a Secret Service man, another was Saul Kohler, of the Newhouse papers. McGovern thought he was saying it in total privacy. But it got out. But by that time he didn't care . . . He was laughing about it, and when I asked him about it on the Dakota Queen, he sort of smiled and said . . . "Well, he was one of these repulsive people, it was . . . one of the types you just want to get your hands on. . . ." He was so loose it was kind of startling. He got very relaxed once he realized what was going to happen. Later he said that he'd known for at least a week, and Gary Hart later said he had known for a month.

Ed: Gary Hart later admitted he had known McGovern would lose for a month before the election?

HST: He told me when I stopped in Denver on the way to the Super Bowl that he'd sensed it as early as September, but when I asked him when he *knew,* he thought for a minute and then said, "Well, I guess . . . it was around October 1. . . ." According to

Pat Caddell's polls they had known—when I say "they," I mean the McGovern top command—had known what kind of damage the Eagleton thing had done and how terminal it was ever since September. Pat said they spent a month just wringing their hands and tearing their hair trying to figure out how to overcome the Eagleton disaster.

Ed: By "the Eagleton disaster," do you mean the question of McGovern's competence in handling the affair?

HST: His whole image of being a . . . first a maverick, anti-politician and then suddenly becoming an expedient, pragmatic hack . . . who talked like any politician in anybody's . . . kind of a . . . Well, he began talking like a used car salesman, sort of out of both sides of his mouth, in the eyes of the public, and he was no longer . . . either a maverick or an anti-politician . . . he was . . . he was no better than Hubert Humphrey and that's not a personal judgment, that's how he was *perceived* . . . and that's an interesting word. "Perceive" is the word that became in the '72 campaign what "charisma" was for the 1960, '64 and even the '68 campaigns. "Perceive" is the new key word.

Ed: What does "perceive" mean?

HST: When you say perceive you imply the difference between what the candidate *is* and the way the public or the voters *see* him.

Ed: What causes the difference between the perception and the reality?

HST: The best example of how *perception* can drastically alter a campaign is the difference between, for instance, how McGovern was perceived by the Wallace voters in the Wisconsin primary as being almost as much of a maverick and an anti-politician as George Wallace himself. He carried the south side of Milwaukee—one of the last places anybody expected him to carry.

Ed: That was primarily a blue-collar district?

HST: Not just blue-collar—hardhat, a really serious hardhat district.

Ed: Weren't they also Polish?

HST: A lot of them, yeah. Muskie was supposed to carry the Fourth but Muskie's campaign was falling apart by that time, and Humphrey was not the kind of person who would go over up there.

Ed: So the voters perceived . . . the blue-collar, Polish, Wallace-style voters perceived McGovern to be as much of a maverick as Wallace.

HST: Yes, at that point he was hitting the tax reform issue, which he picked up from Wallace in Florida.

Ed: What was the difference between the perception and the reality on the Eagleton affair?

HST: The Eagleton affair was the first serious crack in McGovern's image as the anti-politician. He dumped Eagleton for reasons that still aren't . . . that he still refuses to talk about. Eagleton's mental state was much worse than was ever explained publicly. How much worse, it's hard to say right now, but that's something I'll have to work on. . . . In any case there was *no hope* of keeping Eagleton on the ticket.

The Eagleton thing is worth looking at for a second in terms of the difference between perception and reality. McGovern was perceived as a cold-hearted, political pragmatist who dumped this poor, neurotic, good guy from Missouri because he thought people wouldn't vote for him because they were afraid that shock treatments in the past might have some kind of lingering effect on his mind. Whereas, in fact, despite denials of the McGovern staff in the last days of the campaign—when I was one of the five or six reporters who were pushing very aggresively to find out more about Eagleton and the real nature of his mental state—I spent about ten days in late September, early October, in St. Louis trying to dig up Eagleton's medical record out of the Barnes Hospital, or actually the Rennard Hospital in the Washington University medical center. Despite this, Mankiewicz denied knowing anything about it, because he'd promised to protect the person who told him about it in the first place. . . .

Ed: Which person?

HST: The person who called and said . . . several days after the convention . . . who left a note at the headquarters in Washington saying, "There's something you should know about Tom Eagleton—he's a dangerous nut."

Ed: This was back in June, July?

HST: It was about two days after the convention ended in Miami.

Ed: An anonymous person called Mankiewicz . . . ?

HST: And Gary Hart.

Ed: And Gary Hart?!

HST: Both of them got messages about the same time. It was the husband of a woman whose name . . . well, there's no point in going into that—it would probably be libelous . . . but it was the husband of a woman who had been part of the anaesthesiology team, who had participated in Eagleton's second shock treatment, so she knew about it.

Ed: So you were investigating the Eagleton story and Mankiewicz denied knowing anything about it?

HST: Repeatedly, over and over again. I knew he was lying because I had all the facts from other people in the campaign whose names I couldn't use. I couldn't quote them, because I had promised I wouldn't say where I got the information. About three weeks after the election, though, Haynes Johnson of the Washton *Post* wrote a long series on the Eagleton affair, and here's the way he explains how Mankiewicz reacted to the initial shock of this information about Eagleton. . . . He's talking about the fact that two reporters from the Knight newspapers got hold of the information about the same time Gary and Frank did. The same person who called them, called John Knight in Detroit, and two reporters from the Detroit *Free Press*—or the Washington bureau of Knight newspapers—flew out to Sioux Falls with a long memo on the Eagleton situation. They hadn't broken the story yet—but they were about to. They were trying to be . . . first they were trying to be fair with McGovern and, second, they were trying to use what they had to get more—which is a normal journalistic kind of procedure.

Ed: A normal *what* kind of procedure?

HST: Journalistic. If you have half a story and you don't know the rest, you use what you have to pry the rest out of someone.

Ed: Leverage.

HST: Here's what Mankiewicz told Haynes Johnson after the election was over, when it no longer mattered: "As Mankiewicz says, they had come up with a very incoherent and largely unpublishable memo full of rumors and unsubstantiated material—but a memo that was clearly on the right track." The memo contained such things as drinking reports and reports that Eagleton had been hospitalized and given electro-shock treatments for psychiatric problems. "But the real crusher," Mankiewicz said, "was a passage in the memo that had quotations around it as if it had been taken from a hospital record. It said that Tom Eagleton had been treated with electro-shock therapy at Barnes Hospital in St. Louis for, and this was the part that was quoted, 'severe manic-depressive psychosis with suicidal tendencies.' And that scared me."

That was Mankiewicz talking, and here's the explanation he gave for why he lied to all the reporters, including me, who had asked him about this. . . . Because *I knew* . . . I had that exact quote from several people on the McGovern staff, who wanted to release it. They thought that if people knew the truth about the Eagleton situation—that there was no way he could possibly be kept on the ticket—that the *"perception"* of McGovern's behavior with Eagleton might be drastically altered. Eagleton would no longer be the wronged good guy, but what he actually was—an opportunistic liar.

Ed: An opportunistic liar.

HST: With a history of very serious mental disorders and no reason for anyone to believe they wouldn't recur. Here's what Mankiewicz . . . here's the reason Mankiewicz gives for not explaining this to the press at the time. This is Haynes Johnson of the Washington *Post* again: "Mankiewicz says 'he stalled furiously' with the newspaper representatives, appealed to their patriotism and promised them tangible news breaks. Both McGovern and Eagleton would have complete physicals later at Walter Reed Hospital, and challenge the other candidates to do the same and release the medical results. When that happened, he went on, he would try to arrange either an exclusive interview with Eagleton or give them a news cycle break on the Eagleton medical story."

Ed: What's a news cycle break?

HST: I don't know. That's the kind of language Mankiewicz used all through the campaign when he got confused and started treading water.

Ed: So the difference between the perception and the reality was that the public saw McGovern dumping Eagleton for political expedience, when in reality there was no way Eagleton could stay on the ticket. He had deceived McGovern, and Mankiewicz was attempting to break this in the most favorable way but failed.

HST: Right. At that point Mankiewicz was afraid to say anything heavy to the press, and rightly so, I think. Look at what happened to Jack Anderson when he went on the air . . . on the Mutual Radio Network with a story of Eagleton's drunk driving arrests. Then he couldn't prove it. He couldn't get the records. He was told by True Davis, who had run against Eagleton in the Democratic primary for senator in 1968 in Missouri, that the records were in a box in an office in St. Louis, and Davis promised Anderson that he would get them immediately. So Anderson had every reason to believe that he would have the actual drunk driving records or xeroxes of them in his hands by the time he broke the story. After Anderson had broken the story both on the radio and in his column . . . his syndicated column . . . he got desperate for the records because he knew he was going to be challenged. At that point True Davis was the president of a bank owned by the United Mine Workers in Washington.

Ed: Tony Boyle's union? Hubert Humphrey's friend?

HST: Right. Davis told Jack Anderson that unfortunately the box containing the records pertaining to Eagleton's drunk driving arrests had *disappeared* from this room . . . some storage place in St. Louis . . . and contrary to what he told Anderson earlier, he couldn't produce them. So Anderson was left with a story that almost every journalist in Washington still believes to be true.

Ed: How does this get back to what we were talking about before?

HST: I wanted to tell you why Mankiewicz was afraid to break the . . . or help anyone else break the story on Eagleton's mental history. Anderson got burned so badly on that, and was so embarrassed publicly that it appeared—for reasons that he could never explain—that he was just taking a cheap shot at Eagleton, and Eagleton came off looking better than he had before Anderson had started. So Mankiewicz and Gary Hart along with McGovern . . . those were the only people who knew the details about Eagleton's

433

mental disorders. . . . They decided that *they* couldn't break the story. They couldn't help anyone else investigate Eagleton any further than Eagleton himself wanted to be investigated, or it would appear that the McGovern staff was deliberately leaking false information on Eagleton in order to make him look bad, which would then in turn make McGovern look good.

Ed: Which what? Which in turn would make McGovern look good?

HST: Yeah, if Eagleton had turned out . . . if the records had been available . . . See, Eagleton never showed McGovern his medical records. He kept saying he would bring them to South Dakota.

Ed: Did McGovern keep asking him?

HST: Oh, yes. They kept . . . they couldn't believe it when he didn't show up with them in South Dakota.

Ed: He promised that he was going to bring them?

HST: He promised it for about ten days and finally he said that the psychiatrists wouldn't release them, the Mayo Clinic wouldn't release them, the Barnes Hospital wouldn't release them.

Ed: Why wouldn't the hospital release records to a patient?

HST: Well, the answer is . . . the question is the answer.

Ed: So it wasn't true. He just did not bring the records for his own reasons.

HST: Well, would you want to go . . . would you go to a psychiatrist who you thought would release his own personal diagnosis of your condition?

Ed: No, but he promised McGovern the records and he did not produce the records. He could have produced the records.

HST: Yes, he could have.

Ed: Yes, he could have.

HST: By the end of the campaign McGovern had still not seen the records, but at that point . . . he didn't care anymore.

Ed: Okay, now back to perception and reality—and Mankiewicz.

HST: When I talked to Mankiewicz about the Eagleton records, he denied knowing anything about it at all, whereas, in fact, he knew exactly what I'd just said about . . . severe psychosis and so forth . . .

Ed: What he later told Haynes.

HST: I gave him the same words, exactly.

Ed: And he denied it.

HST: Right. He denied it. But what he told me was that I should go out to St. Louis and look . . . and look for the records on my own. He said, "I'm surprised that some of you people haven't gone out there and worked on it," speaking of the journalists. He was hinting that the records were there, but that was as far as he would go. They were afraid, as I said . . . well, they knew that the information had to come from somebody other than from the McGovern camp in order to have any kind of credibility, or otherwise it would look like . . .

Ed: Like they were trying to make Eagleton look bad.

HST: Yeah, and Eagleton kept accusing them of it . . . constantly . . . saying that these bastards have not only spiked my career but now they're trying to make it look worse in order to make themselves look good. Whereas, in fact, McGovern and about six of his top people knew that the information was there to get their hands on, but they couldn't *do* it . . . What I tried to do was to go out and *buy* them or find somebody who would *steal* them out of the safe at Rennard Hospital.

Ed: At what hospital?

HST: Rennard Hospital. That's where they are . . . in St. Louis.

Ed: They're still there?

HST: Yeah, but they're not public "records" in any real public sense.

Ed: I understand, but they could be released at the request of a patient.

HST: Yes, at the request of the patient.

Ed: So the public perceived McGovern to be the bad guy, when in fact it was really Eagleton. And McGovern never recovered from that change in his image.

HST: No, to the extent that it damaged him . . . Pat Caddell has very convincing figures on that. Their polling from July, September to November shows that the Eagleton affair had hurt McGovern so badly that the fact is the figures went off the end of the board. It was totally impossible to recover from that . . . the damage was so great particularly among the younger voters where Mc-

Govern's potential strength lay.

Ed: Why were there so many defections over Eagleton among McGovern's younger supporters?

HST: They were the people who would be more inclined to be sympathetic—because they were more sophisticated—to a person who had been treated for nervous tension, even if he had gone to the extent of having electro-shock treatments. They were not the kind of people who would say, "Oh, that nut—get rid of him." They were also the same kind of people who had earlier seen McGovern as an anti-politician . . . or the "white knight," as some people called him . . . The honest man . . . Not the kind of person who would *say* one thing and *do* another. And at that point with Eagleton, as he said, he was behind him 1000 percent. Then he turned around and asked him to get off the ticket.

Ed: It was at that point McGovern said "1000 percent?"

HST: One of the weird unanswered questions is whether Mc-Govern actually *said* 1000 percent to anyone but Eagleton.

Ed: Well, who reported that McGovern said, "I was behind you 1000 percent?"

HST: Eagleton reported it.

Ed: Eagleton reported it, but McGovern never denied it . . . he couldn't have, of course.

HST: He didn't deny it and Mankiewicz explained to me . . . he said, we *had* to do that. We came to a point where we either had to back him totally, or dump him. There was no middle way.

Ed: So they decided to back him totally. What made them change their minds?

HST: The reaction from all over the country . . . the party hierarchy . . . mainly the financial people. The money flow stopped completely.

Ed: The money flow stopped completely because of Eagleton? Was there ever any . . . in other words, the money people said, you have to get rid of Eagleton or we're not going to put any more money into this campaign.

HST: Oh, it wasn't just the money people . . . They said that . . . But it was also Jean Westwood, Larry O'Brien, Mayor Daley, all the pros, who said we simply can't do it. Mankiewicz had said the same thing. Just as soon as the Eagleton story broke. He said:

"Let's get rid of this guy."

Ed: Frank said that? "Let's get rid of this guy?" Right away?

HST: Yeah. In the Haynes Johnson story Mankiewicz said that he was speaking both for himself and Gary Hart when he went to McGovern right after they found out about the information on Eagleton, the initial information, the stuff that was published. He said, "I remember that night I called him 'George' which I vowed I would not do during the campaign. I indicated I was speaking for Gary and myself." Mankiewicz told McGovern, "Let's get rid of this guy."

Ed: That was the first time he had called Senator McGovern George? That seems unusual.

HST: Yeah, that puzzled me all throughout the campaign, because I remember when I first met McGovern over at Tom Braden's house back in December . . . He came over for dinner, and it seemed like the most natural thing in the world to call him George . . . like I had called Tom Braden, columnist from the Washington *Post* "Tom," and . . . people would call Robert Kennedy "Bobby." One of the . . . sort of . . . consistent indicators of the tone of the McGovern campaign and McGovern's personality was the fact that nobody in the campaign, including Mankiewicz, who was the closest person to him in the campaign, ever called him anything but "The Senator" or addressed him as "Senator," which struck me as very peculiar.

HST: At first I called him George, but then I began to feel weird, because I was the only person that called him that. My wife called him that . . . I never heard anyone else call him "George."

Ed: What did you call Hubert Humphrey? Did you speak to him first face to face.

HST: I didn't get the chance to address Humphrey directly. I was introduced to him once, though . . . He had a habit of wandering up and down the aisle of his plane.

Ed: This was on the Humphrey campaign plane?

HST: In California, yeah. I went out there . . . after I called him all these wretched things. I figured I owed them a free shot at me since I'd taken so many at them. I went out to the Lockheed factory with Hubert . . . whoever makes the L-1011. Yeah, it must be Lockheed . . . in Palmdale, I think it was.

Ed: In California?

HST: Yeah, it was during the California primary. I figured I should spend at least one day on the Humphrey plane . . . so I called his press office at the Beverly Hilton and I said I'd be on it—and I thought, well Jesus, here we go—I'll get a beating now. . . . And when I came on Humphrey was walking up and down the aisle. One of his press aides was sort of escorting him and saying this is so and so, from so and so . . . Then he got to me and said, "Who are you?" And I said I was Hunter Thompson from *Rolling Stone,* and he said how do you *spell* that . . . So at the top of his voice he insisted that I spell Hunter Thompson . . . then I had to spell *Rolling Stone.*

Ed: They'd never heard of you?

HST: Of course they had—*Newsweek* had just quoted me in two consecutive issues, calling Humphrey "a treacherous, gutless old ward-heeler"—that bullshit about spelling was just their way of getting back at me. I guess they thought I'd be embarrassed. The whole Humphrey trip was run by waterheads . . . but there was no way I could avoid that crap and I figured . . . you know . . . they deserved a free shot by that time.

Ed: When you spoke to Nixon, how did you address him?

HST: I don't think I did. I'm very uncomfortable with titles.

Ed: What did Nixon call you?

HST: "Hunter" . . . We were talking about football. He was feeling very relaxed.

Ed: We seem to be getting off the track. We were discussing the difference between "perception" and "reality" in the handling of the Eagleton affair. The public *perceived* Eagleton to be the good guy . . .

HST: Excuse me, but I think I see a mescaline dealer down there in the street.

Ed: No . . . pull the curtains, pull the curtains.

HST: I should call my attorney.

Ed: Maybe we should get your personal physician back here.

You're acting very tense, very nervous . . . we can't even *think* about mescaline dealers right now. We're on a crisis schedule with this book . . . . Do you want to say anything further about the way Mc-Govern handled the Eagleton problem?

HST: I think he handled it very badly. There were two people in the campaign . . . in the sort of top echelon, who made the strongest possible case with George for unloading Eagleton.

Ed: Who? When was this?

HST: Right after it happened, the day the story broke. It was a Tuesday, as I recall—the last Tuesday in July.

Ed: Who argued for dumping Eagleton?

HST: Well . . . Eleanor McGovern was the first one. But that's not what I mean here, because she wanted to dump him in Miami, about two minutes after she heard he'd been selected to be on the ticket. She was the only person in Miami who was openly, out-front opposed to Eagleton right from the start—except me, of course, but people like Hart and Mankiewicz never took my opinions very seriously anyway . . . and in Miami I wasn't down on Eagleton because I knew any foul secrets about him; neither did Eleanor . . . . But when I was talking to Stearns and Bill Dougherty [McGovern advisor, William Dougherty, Lieutenant Governor of South Dakota] on the beach that Saturday afternoon after the convention, I told him Eagleton looked like the first big mistake they'd made, up to then—because he seemed out of place in that campaign; he was a hack, just another one of these cheap hustlers—and Dougherty said it was kind of funny to hear *me* saying almost exactly the same things Eleanor had been saying about Eagleton . . . .

Ed: Bill Dougherty said that? In Miami?

HST: Yeah, but I didn't print it. Stearns and I were out on the beach drinking beer when Bill saw us. . . . He just came over and sat down, without realizing I had my tape recorder going, so I figured it wasn't fair to use some of the brutally frank things he said that day. . . . I edited them out of the tape transcription.

Ed: Too bad—but let's get back to what happened when the Eagleton story actually broke. *Who* wanted to dump him?

HST: Mankiewicz didn't even want him to come to South Dakota—he wanted to dump him the minute he heard about it—the shock treatments.

439

Ed: Mankiewicz wanted to dump Eagleton immediately? And McGovern said no?

HST: McGovern wasn't sure.

Ed: So you say Mankiewicz handled the situation badly.

HST: Well, you can't blame it on Frank. Mankiewicz couldn't dump him; McGovern had to. And Gary Hart was . . . at first . . . under the impression that they should ride it out, or at least, *try* to ride it out. That was the rationale behind the 1000 percent . . . let's back him . . . they couldn't back him 99 percent . . . or 84 percent . . . they had to back him 1000 percent . . . or a million percent, or whatever . . . In other words, they had to back him or dump him.

Ed: And they wound up doing neither, really.

HST: Right, and that was the pattern of their blunders all through the campaign. It happened with welfare, the thousand dollar per person scheme; it happened with the Salinger trip to Paris to talk with the Viet Cong.

Ed: Did Salinger go to Hanoi or did he go to Paris?

HST: To Paris.

Ed: To negotiate with the Viet Cong representatives? To make a deal of some kind?

HST: Not really to make a deal, but to establish a contact. . . . McGovern told him to do it and then denied it.

Ed: I see. McGovern had sent Salinger to Paris and then denied it.

HST: No, he didn't *send* him, he *asked* him to go—Pierre was going to Paris anyway, he lives there. So McGovern asked him to see what he could find out about getting some POW's released.

Ed: So the public's perception of McGovern was distorted—but you think that McGovern essentially was at the root of that distortion.

HST: I think his *indecisiveness* was at the root of that distortion. At every crisis in the campaign McGovern appeared to be—was perceived to be—and, in fact, *was* indecisive . . . for unnatural periods of time.

Ed: Unnatural periods of time?

HST: Well, unsettling periods of time. The selection of a replacement for Eagleton was one of the most heinous botches

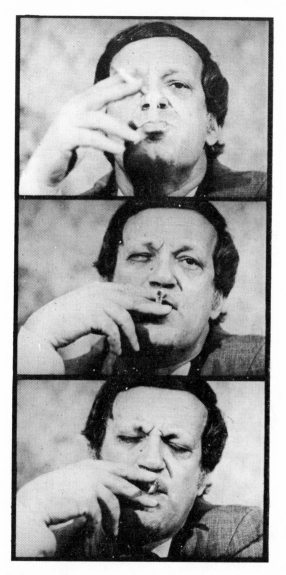

"I had three main reasons. The first was political and personal—he had lied to us and we couldn't have him around . . . the second was the public reaction that inevitably would come from these kinds of reports . . . and the third was patriotism. In other words, did we want this man to be in the position to be President?"

in the history of politics. Here he was calling Humphrey and Muskie and offering it to them *publicly*—and then being turned down . . . He had also offered it to Humphrey at the convention . . . I didn't realize that until later.

Ed: He had offered it to Humphrey before he offered it to Eagleton?

HST: Yeah. Informally. Like a peace offering—symbolic.

Ed: Informally, symbolic. Very subtle, eh?

HST: And Humphrey turned it down informally. Humphrey was in a fit of pique at the convention.

Ed: So throughout the campaign McGovern exhibited these alarming tendencies, which the public perceived to be indecision.

HST: It *was* indecision.

Ed: But nevertheless, you think that Eagleton was really more of a villain than the public ever knew.

HST: Absolutely.

Ed: Let's get back to the airplane . . . The last thing I remember was that the pilot had his clothes off and you were landing in . . . where was it . . . were you back in Sioux Falls?

HST: Sacramento.

Ed: Sacramento?

HST: That was a flashback.

Ed: Well, let's focus on Sioux Falls. The Zoo Plane and the Dakota Queen are landing in Sioux Falls and it's the night before the election. . . . You said previously that everyone's mood was somewhat sober, that most of the key people in McGovern's staff knew at this point there was no chance.

HST: Everybody on both planes knew what was going to happen. But the dimensions of the defeat—that was a real shock —but nobody thought McGovern was going to win. It was out of the question. And because of that, I think, there was a mood of suspended hysteria on the Zoo Plane, which would probably have happened on the other plane too, if McGovern hadn't been there. But in deference to the candidate, his wife, his family, his close personal friends, all those people, the mood there was . . . almost a sort of peaceful resignation.

Ed: Is it true that McGovern has an illegitimate twenty-two-year-old son?

HST: Hmmm . . . Well, I think you'd better . . . ah . . . let's call him and ask. I have his number over here in this book. . . .

Ed: One last question about this trip from Long Beach to Sioux Falls: Why was this second plane called the Zoo Plane and how widespread was the use of dangerous narcotics in the campaign and on this particular trip?

HST: Well, let's first deal with the fact that "drugs" are not necessarily narcotics. We want to get that clear in our minds. The narcotic is one type of drug and . . .

Ed: Excuse me, I . . .

HST: Coffee is a drug . . . yes, there were drugs being used . . . booze is a drug . . . many drugs. . . . They're all around us these days.

Ed: I understand you're an expert. . . .

HST: Well . . . I've been studying drugs for years.

Ed: A student of pharmacology.

HST: I make a point of knowing what I'm putting into myself. Yes. . . . The Zoo Plane: I'm not sure who named it that, but the name derived from the nature of the behavior of the people on it . . . It was very much like a human zoo, and I recall particularly that last flight from Long Beach to Sioux Falls . . . I remember Tim Crouse's description of how the older and straighter press people must have felt when they saw five or six freaks reeling around in the cockpit on takeoff and landing, passing joints around. As Tim said, you can imagine how these guys felt. They had heard all these terrible things, they'd read stories about how people in dark corners gathered to pass drugs around, and they always thought that it happened in urine-soaked doorways around Times Square. But all of a sudden here we were covering a presidential campaign and there were joints being passed up and down the aisle: weird people in the cockpit . . . drug addicts . . . lunatics . . . crowding into the cockpit just to get high and wired on the

443

lights. The cockpit had millions of lights all around it . . . green lights . . . red lights . . . all kinds of blinking things—a wonderful place to be. That surge of power in a jet . . . you don't get any real sense of it back in the passenger seats, but the feeling . . . up in front is like riding God's own motorcycle. You can feel that incredible . . . at takeoff . . . that incredible surge of power behind you . . . in the 727 the engines are way back in the back and you feel like you're just being lifted off the ground by some kind of hellish force. And the climb angle is something like 45 or 50 degrees . . . maybe 60 degrees . . . and then all these green lights blinking and these dials going and there are things buzzing and humming . . . and looking down seeing the lights here and there . . . and cities passing and mountain ranges . . . a wonderful way to go. I think I'm going to have to get a flying license very soon, and maybe one of those Lear jets. Jesus—the possibilities! It beats motorcycles all to hell.

Ed: It's the third dimension. Motorcycles are only two dimensional.

HST: Yeah, right. I think I'd like to get up there at night, all alone—with a head full of mescaline, just roll around in the sky like a big Condor. . . .

Ed: What about drugs on the Zoo Plane?

HST: Christ, you have a one-track mind! I think probably . . . I wish we had a picture of this somewhere . . . I don't think anybody ever got one. If they did, we'll all be arrested for it. But early on in the campaign, I'm not sure at what point, both galleys, which is where on commercial jets the stewardesses kind of station themselves to serve food . . . On the Zoo Plane both of them were immediately converted into bars, one in the front and one in the back. The stewardesses were totally helpless—at the mercy of these lunatics who had taken over the plane. That trip from Long Beach to Sioux Falls was probably the worst . . . after we had left the cockpit, about five of us gathered in the rear galley, there was one overhead light and the rest of the plane was dark. They had turned the lights out—it was practically midnight and . . .

Ed: Midnight?

444

HST: Yeah, we didn't arrive in Sioux Falls until one-thirty in the morning on November 7, election day. And the rest of the plane was dark and here was this one overhead light in this galley, and I had taken my tape recorder back, playing Herbie Mann's *Memphis Underground* album, at top volume in this tiny little room with tin walls and the music was echoing all up and down the plane. Somebody up in front was playing a Rolling Stones album on another tape recorder and we were . . . smoking this very peculiar looking hash pipe . . . passing it around . . .

Ed: Was that your billy club hash pipe?

HST: I'd rather not talk about that. . . . No, this was some kind of strange Lebanese flower pipe which was clearly a drug implement. There was no mistaking it. And right next to us were about four of these rather old-time, straight-looking cameramen from ABC-TV, just looking up in stone horror that here on a presidential campaign these . . . addicts and . . . loonies . . . all of them being paid, presumably well, by respectable or whatever newspapers or media that covered this presidential campaign.

Ed: Union members.

HST: These people were, yes, that sort. And it was funny and very bizarre for a presidential campaign. Behavior like that was consistent for maybe a month on the Zoo Plane . . . the last month. As the McGovern situation got worse, the Zoo Plane became crazier and crazier.

Ed: What happened when you arrived in Sioux Falls?

HST: Well, there was a very sad kind of . . . welcome-home rally for George McGovern and . . . One final note on the Zoo Plane. I think it was a tradition dating back to one of the Kennedy campaigns . . . At every hotel wherever the campaign press corps stopped, there would be maybe a hundred rooms reserved for the press. And everyone upon checking out would keep their keys, and we brought the keys on the plane and taped them along the aisle. The keys jingled like a giant tambourine on every takeoff . . . They were taped next to each other in a solid row along both top racks above the seats. There were maybe five thousand hotel keys . . .

Ed: From the entire campaign?

HST: Every hotel in the country, it looked like. And I think on the last day of the campaign, one of the CBS cameramen put them all in a huge bag. He was going to take them to one mailbox in Washington and dump them all in there. . . . Then they were going to film the behavior of the postman when he opened the box and found five thousand hotel keys . . . it must have weighed two hundred pounds . . . that was the kind of twisted humor that prevailed on the Zoo Plane.

Ed: What happened when you arrived in Sioux Falls?

HST: Well, it was, as I say, it was really a sad kind of rally. It was cold and late. My notes here say: 12:55 and the sign says "Welcome Home, George" . . . erected by the local Jaycees. It was sort of the return of the local boy who made good, but I suspect that even in that crowd there was an ominous sense that some kind of awful beating was about to occur. And as it happened, McGovern didn't even carry South Dakota. He lost it by eight or nine points.

Ed: What did McGovern say when he got off the plane? Did he make a speech?

HST: The only quote I have here in the notebook—yeah, here it is: "When I see these thousands of people standing here I think of words like love and devotion." My own feeling at the time was . . . sort of like "the party's over" and . . . once you got off the Zoo Plane it was almost like being . . . plunged back into reality. Most of us just crashed that night either at the Holiday Inn or the Ramada Inn. And the next morning by about ten o'clock Mc-Govern had a schedule . . . this was his last official campaign schedule and about half of the press corps followed him. I didn't, I slept. Then I had lunch with some of the heavier, straighter reporters . . . Doug Kneeland from the New York *Times,* Bill Greider from the *Post,* and four or five others. We were discussing what bets were safe and I think Kneeland had McGovern and six points, meaning that if McGovern lost by five he would win the bet. He was a little dubious about that one, but we decided that anybody who had McGovern and ten points was pretty safe. There was no question in their minds, even the most enlightened and supposedly . . . inside, hard-core press people—that McGovern would lose by more than ten points. And this was at noon on election day. . . .

Ed: I notice here we have the schedule for Senator George McGovern on Tuesday, November 7, election day. It only runs up to 3:30, where it says private time at Holiday Inn. What happened after that?

HST: There wasn't a hell of a lot to do in Sioux Falls . . .

Ed: We're now on election day and according to what you've told me so far, you and the members of the press were sitting around betting on exactly how much McGovern would lose by. What was McGovern doing during that day? This "Schedule for Senator George McGovern" . . . begins at 8:30 A.M. . . .

HST: Let's just put the goddamn thing in the record . . .

Schedule for Senator George McGovern
Tuesday, November 7, 1972

8:30 A.M. Depart Holiday Inn Downtown. Shuttle buses will pick up people from the other hotels shortly beforehand — bus schedules forthcoming upon arrival Mon. evening at the Holiday Inn.

9:45 A.M. Arrive to vote at Educational Building of Congregational Church, 301 E. 4th Street, Mitchell, S. Dakota. There will only be room inside for press pool.

10:15 A.M. Depart for Dakota Wesleyan.

10:25 A.M. Informal coffee with President Don Messer, University Building, Allen Hall, Dakota Wesleyan University.

11:10 A.M. Depart (walking) for Campus Center.

11:15 A.M. High School Students Seminar — speech, Campus Center Building, 2nd floor cafeteria.

12:00 P.M. Interview with Mitchell Daily Republic. PRESS FILING in Campus Center Building.

12:20 P.M. Drop in at Burg Shoe Store, 216 N. Main Street, followed by visit to Mitchell McGovern Headquarters.

1:00 P.M.	Depart for Sioux Falls (box lunch in cars and buses).
2:15 P.M.	Presentation and press reception, Minnehaha Country Club, W. 22nd Street, Sioux Falls.
3:15 P.M.	Depart for Holiday Inn.
3:30 P.M.	Private time at Holiday Inn.
To be announced:	Election Night Statement, Coliseum, 501 N. Main, Sioux Falls.

Time of Departure of planes back to Washington will be posted in Press Room immediately following Election Night statement.

Ed: What did McGovern do after 3:30? How did he spend his private time? What did he do that day?

HST: Well, he spent most of the afternoon at that Country Club reception . . . it was the first time I'd ever seen him drinking . . . sort of casually and openly in public . . .

Ed: Was he drinking more heavily than usual?

HST: Not *heavily,* but he wasn't worried about walking up to the bar and saying . . . uh . . . let me have . . . a . . . vodka and orange juice. Normally a presidential candidate wouldn't do that. He'd have somebody else go get it for him . . . and if anybody asked what he was drinking, he'd say "orange juice." But by that time McGovern no longer cared what people thought about his minor vices. Particularly the press corps . . . A weird relationship develops when you follow a candidate for a long time. You become sort of a . . . friendly antagonist . . . to the extent sometime where it can get dangerous . . . It certainly did in this campaign during the last month or so . . . In my case I became more of a flack for McGovern than . . . than a journalist. Which is probably why I made that disastrous bet, although there wasn't a reporter in the press corps who thought that George would lose by more than 10 points. . . . except Joe Alsop; he said McGovern wouldn't get more than 40 percent of the vote.

Ed: The others were more optimistic?

HST: Well . . . there was a sense of suspended . . . ah . . .

448

not animation . . . that's the wrong word: it was sort of a sense of limbo, an ominous sense that the night was not gonna be very pleasant. We all knew it but nobody was talking about it. McGovern Headquarters was in the downtown Holiday Inn and there was a sort of false gaiety that prevailed there. There was a bar on the top floor . . . kind of a big, glass-walled dome. People were having a few drinks and pretending that none of them knew what was about to happen. I recall spending a few hours up there with Ron Rosenbaum from the *Village Voice* and Bob Greene from the Chicago *Sun Times* and I don't think we talked about the election at all . . . We just talked about how strange it was to be sitting in Sioux Falls up at the top of the Holiday Inn . . . wondering what songs were on the jukebox . . . It was like going to visit a couple on the verge of a really nasty divorce scene . . . where you know it, and you're invited over for dinner, but nobody mentions it . . . You sit there listening to music . . . and you talk about . . . I don't know . . . the Super Bowl . . . or the pig races . . . or . . .

Ed: Pig races?

HST: Right. Pig races are incredible. Drama. Tension. Speed. I think what we . . . what we all thought would happen would be that . . . They had a giant press room set up with a free bar, about fifty typewriters, and six TV consoles at one end of the room and I think the general impression was that we'd sort of filter in there about 6 o'clock . . . which would be seven, Eastern Time . . . when the polls closed in New York and Massachusetts . . . and we would sort of watch the deal go down *slowly*. I think we all assumed that by midnight it would be over. The only question was how bad it would be . . . But what happened as it turned out was that . . . well, I decided rather than go to the press room, I'd go up and watch the first TV returns with some of McGovern's closest staff people. It seemed more fitting somehow to go up to the ninth floor where most of the staffers were staying and watch the first returns with some of McGovern's key people, the ones who were closest to him. I knew that John Holum and Sandy Berger, two speech writers, were staying in a room up there, so I picked up the house phone in the lobby about 6:15 . . . I'd heard that some of the results had come in but I didn't know what they were at that point . . . and it didn't seem to

449

make much difference . . . Too early, I thought . . . when Holum answered I asked if he was busy and if he wasn't I'd like to come up and have a drink and sit around and wait for the results . . . He said, "Don't bother . . . It's all over . . . We've been *wiped* . . . Shit, we're losing *everything!*"

Ed: What time was this?

HST: Shortly after 6 . . . Central Time. So that was what . . . 5 o'clock Eastern Time . . . No, 7 Eastern Time, excuse me . . . and 4 California time . . . It was really all over by then. By 6:30 there wasn't a person at the Holiday Inn who didn't know what had happened. There was never any question of winning, but the Shock set in when people began to sense the dimensions of it, how *bad* it was. . . . And the tip-off there was . . . I'm not sure . . . but . . . first it was when Ohio went down . . . no, Illinois . . . that's right, it was Illinois . . . When Illinois went by 11 points you could almost feel the shudder that went through the place because Illinois was where they had Gene Pokorny, their best organizer. He was a real wizard. He's the one who did the Wisconsin primary. And Illinois was the key state so they put their best person in. They *had* to have Illinois. If the election had been close Illinois would have been critical, and with Daley coming around there was at least a possibility that Illinois would go for McGovern. But if Pokorny couldn't carry Illinois—when it went down by 11 points, a feeling of shock and doom came over the whole place. Nobody talked. You could see TV people like Frank Reynolds and Bruce Morton doing their interviews . . .

Ed: Frank Reynolds, Bruce Morton?

HST: ABC-TV, and Bruce Morton from CBS . . . Setting up their cameras and their lights out in the lobby, doing on-the-scene reports with a quiet crowd gathered around watching them, and theirs were the only voices you could hear and they were broadcasting . . .

Ed: Who were they interviewing?

HST: They weren't interviewing anybody. It was eerie, you'd walk out of the press room, through the lobby out of the elevators, into the bar . . . There'd be a huge crowd in the lobby and only one person talking and you'd hear this voice saying, "The mood at the McGovern headquarters . . . is extremely solemn and shocked . . . one of shock and depression . . . right now . . . Illinois has just fallen . . . California is gone, New York is gone . . ." They'd read this list of disasters and you knew their faces and what they were saying was on TV screens all over the country . . . It was like a televised funeral.

I think about 8:00 I was sitting in the coffee shop eating a hamburger . . . no, pea soup it was . . . I didn't feel like eating, but somebody insisted I have something . . . I was feeling depressed . . . And John Holum came in. I could see that he'd been crying . . . and . . . he's not the kind of person you'd expect to see walking around in public with tears all over his face. I said why don't you sit down and have a beer, or some pea soup or whatever . . . And he said, "No, I think it's about time to go upstairs and write the statement." He was going up to write McGovern's concession statement and . . . you could see he was about to crack again . . . and that's what he did, he turned and walked out of the coffee shop and into the elevator.

I think McGovern slept through the first returns. Holum woke him up and asked him what he wanted to say . . . and . . . McGovern was very cool for a while till he read the statement that Holum had written . . . he typed a first draft, then woke George up and said, "Here it is . . . we have to go over about 10 o'clock to the coliseum and . . . do it." It was sort of a giant auditorium . . . where a big crowd of mainly young people were waiting for McGovern . . . and all the national press and the network cameras.

Ed: But first he read the statement that Holum had written for him.

HST: Yeah . . . That was the only time that McGovern cracked. For about a minute he broke down and . . . and . . . and couldn't talk for a few minutes. Then he got himself together . . . He was actually the coolest person in the place from then on. Other people were cracking all around. It was . . . spooky to be there later at night.

Ed: What was Mankiewicz's reaction?

HST: Well, Frank had flown out early from Washington. There were plans for *two* planes to fly out . . . Mankiewicz had come out in a small Lear jet . . . with . . . I've forgotten who else came out with him. Most of the top people were supposed to come out on the *second* plane, once the polls closed in the east . . . But when the shittrain started they cancelled that flight . . . Gary Hart never showed up in Sioux Falls, for instance . . . his wife was waiting for him out there, at the Holiday Inn . . . Rick Stearns . . . Eli Segal . . . Hal Himmelman; none of them ever left Washington.

Ed: Why not?

HST: Well . . . the shock was so sudden, so massive . . . that they didn't *want* to come out.

Ed: But Mankiewicz came?

HST: He came out on the first plane . . . the four-person jet . . . and I recall seeing him once or twice, but I didn't talk to him that night . . . It was not the kinda night when you . . . it wasn't the scene where you felt like talking to people.

Ed: How did Mankiewicz look? How did he take it?

HST: Like everybody else . . . stunned, wall-eyed . . . there was nothing to say . . . just a helluva shock . . . you know . . . a fantastic beating . . . and I think about . . . oh . . . ten or fifteen of us stayed in the press room watching the final returns from other races around the country until about 4 or 5 in the morning. I remember, when Agnew came on, throwing something at the television set. It was a beer can . . .

Ed: You threw a beer can at the television set when Agnew came on?

HST: Yeah . . . That was the mood there. I was more extreme, but that was the general mood, even among the press. I think one of the best expressions of that—the feeling of the press, which McGovern has cursed all the way through the campaign and ever since the campaign . . .

Ed: Excuse me, McGovern cursed what?

HST: McGovern places a large part of the blame for his defeat on the press. He did before the election, and even now he's still doing it. The Eagleton affair turned him brutally against the press. He thought they were crucifying him and leaving Nixon alone . . . and he was right, on one level. But what he ignored was the fact that, first, he was out in the open and committing these blunders that the press couldn't ignore . . . while Nixon was *not* out in the open and committing no blunders . . . or at least none that the press could pin on him. The Watergate thing came about as close as anything and the Washington *Post* worked that one about as heavily as any newspaper could. But McGovern throughout the campaign blamed the press for taking advantage of his . . . of what he called his "open campaign" . . . as if . . . he opened up his house to guests and they came in and pissed all over the floor and ripped off his silver and . . . you know . . . raped the children . . . that sort of thing . . . But I think one of the best examples of the way the press people felt that night showed up in these few pieces of paper I found in the typewriter about 5 in the morning in the press room. I was just sort of wandering around . . . There was an odd sense of not wanting to go to sleep . . . because that would have been giving up . . . In a scene like that you get a weird feeling that maybe if you stay up a little longer, maybe something good might happen . . . but Colorado was the only bright spot in the country that night . . .

Ed: Why was that?

HST: Gordon Allot got beaten . . . A Republican senator . . . an arch Nixon supporter . . . He was defeated by Floyd Haskell, a sort of unknown Democrat, by a very small margin . . . and also the Olympics were defeated which was a definite victory . . .

Ed: There had been a referendum?

HST: Oh yeah . . . They actually threw the Winter Olympics out of Colorado . . . Which was a great shock to the Chamber of Commerce people, the greedheads. . . . And then I called Aspen and . . . we carried . . . you know Aspen was the only county in Colorado that went for McGovern . . . And there was one other thing . . . I forget what . . . oh, Pat Schroeder . . . a sort of a liberal woman lawyer who beat the former DA who was the incumbent congressman.

Ed: Where was that?

HST: In Denver.

Ed: Also in Colorado.

HST: Yeah, but the rest of the country—except for Massachusetts—was a sort of a never-ending nightmare. For a while, in the press room, there were people trying to write or . . . half-heartedly poking on typewriters around the edge of the room. . . .

But nobody was writing by five, we were just sort of watching television and drinking, and I saw this abandoned story sort of . . . lying around. One page was still in the typewriter, the others were on the table beside it, and I think it pretty well expresses the feeling of most of the press about the McGovern campaign . . . I have no idea who wrote it . . . There was no byline . . . it was a first draft . . . just left there unfinished on the table . . . and at first I found one page and I thought, . . . hmnnn . . . where's the rest of this? So I shuffled around through the paper on the table and put it together . . .

Ed: Well, let's include this, with the following message to whoever originally wrote it: We hope you'll get in touch with Barbara Burgower at Straight Arrow Books in order that we may properly credit this piece of writing and carry the customary copyright of permissions and acknowledgments in future editions of this book. What follows is the actual manuscript which Dr. Thompson found that morning.

the cruel moment of defeat hurt senator mcgovern more deeply than it might most other ~~men~~. his quest for the presidency was inspired not so much by/ ~~simple~~ desire for power but by ~~xxxxxxxxxxx~~ conviction that the country ~~xxxxxx~~ wanted new spiritual direction, fresh vision about its ideal and perhaps, above all, a   national integrity that he felt was its greatest need.   he talked frequently about a@crisis of spirit@ in the united states but ~~xxx~~ americans overwhelmingly demonstrated that they did not agree with him. not even the country*s young people.

senator mcgovern had hinged his l~~xxxx~~cxx whole campaign on oppostion to the vietnam war, ~~xxxxxxxxxxxx~~ hoping to pursuade americans of its immorality and awakenong in them a sense of outrage and shame. he tried to demonstrate that the continuing american presnece in vietnam, the bombing and the ~~xxxxxx~~ suport of what he denounced as a corrupt dictatorship was an indication of ~~xxx~~ a ~~xxxxx~~ moral collapse in the ~~x~~ united states. he did not balme the people but the nixon administration/ but the people did not ~~xxxxx~~ respond to his appeals. ironically yesterday morning he voted here in support of a local ~~xxxxx~~ proposition to outlwa the

454

Ed: You never left the airport?

HST: Well . . . I was looking for a cab to get across the main terminal . . . it was about a mile away . . . and Sandy Berger . . . appeared in his car . . . he was one of the people who had broken down earlier . . .

Ed: Who is Sandy Berger?

HST: He was one of the speech writers, . . . first-class speech writer, one of the two or three who were with McGovern all the way through from Miami on, and . . . he was in such a state when he picked us up. It was rush hour in Washington and we had to go down one side of a freeway. There was a big grass island about eighteen inches high and twelve feet wide separating the two . . . freeways . . . six lanes, three in each direction . . . Sandy thought he was giving Tim Crouse and me a ride into town but we said we were going over to the main terminal to catch another plane, and he said, "Oh, back *there,* eh?" . . . And right smack in the middle of rush-hour traffic in Washington, right straight across the island . . . up over this huge bump, in a driving rain, he just made a high-speed U-turn right over the island and back into the other lane, and cars were skidding at us, coming sideways and fishtailing, trying to avoid us . . . That was the kind of mood the McGovern people were in. I don't think he cared whether anybody hit us or not. It scared the hell out of me . . . But we made it to the terminal and I bought a ticket for Denver, and . . . just got the hell out of Washington.

Ed: Just got the hell out of Washington? I think that should be the end, that's a good point to end this chapter.

HST: Yeah, I decided to get the hell out . . . give them time to cool off and get themselves together . . . then come back later and get into some serious talk about why . . . why it happened.

Ed: A serious talk?

HST: Yeah—poke into the reasons for it . . .

Ed: Okay, that'll be the end of chapter we'll call "November."

HST: Why not?

Be Angry At The Sun

That public men publish falsehoods
Is nothing new. That America must accept
Like the historical republics corruption and empire
Has been known for years.

Be angry at the sun for setting
If these things anger you. Watch the wheel slope
               and turn,
They are all bound on the wheel, these people,
               those warriors.
This republic, Europe, Asia.

Observe them gesticulating,
Observe them going down. The gang serves lies,
               the passionate
Man plays his part; the cold passion for truth
Hunts in no pack.

You are not Catullus, you know,
To lampoon these crude sketches of Caesar. You
               are far
From Dante's feet, but even farther from his dirty
Political hatreds.

Let boys want pleasure, and men
Struggle for power, and women perhaps for fame,
And the servile to serve a Leader and the dupes
               to be duped.
Yours is not theirs.

—Robinson Jeffers

458

December

Purging the McGovernites . . . Shoot-Out in the
Dung-Heap Corral . . . Where Do We Go
From Here: What Next for the "New Politics"?
. . . A Crude Autopsy & Quarrelsome
Analysis on Why McGovern Got Stomped . . .

"The harvest is past, the summer is ended, and we are not saved."
—Jeremiah 8:20

ON A FRIDAY AFTERNOON in early December I spent about thirty-
three minutes observing the traffic pattern around Times Square
from the co-pilot's seat of a chartered Beechcraft Bonanza. We
were trying to land at LaGuardia airport on Long Island in time
to catch a 6:30 flight to Evansville, Indiana . . . but the runways
were crowded at that hour, and when the Tower put us into the
holding pattern we were faced with a choice between drifting idly
around in circles above the New Jersey shoreline, or doing something different.

I offered the pilot a Harp Ale out of my kitbag and said I'd
just as soon do anything that wouldn't cost him his license—like
maybe swooping down on Manhattan Island to check the size
of the crowd outside of whatever theater was showing "Deep
Throat."

He glanced across at me, refusing the ale, but I could see a
new light in his eyes. "Lissen," he said. "Are you serious? Because we can really *do* that, if you want to." He smiled wickedly.
"We can go right down to five hundred feet and still be legal."

Why not?" I said. "Five hundred feet still gives us plenty of
room to maneuver."

He chuckled and pushed the stick hard left, throwing the plane
into a tight downward spiral. "You'll get a big kick out of this,"
he said. "Five hundred feet ain't much . . . ." He glanced over

at me, keeping the plane aimed straight down at Times Square. "You a pro football fan?"

"Absolutely," I replied.

He nodded. "Well, five hundred feet is about a hundred and seventy yards—and every quarterback in the league can throw a football about half that far."

I tried to raise my ale-bottle for a long drink, but our plunge-angle made it impossible to lift it high enough to overcome the reverse-gravity flow. We were headed straight down at a little over 300 miles an hour . . . and from somewhere behind me in the small cabin I heard a voice; a low keening sound, very much like a moan . . . .

"What's that noise?" the pilot asked.

"That's Frank," I said. "I think he just bit a chunk out of his own liver." I looked back to be sure Mankiewicz was still strapped into his seat—which he was, but his face was grey and his eyes seemed unable to focus. He was sitting with his back to the window, so he couldn't enjoy the view. A⁻ᵈ our engine noise was so loud that he couldn't hear what we were saying up in the cockpit, so he had no way of knowing that our sudden, high-speed power-dive straight down at the vortex of Manhattan Island was anything more or less than what anybody who has spent a lot of time on commercial jetliners would assume it to be—the last few seconds of an irreversible death-plunge that would end all our lives, momentarily, in a terrible explosion and a towering ball of fire in the middle of Broadway.

"Don't worry," I yelled back at him. "We're stuck in a holding pattern."

He stared down at me, clinging to a hand-strap on the roof of the plane: "What? What? I can't *hear* you!"

Just then we began leveling out, and the ale spilled all over my lap. "Nevermind!" I shouted. "We're right over Times Square."

He tried to lean back in his seat, fighting the G's, but I could see that his heart was not in it. Spontaneous night power-dives over metropolitan areas are not lightly dismissed by those who were weaned on "the Friendly Skies of United." Few commercial passengers have ever experienced a rise or drop angle worse than thirty or forty degrees—so a sudden ninety-degree spiraling swoop over midtown Manhattan does serious things to the nerves.

Soon we were standing on our right wing, and the only thing between me and the sidewalk in Times Square was a thick pane of plexiglass. We were flying in very tight circles, so low that if the window had a hole in it I felt like I could reach down and touch the people on the street.

"You see what I mean?" said the pilot. "Five hundred feet ain't much, is it?"

"Jesus!" I muttered

He laughed. "You wanna go around again?"

I glanced back at Frank, but even at a glance I could see that the damage was already done. His face was frozen; his mouth had gone slack and his eyes were locked in a kind of glazed-blank fascination on the toes of his own shoes, which—because of our flight angle—seemed to be floating in a state of weightlessness about fifteen inches off the floor of the plane.

"He looks okay," I said to the pilot. "Let's take another run."

He grinned. "We'll turn a little wider this time, and come in real low—right across Central Park." He eased back on the stick and aimed us out above the docks on the Hudson River. "I don't do this much with passengers," he said. "Most people get scared when I take it down this low." He nodded. "I usually don't even mention it, but you guys looked like the type who'd probably get a boot out of stuff like this."

"You were right," I said. "Frank's acting a little funny right now, but it's only because he's tired. . . . It's been about fifteen months since he had any real sleep."

Now we were bearing down on Times Square again, coming in so low over Central Park and the Plaza Fountain that I was sure if I could lean out the window and yell something vicious, everybody on Fifth Avenue would hear me and look up.

The pilot spoke without taking his eyes off our tree-skimming course: "Fifteen months with no sleep? God *damn!* You guys must have really been whooping it up!"

I shrugged, trying to light a cigarette as we zoomed across 59th Street. "Well . . . I guess maybe you could say that."

"What line of work are you in?" he asked.

461

"Work?" It had been a long time since anybody asked me a thing like that. "Well . . . ah . . . Frank's writing a book about politics, I think . . . and I'm organizing a campaign for the U.S. Senate."

"*Whose* campaign?" he asked.

"Mine," I said.

He glanced over at me and smiled. "Well I'll be damned! So you're gonna be a Senator, eh?" He chuckled. "You think you might want to hire a private pilot?"

I shrugged. "Why not? But you'll have to clear it with Frank. He'll be handling that end of the action—after he gets some sleep."

Now we were circling Times Square, standing on the wing and looking straight down at the New York Times building. The pilot appeared to be thinking. "Frank?" he said. "Frank *Mankiewicz?* . . . I saw that name on the manifest. Didn't he have something to do with that goddamn *McGovern* business?"

I hesitated, reaching around behind me to fetch another bottle of ale out of the kitbag as we leaned left around the Empire State Building.

"Yeah," I said finally. "Frank was McGovern's political director."

He said nothing for a moment, then he slowly turned to look at me again. "So now you want Mankiewicz to run *your* campaign?"

I laughed nervously. Was Frank listening? Was he conscious? Could he *hear* us—above the roar of the engines and the whine of his own nerve ends?

A sudden burst of noise from the radio ended our conversation. It was the voice of an air-traffic controller from the La-Guardia tower, telling us to get back in the landing pattern immediately. We hooked a hard right over Brooklyn, then left & down to the private/charter runway in front of the small yellow Butler Aviation terminal, a painfully familiar docking place to anyone who spent any time on the McGovern campaign plane last fall.

We had about four minutes to make the Eastern flight to Evansville, which was leaving from a gate about a mile across the LaGuardia parking lot in the main terminal . . . but our pilot had radioed ahead for a cab, and it was waiting for us on the runway.

This is the kind of split-second service that you come to take for granted after a year or so on the [presidential] campaign trail. But the cost—for chartered planes, private cars, police escorts, and a small army of advance men and Secret Service guards clearing a path for you—is about $5000 a day, which is nice while it lasts, but the day after the polls close you suddenly understand why Cinderella never stayed out after midnight.

McGoverns Now Ordinary Tourists

St. Thomas, V.I. (UPI)—Sen. George McGovern, his Secret Service protection gone, stood in line with ordinary tourists Thursday to fly to the Virgin Islands for a week of rest after his crushing election defeat . . . . McGovern gave up his 727 jet—which he had dubbed Dakota Queen II, after his World War Two bomber— when he returned to Washington Wednesday from South Dakota. As he left Dulles Airport outside Washington Thursday morning, he stood in line at the ticket counter and rode a bus with the other passengers from the terminal to the plane . . . . A few Secret Service agents accompanied him to the airport, and one who was in the Virgin Islands on other business paid a courtesy call with the local police chief when McGovern arrived. But the agents who hounded his steps for the past nine months were with him no more.

—Rocky Mountain *News,* Nov. 10, 1972

McGovern himself was not as overtly unhinged by this sudden fall from grace as were some of his staff people and journalists who'd been following him back and forth across the country for the past year. In Mankiewicz's case, it had been almost *two* years, and now—a month after the election—he was having a hard time coping with the rigors of public transportation. We were on our way from New Haven to Owensboro, Kentucky where he was scheduled to explain the meaning of the election and McGovern's disastrous defeat to a crowd of dispirited local liberals at Kentucky Wesleyan College. Earlier that afternoon Frank and I had been part of a panel discussion on "The Role of the Media in the Campaign." The moment the Yale gig ended, we sprinted out of the auditorium to a waiting car. Rather than cope with the complexities of airline schedules, Mankiewicz insisted on chartering the Beechcraft. There was no particular reason for me to fly down to Owensboro with him—but it seemed like a good time to spend a few hours talking seriously, for the first time since Election Day, about the reasons and realities that caused McGovern to get stomped so much worse than either he or anybody on his staff had expected.

After his speech in Kentucky that night, Frank and I spent about three hours in a roadside hamburger stand, talking about the campaign. Three weeks earlier, just after the election, he had said that three people were responsible for McGovern's defeat: Tom Eagleton, Hubert Humphrey, and Arthur Bremer—but now he seemed more inclined to go along with the New York *Times*/Yankelovitch poll, which attributed Nixon's lopsided victory to a rising tide of right-bent, non-verbalized racism in the American electorate. The other McGovern staffers I'd talked to had already cited that "latent racism" theory, but there was no consensus on it. Gary Hart and Pat Caddell, for example, felt the Eagleton Affair had been such a devastating blow to the whole campaign machinery that nothing else really mattered. Frank disagreed, but there was no time to pursue it that night in Owensboro; at the crack of dawn the next morning we had to catch a plane back to Washington, where the Democratic National Committee was scheduled to meet the next day—Saturday, December 9—for the long-awaited purge of the McGovernites. There was not much doubt about the outcome. In the wake of McGovern's defeat, the party was careening to the right. John Connally's Texas protegé, Robert Strauss, already had more than enough votes to defeat McGovern's appointee, Jean Westwood, and replace her as Democratic National Chairman. Which is exactly what happened the next day. George's short-lived fantasy of taking over the party and remolding it in his own image had withered and died in the five short months

"This country is going so far to the right that you won't recognize it."

since Miami. Now the old boys were back in charge.

*"Just why the American electorate gave the present adminis-
tration such an overwhelming mandate in November remains something of a mystery to me. I firmly believed throughout 1971 that
the major hurdle to winning the presidency was winning the Democratic nomination. I believed that any reasonable Democrat could
defeat President Nixon. I now think that no one could have
defeated him in 1972."*

—Sen. George McGovern, speaking at
Oxford University two months after the election.

After months of quasi-public brooding on the Whys and
Wherefores of the disastrous beating he absorbed last November,
McGovern seems finally to have bought the Conventional Wisdom
—that his campaign was doomed from the start: conceived in a
fit of *hubris,* born in a momentary power-vacuum that was always
more mirage than reality, borne along on a tide of frustration
churned up by liberal lintheads and elitist malcontents in the
Eastern Media Establishment, and finally bashed into splinters
on the reefs of at least two basic political realities that no
candidate with good sense would ever have tried to cross in the
first place . . . . To wit:

(1) *Any* incumbent President is unbeatable, except in a time
of mushrooming national crisis or a scandal so heinous—and with
such obvious roots in the White House—as to pose a clear and
present danger to the financial security and/or physical safety
of millions of voters in every corner of the country.

(2) The "mood of the nation," in 1972, was so overwhelmingly
vengeful, greedy, bigoted, and blindly reactionary that no presidential candidate who even faintly reminded "typical voters" of the
fear & anxiety they'd felt during the constant "social upheavals"
of the 1960s had any chance at all of beating Nixon last year—
not even Ted Kennedy—because the pendulum "effect" that began
with Nixon's slim victory in '68 was totally irreversible by 1972.
After a decade of left-bent chaos, the Silent Majority was so deep

466

in a behavorial sink that their only feeling for politics was a power-ful sense of revulsion. All they wanted in the White House was a man who would leave them alone and do anything necessary to bring calmness back into their lives—even if it meant turning the whole state of Nevada into a concentration camp for hippies, niggers, dope fiends, do-gooders, and anyone else who might threaten the status quo. The Pendulum Theory is very vogueish these days, especially among Washington columnists and in the more prestigious academic circles, where the conversion-rate has been running at almost epidemic proportions since the night of November 7. Until then, it had not been considered entirely fashionable to go around calling ex-Attorney General John Mitchell a "prophet" because of his smiling prediction, in the summer of 1970, that "This country is going so far to the right that you won't recognize it."

This is the nut of the Pendulum Theory. It is also a recurring theme in McGovern's personal analysis of why the voters rejected him so massively last November. The loss itself didn't really surprise him, but he was deeply and genuinely shocked by the *size* of it. Not even the Eagleton debacle, he insisted, could explain away the fact that the American people had come within an eyelash of administering the worst defeat in the history of presidential politics to a gentle, soft-spoken, and essentially conservative Methodist minister's son from the plains of South Dakota.

I hung around Washington for a few days after the DNC purge, buying up all the cheap smack I could find . . . and on Wednesday afternoon I stopped at McGovern's office in the Old Senate Office Building for an hour or so of talk with him. He was gracious, as always, despite the fact that I was an hour late. I tried to explain it away by telling him that I'd had a bit of trouble that morning: a girl had been arrested in my suite at the Wash-ington Hilton. He nodded sympathetically, without smiling, and said that yes, John Holum had already told him about it.

I shook my head sadly. "You never know these days," I said. "Where will it end?"

He walked around the desk and sat down in his chair, propping his feet up on the middle drawer. I half-expected him to ask me *why* a girl had been arrested in my hotel room, but it was clear from the look on his face that his mind had already moved on to whatever might come next. McGovern is a very private person—which might be part of the reason why not even his friends call him "George"—and you get the feeling, after being around him for a while, that he becomes uncomfortable when people start getting personal.

I was tempted for a moment to push on with it, to keep a straight face and start mumbling distractedly about strange and unsettling events connected with the arrest—pornographic films that had allegedly been made on the Zoo Plane, Ted Van Dyk busted for pimping at the "Issues" desk—but he seemed so down that I didn't have the heart to hassle him, even as a friendly joke . . . . Besides I had my professional reputation to uphold. I was, after all, the National Affairs Editor of *Rolling Stone*.

He was obviously anxious to get on with it, so I set up the tape recorder and asked him about a comment he'd made shortly after the election about the split in the Democratic Party. He had told a group of reporters who flew down to talk with him at Henry Kimmelman's house in the Virgin Islands that he wasn't sure if the two wings of the party could be put back together . . . . But the part of the quote that interested me more was where he said he wasn't sure if they *should* be put back together. "What did you mean by that?" I asked. "Are you thinking about something along the lines of a fourth party?"[1]

McGovern: No, I was not suggesting a major break-up of the Democratic Party. We had been talking earlier about Connally's role, you know, and also about so-called Democrats for Nixon that had formed in the campaign, and they had asked me what I thought could be done to bring those people back in. Well, I don't think they ever really belonged in the Democratic Party. I thought that it wasn't just a matter of personality differences with me or ideological differences with me. I thought that basically they were

---

1. The following McGovern/HST interview is a verbatim transcript of their conversation that day—totally unedited and uncorrected by the author, editor, or anyone else.

more at home in the Republican Party and I wasn't sure that we ought to make the kind of gestures that would bring them back.

HST: Were you talking specifically about . . . ?

McGovern: Well, I was really talking about this organized group rather than the defection of large numbers of blue-collar workers, which I regard as a serious problem. I think those people *do* have to be brought back into the Democratic Party if it's going to survive as a party that can win national elections. But in terms of those that just took a walk, you know, and really came out for Nixon, I'm really not interested in seeing those people brought back into the Democratic Party. I don't think Connally adds anything to the party. I think, as a matter of fact, he's the kind of guy that's always forcing the party to the right and into positions that really turn off more people than he brings with him. What I regard as a much more serious defection is the massive movement of people to Wallace that we saw taking place in the primaries.

HST: Yeah, that's another thing I was going to ask you.

McGovern: I don't think anybody really knows what was at the base of that movement. I suspect that race was a lot more of a factor than we were aware of during the campaign. There wasn't a lot of talk about racial prejudice and the old-fashioned racial epithet, things like that, but I think it was there. There were all kinds of ways that—of tapping that prejudice. The busing issue was the most pronounced one, but also the attacking on the welfare program and the way the President handled that issue. I think he was orchestrating a lot of things that were designed to tap the Wallace voters, and he got most of them. Now what the Democratic Party can do to bring those people back, I'm not sure. I suspect that there should have been more discussion in the campaign of the everyday frustrations and problems of working people, conditions under which they work, maybe more of an effort made to identify with them.

HST: I spent a whole day during the Wisconsin primary on the south side of Milwaukee at a place called Serb Hall . . .

McGovern: Yeah.

HST: I went up there in the afternoon and Wallace was scheduled to be there at five, I think it was—then you and Muskie were coming in later . . . I went out there to talk to those people and I was really amazed to find that you and Wallace were the two people they were . . . kind of muttering and mumbling about who to vote for. Humphrey and Muskie were pretty well excluded. You seemed to have a pretty good grip on it.

McGovern: Yeah.

HST: But at some point you seemed to lose it. I'm not sure why . . .

McGovern: Well, I think there were a number of factors. One, once I became the nominee of the party, they saw me more as a typical Democrat. I mean, I was no longer the challenger taking on the party establishment. I was the nominee at that point. Secondly, instead of competing with Muskie and Humphrey, I was then competing with Nixon, the author of the Southern strategy and the guy who hammered hard against those who were dissenters on the war and hammered on amnesty and busing and those things, so that it was a different type of competition than I had with Muskie and Humphrey in Wisconsin.

HST: But I got the impression that they were actually considering voting for you or Wallace.

McGovern: I know that. I know.

HST: Even though they disagreed with you on a lot of things.

McGovern: If I could just say this to you: I think that probably you may have gotten an exaggerated impression of the numbers of them. I think that it always startled people to find any—and it was easy to assume that when you ran into a guy who said well it's either Wallace or McGovern, that he was typical of large numbers of people. As I think back on it, it always struck me as such a paradox that it made more of an impression on me than was justified by the numbers of people that actually said it. Futhermore, I think we were hurt by the—I think those people were turned off, some of them, by the Eagleton controversy. I think that others were turned off by the attacks on me as a radical. I think they came to perceive me as more radical than they wanted me to be. Also, some of them were offended by the convention. I thought the convention was great, but what came across on television, apparently, to many of these guys was they saw a lot of aggressive women, they saw a lot of militant blacks, they saw long-haired kids, and I think that combination, which helped win the nomination for me, I think it offended a lot of them.

HST: John Holum and I were talking about that the other night. There should have been somebody assigned to sit in a room in Ft. Lauderdale and just watch the whole show on television, to see how it came across . . .

McGovern: Yeah, I thought one of the highlights of that convention was that ringing peroration of Willie Brown's when he said "Give me back my delegation!"—screamed that into the television networks of the country, and it scared the hell out of a lot of people who saw that as a wild militant cry of the blacks, you see, they're going to take over the country. And so that what seemed to be powerful and moving and eloquent to us was terrifying to many people.

HST: Did you get any kind of feedback on that?

McGovern: I did, yeah.

HST: During the convention?

McGovern: Not during the convention, but afterward I ran into people who weren't nearly as impressed with it as I was, and who, in fact, were turned off by it. And that was one of the most celebrated incidents of the convention . . . You need a bottle opener?

HST: Yeah, but I only have one beer. Would you like some? Do you have a glass? . . . I haven't even eaten breakfast yet. I had a disturbing sort of day. I was up until eight o'clock.

McGovern: Was that when they arrested the gal in your room?

HST: Yeah, but I'd rather not get into that right now . . . actually I got so wound up in the last few weeks that I went to the doctor in Aspen on Tuesday to find out what the hell was wrong with me . . . why I was so knotted up. I had a cold and I had all kinds of things wrong. We went through about six hours of tests at the hospital, the whole works, then I went back to his office and he said I had this and that, a virus, nothing serious but he said in all of his years in medicine, about fifteen or twenty years, he's one of those people, one of those high-powered Houston Medical Center doctors who dropped out and came to Aspen, he said he'd never seen anybody with as bad a case of anxiety as I had. He said I was right on the verge of a complete mental, physical, and emotional collapse. At that point I began to wonder how the hell you or anyone else survived be-

471

cause . . . I really am amazed, I think I said that to you on Monday on the plane.

McGovern: Well, it is a fantastic physical and emotional beating.

HST: Yeah, but it never seemed to show on you—it showed on some people, God knows it showed on me.

McGovern: Well, I wouldn't want to go through it again, I don't think.

HST: No, once every four years just to recover. Here's the main question I want to get to and I think it's something that I have a very personal interest in. I don't see any need for me to stay in politics at all or getting my head involved or running for anything, which I'm kind of thinking of doing. I was thinking of running for the Senate in Colorado, running against Gary in the primary. I'm not sure how serious I am about that, but here's a question that sort of haunts me now, talking to John and everyone else in the campaign about it just in the last two-three days, is whether this kind of campaign could have worked? Were the mistakes mechanical and technical? Or was it either flawed or doomed from the start by some kind of misconception or misdirection?

McGovern: I think that there was just a chance, coming out of Miami, that we could have ignited the public. There was a period there right after I got the nomination when I'm sure that the majority of the American people really weren't sure what they were going to do about me. But the impressions that they had were rather favorable.

HST: I would have bet dead even coming out of the convention . . . I was optimistic.

McGovern: Yeah, I was, too. Now I think the first thing they saw was the Eagleton thing, which turned a lot of people off. No matter what I'd have done, you see, we were in trouble there. And so that was an unfortunate thing. And then there were some staff squabbles that the press spotlighted, which gave the impression of confusion and disarray and lack of direction, and I think that hurt.

HST: I know it hurt. At least among the people I talked to.

McGovern: So those two factors were related and the Eagleton

472

thing upset the morale of the staff and people were blaming each other, and there was no chance to recover from the fatigue of the campaign for the nomination—we had to go right into that Eagleton battle, and so I think that—if there was a chance, at that point, to win the election—we probably lost it right there. And then other factors began to operate, Kissinger's "peace is at hand" business, the negotiations sort of blunted and killed it; actually, I think the war issue was working for the President. And then the accommodation of—at least the beginning of the accommodation of Peking and Moscow seemed to disarm a lot of moderates and liberals who might otherwise have been looking in another direction.

HST: But that was happening even before the convention.

McGovern: Yeah, it was, but it happened far enough ahead so that the impact of it began to sink in then. And I think—I don't think we got a break after Miami. I think that from then on in the breaks were with the President. I mean—and he orchestrated his campaign very cleverly. He stayed out of the public eye, and he had all the money he needed to hire people to work on direct mail and everybody got a letter tailored to their own interests nad their own groove, and I think their negative TV spots were effective in painting a distorted picture of me.

HST: The spinning head commercial?

McGovern: Yeah, the spinning head commercial, knocking over the soldiers. The welfare thing. They concentrated on those themes. I suppose maybe I should have gone on television earlier with thoughtful Q and A sessions, the kind of speeches I was doing there the last few weeks. I think maybe that might have helped to offset some of the negatives we got on the Eagleton thing . . . Another problem: There was a feeling on the part of a lot of the staff that after Miami there wasn't the central staff direction that should have been. Whose fault that is I don't know . . . I found in the field a lot of confusion about who was really in charge, pushing and pulling as to where you got things cleared, who had the final authority. That could have been handled more smoothly than it was. When you add all of those things up, none of them, in my opinion, comes anywhere near as serious as the fact that the Republicans were caught in the middle of the night burglarizing our headquarters. They were killing people in Vietnam with bombing raids that were pointless from any military point of view. They were making secret deals to sell out the public interest for campaign contributions, you know, and routing money through Mexican banks and all kinds of things that just seemed to me to be scandalous.

HST: Wasn't there a Harris Poll that showed that only 3 percent of the electorate considered the Watergate thing important?

McGovern: Yeah. That's right. Mistakes that we made seemed to be much more costly. I don't know why, but they were. I felt it at the time, that we were being hurt by every mistake we made, whereas the most horrendous kind of things on the other side somehow seemed to—because, I suppose, of the great prestige of the White House, the President's shrewdness in not showing himself to the press or the public—they were able to get away with things that we got pounded for.

HST: Do you think it would be possible to, say, discount . . . if you could just wipe out the whole Eagleton thing, and assume that, say, Mondale or Nelson had taken it and there had been no real controversy, and try to remove the vice-presidential thing as a factor. What do you think . . .

McGovern: I think it would have been very close. I really do. I think we'd have gotten off the ground fast, and I think we'd have capitalized on those early trips and that the press would have been more enthusiastic about it and they'd have been reporting the size of the crowds and the enthusiasm instead of looking at the staff problem. See, once we got into the Eagleton thing, they seemed to feel almost a constraint to report that everything was unfortunate about the campaign. The campaign, actually, was very well run, compared to others that I've seen. The fund-raising was a miracle the way that was run. The crowds were large and well advanced, and the schedules went off reasonably well day after day. I didn't think there were major gaps being made in the campaign, but there were some right at the beginning that haunted us all the way through. I think if we'd have gotten off to a better start just like a —I remember when I was at Northwestern there was a great hurdler that was supposed to win the U.S. competition and probably win the Olympics, and he hit the first hurdle with his foot, and then he hit about the next four in a row, you know, and just petered out. After he hit that first hurdle, that's kind of what happened to us. We got off—we broke stride on that thing right after the convention, and from then on in, I think millions of people just kind of turned us off. They were skeptical and I think the mood of the country was much more conservative than we had been led to believe in the primaries. We were winning those primaries on a reform program and rather blunt outspoken statement of what we were going to do.

HST: That was the next question I was going to ask. Have you thought about what might have happened if you'd kept up that approach?

McGovern: Well, I think we did keep it up. I never did buy the line that we really changed our positions very much from the primary to the general. I can't see where there was all that much of a shift.

HST: I think it was a perceived shift. There was a definite sense that you had changed your act.

McGovern: I'm not sure how much different we *really* were. I think we were pretty much hitting the same issues. What did you perceive as the difference? Maybe I can answer your question better if I . . .

HST: Well it seemed to me, when you'd selected Eagleton it was the first step sort of backwards. If we assume that your term "new politics" had any validity, your choice of Eagleton was the point where it turned around and you decided that the time had come to make friends with the people you'd been fighting the whole time. And without questioning the wisdom of it I . . .

McGovern: You mean because he'd been with Muskie and . . .

HST: Yeah, Eagleton struck me as being a cheap hack and . . . he still does, you know, he strikes me as being a useless little bastard . . . When I went up to St. Louis to do what I could to get hold of some of those records to try to find out more about it, I was treated like someone who'd come up to the North Pole to blackmail Santa Claus, even by your people. But I kept hearing, from what I considered pretty reliable sources, that there's more to Eagleton's mental problems than you or anybody . . .

McGovern: Well, see, nobody'll ever know that for sure, 'cause those records are never gonna be available. I think the FBI has them.

HST: How the hell does the FBI have them? On what pretext did they get them?

McGovern: I don't know. But I was told by Ramsey Clark that the FBI had a very complete medical file on Eagleton, and that he (Clark) knew it at the time he was Attorney General.

HST: Including the shock?

McGovern: Yeah, but I never saw the records. I was never able to get access to them.

HST: Do you think that original leak to the press, Frank, and Gary came from the FBI?

McGovern: They might have been directly, they might have, they've been known to leak things like that to the press, and it may very well have been an FBI leak, but the Knight newspapers never would divulge the source.

HST: Frank knew the name of that anaesthesiologist, that woman who gave him the gas during one of the shock treatments, but he wouldn't tell me . . .

McGovern: There were a number of journalists that were trying to get more information on it, but it's tough, very hard to do.

HST: Did you ever find out what those little blue pills were that he was eating?

McGovern: No.

HST: I think I did. It was Stelazine, not Thorazine like I heard originally. I did everything I could to get hold of the actual records, but nobody would even talk to me. I finally just got into a rage and just drove on to Colorado and said to hell with it. It seemed to me that the truth could have had a hell of an effect on the election. It struck me as being kind of tragic that he would be perceived as the good guy . . .

McGovern: I know, it was really unfair. What he should have done, he should have taken the responsibility for stepping down rather than putting the responsibility on me.

HST: He almost threatened not to, didn't he? As I recall, he wasn't going to do it . . .

McGovern: That's right. That's right.

HST: Was it true that he actually told you at one point not to worry about those pills, because the prescription was in his wife's name?

McGovern: He told me they were in his wife's name.

HST: Let me ask you this: Sioux Falls was such a bummer I didn't even want to talk to you up there, but how much of a surprise was the overall result?

McGovern: I was very surprised at the landslide proportions of it. I had felt . . . the last couple of days, I'd pretty well gave up. I thought we—we kept going hard, but I thought we were gonna get beat, but it never occurred to me that we'd only carry a couple of states, you know, the District and Massachusetts. I thought we'd carry a minimum of eight or ten states.

HST: Which ones?

McGovern: Well, I thought we'd carry both California and New York which would have given us some big electoral blocs. I thought we'd carry Illinois. I thought we'd carry Wisconsin, and I thought we'd probably carry my state.

HST: That was a shock . . .

McGovern: Those were all ones that I thought we'd get, and I thought we'd get Rhode Island, Connecticut—you know, I was surprised at the landslide character of it.

HST: Did you go into a kind of brooding or thinking about exactly why there'd been so much difference in the proportions than you'd thought . . .

McGovern: No, and I still haven't figured it out. I mean, I still haven't really figured out the dimensions of it. I think the war thing had a big impact at the end there, the fact that Kissinger was able to say that peace was at hand, just give us a few more days. It almost looked like if we threw them out it would disrupt all this effort that has gone on over the last months. You know, they kept him in orbit for weeks ahead of the election. I think that had an impact. And then the way they threw money into the economy. They ran up a hundred billion dollar deficit in four years he was in office. That's the old FDR deficit-financing technique, and obviously that money ended up in somebody's pockets. So I think that is a subtle factor there, that the economy wasn't good, but it was much better than it would have been had they not been pumping that kind of deficit financing into circulation.

HST: Do you think the kind of campaign you ran in the primaries, a real sort of anti-politician campaign—would have any chance in '76, or do you think we all misconceived the whole thing —not just the temper of the time but the whole basic nature of the electorate.

McGovern: I don't think there ever was a majority for the approach I was using. I think we had a fighting chance.

HST: No better than that? Even with all those new voters? That was a hell of a natural power base for you, wasn't it? What happened?

McGovern: I think we exaggerated the amount of the enthusiasm for change among young people. We saw the activists in the primaries, but it's always·a small percentage that were really working, and you'd see those stadiums packed Saturday after Saturday with tens of thousands of people. There really are a great number of people in this country that are a helluva lot more interested in whether the Dolphins beat the Redskins than they are in whether Nixon or George McGovern ends up in the White House. I think there was a lot of apathy and a lot of feeling—also a lot of kind of weariness over the activism of the sixties—the civil rights movement, the peace movement, the crusades, the marches, the demonstrations. Nixon kind of put all that behind us. Things quieted down. He disarmed the peace movement—there were no riots, no demonstrations, and I think that people were afraid of anything that kind of looked like a fundamental change—that maybe we'd be right back into that same kind of energetic protest, dissent, and demonstrations that they'd grown weary of in the sixties.

HST: Do you think the sixties ended in '68 or '72, just using very rough kind of numbers.

McGovern: I think they were beginning to—I think Nixon's election in '68 really signalled the end of that.

HST: In a sense you were running a sixties campaign in the seventies.

McGovern: Yeah.

HST: I've heard that said. I've thought about that.

McGovern: We were running a campaign that might have won in 1968. *Might* have won. Might have . . . You know, all

478

any kind of consensus—no hard figures or any kind of real analysis —except the kind of things that McGovern said in his interviews which were mainly speculation. . . . He was saying, I *think* this, and that *might* work, and I'm sure this *could* happen if. . . .

But when I asked him, for instance, who the 45 percent of the voters were—eligible voters who didn't vote this year—he said he had no idea. And when I asked that same question to Mankiewicz, he said I should ask Pat Caddell. . . . I just talked to Pat on the phone yesterday, and he said it would take him a long time to get the figures together on a nationwide basis, but the one thing he could say was one of the most noticeable hard facts of this '72 presidential campaign was that, for the first time in almost anyone's memory, fewer people voted for the President in, I think it was, half the states, than had voted for the state level offices—which on the average runs about 15 percent higher in terms of voter turn-out . . . no, excuse me, the *presidential* vote runs on an average about 15 percent higher.

Ed: Usually.

HST: In most states—between ten and fifteen percent higher.

Ed: But not this year?

HST: No, the presidential vote was *lower* in '72. I have the figures . . . but here's Pat Caddell on tape, from our phone talk yesterday. . . .

[*Editor's Note: What follows is a tape recording of Doctor Thompson and Pat Caddell discussing the statistics of the McGovern defeat.*]

HST: (to Caddell): 10 or 15 percent ahead of the state vote? When you say that, you mean Senator and Governor?

Pat: Right.

HST: And this year there were thirty-nine states that had both presidential and senator/governor races?

Pat: A senator *or* governor race. Some had both. Most of them had one or the other. In a statewide race that's the thing to look at.

HST: In twenty of those, the state-office vote was higher than the presidential vote?

Pat: Right.

HST: And in eight states it was just 1 percent less . . . and in five others it was 2 percent less?

Pat: Yeah—despite the *increase* in the number of people that voted this year, which is the highest number of all time . . .

[*end Caddell phone tape*]

Ed: I get a little confused with all these numbers. What's the bottom line? If more people were voting for Governor and Senator than for President, you think this showed a lack of interest in the outcome of the presidential election or a definite decision on the part of some voters not to vote for either Nixon *or* McGovern?

HST: According to Pat's polls, based on repeat interviews with the same people all year long, it shows a conscious decision on the part of an incredibly large number of people *not to vote for President,* but to go in and vote for state-level offices. I'm not sure just what that means . . . if they felt that they had no choice, despite what somebody said that this was supposed to be the clearest choice of the century. . . .

Ed: What were Caddell's statistical explanations for McGovern's defeat? Why did he think McGovern lost?

HST: He disagreed with both McGovern and Mankiewicz, and tended to agree more with Gary Hart. There is a definite split in the McGovern camp over the explanation for the loss.

Ed: What is the Caddell/Hart position?

HST: It has to do with two words: *Eagleton* and *competence.*

Ed: "Eagleton and competence?"

HST: Right. The Eagleton Affair was so damaging to McGovern's image—not as a humane, decent, kind, conservative man who wanted to end the war—but as *a person who couldn't get those things done even though he wanted to.* He was perceived, then, as a dingbat—not as a flaming radical—a lot of people seem to think that was one of the images that hurt him. But according to Pat, that "radical image" didn't really hurt him at all. . . . The same conclusion appeared in a Washington *Post* survey that David Broder and Haynes Johnson did. . . . They agreed that the Eagleton Affair was almost immeasurably damaging. . . . and according to Gary Hart, it was so damaging as to be *fatal.* Gary understood this as early as mid-September; so did

482

Frank—they all knew it.

Ed: McGovern too?

HST: Sure. They could all see it happening, but they couldn't figure how to deal with it—because the damage was already done, and there was no way McGovern could prove that he was not as dangerously incompetent as the Eagleton Affair made him seem to be. They couldn't figure out . . . there was nothing they could do . . . no issue they could manufacture, no act that they could commit . . . or anything they could say . . . that would change people's minds on the question of McGovern's *competence* to get anything done, regardless of what he wanted to get done. In other words, there were a lot of people who liked him, liked what he said —but who wouldn't vote for him, because he seemed like a bumbler.

Ed: You say Mankiewicz knew this, but he didn't agree with Caddell and Hart?

HST: Well, it's never easy to be sure of what Frank really thinks . . . . But he was at least half convincing when he told me down in Owensboro that night . . .

Ed: Down where?

HST: In Owensboro, Kentucky—when I went down to listen to his speech at Kentucky Wesleyan. He seemed convinced that the Swing to the Right and the sort of silent, anti-nigger vote—the potential Wallace vote—was the issue that cost McGovern the election. And at one point—I'm not sure exactly when—the McGovern campaign was fairly well convinced—not the entire staff, but the theorists at the top—that if Wallace had stayed in the campaign, if he hadn't been shot, if he had run as an Independent American . . . whatever the hell that party was in '68, and if he'd run as the same healthy, feisty little judge from Alabama, that he would have *split the vote that Nixon had ended up with* . . . about 60 percent.

Ed: How many percent?

HST: 61 or 62 percent. . . . That Wallace would have split that vote with Nixon, leaving McGovern with a plurality—the largest popular vote among the three candidates—but not enough electoral votes to actually become President, at which point the election would have been thrown into the House of Representatives.

Ed: Mankiewicz & McGovern really believed that possibility?

483

HST: George seemed to . . . I'm not sure how strong he thought the possibility really was. But I know that was sort of a private fear of theirs—a pretty dark view of the American electorate, I'd say: that half of the Nixon vote, given the chance, would have gone *even further to the right.* I suspect that's really one of the roots of the thinking of at least half of the ranking staff people in McGovern's campaign, even now. . . . The Hart/Caddell theory was a less ominous view of the potential of the electorate. Both Gary and Pat were convinced *that McGovern could have won.* That was the question I asked almost every one of the staff people I talked to at any length.

Ed: What makes Caddell and Hart think he could have won?

HST: Primarily the provable damage that the Eagleton Affair did to the actual numbers of the McGovern constituency—the potential constituency. In July, for instance, nationally, the polls . . .

Ed: Caddell's polls?

HST: Caddell's, and I think there were two more, Gallup and Harris. It was a rough consensus among the polls in July that Nixon had 52 percent of the vote, McGovern had 37 percent, and 11 percent were undecided. In September the figures were Nixon 56 percent, McGovern 34 percent, and 10 percent undecided.

Ed: That indicates no change.

HST: On paper it indicates no change, but what it doesn't show is . . . Nixon lost 9 percent of his vote in that period of time . . . 9 out of the original 52. He gained 15 percent from elsewhere but he lost 9 percent of his first group. Meanwhile McGovern lost *13* points of *his* vote, his original 37 percent . . . But the McGovern loss was apparently, according to the figures, almost *entirely due to the Eagleton Affair,* whereas the Nixon loss would have happened anyway, because they were mainly people who in July had said that they were Democrats—Humphrey Democrats—who refused to vote for McGovern, but as the election drew closer they began to filter back. So Nixon's 9 percent loss was inevitable, more or less. What Nixon did was pick up a tremendous amount of mainly young, not necessarily liberal Democrats—but young, sort of educated, relatively sophisticated voters *who would have stayed with McGovern,* according to the polls . . . according to the answers they gave the poll-takers, *if it had not been for the Eagleton disaster.* That's when his image as a different kind of politician, an anti-politician, just cracked and shattered and there was no way to put it back together. According to the Hart/Caddell theory, if that hadn't happened, the race would have been at least very close . . . And that's where you get into another powerful factor: What the Eagleton disaster did, the *worst* thing it did, was to *prevent the race from ever getting close,* which allowed Nixon to hide . . . . There was no pressure on him, and that altered McGovern's strategy to the point that he was always fighting with his back to the wall, more or less . . . . They were on the defensive the whole time, facing this ever increasing erosion of their vote, massive margins between him and Nixon. . . . McGovern's main strength in the primaries—up until in California I think . . . he was always the underdog, always trailing, but he always closed very fast, by picking up a big chunk of the undecided vote . . . .

In this case—there was almost nothing he could have done. To close that kind of gap was beyond the realm of possibility . . . . And therefore Nixon, who has never been good under pressure, was never put under any sort of pressure . . . . He could afford to just sit in the White House and watch McGovern sort of fumbling around the country. Had the race been close—anything under 10 points—the McGovern strategy, they say, would have been entirely different . . . . But they spent the whole time trying to overcome this massive fistula on their image, as it were . . . . which runs counter to the Mankiewicz/McGovern theory that it was basically a right-wing tide with heavy racist undertones, or undercurrents, rip tides. . . . The basic question in '72 was: Could McGovern have won, under any circumstances?

Ed: I don't know how deeply you want to get into this, but these numbers are very interesting to me. In July Nixon had 52 percent of the vote and in September he had 56.

HST: Those polls were taken before the Democratic Convention.

Ed: And yet you say he was losing steadily . . . . So if he was losing some of his constituency, where was Nixon gaining his votes from?

HST: According to Caddell, he was gaining them from the

people who would have voted for McGovern, had he not . . . .

Ed: Were it not for the Eagleton Affair . . . . All right, meanwhile, you have McGovern losing 13 percent of his 37 percent in July, and still winding up with 34 percent in September. Where did he gain his strength from?

HST: According to Caddell, he picked up almost all the Nixon defectors, because they were people who were angry in July over the spectacle of a gang of freaks taking over the party that even though they said they were Democrats, they wouldn't vote for McGovern.

Ed: In other words, were it not for the Eagleton Affair, Nixon was actually steadily losing, and McGovern was slowly but surely picking up the Humphrey voters . . . so the deciding factor, according to Caddell's statistics, was the massive defection from McGovern to Nixon resulting from the Eagleton Affair. I just wanted to clarify this.

HST: Yes, that's it.

Ed: Now the question is: Now that we've established these two schools of thought, to which do you subscribe or do you have your own theory?

HST: Well . . . I'm not sure, but I doubt that McGovern himself could have won with *any* kind of campaign, even without the Eagleton incident.

Ed: Why?

HST: Well, that doesn't mean another candidate with the same views as McGovern might not have been able to win . . . . or even a candidate with views more radical than McGovern's.

Ed: So you think it was something personal about McGovern himself?

HST: I think that element of indecisiveness, and the willingness—as he said in his interview—to do anything possible to forge a "winning coalition" didn't do him any good at all . . . . I think it hurt him. It hurt him drastically with the so-called "youth vote," for instance. And I think it hurt him with the Wallace-type Democrats that I talked to up in Serb Hall in Milwaukee that day; who disagreed with him, but *perceived* him—that word again—as a straight, honest, *different type of politician,* a person who would actually *do* what he said, make some real changes.

486

Ed: Do you think Eagleton was the chief reason for them changing their minds? Those Wallace people?

HST: No—not the Wallace people. But there was a whole series of things that hurt him all across the board: that trip to the LBJ Ranch, the sucking up to Mayor Daley, the endorsement of Ed Hanrahan, state's attorney in Chicago—who was indicted for the murder of Fred Hampton, the Black Panther leader. . . .

Ed: McGovern endorsed Hanrahan?

HST: Yeah. He also endorsed Louise Day Hicks in Boston.

Ed: Oh, no!

HST: The racist woman, who was running for Congress . . .

Ed: Did she win?

HST: No, I think she lost. And Hanrahan lost, despite the McGovern endorsement . . . all that hurt McGovern and also having his own so-called campaign director, Larry O'Brien, denounce him just before Labor Day. O'Brien denounced the whole McGovern campaign as a can of worms, a rolling ball of madness . . . *incompetence,* a bunch of ego freaks running around in circles with nobody in charge. That kind of thing couldn't possibly have helped.

Ed: O'Brien said all that?

HST: Yeah. He went totally around the bend.

Ed: Did you vote for McGovern?

HST: Yeah, I did.

Ed: Why?

HST: It was essentially an anti-Nixon vote. McGovern, I don't think, would have been a bad President. He's a better Senator. But I don't think that the kind of standard-brand Democrat that he came to be—or that he actually was all along, and finally came out and admitted he was toward the end, more by his actions than by what he said—I'm not sure that kind of person is ever going to win a presidential campaign again. What was once the natural kind of constituency for that kind of person—the Stevenson constituency, the traditional liberal—has lost faith, I think, in everything that Liberalism was supposed to stand for. Liberalism itself has failed, and for a pretty good reason. It has been too often compromised by the people who represented it. And the fact is people like Nixon—candidates like Nixon—have a running start which gives them a tremendous advantage. My own theory, which sounds like madness, is that McGovern would have been better off running against Nixon with the same kind of neo-"radical" campaign he ran in the primaries. Not radical in the left/right sense, but radical in a sense that he was coming on with . . . a new . . . a different type of politician . . . a person who actually would grab the system by the ears and shake it. And meant what he said. Hell, he certainly couldn't have done any *worse*. It's almost impossible to lose by more than 23 percent . . . . And I think that conceivably this country is ready for a kind of presidential candidate who is *genuinely* radical, someone who might call for the confiscation of all inherited wealth, for instance, or a 100 percent excess-profits tax . . . . For example, Wallace, if he'd understood how much potential strength he had, and if he hadn't been shot, could have gone to the Democratic Convention with a nasty block of votes—enough to probably dominate the convention, not to win the nomination, but enough to give him veto power on the candidate. Wallace did so much better in the primaries than even *he* expected, but by the time he realized what was happening, it was too late for him to file delegate slates in the states where he was running. . . . He came in second in Pennsylvania, beating both McGovern and Muskie, but he didn't get a single delegate. He came in second in Wisconsin, but I don't think he got *any* delegates up there either. . . . Whereas McGovern, in Pennsylvania, finishing in a virtual tie with Muskie for third— or fourth—got seventeen delegates, as I recall.

Ed: Simply because Wallace failed to file?

HST: He was very erratic about it. He wound up with more than 300 delegates in Miami, but with any planning he could have won twice that—more than Humphrey. . . . That was just an oversight, a lack of real confidence. But I think the Wallace people were stunned at the energy they set off and by the time they realized what was there, it was too late to put it together.

Ed: And you think that this was the kind of energy which will bring forward a new candidate in '76 who could win?

HST: No necessarily. There's all kinds of weird energy out there. The Youth Vote, for instance—the first-time voters, the people between eighteen and twenty-four—could have altered the outcome drastically in states like California, Illinois, New York, Michigan, Missouri . . . . McGovern could have won those states with a big turnout among first-time voters—not to mention the huge drop-out vote, the people between twenty-five and forty who didn't vote at all.

Ed: Caddell's figures showed this?

HST: Right. There were states . . . where he compared Humphrey's margin or his loss—whatever the figures were in '68 —to the number of new voters coming into the electorate this time around . . . and there were an incredible number of states where Pat's figures showed that even if McGovern could get at least half of them, he'd carry something like twelve states with this Youth Vote.

Ed: You have said already that you doubt McGovern could have won. What do you think is going to happen in '76?

HST: McGovern *could* have won—but it was unlikely, given the nature of his organization. For one thing, it was technically oriented . . . or at least the best part of it was technically oriented. The best people in the campaign were technicians: at the staff command level there was almost constant confusion, and McGovern's indecisiveness compounded that confusion and left the technicians often wandering around in circles wondering what the hell to do . . . . He had people who could do the work and could turn the vote out, but they weren't always sure what he was doing. The campaign plane would fly into a state and the staffers would have conflicting things set up for him to do. The people on the plane— Mankiewicz, Dutton, Dick Dougherty, the press secretary—were running a different campaign than the one on the charts in the Washington headquarters, or in most of the state offices . . . .

Ed: You think he failed to provide his staff with the necessary direction or leadership?

HST: Yeah, I think you either have to have a very strong decisive person at the top or else a really brilliant staff command. And he didn't have either one, actually. But he *did* have the troops in the field . . . .

Ed: Is there a possibility for marshalling those troops again in '76?

HST: Yeah, definitely, but I doubt if a candidate like Mc-

Govern can marshal them again. The McGovern/McCarthy type candidacies have disappointed too many people, because of a disillusionment with the candidates themselves.

Ed: Do you have any candidate in mind that you think could marshal those forces—as opposed to the old liberal candidates, such as Stevenson, McCarthy, McGovern?

HST: Gary Hart said the other day that . . .

Ed: Gary Hart?

HST: Yeah, he said that the only person he could think of who might have been able to do it this year—who could have won by being "radical" but without being perceived as a left, knee-jerk liberal—was Harold Hughes, because he has a kind of kinky anarchistic streak in him . . . . Maybe Wallace with a little help this year—if he'd gotten his campaign organized two years ago, like McGovern did, and if he'd changed his racist tune a bit—would have been very dangerous. But he never got his act together; he's finished now.

Ed: Wallace is finished in politics?

HST: Yeah, but a candidate like Wallace could be very dangerous in '76—like any candidate who can convince the voters that he really intends to change the system drastically, in almost any direction, could be dangerous. I think what most people seem to be tired of are the sort of lint-headed, wooly-minded—what a lot of people call do-gooders—people who would *like* to do the right thing, but who just can't get it up. That kind of candidate is going out of style. I don't think Ted Kennedy, for instance, is going to win in '76. He's too much of an "old politician," in the sense that McGovern eventually ended up an "old potitician." All this running around the country endorsing Hanrahan and Hicks. For instance, in Minnesota, Mondale was one of the people that . . .

Ed: He's the Senator from Minnesota? Fritz Mondale?

HST: Mondale ran almost 15 points ahead of McGovern in Minnesota, but on paper there's very little difference between their points of view or in what they stand for.

Ed: Are you considering running for office yourself?

HST: Yeah, I was thinking of running for the Senate in Colorado.

Ed: The Senate in Colorado?

HST: Yeah—the U.S. Senate from Colorado. But I might end up running against Gary Hart in the primary. That would be interesting . . . . I might not run as a Democrat, or I might not run at all. It's a grueling, rotten ordeal to go through.

Ed: Well, you've run for office before . . . on the Freak Power ticket, when you were running for Sheriff in Aspen. What were your campaign promises during that election?

HST: There were several. I was going to rip up the streets for one.

Ed: Rip up the streets?

HST: With jackhammers.

Ed: With jackhammers?

HST: Send a horde of freaks into the streets on the morning after the election to tear up the streets and sod them . . . . use all the asphalt to build a huge parking lot at the edge of town. . . . And there was a certain heavy drug element in the campaign which the Washington *Post* was responsible for.

Ed: Did you make any campaign promises regarding the legalization of any drugs?

HST: Well, under state law I couldn't say that I wouldn't arrest people for breaking the law. However I agreed—in three consecutive debates with the incumbent Sheriff, I found myself in front of huge audiences defending the use of mescaline by the sheriff; saying that . . . well, finally I made *one* compromise: I said I wouldn't eat mescaline while *on duty,* if I won.

Ed: What were the final numbers on that election?

HST: I won the city of Aspen.

Ed: You won the city of Aspen, but you lost the election?

HST: I lost heavily in the suburbs, the Agnew vote.

Ed: What was the final percentage?

HST: I think it was something like I got 44 percent of the vote as opposed to the 51 percent for the incumbent Democrat. What the bastards did was—which I'll never forget and I think everyone should keep it in mind in terms of trying to run a third party candidacy nationally or anywhere else—rather than see us win . . . the other two parties did a massive telephone blitz the night before the election, and combined their votes against us.

Ed: If you were to run for Senate in Colorado what kind of a campaign would you conduct? Would you run as a Democrat?

HST: Only if proved to be absolutely impossible to win as a third party candidate. I'd have to check and see. I don't see any point in running for anything any more unless I was serious about winning.

Ed: And what would your platform be?

HST: I haven't thought about it. But it would naturally have to involve a drastic change of some kind . . . . Maybe just an atavistic endeavor, but there's no point in getting into politics at all unless you plan to lash things around.

Ed: Lash things around?

HST: That's one of the secrets. The other . . . well, it depends on who you're running against. But because of the Eagleton thing, Nixon didn't really have to run at all. Any candidate who'd offered a real possibility of an alternative to Nixon—someone with a different concept of the presidency—could have challenged him and come very close to beating him. That was the prevailing theory among the Democrats all along in the primaries, which is why there were so many people getting into it early . . . Nixon was so vulnerable, he was such a wretched President, that almost any Democrat could beat him.

Ed: If you were to run for Senate in Colorado and win, would you then consider running for the presidency itself?

HST: Yeah, I'd do almost anything after that, even run for President—although I wouldn't really *want* to be President. As a matter of fact, early on in the '72 campaign, I remember telling John Lindsay that the time had come to abolish the whole concept of the presidency as it exists now, and get a sort of City Manager-type President. . . . We've come to the point where every four years this national fever rises up—this hunger for the Saviour, the White Knight, the Man on Horseback—and whoever wins becomes so immensely powerful, like Nixon is now, that when you vote for President today you're talking about giving a man dictatorial power for four years. I think it might be better to have the President sort of like the King of England—or the Queen—and have the real business of the presidency conducted by . . . a City Manager-type, a Prime Minister, somebody who's directly answerable to Congress, rather than a person who moves all his friends into the

White House and does whatever he wants for four years. The whole framework of the presidency is getting out of hand. It's come to the point where you almost can't run unless you can cause people to salivate and whip on each other with big sticks. You almost have to be a rock star to get the kind of fever you need to survive in American politics.

Ed: One last question, Dr. Thompson, will you be covering the 1976 election as a journalist if you are not actually a candidate?

HST: I think so, yeah. There's a sort of weird, junkie, addictive quality about covering a presidential campaign. You can see it in almost everybody in the press corps. I noticed it particularly in Tim Crouse who got hooked so fast it was just like somebody getting hooked on one shot of heroin . . . . I doubt if Crouse will miss another campaign as long as he lives; there's a tremendous adrenalin rush, a hell of a high in politics, particularly when you're winning or you think you have a chance to win . . . .

Ed: Even for the reporter?

HST: Yeah. There's an excitement and a pace to the presidential campaign that definitely keeps you wired. It's a grueling trip, but that insane kind of zipping from place to place . . . on the Monday before the election we did Kansas and both coasts. . . . I crossed over my own house in Colorado three times. It's frantic, kind of chasing after the Golden Fleece, and probably a lot more fun if you don't win or if you have no real stake in it . . . . Yeah, it's one of the best assignments I can think of.

Here's a thing I want to hit—one of the unanswered questions of this campaign—a real key question is whether or not the *potential* McGovern vote came out. So far nobody's been able to say. I don't think it did. But *if* it did—if all the people who were *likely* to vote for McGovern actually voted for him—then the implications are nasty. There's no hope for that kind of candidacy again. Something totally different will have to be done.

Ed: Haven't Caddell's statistics proven that, in fact, the Mc-Govern vote *did not come out?* Either it didn't vote at all, or it changed its vote to Nixon.

HST: It's hard to say exactly who the potential McGovern vote was. Pat's theory is based on the assumption that McGovern could appeal in the end to the people who might have voted for Wallace, and the Humphrey Democrats. Forty-eight percent of the people who said they voted for Humphrey in California in the primary, ended up voting for Nixon in the general election. Pat says those figures are kinky . . . he says it's more like 30 percent, but even so that's a hell of a defection.

Ed: But you don't seriously believe that the McGovern vote came out, do you? The people who might have voted for the candidate McGovern *wasn't* didn't really come out did they?

HST: Maybe the McGovern constituency came out, but I doubt it. The people who might have voted for the candidate McGovern wasn't, like you said, they didn't turn out. Half the people I know didn't vote . . . .

Ed: Half the people *you* know didn't vote?

HST: Yeah. And besides that, the black vote was very low, the chicano vote was negligible . . . and it was only 47 percent of the new voters voting. McGovern was counting on at least two-thirds of those people . . . and he was getting it consistently in the primaries, but of course those were Democratic primaries . . . . One of the odd things about the McGovern campaign is that nobody has any figures to explain the disastrous result. Nobody involved in the campaign seems to really have the *will* to understand. I don't think we learned much from the McGovern campaign.

Ed: How many months were you on the road? Nearly a year?

HST: It was almost exactly a year . . . .

Ed: Nevertheless you plan to do this again in '76. Why?

HST: I cursed and groaned and shouted and actually quit as National Affairs Editor about four times but . . . that's because your nerves get stretched so raw, you get so hellishly tense . . . that . . . like anything else when you're that wired, good things are *very* good and bad things are *very* bad. It's a strange kind of high . . . that's the reason you get so many volunteers into politics:

494

campaign groupies, politics junkies, people all around with all this energy and talent.

Ed: Would you describe yourself as a political junkie?

HST: I guess I have the potential for it. At the moment I'm not, but now I'm just exhausted . . . you know . . . you know . . . any time you've been involved in it, I mean *really* involved in it . . . on a level where you have some control over it . . . that Sheriff's campaign in Aspen was a high that I've never gotten from any kind of a drug. It's mainly an *adrenalin high,* that's what it is . . .

Ed: The other day I reread the end of *Hell's Angels,* one of my favorite books . . . and you talked about The Edge . . . you know . . . that moment that I've experienced . . . I was a . . . minor league bike-rider in my youth . . . that moment of being on the edge . . . and you talk about that a lot throughout your coverage this past year. You said the candidates . . . the staff, and the press . . . were all on The Edge . . . is politics the greatest Edge you've discovered? Is that the sharpest Edge that you've personally experienced and would like to continue to experience? Politics?

HST: That depends on what kind of campaign it is. I couldn't think of anything . . . it'd be hard to imagine anything stranger or weirder or higher or closer to that Edge you're talking about than a flat-out Freak Power campaign for President of the United States. The energy you could put behind that . . . the frenzy you'd stir up would probably get you killed, but Jesus Christ, it would be something that nobody'd ever forget. In Aspen, that theme song we had . . . Herbie Mann's "Battle Hymn of the Republic."

Ed: That was the theme song of your campaign?

HST: I used it on all spots . . .

Ed: Radio spots?

HST: There *is* no local television in Aspen, so we used the radio. And we got the people very frightened by that song . . . . Like I say, the two parties combined against us. All the incumbents won. Both the Democrats and the Republicans dumped their challengers, to make sure the Freak Power candidates didn't win.

My thinking was based on the asumption of a natural con-

495

stituency of about 35 percent, so if we could make it a three-way race, all we had to do was get about 10 percent more . . . which we did but it never occurred to me that the bastards would actually combine against us. I doubt if they could do that nationally, but it's easy in a small town. Not even on the state level. That's one of the factors I'm considering in terms of running for the Senate. I've been talking to people like Rick Stearns, Carl Wagner, Sandy Berger—some of the best people in the McGovern campaign, and sort of half-seriously asking if they'd like to come out and run a neo-Freak Power campaign for the U.S. Senate in Colorado. I don't think we'd have to talk about eating mescaline on the Senate floor . . . but . . . there's a tremendous void between the outright Freak Power and conventional politics. In Aspen I had a set of stocks built . . . .

Ed: Stocks? You mean the old fashioned hands and legs and . . .

HST: Right, stocks—three holes, one for the neck, one for each wrist. They were going to be installed on the courthouse lawn for dishonest drug dealers.

Ed: Stocks for dishonest drug dealers? What else was in the platform?

HST: Immediate and unceasing harassment of real estate developers . . . anybody who fouled the air with asphalt smoke or dumped scum into the river. And people went along with this platform even though—on top of everything else—I'd shaved my head completely bald. The people who voted against me thought I was the Anti-Christ, finally come back . . . finally arrived once again on earth—right there in Aspen, Colorado.

Ed: So the Edge we're talking about would be really the greatest if one were the candidate himself?

HST: Yeah, but then the punishment would be the greatest too . . . it's much more fun to run a political campaign than it is to be the candidate.

Ed: How about writing about it?

HST: That actually isn't much fun, writing about it . . . the High is in the participation, and particularly if you identify with one candidate . . . . I don't think that I could do it if I didn't

The author discussing the 1974 race in Colorado with Carl Wagner, "one of the best field organizers in the business," according to Senator McGovern.

care who won. It's the difference between watching a football game between two teams you don't care about, and watching a game where you have some kind of personal identity with one of the teams if only a huge bet. You'd be surprised how fast the adrenalin comes up, if you stand to lose $1,000 every time the ball goes up in the air. That's why the Aspen Freak Power campaign developed all that fantastic voltage. Any kind of political campaign that taps the kind of energy that nothing else can reach . . . . There are a lot of people just walking around bored stupid . . . .

Ed: Any kind of campaign that taps that energy would . . .

HST: Would generate a tremendous high for everybody involved in it.

Ed: And would ultimately for you be another paramount experience—out there on the Edge?

HST: Oh, absolutely. But you know you'd be killed, of course, and that would add to it considerably—never knowing when the bullet was coming.

Poor Losers.

Epitaph

Four More Years . . . Nixon Uber Alles . . . Fear and Loathing at the Super Bowl . . .

PRESIDENT NIXON *will be sworn into office for a second term today, emboldened by his sweeping electoral triumph of last November and a Vietnam peace settlement apparently within his grasp . . . In the most expensive inauguration in American history—the cost is officially estimated at more than $4 million—Mr. Nixon will once again take the oath on a temporary stand outside the east front of the Capitol, then ride in a parade expected to draw 200,000 people to Pennsylvania Avenue and its environs, and millions more to their television sets . . . It will be the President's first statement to the American people since his television appearance on November 6, election eve. Since then the peace talks have collapsed, massive bombing of North Vietnam has been instituted and then called off, and the talks have resumed without extended public comment from Mr. Nixon . . .* —San Francisco *Chronicle,* January 20, 1973

> *When the Great Scorer comes to write*
> *against your name—he marks—*
> *Not that you won or lost—*
> *But how you played the game.*

—Grantland Rice: who was known—prior to his death in the late fifties—as "The Dean of American Sportswriters," and one of Richard Nixon's favorite authors.

They came together on a hot afternoon in Los Angeles, howling and clawing at each other like wild beasts in heat.

Under a brown California sky, the fierceness of their struggle brought tears to the eyes of 90,000 God-fearing fans.

They were twenty-two men who were somehow more than men.

They were giants, idols, titans . . . .

Behemoths.

They stood for everything Good and True and Right in the American Spirit.

Because they had guts.

And they yearned for the Ultimate Glory, the Great Prize, the Final Fruits of a long and vicious campaign.

Victory in the Super Bowl: $15,000 each.

They were hungry for it. They were thirsty. For twenty long weeks, from August through December, they had struggled to reach this Pinnacle . . . and when dawn lit the beaches of Southern California on that fateful Sunday morning in January, they were ready.

To seize the Final Fruit.

They could almost taste it. The smell was stronger than a ton of rotten mangoes. Their nerves burned like open sores on a dog's neck. White knuckles. Wild eyes. Strange fluid welled up in their throats, with a taste far sharper than bile.

Behemoths.

Those who went early said the pre-game tension was almost unbearable. By noon, many fans were weeping openly, for no apparent reason. Others wrung their hands or gnawed on the necks of pop bottles, trying to stay calm. Many fist-fights were reported in the public urinals. Nervous ushers roamed up and down the aisles, confiscating alcoholic beverages and occasionally grappling with drunkards. Gangs of Seconal-crazed teenagers prowled through the parking lot outside the stadium, beating the mortal shit out of luckless stragglers . . . .

What? No . . . . Grantland Rice would never have written weird stuff like that: His prose was spare & lean; his descriptions came straight from the gut . . . and on the rare and ill-advised occasions when he wanted to do a "Think Piece," he called on the analytical powers of his medulla. Like all great sportswriters, Rice understood that his world might go all to pieces if he ever dared to doubt that his eyes were wired straight to his lower brain—a sort of de facto lobotomy, which enables the grinning victim to operate entirely on the level of Sensory Perception. . . .

Green grass, hot sun, sharp cleats in the turf, thundering cheers from the crowd, the menacing scowl on the face of a $30,000-a-year pulling guard as he leans around the corner on a Lombardi-style power sweep and cracks a sharp plastic shoulder into the linebacker's groin . . . .

Ah yes, the simple life: Back to the roots, the basics—first a Mousetrap, then a Crackback & a Buttonhook off a fake triple-reverse Fly Pattern, and finally The Bomb. . . .

Indeed. There is a dangerous kind of simple-minded Power/Precision worship at the root of the massive fascination with pro football in this country, and sportswriters are mainly responsible for it. With a few rare exceptions like Bob Lypsyte of The New York *Times* and Tom Quinn of the (now-defunct) Washington *Daily News,* sportswriters are a kind of rude and brainless subculture of fascist drunks whose only real function is to publicize & sell whatever the sports editor sends them out to cover. . . .

Which is a nice way to make a living, because it keeps a man busy and requires no thought at all. The two keys to success as a sportswriter are: (1) A blind willingness to believe anything you're told by the coaches, flacks, hustlers, and other "official spokesmen" for the team-owners who provide the free booze . . . and: (2) A Roget's Thesaurus, in order to avoid using the same verbs and adjectives twice in the same paragraph.

Even a sports editor, for instance, might notice something wrong with a lead that said: "The precision-jackhammer attack of the Miami Dolphins stomped the balls off the Washington Redskins today by stomping and hammering with one precise jack-thrust after another up the middle, mixed with pinpoint-precision passes into the flat and numerous hammer-jack stomps around both ends . . . .

Right. And there was the genius of Grantland Rice. He carried a pocket thesaurus, so that "The thundering hoofbeats of the Four Horsemen" never echoed more than once in the same paragraph, and the "Granite-grey sky" in his lead was a "cold dark dusk" in the last lonely line of his heart-rending, nerve-ripping stories . . . .

There was a time, about ten years ago, when I could write like

501

Grantland Rice. Not necessarily because I believed all that sporty bullshit, but because sportswriting was the only thing I could do that anybody was willing to pay for. And none of the people I wrote about seemed to give a hoot in hell what kind of lunatic gibberish I wrote about them, just as long as it *moved*. They wanted Action, Color, Speed, Violence . . . . At one point, in Florida, I was writing variations on the same demented themes for three competing papers at the same time, under three different names. I was a sports columnist for one paper in the morning, sports editor for another in the afternoon, and at night I worked for a pro wrestling promoter, writing incredibly twisted "press releases" that I would plant, the next day, in both papers.

It was a wonderful gig, in retrospect, and at times I wish I could go back to it—just punch a big hatpin through my frontal lobes and maybe regain that happy lost innocence that enabled me to write, without the slightest twinge of conscience, things like: "The entire Fort Walton Beach police force is gripped in a state of fear this week; all leaves have been cancelled and Chief Bloor is said to be drilling his men for an Emergency Alert situation on Friday and Saturday night—because those are the nights when 'Kazika, The Mad Jap,' a 440-pound sadist from the vile slums of Hiroshima, is scheduled to make his first—and no doubt his last—appearance in Fish-head Auditorium. Local wrestling impresario Lionel Olay is known to have spoken privately with Chief Bloor, urging him to have 'every available officer' on duty at ringside this weekend, because of the Mad Jap's legendary temper and his invariably savage reaction to racial insults. Last week, in Detroit, Kazika ran amok and tore the spleens out of three ringside spectators, one of whom allegedly called him a 'yellow devil.' "

"Kazika," as I recall, was a big, half-bright Cuban who once played third-string tackle for Florida State University in Tallahassee, about 100 miles away—but on the fish-head circuit he had no trouble passing for a dangerous Jap strangler, and I soon learned that pro wrestling fans don't give a fuck anyway.

Ah, memories, memories . . . and here we go again, back on the same old trip: digressions, tangents, crude flashbacks . . . . When the '72 presidential campaign ended I planned to give up this kind of thing . . . .

But what the hell? Why not? It's almost dawn in San Francisco now, the parking lot outside this building is flooded about three inches deep with another drenching rain, and I've been here all night drinking coffee & Wild Turkey, smoking short Jamaican cigars and getting more & more wired on the Allman Brothers' "Mountain Jam," howling out of four big speakers hung in all four corners of the room.

Where is the MDA? With the windows wide open and the curtains blowing into the room and the booze and the coffee and the smoke and the music beating heavy in my ears, I feel the first rising edge of a hunger for something with a bit of the crank in it.

Where is Mankiewicz tonight?

Sleeping peacefully?

No . . . probably not. After two years on The Edge, involuntary retirement is a hard thing to cope with. I tried it for a while, in Woody Creek, but three weeks without even a hint of crisis left me so nervous that I began gobbling speed and babbling distractedly about running for the U.S. Senate in '74. Finally, on the verge of desperation, I took the bush-plane over to Denver for a visit with Gary Hart, McGovern's ex-campaign manager, telling him I couldn't actually put him on the payroll right now, but that I was counting on him to organize Denver for me.

He smiled crookedly but refused to commit himself . . . and later that night I heard, from an extremely reliable source, that Hart was planning to run for the Senate himself in 1974.

Why? I wondered. Was it some kind of subliminal, un-focused need to take vengeance on the press?

On *me?* The first journalist in Christendom to go on record comparing Nixon to Adolph Hitler?

Was Gary so blinded with bile that he would actually run against me in The Primary? Would he risk splitting the "Three A's" vote and maybe sink us both?

I spent about twenty-four hours thinking about it, then flew to Los Angeles to cover the Super Bowl—but the first person I ran into down there was Ed Muskie. He was wandering around in the vortex of a big party on the main deck of the Queen Mary, telling anybody who would listen that he was having a hell of a hard time deciding whether he was for the Dolphins or the Redskins. I introduced myself as Peter Sheridan, "a friend of Donald Segretti's." "We met on the 'Sunshine Special' in Florida," I said. "I was out of my head . . . ." But his brain was too clouded to pick up on it . . . so I went up to the crow's nest and split a cap of black acid with John Chancellor.

He was reluctant to bet on the game, even when I offered to take Miami with no points. A week earlier I'd been locked into the idea that the Redskins would win easily—but when Nixon came out for them and George Allen began televising his prayer meetings I decided that any team with both God and Nixon on their side was fucked from the start.

So I began betting heavily on Miami—which worked out nicely, on paper, but some of my heaviest bets were with cocaine addicts, and they are known to be very bad risks when it comes to paying off. Most coke freaks have already blown their memories by years of over-indulgence on marijuana, and by the time they get serious about coke they have a hard time remembering what day it is, much less what kind of ill-considered bets they might or might not have made yesterday.

Consequently—although I won all my bets—I made no money.

The game itself was hopelessly dull—like all the other Super Bowls—and by half time Miami was so clearly in command that I decided to watch the rest of the drill on TV at Cardoso's Hollywood Classic/Day of the Locust-style apartment behind the Troubadour . . . but it was impossible to keep a fix on it there, because everybody in the room was so stoned that they kept asking each other things like "How did Miami get the ball? Did we miss a kick? Who's ahead now? Jesus, how did they get 14 points? How many points is . . . ah . . . *touchdown?*"

Immediately after the game I received an urgent call from my attorney, who claimed to be having a terminal drug experience in his private bungalow at the Chateau Marmont . . . but by the time I got there he had finished the whole jar.

Later, when the big rain started, I got heavily into the gin and read the Sunday papers. On page 39 of *California Living* magazine

504

I found a hand-lettered ad from the MacDonald's Hamburger Corporation, one of Nixon's big contributors in the '72 presidential campaign:

PRESS ON, it said. NOTHING IN THE WORLD CAN TAKE THE PLACE OF PERSISTENCE. TALENT WILL NOT: NOTHING IS MORE COMMON THAN UNSUCCESSFUL MEN WITH TALENT. GENIUS WILL NOT: UNREWARDED GENIUS IS ALMOST A PROVERB. EDUCATION ALONE WILL NOT: THE WORLD IS FULL OF EDUCATED DERELICTS. PERSISTENCE AND DETERMINATION ALONE ARE OMNIPOTENT.

I read it several times before I grasped the full meaning. Then, when it came to me, I called Mankiewicz immediately.

"Keep your own counsel," he said. "Don't draw any conclusions from anything you see or hear."

I hung up and drank some more gin. Then I put a Dolly Parton album on the tape machine and watched the trees outside my balcony getting lashed around in the wind. Around midnight, when the rain stopped, I put on my special Miami Beach nightshirt and walked several blocks down La Cienega Boulevard to the Losers' Club.

Photo Credits
Terry Arthur, 22, 122 (top), 506; Robert C. Scheu, 44; Neil Benson, 51;
Annie Leibovitz, 51, 122 (bottom), 145, 153 (top), 155, 200 (top), 206,
224, 232, 239, 249 (bottom), 423, 441; Dave Randolph, 68; Michael Dobo,
80; Stuart Bratesman, 94, 170, 179, 200 (bottom), 257, 262, 288, 296, 369,
407, 498; Boyd Hagen, 99; *The Islander News,* 126; Owen Franken, 138,
308; Elihu Blotinck, 153 (center); Arthur Pollock, 153 (bottom); Mark
Perlstein, 181, 249 (top); Wide World Photos, 212, 353; Mark Diamond,
344, 389; Hank Lebo, 398; J. Anthony Lukas, 412; Tom W. Benton, 415;
UPI, 325, 465.

Special thanks from Straight Arrow Books to: The Seal Rock Inn,
Sabine Gnittke, Sandra MacDonald, Margaret Wolf, Mercury
Printing Co., Inc., Chong Lee, Linda Gunnarson, Bill
Burgower, John Clancy, Tom Benton, Ralph
Steadman, Sandy Thompson, Jane Wenner,
Lynn Nesbit, Jim Naughton, Bill Greider,
Angelo Scaramastra, David Charlesen,
John Chancellor, Alexander Pushkin,
Suzanne Lipsett, Stephanie Franklin,
Cathy Crosby, Sarah Lazin, Charles
Perry, Paul Scanlon, Tim Crouse,
Annie Leibovitz, Barbara Ziller,
Robert Kingsbury, Rosemary
Powell, the rest of the staff
of **Rolling Stone** and
above all, Jann
Wenner.

BOOK DESIGN   JON GOODCHILD

Straight Arrow Books: Dian-Aziza Ooka,
Lawrence Ratner, Douglas Mount,
Darlene Gremli, Rosemary
Nightingale, Barbara
Burgower. Editor:
Alan Rinzler